W9-CZR-592

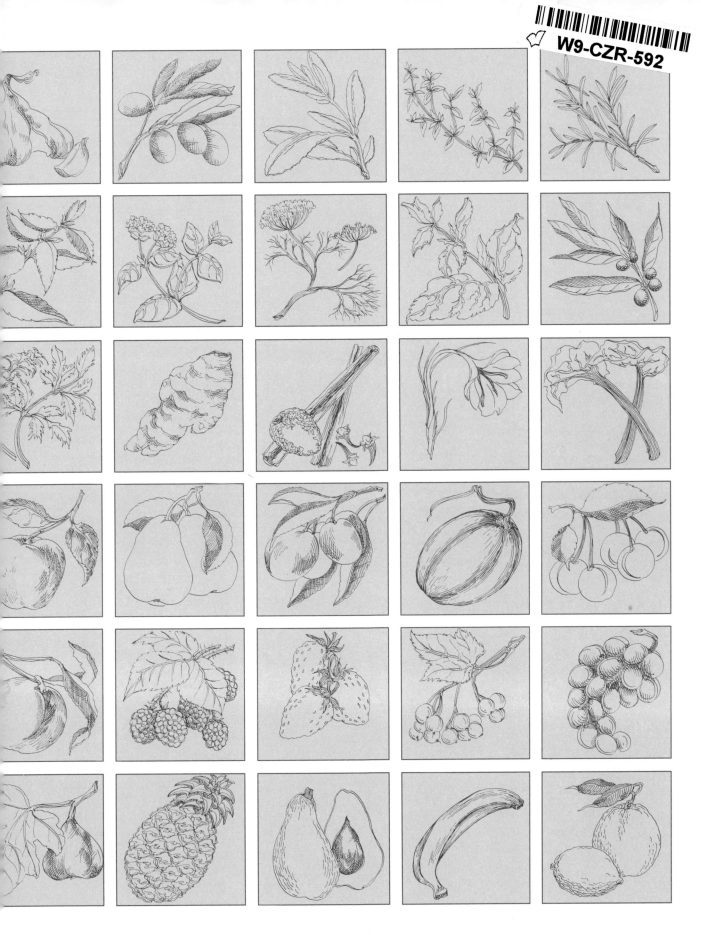

The Best Of Family Circle
COOKBOOK

Other Books by Family Circle

Recipes America Loves Best
Family Circle Hints Book
Delicious Desserts
Great Meals on a Tight Budget

To order a subscription to **FamilyCircle** Magazine, write to Family Circle subscriptions, 488 Madison Avenue, New York, NY 10022.

The Best Of FamilyCircle® COOKBOOK

The Editors of Family Circle

Special Project Staff

Project Editor—Diane Mogelever
Family Circle Food Editor—Jean Hewitt
Family Circle Senior Associate Food Editor—David Ricketts
Production Editor—Rosalyn Badalamenti
Type Supervisor—Wendy Hylfelt
Typesetting—Vickie Almquist
Assistants—Helen Russell and Joanne Hajdu
Illustrations—Lauren Jarrett
Text Design—Levavi & Levavi
Cover Photograph—Gordon Smith
Cover Design—Marcon Dynamics

Project Manager—Annabelle Grob
Associate Project Manager—Margie Chan Yip

Photographers—Dennis Gottlieb, Laszlo, Bill McGinn, Rudy Muller, Ron Schwerin and Gordon Smith

Published by The Family Circle, Inc.
488 Madison Avenue, New York, NY 10022

Copyright ©1985 by The Family Circle, Inc.

All rights reserved. No part of this book may be reproduced in any form or by any electronic or mechanical means, including information storage and retrieval systems, without permission in writing from the publisher, except by a reviewer who may quote brief passages in a review.

Manufactured in the United States of America

10 9 8 7 6 5 4 3 2 1

Library of Congress Cataloging in Publication Data
Main entry under title:

The Best of Family circle cookbook.
Includes index.

1. Cookery.	I. Family circle (Mount Morris, Ill.)		
TX715.B485555	1985	641.5	85-4465

ISBN 0-933-58500-4

Published and distributed to the trade by

HPBooks
P.O. Box 5367
Tucson, AZ 85703
(602) 888-2150

Trade edition ISBN 0-89586-428-2

Contents

The Best Of Family Circle
COOKBOOK

Introduction

*T*oday's busy life-style combined with an ever-growing interest in physical fitness and healthful eating make the need for nourishing but delicious meals a top priority in our lives. This book will take you right through the meal, starting with a taste-stimulating appetizer, soup or salad, on to the mouth-watering main dish, and ending with a delectable dessert. Piping hot breads, vegetables and other accompaniments are added for good measure.

To help with meal planning we offer a chapter of menus. There are quick and easy menus for those busy, little-time-to-cook days and make-ahead menus for the days when there is no time to cook. Menus with dishes families love to eat and menus for company and other special occasions are also included.

Parties and extra-special meals for entertaining are covered in the last chapter. Most of the recipes are either totally or partially made ahead with little last-minute preparation so *everyone* can enjoy the party.

The recipes included here may be quick and easy to make, make-ahead, special and/or family-type. Each is coded for fast identification. The nutritional value of each recipe is given at the top. Check this to find the number of calories and the amount of protein, fat, sodium and cholesterol, and to help plan nutritious, well-balanced meals. Helpful tips are included throughout the book.

In This Book

Recipes and menus are coded by type, using the following symbols:

 for Quick

 for Make-Ahead

 for Special

 for Family

Eggs are large.
Milk is whole homogenized.
Flour, cake or all-purpose, is sifted before measuring.

Heavy cream for whipping is 40 percent butterfat.
Baking powder is double action.
Measurements are level.
Brown sugar is firmly packed.
Herbs and spices are dried unless noted otherwise.
Vinegar is cider.
Corn syrup, unless specified, can be either light or dark.
Doubling recipes is not wise. It is best to make the recipe a second time.
Vegetable shortening is used for greasing pans.

Emergency Ingredient Substitutes

WHEN THE RECIPE CALLS FOR:	YOU MAY SUBSTITUTE:
1 square unsweetened chocolate	3 tablespoons unsweetened cocoa powder plus 1 tablespoon butter or margarine
1 cup sifted cake flour	⅞ cup sifted all-purpose flour (1 cup less 2 tablespoons)
1 cup all-purpose flour	1 cup whole-wheat flour or ⅝ cup potato flour or ⅞ cup rice flour
2 tablespoons flour (for thickening)	1 tablespoon cornstarch
1 cup sweet milk	½ cup evaporated milk plus ½ cup water
1 cup buttermilk	1 tablespoon vinegar plus enough sweet milk to make 1 cup
1 cup sour cream (in baking)	⅞ cup buttermilk or sour milk plus 3 tablespoons butter
1 cup sour cream	1 cup plain yogurt
1 egg (for custards)	2 egg yolks
1 cup brown sugar (packed)	1 cup sugar or 1 cup sugar plus 2 tablespoons molasses
1 teaspoon lemon juice	½ teaspoon vinegar
¼ cup chopped onion	1 tablespoon instant minced onion
1 clove garlic	⅛ teaspoon garlic powder
1 cup zucchini	1 cup summer squash
1 cup tomato juice	½ cup tomato sauce plus ½ cup water
2 cups tomato sauce	¾ cup tomato paste plus 1 cup water
1 tablespoon fresh snipped herbs	1 teaspoon dried herbs
1 tablespoon prepared mustard	1 teaspoon dry mustard

Food Equivalents

Bread
Bread crumbs, soft, 1 cup	2 slices
Bread cubes, 1 cup	2 slices
Bread, 1 pound, sliced	22 slices

Butter or Margarine
½ stick	¼ cup or 4 tablespoons
1 pound	4 sticks or 2 cups

Cream and Milk
Cream, heavy, 1 cup whipped	2 cups
Milk, evaporated, small can	⅔ cup
Milk, sweetened condensed, 14 ounce can	1⅔ cup
Milk, instant, non-fat dry, 1 pound	5 quarts, liquid skim milk

Cheese
Cheese, cream, 8-ounce package	1 cup
Cheese, cottage, 8 ounces	1 cup
Cheese, Cheddar or Swiss, 1 pound, shredded	4 cups
Cheese, blue, crumbled, 4 ounces	1 cup
Cheese, Parmesan or Romano, ¼ pound, grated	1¼ cups

Cookies
Chocolate wafers, 1 cup crumbs	19 wafers
Vanilla wafers, 1 cup fine crumbs	22 wafers
Graham crackers, 1 cup fine crumbs	14 square crackers

Dried Beans and Peas
1 cup	2¼ cups, cooked

Eggs (large)
Eggs, whole 1 cup	5 to 6
Egg yolks, 1 cup	13 to 14
Egg whites, 1 cup	7 to 8

Flour
Flour, all-purpose, sifted, 1 pound	4 cups
Flour, cake, sifted, 1 pound	4¾ to 5 cups

Nuts
Almonds, 1 pound, shelled	3½ cups
Peanuts, 1 pound, shelled	3 cups
Walnuts, 1 pound, shelled	4 cups
Pecans, 1 pound, shelled	4 cups

Pasta
Macaroni, elbow, uncooked, 8 ounces	4 cups, cooked
Spaghetti, 8 ounces, uncooked	4 cups, cooked
Noodles, medium width, 8 ounces, uncooked	3¾ cups, cooked

Rice
Long-grain white rice, 1 cup	3 cups, cooked
Enriched pre-cooked rice, 1 cup	2 cups, cooked

Sugar
Sugar, granulated, 1 pound	2 cups
Sugar, brown, firmly packed, 1 pound	2¼ cups
Sugar, 10X (confectioners'), sifted, 1 pound	3⅓ to 4 cups

Vegetables and Fruits
Apples, 1 pound	3 medium size
Bananas, 1 pound	3 medium size
Carrots, 1 pound, sliced	2½ cups
Cabbage, 1 pound, shredded	4 cups
Herbs, chopped fresh, 1 tablespoon	1 teaspoon dried
Lemon, 1 medium size, grated	2 teaspoons lemon rind
Lemon, 1 medium size, squeezed	2 tablespoons lemon juice
Orange, 1 medium size, grated	2 tablespoons orange rind
Orange, 1 medium size, squeezed	⅓ to ½ cup orange juice
Onions, yellow cooking, 1 pound	5 to 6 medium size
Onions, small white silverskins, 1 pound	12 to 14
Potatoes, all-purpose, 1 pound	3 medium size
Peaches, 1 pound	4 medium size
Mushrooms, 1 pound, sliced	3 cups
Tomatoes, 1 pound:	
Large	2
Medium size	3
Small	4

Important Measures

½ tablespoon	1½ teaspoons
1 tablespoon	3 teaspoons
1 ounce liquid	2 tablespoons
1 jigger	1½ ounces
¼ cup	4 tablespoons
⅓ cup	5 tablespoons plus 1 teaspoon
½ cup	8 tablespoons
⅔ cup	10 tablespoons plus 2 teaspoons
¾ cup	12 tablespoons
1 cup	16 tablespoons
1 pint	2 cups
1 quart	2 pints
1 gallon	4 quarts
1 pound	16 ounces

Oven Temperatures

Ovens need not be preheated for meats, vegetables and most casserole dishes. Recipes that *need* preheated ovens, have the direction inserted in the recipe to allow the 15-minute margin for preheating either gas or electric ovens.

Very Slow	250°-275°
Slow	300°-325°
Moderate	350°-375°
Hot	400°-425°
Very Hot	450°-475°
Extremely Hot	500°+

Emergency Baking Dish and Pan Substitutes

WHEN THE RECIPE CALLS FOR:	YOU MAY SUBSTITUTE:
4-cup baking pan or dish	9-inch pie plate, or 1-quart soufflé dish
6-cup baking pan or dish	9-inch round layer cake pan, or 8 x 4 x 3-inch loaf pan, or 10-inch pie plate
8-cup baking pan or dish	8 x 8 x 2-inch dish or cake pan, or 11 x 7 x 1½-inch pan, or 9 x 5 x 3-inch loaf pan
three 8-inch round pans	two 9 x 9 x 2-inch cake pans
two 9-inch round layer-cake pans	two 8 x 8 x 2-inch cake pans, or 13 x 9 x 2-inch pan
9 x 5 x 3-inch loaf pan	9 x 9 x 2-inch cake pan
9-inch angel-cake tube pan	10 x 3¾-inch Bundt® pan, or 9 x 3½-inch fancy tube pan

Availability of Fresh Fruits and Vegetables

Today, thanks to refrigeration and the speedy transportation of produce, many fruits and vegetables are available all year. They may come to your local market from the farmer down the road or from a farmer in another country. Because shipping is costly, your best buys will be the fruits and vegetables purchased during their growing season in your section of the country.

The following fruits and vegetables are usually available all year:

Apples	Cucumbers	Parsley & herbs
Artichokes	Eggplant	Parsnips
Avocados	Escarole	Pears
Bananas	Garlic	Peas, green
Beans, green	Grapefruit	Peppers, sweet
Beets	Grapes	Pineapples
Broccoli	Greens	Plantains
Brussels sprouts	Lemons	Potatoes
Cabbage	Lettuce	Radishes
Carrots	Limes	Spinach
Cauliflower	Mushrooms	Squash
Celery	Onions	Strawberries
Chinese cabbage	Onions, green	Sweet potatoes
Coconuts	Oranges	Tomatoes
Corn, sweet	Papayas	Turnips-rutabagas

The following are available in the markets only during the months indicated:

Apricots—June to August
Asparagus—March to July
Blueberries—June to August
Cantaloupes—April to October
Cherries—May to August
Cranberries—September to December
Honeydews—February to October
Mangoes—March to August
Nectarines—January and February, June to September
Okra—April to November
Peaches—May to September
Persimmons—October to February
Plums and Prunes—June to October
Pomegranates—September to December
Pumpkins—September to December
Tangelos—October to February
Tangerines—November to March
Watermelons—April to September

Refrigerator Storage

EGGS

Eggs should be stored in the refrigerator large end up in their original carton for up to one week. Soiled eggs should be wiped clean with a dry cloth before storing. A wet cloth would wash off the natural protective film and allow other flavors, odors, bacteria and molds to enter the egg.

FISH

Fresh fish and shellfish should not remain at room temperature for longer than 2 hours. Wrap them well and store in the coldest part of the refrigerator for up to 2 days.

FRUITS AND VEGETABLES

Fruits and vegetables may be stored in the refrigerator for several days. The longer they are refrigerated the greater the vitamin loss, so it is best to eat them as soon after purchase as possible.

Asparagus, broccoli, cabbage, cauliflower, celery, cucumbers, green beans, green onions, green and red peppers, radishes, and greens (kale, spinach, turnip greens, chard and salad greens) should be promptly refrigerated in a covered container, moisture-proof bag or a vegetable crisper.

Apples, apricots, berries, cherries, corn (in husks), grapes, nectarines, peaches, pears, peas (in shell), and plums should be refrigerated loosely covered or in a plastic produce bag with air holes.

MEAT AND POULTRY

Meat and poultry should be stored, wrapped, in the coldest part of the refrigerator. For the best flavor and nutritive value, meat should be used in 2 to 3 days. (Ground meat should be used within 24 hours to prevent spoilage.) Poultry should be used within 1 or 2 days. Information on the recommended maximum length of time meat and poultry should be stored in the refrigerator may be found in the Meat and Poultry Refrigerator Storage Chart.

FRESH, UNCOOKED MEAT	STORAGE TIME
BEEF	
roasts	**4 days**
steaks	**3 days**
stew meat, liver, kidney	**2 days**
ground	**1 day**
VEAL	
roasts	**3 days**
chops, slices, liver, kidney	**2 days**
ground	**1 day**
LAMB	
roasts	**3 days**
chops, shanks, kidney	**2 days**
ground	**1 day**
PORK	
fresh roasts, chops, spareribs	**3 days**
fresh, ground	**1 day**
salt pork	**30 days**
slab bacon	**14 days**
sliced bacon	**7 days**
hams, whole, picnic	**7 days**
ham steak	**4 days**
POULTRY	
chicken, whole or cut up	**2 days**
chicken livers	**2 days**
turkey, whole or cut up	**3 days**
Cornish game hens	**2 days**
duck	**2 days**
goose	**2 days**

Good Meals— Good Health

We all want to be physically and mentally alert and have a happy outlook on life. Good nutrition is the key. A well-developed body of ideal weight, smooth skin, glossy hair and clear eyes are the signs of a well-nourished person.

Eat a variety of foods in moderation to provide a complete range of vitamins and minerals. Eat foods that provide plenty of starch (your body's main energy source), such as pasta, and fiber (assists elimination), such as apples. Avoid eating foods containing a lot of fat, cholesterol, sodium and sugar.

The Nutrient Value Per Serving is included with each recipe in this book to help you plan daily menus that are well balanced and healthful. Refer to the Daily Nutrition Countdown Chart for the daily requirements of average adult men and women.

DAILY NUTRITION COUNTDOWN CHART

| | AVERAGE HEALTHY ADULT | |
	Women	Men
Calories[1]	2,000	2,700
Protein[2]	46 gms (184 cal.)	56 gms (224 cal.)
Fat[3]	66 gms (594 cal.)	90 gms (810 cal.)
Sodium[4]	1,100 - 3,300 mg	1,100 - 3,300 mg
Cholesterol[5]	300 mg	300 mg

Calories (cal.) that do not come from protein or fat should be derived from complex carbohydrates found in whole grains, fresh fruits, vegetables, pasta, etc.

[1]RDA [2](12% of calories) RDA [3](30% of calories) Amer. Heart Assoc. and Nat'l Acad. of Science [4](USDA) [5]Amer. Heart Assoc.

Did You Know

Cucumbers and tomatoes are classified as fruits not vegetables.

Pears ripen from the inside out. Choose pears that are a little firm and have a slight fruity aroma.

Pineapples do not ripen after they are picked, so don't buy them if they are underripe and expect them to ripen when you get them home.

Root vegetables are those that mature underground like potatoes and carrots.

Zucchini, yellow crookneck and straightneck squash share many of the same cooking qualities and may be interchanged in most recipes.

Potatoes will roast in half the time if they are boiled for 5 minutes, then put into a hot oven.

Pea soup and other starchy foods will not boil over if the top inch or two of the inside of the pot is rubbed with oil.

Frozen ground meat should be removed from the freezer and placed, wrapped, in the refrigerator to thaw the night before you wish to serve it.

Processed meats are an excellent source of high-quality protein.

"Marbling," the fine flecks of fat within the lean of the meat, is the key to selecting top-quality meat. The fat cooks away, leaving a tender, juicy piece of meat.

Chicken is a great choice if you are counting calories. a 3½-ounce serving (without skin) has only 136 calories.

Thighs and other less expensive chicken parts may be substituted in many recipes calling for chicken breasts.

Sliced chicken or turkey breast can be substituted for veal for a less expensive dish.

Eggs are graded by the U.S. Department of Agriculture according to appearance. Grade AA or Fresh Fancy Eggs are the highest quality, with thick, high whites and firm, high yolks.

Eggshell color is determined by the breed of the hen and has no effect on the quality, taste or nutrient value of the egg.

Eggs perform best at room temperature (they separate easier, beat faster and yield greater volume). Take them out of the refrigerator about 1 hour before using.

Cakes may turn out heavy and soggy if the oven temperature is too low.

Cakes may fall if the oven door is opened too soon, if the oven is too hot or if there is not enough flour in the batter.

Nuts and fruits will not sink to the bottom of a cake if they are lightly coated with flour before they are added to the batter.

Cooking Terms

Brown sugar may be softened by adding a piece of bread to the sugar in a plastic bag or an airtight container.

Flat champagne may be used for poaching fish or poultry. The cooking liquid will make a delicious sauce.

Dry vermouth may be substituted for dry white wine when braising meat or poultry.

The alcohol content of wine boils off during cooking. All that remains is the flavor.

Ham may be basted with port or Marsala wine. The drippings may then be used for a flavorful sauce.

Domestic jug wines are great for cooking—you don't need an expensive wine.

A

À la in the manner of *à la maison,* in the style of the house—"the house specialty."

Al dente An Italian phrase meaning "to the tooth," used to describe spaghetti or other pasta at the perfect stage of doneness— tender, but with enough firmness to be felt between the teeth.

Antipasto Another Italian word, this one meaning "before the meal." Antipasto is a selection of hors d'oeuvres, such as salami, marinated mushrooms, tuna or anchovies.

Aspic A jelly made from the cooking liquids of beef or poultry, principally. It will jell by itself, but is often strengthened with additional gelatin and used for coating and garnishing cold foods.

Au gratin Usually a creamed mixture topped with bread crumbs and/or cheese and browned in the oven or broiler.

Au naturel A French phrase referring to foods that are cooked simply or served in their natural state.

B

Bake To cook cakes, pies, cookies, breads and other pastries and doughs in the oven by dry heat.

Barbecue To roast meat, poultry or fish over hot coals or other heat, basting with a highly seasoned sauce. Also the food so cooked and the social gathering.

Baste To ladle pan fat, marinade or other liquid over food as it roasts in order to add flavor and prevent dryness.

Batter A flour-liquid mixture, as for pancakes, thin enough to pour.

Beat To stir vigorously with a spoon, eggbeater or electric mixer.

Blanch To plunge foods, such as tomatoes and peaches, quickly into boiling water, then into cold water, to loosen skins for easy removal. Also, a preliminary step to freezing vegetables.

Blend To mix two or more ingredients until smooth.

Boil To cook in boiling liquid.

Bone To remove the bones from meat, fish or poultry. This is usually done to make eating, carving or stuffing easier.

Bouillon A clear stock made of poultry, beef or veal, vegetables and seasonings.

Bouquet garni A small herb bouquet, most often sprigs of fresh parsley and thyme plus a bay leaf, tied in cheesecloth. Dried herbs can be used in place of the fresh. The *bouquet garni* is dropped into stocks, stews, sauces and soups as a seasoner and is removed before serving—usually as soon as it has flavored the dish.

Braise To brown in fat, then to cook, covered, in a small amount of liquid.

Bread To coat with bread crumbs, usually after dipping in beaten egg or milk.

Broil To cook under a broiler or on a grill by direct dry heat.

Broth A clear meat, fish, poultry or vegetable stock made of a combination of them.

Brush To spread with melted butter or margarine, beaten egg, water or other liquid, using a small brush.

C

Calorie The measure of body heat energy produced by the burning (oxidation) of the food we eat.

Candy To cook fruit, fruit peel or ginger in a heavy syrup until transparent, then drain and dry. To cook vegetables, such as carrots or sweet potatoes, in sugar or syrup.

Caramelize To melt sugar in a skillet, over low heat, until it becomes golden brown.

Chantilly Heavy cream whipped until soft, not stiff; it may be sweetened or not.

Chop To cut into small pieces.

Coat To cover with flour, crumbs or other dry mixture before frying.

Coat the spoon A term used to describe egg-thickened sauces when cooked to a perfect degree of doneness; when a custard coats a metal spoon; it leaves a thin, somewhat jelly-like film.

Combine To mix together two or more ingredients.

Crimp To press edges of piecrust together with the tines of a fork or your fingertips.

Croutons Small, fried bread cubes.

Crumb To coat food with bread or cracker crumbs. So that the crumbs will stick, the food should be first be dipped in milk or beaten egg.

Crumble To break between the fingers into small, irregular pieces.

Crush To pulverize food with a rolling pin or whirl in a blender until it is granular or powdered.

Cube To cut into cubes.

Cut in To work shortening or other solid fat into a flour mixture with a pastry blender or two knives until the texture resembles coarse meal.

Cutlet A small thin, boneless piece of meat—usually cut from the leg of veal or chicken or turkey breast.

D

Dash A very small amount–less than $\frac{1}{16}$ teaspoon.

Deep-fry To cook in hot, deep, temperature-controlled fat.

Deglaze To loosen the browned bits in a skillet or roasting pan by adding liquid while stirring and heating. A glaze is used as a flavor base for sauces and gravies.

Demitasse French for "half cup," it refers to the small cups used for after-dinner coffee and also to the strong, black coffee served in them.

Devil To season with mustard, pepper and other spicy condiments.

Dice To cut into small, uniform pieces.

Dissolve To stir a powder or solid ingredient into a liquid to make a solution.

Dot To scatter bits of butter or margarine or other seasoning over the surface of a food to be cooked.

Dough A mixture of flour, liquid and other ingredients stiff enough to knead.

Drain To pour off liquid. Also, to place fried foods on paper toweling to soak up the excess fat.

Drawn butter Melted, clarified butter or margarine; often served with boiled shellfish.

Dredge To coat with flour prior to frying.

Drizzle To pour melted butter or margarine, marinade or other liquid over food in a thin stream.

Duchess Mashed potatoes mixed with egg, butter or margarine and cream, piped around meat, poultry or fish dishes as a decorative border, then browned in the oven or broiler just before serving.

Dust To cover lightly with flour, 10X (confectioners') sugar or other dry ingredient.

Dutch oven A large, heavy, metal cooking pot with a tight-fitting cover; used for cooking pot roasts and stews and for braising large cuts of meat and poultry.

E

Entrée A French term applying to the third course in a full French dinner. We use the term to designate the main dish of a meal.

Espresso Robust, dark, Italian coffee brewed under steam pressure. It is traditionally served in small cups and, in this country (though usually not in Italy), accompanied by twists of lemon rind.

F

Fillet A thin, boneless piece of meat or fish.

Fines herbes A mixture of minced fresh or dried parsley, chervil, tarragon and, sometimes, chives, used to season salads, omelets and other dishes.

Flake To break up food (salmon or tuna, for example) into smaller pieces with a fork.

Flambé, flambéed French words meaning "flaming." In the culinary sense, the verb *flamber* means to pour warm brandy over a food and to set it afire with a match.

Florentine In the style of Florence, Italy, which usually means served on a bed of spinach, topped with a delicate cheese sauce and browned in the oven. Fish and eggs are often served Florentine style.

Flour To coat with flour.

Flute To form a fluted edge with the fingers, on a piecrust edging.

Fold in To mix a light, fluffy ingredient, such as beaten egg white, into a thicker mixture, using a gentle under-and-over motion.

Fondue Switzerland's gift to good eating: A silky concoction of melted cheese, white wine and kirsch served in an earthenware crock set over a burner. To eat the fondue, chunks of bread are speared with special, long-handled fondue forks and then twirled in the semiliquid cheese mixture. *Fondue Bourguignonne* is a convivial Swiss version of a French dish: Cubes of raw steak are speared with the fondue forks, fried at the table in a pot of piping hot oil, then dipped into assorted sauces.

Frappé A mushy, frozen dessert.

Fricassee To simmer a chicken covered in water with vegetables and often wine. The chicken may be browned in butter first. A gravy is made from the broth and served with the chicken.

Fritter A crisp, golden, deep-fried batter bread, often containing corn or minced fruits or vegetables. Also, pieces of fruit or vegetable, batter-dipped and deep-fried.

G

Garnish To decorate with colorful and/or fancily-cut pieces of food.

Glaze To coat food with honey, syrup or other liquid so it glistens.

Gluten The protein of wheat flour that forms the framework of cakes, breads, cookies and pastries.

Goulash A beef stew, flavored with paprika.

Grate To shred into small pieces with a grater.

Grease To rub butter, margarine or other fat over a food or container.

Grill To cook on a grill, usually over charcoal.

Grind To put through a food grinder.

H

Hors d'oeuvres Bite-size appetizers served with cocktails.

Hull To remove caps and stems from berries.

I

Ice To cover with icing. Also, a frozen, water-based, fruit-flavored dessert.

Italienne, á la Served Italian style with a garnish of pasta.

J

Julienne To cut food into uniformly long, thin slivers (1½ x ¼-inches).

K

Kabob Cubes of meat, fish or poultry and/or vegetables threaded on long skewers and grilled over coals or under the broiler.

Kasha Buckwheat groats braised or cooked in liquid and usually served in place of rice, potatoes or another starch.

Knead To work dough with the hands until it is smooth and springy. Yeast breads must be kneaded to develop the gluten necessary to give them framework and volume.

L

Lard Creamy white rendered pork fat.

Line To cover the bottom, and sometimes sides, of a pan with paper or thin slices of food.

Lyonnaise Seasoned in the style of Lyons, France, meaning with parsley and onions.

M

Macerate To let food, principally fruits, steep in wine or spirits (usually kirsch or rum).

Maître d'hôtel Simply cooked dishes seasoned with minced parsley, butter and lemon, *Maître d'hôtel* butter is a mixture of butter (or margarine), parsley, lemon juice and salt. It is most often used to season broiled fish, grilled steaks or chops or boiled carrots.

Marinade The liquid in which food is marinated.

Marinate To let food, principally meats, steep in a piquant sauce prior to cooking. The marinade serves to tenderize and add flavor.

Marzipan A confection made from almond paste, sugar and egg whites—often colored and shaped into tiny fruit and vegetable forms.

Mash To reduce to a pulp.

Mask To coat with sauce or aspic.

Melt To heat a solid, such as chocolate or butter, until liquid.

Meringue A stiffly beaten mixture of sugar and egg white.

Mince To cut into fine pieces.

Mix To stir together.

Mocha A flavoring for desserts, usually made from coffee or a mixture of coffee and chocolate.

Mold To shape in a mold.

Mousse A rich, creamy, frozen dessert; also, a velvety hot or cold savory dish, rich with cream, bound with eggs or—if cold—with gelatin.

Mull To heat a liquid, such as wine or cider, with whole spices.

N

Niçoise Prepared in the manner of Nice, France—with tomatoes, garlic, olive oil and ripe olives.

O

Oil To rub a pan or mold with cooking oil.

P

Panbroil To cook in a skillet in a small amount of fat; drippings are poured off as they accumulate.

Parboil To cook in water until about half done; vegetables to be cooked *en casserole* are usually parboiled.

Pare To remove the skin of a fruit or vegetable with a swivel-blade vegetable peeler.

Pasta The all-inclusive Italian word for all kinds of macaroni, spaghetti and noodles.

Pastry A stiff dough, made from flour, water and shortening, used for piecrusts, turnovers and other dishes; it is also a rich cookie-type dough used for desserts.

Pastry bag A cone-shaped fabric, parchment or plastic bag with a hole at the tip for the insertion of various decorating tubes. Used to decorate cakes, pastries, etc.

Pâté A well-seasoned mixture of finely minced or ground meats and/or liver. *Pâté de foie gras* is made of goose livers and truffles.

Petits fours Tiny, fancily-frosted cakes.

Pilaf Rice cooked in a savory broth, often with small bits of meat or vegetables, herbs and spices.

Pinch The amount of a dry ingredient that can be taken up between the thumb and index finger—less than ¼ teaspoon.

Pipe To press frosting, whipped cream, mashed potatoes or other soft mixtures through a pastry bag fitted with a decorative tube to make a fancy garnish or edging.

Plank A well-seasoned (oiled) hardwood plank used to serve a broiled steak or chop, usually edged with Duchess potatoes.

Plump To soak raisins or other dried fruits in liquid until they are softened and almost returned to their natural state.

Poach To cook in simmering liquid, as fish fillets for example.

Polenta A cornmeal porridge popular in Italy. Usually cooled, sliced or cubed, then baked or fried with butter and Parmesan cheese.

Pound To flatten by pounding.

Preheat To bring an oven or broiler to the correct temperature before cooking food.

Purée To reduce food to a smooth, velvety texture by whirling in an electric blender or pressing through a sieve or food grinder. Also, the food so reduced.

R

Ragôut A stew.

Ramekin A small, individual-size baking dish.

Reduce To boil a liquid, uncovered, until the quantity is concentrated.

Render To melt solid fat.

Rice To press food through a container with small holes. The food then resembles rice.

Risotto An Italian dish made with rice browned in fat and combined with tomatoes, mushrooms, onions or truffles. It is usually thick and topped with grated cheese.

Roast To cook meat or poultry in the oven by dry heat.

Roe The eggs of fish, such as sturgeon, salmon (caviar) or shad; considered delicacies.

Roll To press and shape dough or pastry with a rolling pin.

Roux A cooked, fat-flour mixture used to thicken sauces and gravies.

S

Sauté To cook food quickly in a small amount of hot fat in a skillet.

Scald To heat a liquid just until bubbles form around the edge of the pan, but the liquid does not boil.

Scallop To bake small pieces of food *en casserole,* usually in a cream sauce. Also a thin, boneless slice of meat, such as veal.

Score To make shallow, crisscross cuts over the surface of a food with a knife.

Scramble To stir eggs or an egg mixture while cooking until the mixture sets.

Scrape To remove fruit or vegetable skin by scraping with a knife.

Shirr To cook whole eggs in ramekins with cream and crumbs.

Short An adjective used to describe a bread, cake or pastry that has a high proportion of fat and is ultra-tender or crisp.

Shortening A solid fat, usually of vegetable origin, used to add tenderness to pastry, bread or cookies.

Shred To cut in small, thin slivers by rubbing food, such as Cheddar cheese, over the holes in a shredder-grater.

Sift To put flour or another dry ingredient through a sifter. (*Note:* In this book, recipes that call for *sifted* flour require that you sift the flour and then measure it, even if you use a flour that says "sifted" on the bag.)

Simmer To cook in liquid just below the boiling point.

Skewer To thread food on a long wooden or metal pin before cooking, also, the pin itself.

Skim To remove fat or scum from the surface of a liquid or sauce.

Sliver To cut in long, thin strips.

Soak To let stand in liquid.

Spit To thread food on a long rod and roast over glowing coals or under a broiler; also the rod itself.

Steam To cook, covered, on a trivet over a small amount of boiling water.

Steep To let food soak in liquid until the liquid absorbs its flavor, as in steeping tea in hot water.

Stew To cook, covered, in simmering liquid.

Stir To mix with a spoon using a circular motion.

Stir-fry To cook in a small amount of oil, in a wok or skillet, over high heat, stirring or tossing constantly, for a short period of time.

Stock A liquid flavor base for soups and sauces made by long, slow cooking of meat, poultry or fish with their bones. Stock may be brown or white, depending on whether the meat and bones are browned first.

Stud To press whole cloves, slivers of garlic or other seasoning into the surface of a food to be cooked.

T

Thicken To make a liquid thicker, usually by adding flour, cornstarch or beaten egg.

Thin To make a liquid thinner by adding liquid.

Timbale A savory meat, fish, poultry or vegetable custard, baked in a small mold. Also, pastry shells made on special iron molds—Swedish Rosettes, for example.

Torte A very rich, many-layered cake made with eggs, and, often, grated nuts. Usually it is filled, but frequently it is not frosted.

Toss To mix, as a salad, by gently turning ingredients over and over in a bowl, either with the hands or with a large fork and spoon.

Truss To tie into a compact shape before roasting.

Turnover A folded pastry usually made by cutting a circle or square, adding a dollop of sweet or savory filling, folding into a semi-circle or triangle, then crimping the edges with the tines of a fork. Most turnovers are baked, but some are deep-fat fried.

Tutti-Frutti A mixture of minced fruits used as a dessert topping.

V

Véronique A dish garnished with seedless green grapes.

Vinaigrette A sauce, French in origin, made from oil, vinegar, salt, pepper and herbs; usually served on cold meat, fish or vegetables.

W

Whip To beat until frothy or stiff with an eggbeater or an electric mixer.

Wok A round-bottomed, bowl-shaped Chinese cooking utensil used for stir-frying.

Z

Zest The oily, aromatic, colored part of the rind of citrus fruits.

1. What's Cooking

*I*f variety is the spice of life then varied menus are the spark of home cooking. Here we offer you a variety of menu plans using many recipes from the chapters that follow. Each menu is coded as to the type of meal. They may be quick meals, make-ahead meals, special meals, family meals, or any combination of these categories.

Quick meals are usually ready to be served in under an hour. The menus are rounded out with items that are easily prepared (celery and carrot sticks), may be purchased at the store ready-to-cook (green beans), or purchased ready-to-eat (marble cake).

Make-ahead meals offer recipes that are made from several hours to several days before serving and require a minimum of last-minute preparation. Again, the menus are rounded out with easily prepared and purchased dishes.

Special meals help you go all-out for your family, friends and relatives. The recipes are fancier and may take a little more time to prepare. Here you will find menus for special brunches, luncheons, an afternoon tea and teen gatherings. For entertaining ideas, see Chapter 9: Elegant Meals and Festive Parties for Holidays and Entertaining.

Family meals include recipes for more traditional family fare. The main dish may use less tender cuts of meat or dried beans, which are less expensive, but may require a longer cooking time.

Many of these menus fall into two or even three different meal categories. A Quick Meal might also be considered a Special Meal, a Family Meal, or even both! Each menu is marked with symbols designating the meal categories.

Throughout the book, every recipe is categorized, and marked with the same symbols, indicating if it is a Quick, Make-Ahead, Special and/or Family recipe.

The menus are planned to feed a specified number of people with average appetites. When choosing a menu for heavy or light eaters keep this in mind and plan accordingly.

Occasionally a menu calls for a recipe that makes more servings than the number of people to be served. This allows for extra servings and even leftovers to be properly stored and used for another meal.

...And now the menu!

Meals for Four

◩◻ *BREAKFAST FOR 4*
Orange Juice with Fresh Mint
Apple Griddle Cakes, page 44
Honey   Maple Syrup   Butter
Sausage Patties
Hot Chocolate   Coffee

◩▼ *BRUNCH FOR 4*
Champagne and Orange Juice
French Omelets, page 164
with Sausage and Pepper Filling, page 165
or Grated Swiss Cheese
Croissants   Strawberry Jam
Bananas Flambé, page 253
Coffee   Tea

◩▼ *LUNCH FOR 4*
Quick Gazpacho, page 70
Chicken Livers and Peppers, page 130, in Patty Shells
Crisp Zucchini and Carrot Sticks
Lemon Sherbet with Kiwi Slices
White Wine   Tea

◻ *LUNCH FOR 4*
Pear Halves on Leaf Lettuce Cups
Hot Reuben Sandwiches, page 92
Lemon Sponge Cake
Seltzer

■ ▼ *SUMMER LUNCH FOR 4*

Chicken Broth with Green Onion Slices
Turkey Alfredo-Stuffed Artichokes, page 173
Swedish Limpa Breads, page 49
Fresh Strawberry Ice, page 268
White Wine Spritzers

■ *SUMMER LUNCH FOR 4*

Herring Salad, page 82
Tomato Slices
Swedish Limpa Breads, page 49
Chocolate-Pecan Refrigerator Cookies, page 234
Beer

■ *WINTER LUNCH FOR 4*

Monastery Lentil Soup, page 73
Quick Basil Biscuits, page 41
Sliced Tomato and Lettuce Salad
Apple Crisp, page 254
Milk

■ ■ *DINNER FOR 4*

Cassoulet Alsace, page 160
Peas with Mushrooms
French Bread   Butter
Green Grapes   Gruyère Cheese
White or Light Red Wine

◼◻ *DINNER FOR 4*

Lemon Chicken, page 126
Rice
Stir-Fried Snow Peas
Fresh Pineapple and Oranges
Seltzer   Milk   Iced Tea

◼◻ *DINNER FOR 4*

Quick Chili con Carne California Style, page 98
Green Beans Oregano
Cornbread   Butter
Individual Caramel Flans
Beer   Milk

◼◻ *DINNER FOR 4*

Braised Pork Chops with Cabbage, page 104
Fried Potato Rounds
Black Bread   Butter
Marble Cake with Strawberries
Milk   Coffee   Tea

◼▼◻ *DINNER FOR 4*

Broiled Minute Steaks with Basil Butter, page 197
Sliced Boiled Potatoes
Ratatouille, page 190
Whole-Grain Rolls
Cherry Cheesecake
Milk   Coffee

■ ▾ *DINNER FOR 4*

Chicken Broth with Spinach and Lemon to taste
Broccoli-Stuffed Sole with Hollandaise Sauce, page 136
Rice
Apple-Walnut Muffins, page 43
Chocolate Frosted Eclairs
White Wine

■ ▾ *DINNER FOR 4*

Fillet of Flounder with Lobster and Julienned Vegetables, page 134
Mixed Green Salad
Croissants   Butter
Fresh Pears with Roquefort Cheese
White Wine

■ ▾ □ *DINNER FOR 4*

Chicken Provençal, page 125
Buttered New Potatoes
Spinach and Mushroom Salad, (half the recipe) page 75
Garlic Bread
Fresh Berry and Whipped Cream Parfaits
Red Wine   Coffee

■ □ *DINNER FOR 4*

Beef Burgers Paprika with
Noodles and Cabbage, page 98
Cucumber Salad, page 76
Cherry Cheesecake
Milk   Coffee   Tea

■▼■ *DINNER FOR 4*

Ragôut of Chicken with Garlic, page 130
Steamed Green Beans
Toasted French Bread Slices
Chocolate Cake
White Wine   Coffee

■■ *DINNER FOR 4*

Sausage, Cheese and Noodle Pie, page 155
Broccoli and Cauliflower Amandine
Sesame Seed Rolls   Basil Butter, page 197
Log Jam Cookies, page 227
Milk   Coffee   Tea

■■ *DINNER FOR 4*

Pork and Eggplant Casserole, page 157
Italian Green Beans Oregano
Corn Muffins   Butter
Neapolitan Cookies, page 232
Milk   Coffee

▼ *DINNER FOR 4*

Roast Duck with Orange Sauce, page 131
Rice Pilaf, page 192
Baked Acorn Squash Halves with Buttered Peas
Early Autumn Barley Loaf, page 47
Vacherine Stars with Lemon Crème, page 265
Red Wine   Coffee   Tea

▮ DINNER FOR 4
Lettuce and Tomato Salad with Vinaigrette Dressing, page 75
Crab-Stuffed Flounder, page 133
Herb-Seasoned Rice
Scalloped Asparagus, page 180
Mimosa Cake, page 210
White or Light Red Wine   Coffee

▮ DINNER FOR 4
Hot Clam Broth with Julienned Carrots
Beef Sukiyaki, page 93
Rice
Fresh Strawberry Ice, page 268
Vanilla Wafers
Beer

▮▮ DINNER FOR 4
Chicken Breasts with Yogurt Sauce, page 122
Chutney   Peanuts   Raisins   Kumquats
Steamed Cauliflower and Zucchini
Bananas with Coconut and Honey
Beer   Tea

▮▮▮ SUMMER DINNER FOR 4
Cool Avocado Soup (half the recipe), page 68
Shrimp and Scallops in Mustard-Dill Sauce, page 138
Linguini
Sautéed Zucchini and Yellow Squash
Fresh Blueberries with Sour Cream and Brown Sugar
White Wine Spritzers with Galliano Liqueur

◼◻ *FALL DINNER FOR 4*

Thyme Pork Chops with Stuffing, page 106
Hot Applesauce with Cinnamon
Brussels Sprouts and Carrots Sauté, page 182
Peach Crisp, page 254   Whipped Cream
Light Red Wine   Apple Cider

◻ *CALORIE-LIGHT DINNER FOR 4*

Tomato Juice with Lemon Slices
Stir-Fried Vegetables and Tofu, page 177   Rice
Peach Melba Crêpes (2 per serving), page 272
Coffee   Tea

◼◻ *BARBECUE FOR 4*

Barbecued Chicken, page 143
Marinated Tomato-Rice Salad, page 84 in Crisp Lettuce Cups
Corn Sticks   Butter
Marble Cake
Beer   Iced Tea

◻ *SUPPER FOR 4*

Split Pea Soup, page 73 (Freeze the remainder for another meal.)
Cheese Waffles with Ratatouille, page 172
Green Apple Pie, page 243   Vanilla Ice Cream
Milk   Coffee

◼◻ *SUMMER SUPPER FOR 4*

Spaghetti Squash with Picadillo, page 176
Lettuce and Tomato Slices   Hot Buttered Tortillas
Orange Sherbet with Kiwi Slices
Beer   Iced Coffee

Meals for Six

■ *BREAKFAST FOR 6*
Grapefruit and Orange Sections
Whole-Wheat Granola Waffles with Honey Butter, page 45
Canadian Bacon Slices
Milk   Coffee   Tea

■ *BREAKFAST FOR 6*
Cranberry Juice
Eggs Scrambled with Ham and Cheese
Applesauce Doughnuts, page 44
Milk   Coffee   Tea

■ *BREAKFAST FOR 6*
Fresh Peaches and Strawberries in Orange Juice Compote
Crispy Bacon
Fresh Corn Fritters, page 184
Maple Syrup
Milk   Coffee   Tea

■ ■ *LUNCH FOR 6*
Norwegian Fish Chowder, page 74
Whole-Grain Bread and Flat Bread
Bundt Cake
Tea

◧ ▢ LUNCH FOR 6
Fresh Tomato-Basil Soup, page 71
Melba Toast   Herbed Cheese Spread
Macaroni and Chicken Salad with Tuna Dressing, page 79
Pound Cake with Sliced Fresh Fruit
Milk   Coffee

◧ ▢ LUNCH FOR 6
Garden Vegetable Soup, page 71
Curried Lamb Piroshki, page 114
Gingerbread
Milk   Coffee   Tea

◧ ▼ ▢ LUNCH FOR 6
Vegetable Juice Cocktails
Jellied Chicken and Basil Salad, page 78
Orange-Cranberry Relish, page 192
Celery and Carrot Sticks
Parkerhouse Rolls   Butter
Citrus Ice, page 268
Rosé Wine   Iced Espresso

▼ LUNCH FOR 6
Roasted Red and Green Pepper Platter, page 175
Poppy Seed Buns
Stuffed Peaches, page 254
Iced Beef Broth and Tomato Juice (Combine in a tall glass over ice.)

◼️🍸◻️ *LUNCHEON FOR 6*

Onion-Tomato Frittata, page 167
Spinach Salad
Italian Bread   Butter
Peaches in Marsala
Crispy Bow Tie Cookies, page 239
Coffee

🍸 *LADIES' LUNCHEON FOR 6*

Cool Avocado Soup, page 68
Fontina and Ham Crêpe Cake, page 113
Spinach Mimosa
Blueberry Cream in Meringue Nests, page 264
Tea

◼️◻️ *DINNER FOR 6*

Ginger-Beef Stir-Fry with Vegetables, page 94
Rice Noodles
Mandarin Orange and Spinach Salad
Carrot-Raisin Cake
Tea

◼️◻️ *DINNER FOR 6*

Potato and Chorizo Fritatta, page 168
Sautéed Okra
Whole-Wheat Bread   Butter
Brownies   Ice Cream
Milk   Coffee

DINNER FOR 6
Baked Ham Slice
Baked Beans and Apples, page 160
Brown Bread
Tossed Green Salad
Espresso Tortoni, page 271
Pineapple Spritzers (Pineapple juice concentrate mixed with club soda.)

DINNER FOR 6
Quick Gazpacho, page 70
Ziti with Fresh Broccoli Sauce, page 153
Onion Rolls   Butter
Spumoni Ice Cream with Chocolate Sauce
Milk   Espresso

DINNER FOR 6
Papaya with Lime Slices
Spanish Rice and Seafood Stew, page 138
Buttered Lima Beans
Hot Buttered Tortillas
Vanilla Pudding with Toasted Flaked Coconut
Red Wine Coolers with Apple and Orange Slices

DINNER FOR 6
Quick Crispy Skillet Chicken with Sherry Pan Gravy, page 120
Crisp-Cooked Vegetables, page 191
Cheese Biscuits
Honeyed Fruit Compote, page 256
Milk   Coffee   Tea

■**Ⅰ**□ *DINNER FOR 6*
Beef Broth with Mushroom Slices
Sesame Seed Breadsticks
Spaghetti Gorgonzola, page 149
Fudge-Mint Torte, page 209
Red Wine

■□ *DINNER FOR 6*
Old-Fashioned Beef Stew in a Slow Cooker, page 90
Green Salad
Basil Breads, page 56   Butter
Chocolate-Currant-Bourbon Squares, page 235
Milk   Coffee   Tea

■□ *SUMMER DINNER FOR 6*
Marinated Black-Eyed Peas with Ham and Cheese, page 162
Chilled Fluffy Rice
Avocado, Tomato and Lettuce Salad
Orange Cream, page 260
Seltzer   Iced Coffee

■**Ⅰ**□ *DINNER FOR 6*
Individual Green Noodle and Beef Casseroles, page 158
Marinated Artichoke Hearts and Pitted Ripe Olives on Boston Lettuce
Breadsticks
Port Wine Gelatin with Strawberries, page 262
Red Wine   Coffee

◧◧◧ *DINNER FOR 6*

Chicken Breasts with Lemon Parsley, page 126
Scalloped Tomato and Cheese Bake, page 190
Hot Buttered Rice
Mixed Vegetables
Spiced Rhubarb, page 255   Vanilla Ice Cream
White Wine   Coffee

◧ *DINNER FOR 6*

Cream of Pumpkin Soup with Cinnamon Croutons, page 72
Roast Chicken with Apple-Celery Stuffing and Cream Gravy, page 122
Mashed Potatoes
French-Style Green Beans
Chocolate-Chestnut Roll, page 208
White Wine   Coffee

◧ *DINNER FOR 6*

Baked Pineapple Slices
Scalloped Potatoes and Ham, page 112
Brussels Sprouts
Toasted Cheese Bread   Butter
Sour Cream-Walnut Cake, page 202
Milk   Coffee

◻ *WINTER'S EVE DINNER FOR 6*

Cheese and Wine Fondue, page 171
with Vegetables and French Bread
Strawberries (or Orange Slices) in Champagne
Hot Chocolate

▢ *DINNER FOR 6*

Fruit Salad
Lamb Chops Provençal, page 116
Orzo
Sautéed Zucchini with Grated Parmesan Cheese
Mocha Lace Roll-Ups, page 240
Red Wine   Milk   Coffee

▢ *DINNER FOR 6*

Onion Soup au Gratin.
Carrot and Meat Pie, page 96
Mixed Green Salad
Rhubarb Upside-Down Cake, page 212
Vanilla Ice Cream
Milk   Coffee   Tea

▢ *WINTER DINNER FOR 6*

Mugs of Tomato Soup
No-Fuss Meatloaf, page 95 Filled with Broccoli Flowerets
Fresh Corn Fritters, page 184
Upside-Down Cake, page 212
Coffee   Tea

◣ ▾ ▢ *JAPANESE DINNER FOR 6*

Chicken Broth with Tofu and Spinach
Beef Teriyaki and Vegetables, page 94
Cellophane Noodles or Rice
Vanilla Ice Cream
Tea

◧▣▢ *BARBECUE FOR 6*

Pork and Vegetable Kabobs, page 139
Kasha
Tomatoes Stuffed with Gruyère and Mozzarella, page 288
Asparagus Vinaigrette
Summer Pudding, page 258
Seltzer with Lime Wedges

▣ *BARBECUE FOR 6*

Skewered Shrimp with Vegetables, page 146
Brown Rice Salad, page 84
Stir-Fried Chinese Pea Pods
Citrus Ice, page 268   Vanilla Wafers
Iced Orange and Spice Tea

▣ *BARBECUE FOR 6*

Butterfly Shrimp (as an appetizer), page 147
Loin of Pork with Apple Glaze, page 140
Wild and Long-Grain White Rice
Tomato and Spinach Salad with Herbed Croutons
Raspberry Roll, page 210
Light Red Wine   Iced Tea

▢ *BARBECUE FOR 6*

Fish Fillets Grilled in Lettuce, page 146
Marinated Tomato-Rice Salad, page 84
Corn with Peppers and Cream (half of the recipe), page 185
French Bread   Herbed Butter
Pound Cake with Sliced Strawberries and Whipped Cream
Beer   Milk   Iced Coffee

Meals for Eight

♈ *COUNTRY BUFFET BRUNCH FOR 8*

Orange-Avocado Salad with Molasses Dressing, page 76
Country Smoked Meats and Sausages with Apples, page 112
Creamy Corn Pudding, page 184
Assorted Rolls and Muffins
Butter   Honey   Jams
"Roman Punch" Cups, page 269
Coffee

◀◀ ♈ *LUNCHEON BUFFET FOR 8*

Marinated Roquefort and Onion Hors d'Oeuvre Sandwiches, page 64
Basil, Carrot and Chicken Pâté, page 62
Tuna-White Bean Salad, page 82
Spinach, Belgian Endive and Walnut Salad
with Mustard Vinaigrette Dressing, page 75
Brioche
Summer Fruit Compote
Make-Ahead Punch, page 306

♈ *AFTERNOON TEA FOR 8*

Tiny Hot Biscuits   Butter   Basil Jelly, page 197
Frozen Cranberry Cheesecake Minis
Norwegian Honey Cake, page 215
Tea
Milk   Lemon   Sugar

▦ 🍸 *SUMMER DINNER FOR 8*
Tomato Juice Cocktails
Cold Roast Beef au Poivre, page 88
Green Potato Salad, page 81
Chilled Crisp-Tender Green Beans with Melted Lemon Butter
Chocolate-Orange Marble Cheesecake, page 217
Red Wine Coolers   Iced Tea   Lemonade

▦ ◻ *FALL DINNER FOR 8*
Fruited Pork Stew in a Slow Cooker, page 106
Spinach and Carrot Salad
Pumpkin Bread, page 39   Butter
Chocolate Pound Cake, page 213
Dark Beer   Milk

▦ 🍸 ◻ *DINNER FOR 8*
Sausage and Linguini Torte, page 154
Chilled Crisp-Tender Cooked Broccoli with Herb Vinaigrette, page 75
Italian Bread   Butter
Refrigerator Chocolate Ice Cream, page 267
with Chocolate Sauce and Chopped Pistachio Nuts
White Wine   Coffee

🍸 *DINNER FOR 8*
Honeydew Melon Balls with Fresh Mint
Apricot-Mustard-Glazed Turkey Breast, page 132
Curried Rice   Green Beans
Chocolate Fudge Layer Cake, page 203
White Wine   Coffee   Tea

🍸 *DINNER FOR 8*

Creamy Herb Dip, page 59
Assorted Vegetables for Dipping
Flounder and Salmon Roulade with Crab Sauce, page 134
Wild and Long-Grain White Rice   Steamed Asparagus
Lime Soufflé, page 256
Light Red Wine   Coffee   Tea

🍸 *SPRING DINNER FOR 8*

Chilled Madrilène
Leg of Lamb Roulade, page 114
Herbed Rice   Spring Vegetable Salad, page 286
Hot Cross Buns
Pineapple-Mint Sorbet, page 268
Rosé or Light Red Wine

🗖 *DINNER FOR 8*

Pan-Fried Pork Chops
Red Cabbage with Apples, page 183   Peas
Cornmeal-Rye Bread, page 46   Butter
Orange Chiffon Cake, page 211
Apple Cider   Coffee

🗖 *DINNER FOR 8*

Baked Chicken and Pork Loaf with Herbed Tomato Sauce, page 128
Buttered Spinach Fettuccine
Peas and Pearl Onions
Chocolate Chiffon Pie, page 249
White Wine   Coffee

🍸 *CALORIE-LIGHT DINNER FOR 8*

Crab-Stuffed Flounder, page 133 (Make the recipe twice.)
Lemon-Parslied New Potatoes and Green Beans
Cucumber and Lettuce Plate
No-Bake Black Forest Refrigerator Cake, page 276
Seltzer   Coffee

🔲 *CALORIE-LIGHT DINNER FOR 8*

Sliced Fresh Peaches in Orange Juice
Green Beans with Beef Sauce, page 174 (Make the recipe twice.)
on Cooked Shredded Cabbage
Thin-Sliced Whole-Wheat Bread
Marbled Jamaica Chomocha Pie, page 278
Coffee   Tea

🔲 *ITALIAN DINNER FOR 8*

Top-of-the-Stove Beans with Italian Sausage, page 163
Spinach and Mushroom Salad, page 75
Italian Bread   Butter
Pear Cream Tart, page 251
Chianti   Milk   Instant Espresso Coffee

🔲 *MEXICAN DINNER FOR 8*

Nacho Gigante, page 161
Marinated Cauliflower Salad, page 76
Chili-Cheese Casserole Bread, page 42
Flan, page 272
Sangria, page 306

⊞ ⊻ *TEEN PATIO PARTY FOR 8*
Stuffed Edam with Crisp Vegetables, page 60
Assorted Crackers
Tuna or Chicken Salad-Stuffed Pita Breads, page 83
(Make the recipe twice.)
Creamy Coleslaw, page 288
Make-Your-Own-Sundaes with All the Fixings
Lots of Cold Soda and Fruit Drinks

⊻ *TEEN BARBECUE FOR 8*
Chicken Wings with Mustard Glaze, page 144
Marinated Steak Sandwiches, page 141
Pasta Verde Salad, page 81 (Make the recipe twice.)
Marinated Cauliflower Salad, page 76
Chocolate Cupcakes
Watermelon Wedges
Fruit Punch   Soft Drinks

⊞ ☐ *SUNDAY SUMMER SUPPER FOR 8*
Cold Cucumber and Yogurt Soup, page 68
Festive Layered Salad, page 77
Assorted Cold Cuts
Hard Rolls
Lace Cookie Sundaes, page 237
Mixed Fruit Punch

2. Still Warm from the Oven: Quick Breads and Yeast Breads

othing fosters a feeling of well-being like the aroma of freshly baked bread. In this chapter we present a variety of mouth-watering recipes for everything from breakfast breads to special holiday breads.

Quick breads are made with leavening agents like baking powder and baking soda, which require no rising time. They are easily mixed and baked immediately, yielding delicious homemade bread in a very short time. Many cherished breakfast treats, like muffins, doughnuts and pancakes, as well as family favorite sweet breads, are quick breads that can be stirred up in minutes.

Yeast breads involve more preparation time due to the yeast's rising process, but most are actually as simple to make as the quick breads. Our batter bread recipes don't even require kneading—just beat the ingredients together, pour the batter into a prepared pan, let rise and then bake.

If you don't have the time to prepare fresh bread often, consider planning a "baking day." Bake several types of bread, some to use immediately and some to freeze for later, when you are pressed for time.

Remember, when you want to add that extra-caring touch to any meal, serve a loaf of bread warm from the oven.

Quick Breads

◀*Clockwise from bottom:* **Basic Beer Bread (page 41), Chili-Cheese Batter Cornbread (page 52), Orange-Currant Batter Bread (page 50) and Onion-Parsley Batter Bread (page 51).**

〰 ⌂ *Pumpkin Bread*

Bake at 350° for 65 minutes.
Makes 8 servings.

Nutrient Value Per Serving: 444 calories, 5 gm. protein, 15 gm. fat, 228 mg. sodium, 69 mg. cholesterol.

  2 **cups** sifted *all-purpose flour*
 $\frac{1}{2}$ **teaspoon** each *ground cinnamon, ground ginger, ground nutmeg, salt*
  1 **teaspoon** *baking soda*
  1 **tablespoon** *wheat germ (optional)*
 $1\frac{1}{2}$ **cups** *sugar*
  1 **cup** *canned pumpkin*
 $\frac{1}{2}$ **cup** *vegetable oil*
  2 **eggs**

39

3   *tablespoons molasses*
½   *cup water*
½   *cup raisins*
½   *cup chopped nuts (optional)*

1. Grease a 9 x 5 x 3-inch loaf pan. Preheat the oven to moderate (350°).
2. Sift the flour, cinnamon, ginger, nutmeg, salt, baking soda and wheat germ, if you wish, into a medium-size bowl.
3. Beat the sugar, pumpkin, oil, eggs and molasses in a second medium-size bowl until well blended. Stir in the dry ingredients until well mixed. Stir in the water; fold in the raisins and nuts, if you wish; mix well. Turn into the prepared pan.
4. Bake in the preheated moderate oven (350°) for 65 minutes or until the center springs back when lightly pressed with a fingertip.
5. Cool in the pan on a wire rack for 10 minutes; remove from the pan onto the wire rack. Cool to room temperature.

MAKE AHEAD FOR EASY SLICING
This loaf slices best if it is stored overnight after baking. Cool the loaf completely and wrap it in plastic wrap. Use a knife with a serrated edge to slice the loaf.

Apple-Oatmeal Bread

A moist, lightly spiced loaf that is delicious spread with softened butter.

Bake at 350° for 1 hour and 5 minutes.
Makes 1 loaf (8 servings).

Nutrient Value Per Serving: 374 calories, 8 gm. protein, 18 gm. fat, 165 mg. sodium, 85 mg. cholesterol.

1½ *cups* sifted *all-purpose flour*
1   *teaspoon baking powder*
1   *teaspoon baking soda*
1   *teaspoon salt*
1   *teaspoon ground cinnamon*
½   *teaspoon ground nutmeg*
⅔   *cup firmly packed light brown sugar*
1   *cup quick oats, uncooked*
1   *cup coarsely chopped walnuts*
2   *eggs*
¼   *cup milk*
¼   *cup butter or margarine, melted and cooled*
2   *medium-size apples (¾ pound), halved, cored and coarsely shredded (1½ cups)*

1. Preheat the oven to moderate (350°). Lightly grease and flour an 8½ x 4½ x 2¾-inch loaf pan.*
2. Sift the flour, baking powder, baking soda, salt, cinnamon and nutmeg in a large bowl. Stir in the brown sugar, oats and walnuts.
3. Mix the eggs, milk and butter in a small bowl; add all at once to the oatmeal mixture; add the apples; stir lightly with a fork just until the liquid is absorbed and the mixture is thoroughly moistened (do not overmix). Spoon into the prepared baking pan.
4. Bake in the preheated moderate oven (350°) for 1 hour and 5 minutes or until a wooden pick inserted in the center comes out clean. Cool in the pan on a wire rack for 10 minutes. Loosen the edges with a knife; turn out onto the rack. Cool completely. Wrap; store overnight.

Note: Bread can be baked in a 9 x 5 x 3-inch loaf pan. Bake in preheated moderate oven (350°) for 55 minutes or until a wooden pick inserted in the center comes out clean.

Basic Beer Bread

Bake at 350° for 45 minutes.
Makes 1 loaf (12 slices).

Nutrient Value Per Slice: 131 calories, 3 gm. protein, 0.3 gm. fat, 347 mg. sodium, 0 mg. cholesterol.

3   cups unsifted self-rising flour
1   can (12 ounces) beer
1   tablespoon honey

1. Grease a 9 x 5 x 3-inch loaf pan. Preheat the oven to moderate (350°).
2. Combine the flour, beer and honey in a large bowl; stir together until well mixed. Spread the batter in the prepared pan.
3. Bake in the preheated moderate oven (350°) for 45 minutes or until browned and a wooden pick inserted in the center comes out clean. Turn out onto a wire rack to cool.

ALL-PURPOSE FLOUR MAY BE USED FOR SELF-RISING FLOUR
To substitute regular all-purpose flour for the self-rising flour, stir together 3 cups *unsifted* all-purpose flour, 3¾ teaspoons baking powder and 2¼ teaspoons salt.

Raisin-Cinnamon Beer Bread

A delightfully different variation on the Basic Beer Bread.

Bake at 350° for 45 minutes.
Makes 1 loaf (12 slices).

Nutrient Value Per Slice: 165 calories, 4 gm. protein, 1 gm. fat, 234 mg. sodium, 0 mg. cholesterol.

2   cups unsifted self-rising flour
1   cup unsifted whole-wheat flour
1½ teaspoons baking powder
1   teaspoon ground cinnamon
½   teaspoon ground nutmeg
⅛   teaspoon ground cloves
1   can (12 ounces) beer
1   tablespoon honey
1   cup raisins

1. Grease a 9 x 5 x 3-inch loaf pan. Preheat the oven to moderate (350°).
2. Combine the self-rising flour, whole-wheat flour, baking powder, cinnamon, nutmeg and cloves in a large bowl; stir together until well mixed. Add the beer, honey and raisins; mix until well blended. Spread the batter in the prepared pan.
3. Bake in the preheated moderate oven (350°) for 45 minutes or until nicely browned and a wooden pick inserted in the center comes out clean. Turn out onto a wire rack to cool.

BASIL QUICK-BREAD ACCENTS
● **Quick Basil Biscuits: Add 3 tablespoons finely chopped fresh basil to every 2 cups of biscuit mix. Make biscuits following label directions.**
● **Basil Cheese Straws: Add 2 tablespoons finely chopped fresh basil leaves to 1 package (11 ounces) piecrust mix or to any pastry for a double-crust pie. Prepare the pastry as you would normally. Roll out into a 12-inch square. Sprinkle with 2 tablespoons of freshly grated Parmesan cheese. Fold into quarters to make a 6-inch square. Roll the pastry out to make a square ⅛ inch thick. Cut into ½-inch-wide strips. Twist the strips and place on cookie sheets. Bake in a preheated moderate oven (375°) for about 8 minutes or until golden.**

◪ *Chili-Cheese Casserole Bread*

Delicious with or without butter and great with a bowl of chili.

Bake at 350° for 50 minutes.
Makes 8 servings.

Nutrient Value Per Serving: 469 calories, 24 gm. protein, 28 gm. fat, 1091 mg. sodium, 154 mg. cholesterol.

- 4 **eggs**
- 4 **cups milk**
- 2 **cups buttermilk baking mix**
- 1 **teaspoon salt**
- 2 **cans (4 ounces each) green chilies, drained, seeded and chopped**
- 1 **pound Monterey Jack cheese, shredded (4 cups)**

1. Preheat the oven to moderate (350°). Grease a 13 x 9 x 2-inch baking pan.
2. Beat the eggs, milk, baking mix and salt in a large bowl until foamy. Add the chilies and cheese to the milk mixture. Pour into the prepared baking pan.
3. Bake in the preheated moderate oven (350°) for 50 minutes or until golden brown.

▣ *Soufflé Bread*

Bake in the oven and quickly serve, since the bread will fall if it stands.

Bake at 400° for 15 minutes.
Makes 6 servings.

Nutrient Value Per Serving: 123 calories, 5 gm. protein, 10 gm. fat, 264 mg. sodium, 198 mg. cholesterol.

- 4 **eggs, separated**
- 3 **tablespoons melted butter**
- ¼ **cup sifted all-purpose flour**
- 1 **teaspoon baking powder**
- ¼ **teaspoon salt**

- ¼ **teaspoon sugar**
- 1 **tablespoon milk**

1. Preheat the oven to hot (400°).
2. Beat the egg whites in a small bowl until they form firm peaks.
3. In a clean bowl with the same beaters used to beat the whites, beat the yolks until thick and lemon colored. Add 2 tablespoons of the melted butter, the flour, baking powder, salt, sugar and milk. Beat until smooth.
4. Add the remaining 1 tablespoon melted butter to a heavy 8-inch skillet with ovenproof handle. Turn the skillet to coat the bottom with butter.
5. Gently fold the egg yolk mixture into the beaten whites until no streaks of white remain. Pour into the skillet.
6. Bake in the preheated hot oven (400°) for 15 minutes or until the soufflé is puffed and golden and set. Serve immediately; otherwise the bread will begin to fall.

> **KEEP YOUR FLOUR FRESH**
> **Regular all-purpose flour can be stored in an airtight container at room temperature. Whole-wheat flour and rye flour should be stored in the freezer in an airtight freezer bag or container if you will not be using them right away.**

◪ *Bantry Brown Bread*

South of Cork lies Bantry Bay, a land of seafaring men who keep warm with large mugs of strong tea and wedges of soda bread.

Bake at 375° for 45 minutes.
Makes 1 seven-inch round (12 generous slices).

Nutrient Value Per Slice: 179 calories, 5 gm. protein, 5 gm. fat, 294 mg. sodium, 1 mg. cholesterol.

1   **cup unsifted all-purpose flour**
¼   **cup sugar**
2   **teaspoons baking powder**
1   **teaspoon baking soda**
1   **teaspoon salt**
2   **cups unsifted whole-wheat flour**
¼   **cup currants**
¼   **cup vegetable shortening**
1¼ **cups buttermilk**
2   **tablespoons sugar**
1   **tablespoon water**

1. Preheat the oven to moderate (375°).
2. Sift together the flour, ¼ cup sugar, baking powder, baking soda and salt into a medium-size bowl. Stir in the whole-wheat flour and currants. Cut in the shortening with a pastry blender or fork until the mixture resembles small peas. Stir in the buttermilk.
3. Turn the dough out onto a lightly floured pastry cloth or board. Knead 10 times. Shape into a 7-inch round loaf. Place on a cookie sheet. Cut a cross in the top of the dough.
4. Bake in the preheated moderate oven (375°) for 40 minutes; remove from the oven.
5. Combine the 2 tablespoons of sugar and the water in a saucepan; bring to boiling. Brush over the hot loaf. Return to the oven and bake for 5 minutes or until golden.

◼ ☐ *Apple-Walnut Muffins*

Bake at 375° for 15 minutes.
Makes 16 muffins.

Nutrient Value Per Serving: 168 calories, 3 gm. protein, 7 gm. fat, 159 mg. sodium, 44 mg. cholesterol.

2   **cups unsifted all-purpose flour**
½   **cup sugar**
1   **tablespoon baking powder**
1   **teaspoon ground cinnamon**
½   **teaspoon salt**
¾   **cup milk**
2   **eggs**
¼   **cup (½ stick) unsalted butter or margarine, melted and cooled**
1½ **cups coarsely grated apple (2 apples)**
½   **cup chopped walnuts**
¼   **cup sugar**
½   **teaspoon ground cinnamon**

1. Preheat the oven to moderate (375°). Grease the bottoms of sixteen 2½-inch muffin-pan cups.
2. Combine the flour, sugar, baking powder, cinnamon and salt in a bowl; stir to mix.
3. Whisk the milk, eggs and butter in another bowl until blended. Pour over the flour mixture; stir just until the dry ingredients are moistened. Stir in the grated apple. Spoon the batter into the prepared muffin-pan cups, filling each two-thirds full.
4. Combine the walnuts, sugar and cinnamon in a small bowl. Sprinkle over the batter.
5. Bake in the moderate oven (375°) for 15 minutes or until a wooden pick tests clean. Cool in the pans for 5 minutes. Unmold onto a wire rack.

MIXING MUFFINS
When adding the liquid to the dry ingredients, stir as little as possible, just enough to moisten the dry ingredients. The batter will be slightly lumpy. Over-stirring will produce a muffin that is coarse textured and full of tunnels. A good muffin should have straight sides, a rounded top and a uniform grain.

▢ *Applesauce Doughnuts*

Makes 4 dozen.

Nutrient Value Per Doughnut: 64 calories, 1 gm. protein, 3 gm. fat, 30 mg. sodium, 12 mg. cholesterol.

> **Vegetable oil for frying**
> 2¼ **cups sifted all-purpose flour**
> 1½ **teaspoons baking powder**
> ½ **teaspoon baking soda**
> ½ **teaspoon ground cinnamon**
> ½ **teaspoon ground nutmeg**
> ¼ **teaspoon ground cloves**
> ¼ **teaspoon salt**
> ½ **cup granulated sugar**
> ¼ **cup firmly packed light brown sugar**
> 2 **eggs**
> 2 **tablespoons vegetable oil**
> ¼ **cup milk**
> 1 **cup unsweetened applesauce**
> ½ **teaspoon vanilla**
> **10X (confectioners') sugar (optional)**

1. Fill a large heavy saucepan or electric skillet two-thirds full with vegetable oil. Heat to 360° on a deep-fat frying thermometer.
2. Sift together the flour, baking powder, baking soda, cinnamon, nutmeg, cloves and salt onto a piece of wax paper.
3. Beat together the granulated sugar, brown sugar and eggs in large bowl with an electric mixer at medium speed until fluffy. Beat in the 2 tablespoons oil. Stir in the flour mixture, alternately with the milk, beginning and ending with the dry ingredients, until well blended. Stir in the applesauce and vanilla.
4. Carefully drop the batter by level tablespoonfuls, 3 or 4 at a time, into the hot oil. Do not overcrowd the pan or the oil may overflow. Fry, turning once with tongs, for 3 minutes or until golden. Transfer with tongs to paper toweling to drain. Cool completely. Sprinkle with 10X (confectioners') sugar, if you wish.

▲Applesauce Doughnuts

◣ ▢ *Apple Griddle Cakes*

Makes 5 servings.

Nutrient Value Per Serving: 334 calories, 10 gm. protein, 11 gm. fat, 333 mg. sodium, 122 mg. cholesterol.

> 2 **cups sifted all-purpose flour**
> 2 **tablespoons sugar**
> 1 **teaspoon baking soda**
> ½ **teaspoon salt**
> 2 **eggs**

1 **cup milk**
1 **cup plain yogurt**
2 **tablespoons vegetable oil**
1 **medium-size apple, pared and
   finely chopped**

1. Sift the flour, sugar, baking soda and salt into a medium-size bowl.
2. Beat the eggs lightly in another medium-size bowl; stir in the milk, yogurt and oil.
3. Add the milk mixture all at once to the dry ingredients; stir just until smooth. Gently stir in the apples.
4. Spoon the batter onto a hot, lightly greased griddle to form 5-inch circles. Cook over medium heat until brown on the underside. Turn; cook until the other side is brown. Keep warm in a slow oven until all the batter is used.

GRIDDLE TEST
Shake a few drops of water from your fingers over the hot griddle. If the drops sizzle, sputter and jump around over the surface, the griddle is ready.

Whole-Wheat Granola Waffles with Honey Butter

Makes 6 servings.

Nutrient Value Per Serving: 612 calories, 14 gm. protein, 43 gm. fat, 423 mg. sodium, 119 mg. cholesterol.

1 **cup unsifted whole-wheat flour**
1 **cup quick oats, uncooked**
½ **cup wheat germ**
2 **teaspoons baking powder**
2 **cups milk**
¼ **cup (½ stick) butter, melted**
2 **tablespoons honey**
1 **egg**
1 **cup chopped pecans**
   Honey Butter (recipe follows)

1. Combine the flour, oats, wheat germ and baking powder in a medium-size bowl. Beat in the milk, butter, honey and egg until well blended. Fold in the pecans.
2. Heat a double waffle maker to medium-hot. Pour the batter, a heaping ½ cup for two waffles, onto the medium-hot waffle maker. Spread the batter to the edges. Cook until the waffle stops steaming; the waffle should be cooked through. If not, close the waffle maker and cook a little longer. Serve hot with Honey Butter.

Honey Butter: Beat ½ cup (1 stick) softened butter, 1 tablespoon honey and ⅓ cup raisins together until well blended. Spread on hot waffles.

WAFFLES ANY TIME
Make a double batch and wrap leftover waffles in aluminum foil with 2 pieces of wax paper between the layers. Freeze. Reheat the frozen waffles in a toaster whenever you want one!

Yeast Breads

🔲 Cornmeal-Rye Bread

Bake at 375° for 45 minutes.
Makes 2 loaves.

Nutritional Value Per Loaf: 1942 calories, 49 gm. protein, 33 gm. fat, 23 mg. sodium, 0 mg. cholesterol.

 2 **envelopes active dry yeast**
 ½ **teaspoon sugar**
 2½ **cups very warm water**
 ½ **cup cornmeal**
 ⅓ **cup firmly packed light brown sugar**
 ¼ **cup vegetable oil**
 1¼ **cups unsifted rye flour**
 ¼ **cup wheat germ**
 5½ **to 6 cups sifted all-purpose flour**

1. Sprinkle the yeast and sugar into ½ cup of very warm water in a 1-cup glass measure. ("Very warm water" should feel comfortably warm when dropped on your wrist.) Stir to dissolve the yeast. Let stand until bubbly, about 10 minutes.
2. Combine the cornmeal and brown sugar in a large bowl. Heat the remaining 2 cups of water to boiling; pour the water, then the oil, over the cornmeal mixture. Stir to blend. Cool the mixture to lukewarm; stir in the yeast mixture.
3. Beat in the rye flour, wheat germ and 4 cups of the all-purpose flour until smooth. Stir in enough of the additional flour to make a soft dough.
4. Turn out onto a lightly floured surface; knead until smooth and elastic, about 10 minutes, using only as much flour as needed to keep the dough from sticking.
5. Place in a large greased bowl, turn to coat. Cover; let rise in a warm place away from drafts for 1 hour or until double in volume.

▲ **Cornmeal-Rye Bread**

6. Grease two 9 x 5 x 3-inch or two 8½ x 4½ x 3-inch loaf pans. Punch the dough down; turn out onto a lightly floured surface; knead several times. Divide the dough in half; shape into two loaves. Place the loaves into the prepared pans. Cover; let rise in a warm place away from drafts until double in volume, about 45 minutes.
7. Preheat the oven to moderate (375°).
8. Bake in the preheated moderate oven (375°) for 40 to 45 minutes or until the loaves are brown and sound hollow when they are tapped on the bottom. Remove the bread from the pans; cool on wire racks.

TO KNEAD YEAST BREADS
Place the dough on a lightly floured surface. Grasp the back edge of the dough and fold it in half toward you; then push down and back with the heel of your hand. Give the dough a quarter turn, and repeat the process until the dough is smooth and elastic.

◨ *Early Autumn Barley Loaf*

An extremely soft bread that holds up well in sandwiches.

Bake at 325° for 1¼ hours.
Makes 2 loaves.

Nutritional Value Per Loaf: 2594 calories, 70 gm. protein, 19 gm. fat, 1249 mg. sodium, 0 mg. cholesterol.

⅓ **cup barley**
4 **cups water**
2 **envelopes active dry yeast**
⅓ **cup firmly packed light brown sugar**
¼ **cup very warm water**
2 **tablespoons butter or margarine**
1 **teaspoon salt**
3 **cups unsifted whole-wheat flour**
1½ **cups raisins, finely chopped with**
    1 tablespoon flour
5 **to 6 cups unsifted all-purpose flour**

1. Rinse the barley in a coarse strainer under cold running water; turn into a large saucepan; cover with the 4 cups of water. Cover the saucepan with a lid or plastic wrap. Let stand overnight at room temperature.
2. Next day, bring the barley and soaking liquid to boiling; lower the heat; simmer for 45 minutes or until the barley is tender. Reserve 2 cups of the barley water; drain and discard the remaining water.
3. Place the barley in the container of an electric blender; cover. Whirl until smooth; reserve.
4. Sprinkle the yeast and 1 teaspoon of the sugar over ¼ cup of very warm water in a 1-cup glass measure. ("Very warm water" should feel comfortably warm when dropped on your wrist.) Stir to dissolve the yeast. Let stand until bubbly, about 10 minutes.
5. Heat the reserved barley water, butter, remaining sugar and salt in a medium-size

saucepan until the butter melts. Pour into a large bowl; add the reserved puréed barley; cool to lukewarm. Stir in the yeast mixture.
6. Stir in the whole-wheat flour and raisins until smooth; beat in enough of the all-purpose flour to make a soft dough.
7. Turn out onto a lightly floured surface. Knead until smooth and elastic, about 10 minutes, using only as much flour as needed to keep the dough from sticking.
8. Place in a buttered large bowl; turn to bring the buttered side up. Cover with a damp towel. Let rise in a warm place, away from drafts, for 1 hour or until doubled in volume.
9. Punch the dough down; turn out onto a lightly floured surface; knead a few times; invert a bowl over the dough; let rest for 10 minutes.
10. Grease two 9 x 5 x 3-inch loaf pans. Divide the dough in half and knead each half a few times. Shape into two loaves. Place the loaves in the prepared pans. Cover with a damp towel.
11. Let rise again in a warm place, away from drafts for 45 minutes or until doubled in volume.
12. Place a rack in the lowest position in the oven. Preheat the oven to slow (325°).
13. Bake in the preheated slow oven (325°) for 1¼ hours or until golden brown and the loaves sound hollow when tapped on the bottom of the loaves. Cover the loaves loosely with aluminum foil after 30 minutes to prevent over-browning. Remove from the pans to wire racks to cool completely.

BE SURE TO USE FRESH YEAST
All packages of yeast are dated. For the best results, be sure to use the yeast before that date.

◼ *Honey and Cream Cheese-Whole-Wheat Bread*

Bake at 325° for 45 minutes.
Makes 2 loaves.

Nutrient Value Per Loaf: 1956 calories, 64 gm.
protein, 36 gm. fat, 1889 mg. sodium, 63 mg.
cholesterol.

2 **envelopes active dry yeast**
½ **cup very warm water**
½ **cup honey**
1 **can (5.33 ounces) evaporated milk**
    (⅔ cup)
    Water
4 **ounces cream cheese, softened**
    (from an 8-ounce package)
3 **cups unsifted whole-wheat flour**
½ **cup wheat germ**
1½ **teaspoons salt**
2½ **to 3 cups unsifted all-purpose flour**
1 **tablespoon water**
½ **teaspoon honey**
2 **teaspoons sesame seeds**

1. Sprinkle the yeast over the very warm
   water in a 1-cup glass measure; stir in 1
   teaspoon of the honey. ("Very warm water"
   should feel comfortably warm when
   dropped on your wrist.) Stir to dissolve
   the yeast; let stand until bubbly, about 10
   minutes.
2. Pour the evaporated milk into a 2-cup
   measure; add water to make 1½ cups of
   liquid. Pour into a medium-size saucepan;
   add the remaining honey and cream
   cheese. Heat slowly until the cheese starts
   to melt; beat slightly with a wire whisk
   until the mixture is blended. Pour into a
   large bowl; cool to lukewarm. Stir in the
   yeast mixture.
3. Stir in the whole-wheat flour, wheat germ
   and salt until smooth; beat in enough all-
   purpose flour to make a soft dough.
4. Turn out onto a lightly floured surface;
   knead until smooth and elastic, about 10

minutes, using only as much flour as
needed to keep the dough from sticking.
5. Place the dough in a buttered large bowl;
   turn to bring the buttered side up. Cover
   with a damp towel. Let rise in a warm
   place, away from drafts, for 1 hour or until
   doubled in volume.
6. Punch the dough down; turn out onto a
   lightly floured surface; knead a few times;
   invert a bowl over the dough; let rest for
   about 10 minutes.
7. Butter two 8 x 4 x 3-inch loaf pans. Divide
   the dough in half and knead each half a
   few times; shape into two loaves. Place the
   loaves into the prepared pans; cover with a
   towel.
8. Let rise again in a warm place, away from
   drafts, for 45 minutes or until double in
   volume.
9. Combine the 1 tablespoon water with the
   ½ teaspoon honey in a small cup; brush
   over the loaves after the second rising;
   sprinkle with the sesame seeds.
10. Place a rack in the lowest position in the
    oven. Preheat the oven to slow (325°).
11. Bake in the preheated slow oven (325°) for
    45 minutes or until browned and the
    loaves sound hollow when tapped on the
    bottom of the loaves. Cover the loaves
    loosely with a piece of aluminum foil after
    30 minutes to prevent over-browning.
    Remove from the pans to wire racks to
    cool completely.

FOR ONE SLICE
**This is an excellent bread to slice into
¾-inch-slices, wrap in aluminum foil and
freeze. The individual slices can then be
removed and warmed or toasted for
breakfast, slathered with peanut butter, jam
or cream cheese. And it's great with soup.**

☖ *Nut and Raisin Batter Bread*

Bake at 375° for 50 minutes.
Makes 1 loaf (16 slices).

Nutrient Value Per Slice: 210 calories, 6 gm. protein, 7 gm. fat, 161 mg. sodium, 5 mg. cholesterol.

    2   *envelopes active dry yeast*
    ⅓   *cup nonfat dry milk powder*
    ⅓   *cup firmly packed dark brown sugar*
    1   *teaspoon salt*
    ¼   *cup vegetable oil*
    2   *cups very warm milk*
    2   *cups* sifted *all-purpose flour*
    1½ *cups* unsifted *whole-wheat flour*
    ½   *cup raisins*
    ½   *cup walnuts, chopped*

1. Grease a 10-cup Kugelhopf mold or 9-inch angel-cake tube pan.
2. Combine the yeast, milk powder, brown sugar, salt and oil in a large bowl. Stir in the very warm milk. ("Very warm milk" should feel comfortably warm when dropped on your wrist.) Beat the mixture until well blended, about 30 seconds.
3. Mix together the all-purpose and whole-wheat flours in a medium-size bowl. Stir 1½ cups of the flour mixture into the yeast mixture. Beat with an electric mixer at medium speed for 2 minutes. Stir in another ½ cup of the flour mixture; beat for 1 minute. Stir in the raisins, walnuts and remaining flour until well mixed; the dough will be heavy and sticky.
4. Turn the dough into the prepared pan. Cover with buttered wax paper and a towel. Let rise in a warm place, away from drafts, until doubled in bulk, about 20 minutes. Preheat the oven to moderate (375°).
5. Bake in the preheated moderate oven (375°) for 50 minutes or until the loaf sounds hollow when tapped on the bottom of the loaf. Remove the bread from the pan; cool on a wire rack.

◁◁◁ ☖ *Swedish Limpa Breads*

Bake at 375° for 30 minutes.
Makes four 6-inch loaves (10 slices per loaf).

Nutrient Value Per Slice: 62 calories, 1 gm. protein, 0.8 gm. fat, 162 mg. sodium, 0 mg. cholesterol.

    2   *envelopes active dry yeast*
    1½ *cups very warm water*
    ⅓   *cup sugar*
    ¼   *cup molasses*
    1   *tablespoon salt*
    3   *tablespoons grated orange rind*
    2⅓ *cups* sifted *all-purpose flour,*
         or as needed
    2½ *cups* sifted *rye flour*
    2   *tablespoons vegetable shortening*
         Cornmeal

1. Sprinkle the yeast over the very warm water in a large bowl. ("Very warm water" should feel comfortably warm when dropped on your wrist.) Stir to dissolve the yeast.
2. Stir in the sugar, molasses, salt and orange rind until well blended. Stir in the all-purpose and rye flours; beat until smooth. Beat in the shortening. Gradually stir in enough additional all-purpose flour, if necessary, to make a soft dough.
3. Turn the dough out onto a lightly floured surface. Knead until smooth and elastic, about 10 minutes, adding all-purpose flour as needed to prevent sticking.
4. Place the dough in a greased bowl, turn to bring the greased side up. Cover with a damp towel. Let rise in warm place, away from drafts, for 1 hour or until doubled in volume.
5. Generously grease two cookie sheets and sprinkle with cornmeal. Punch the dough down. Shape into a ball. Cut into 4 equal portions. Shape each portion into a rounded loaf. Place the loaves on opposite ends of the prepared cookie sheets. Cover the loaves with a damp towel. Let rise again

in a warm place, away from drafts, for 1 hour or until the loaves are doubled in volume.
6. Preheat the oven to moderate (375°).
7. Bake in the preheated moderate oven (375°) for 30 minutes or until the loaves are lightly browned and sound hollow when tapped on the bottom of the loaves. Remove from the cookie sheets to wire racks to cool completely.

MAKE AHEAD FOR GREAT GIFTS
Wrap the cooled, baked loaves in freezer wrap or aluminum foil; freeze. Wonderful to have on hand for holiday gifts.

Store for up to 4 months in the freezer. Let stand at room temperature for 1 hour before serving.

⧖ *Orange-Currant Batter Bread*

Bake at 350° for 40 minutes.
Makes 1 loaf (16 slices).

Nutrient Value Per Slice: 192 calories, 4 gm. protein, 5 gm. fat, 124 mg. sodium, 63 mg. cholesterol.

3/4 **cup milk**
6   **tablespoons sugar**
1/2 **teaspoon salt**
5   **tablespoons butter**
1   **tablespoon grated orange rind**
1   **envelope active dry yeast**
1/2 **teaspoon sugar**
1/4 **cup very warm water**
1   **cup currants**
1   **tablespoon all-purpose flour**
3   **eggs, slightly beaten**
3   **cups** sifted **all-purpose flour**
1   **tablespoon orange juice**
1/2 **cup 10X (confectioners') sugar**

1. Grease a 6½-cup ring mold.
2. Combine the milk, the 6 tablespoons sugar, salt and butter in a small saucepan. Heat, stirring, just until the butter is melted. Pour into a large bowl. Cool to lukewarm. Stir in the orange rind.
3. Sprinkle the yeast and the ½ teaspoon sugar over very warm water in 1-cup glass measure. ("Very warm water" should feel comfortably warm when dropped on your wrist.) Stir to dissolve the yeast. Let stand until bubbly, about 10 minutes.
4. Toss the currants with the 1 tablespoon flour in a small bowl.
5. Stir the eggs, yeast mixture and 1 cup of the flour into the cooled milk mixture. Beat with an electric mixer at medium speed until smooth. Mix in the remaining 2 cups of flour, 1 cup at a time, until smooth. Stir in the currants. Turn into the prepared mold. Cover with buttered wax paper and a towel. Let rise in a warm place, away from drafts, until doubled in bulk, about 45 minutes. Preheat the oven to moderate (350°).
6. Bake in the preheated moderate oven (350°) for 40 minutes or until the loaf is golden brown and sounds hollow when tapped on the bottom of the loaf. Cool in the pan on a wire rack for 10 minutes. Remove the bread from the pan; cool to room temperature.
7. Gradually stir the orange juice into the 10X (confectioners') sugar in small bowl until the glaze is a good pouring consistency. Drizzle over the bread.

▼ *Onion-Parsley Batter Bread*

Bake at 375° for 35 minutes.
Makes 1 large loaf (20 slices).

Nutrient Value Per Slice: 153 calories, 4 gm. protein, 3 gm. fat, 146 mg. sodium, 22 mg. cholesterol.

> 1 **cup chopped onion (1 large onion)**
> ¼ **cup (½ stick) butter or margarine**
> 2 **envelopes active dry yeast**
> 4 **tablespoons light brown sugar**
> ½ **cup very warm water**
> 1½ **cups milk**
> 1 **teaspoon salt**
> 1 **egg, slightly beaten**
> 5 **cups sifted all-purpose flour**
> ⅓ **cup chopped parsley**
> **Melted butter**

1. Grease a 2-quart soufflé dish or glass casserole.
2. Sauté the onion in the butter in a medium-size skillet, stirring often, until lightly browned. Reserve.
3. Sprinkle the yeast and 2 tablespoons of the brown sugar over very warm water in 2-cup glass measure. ("Very warm water" should feel comfortably warm when dropped on your wrist.) Stir to dissolve the yeast. Let stand until bubbly, about 10 minutes.
4. Heat the milk in a small saucepan until bubbles appear around the edge. Combine the milk, salt, and the remaining 2 tablespoons of brown sugar in a large bowl. Cool to room temperature.
5. Add the yeast mixture, sautéed onions, egg and flour to the milk mixture in the bowl. Mix with an electric mixer at low speed until blended; beat at medium speed for 3 minutes longer. Mix in the parsley. Spread the batter in the prepared dish. Cover with buttered wax paper and a towel. Let rise in a warm place, away from drafts, until double in bulk, about 45 minutes. Preheat the oven to moderate (375°).

6. Bake in the preheated moderate oven (375°) for 35 to 40 minutes or until the bread sounds hollow when tapped on the bottom of the loaf. Turn out onto a wire rack. Brush the top with melted butter. Serve warm.

▼ ▢ *Dill-Cottage Cheese Batter Bread*

Bake at 350° for 60 minutes.
Makes 1 loaf (12 slices).

Nutrient Value Per Slice: 134 calories, 6 gm. protein, 3 gm. fat, 290 mg. sodium, 31 mg. cholesterol.

> 1 **envelope active dry yeast**
> ½ **teaspoon sugar**
> ¼ **cup very warm water**
> 1 **egg**
> 1 **tablespoon dried instant toasted onions**
> 1 **tablespoon butter or margarine, softened**
> 2 **teaspoons dried dillweed**
> 1 **teaspoon salt**
> 1 **cup small curd cottage cheese**
> ¼ **teaspoon baking powder**
> 2½ **cups unsifted all-purpose flour**
> **Melted butter**

1. Grease a 1-quart baking dish.
2. Sprinkle the yeast and sugar over the very warm water in 1-cup glass measure. ("Very warm water" should feel comfortably warm when dropped on your wrist.) Stir to dissolve the yeast. Let stand until bubbly, about 10 minutes.
3. Beat egg slightly in a large bowl. Add the dried instant toasted onions, butter, dillweed, salt, cottage cheese and baking powder; beat until well blended. Stir in the yeast mixture until well blended. Stir in enough of the flour to make a soft dough. Place the dough in the prepared baking

dish. Cover with buttered wax paper and a towel. Let rise in a warm place, away from drafts, until doubled in bulk, about 1 hour. Preheat the oven to moderate (350°).

4. Bake in the preheated moderate oven (350°) for 60 minutes or until the loaf sounds hollow when tapped on the bottom of the loaf. Turn the bread out onto a wire rack. Brush with melted butter. Serve warm.

Chili-Cheese Batter Cornbread

Bake at 350° for 35 minutes.
Makes 1 loaf (12 slices).

Nutrient Value Per Slice: 182 calories, 5 gm. protein, 7 gm. fat, 269 mg. sodium, 51 mg. cholesterol.

  ½ cup water
  3 tablespoons sugar
  1 teaspoon salt
  *¼ cup (½ stick) margarine,
      at room temperature*
  1 envelope active dry yeast
  ½ teaspoon sugar
  ¼ cup very warm water
  1¾ cups unsifted all-purpose flour
  ¾ cup yellow cornmeal
  2 tablespoons nonfat dry milk powder
  2 eggs, slightly beaten
  ½ cup shredded Cheddar cheese (2 ounces)
  *2 tablespoons chopped canned green
      chilies*

1. Grease a 8½ x 4½ x 2½-inch glass or ceramic loaf pan.
2. Combine the ½ cup water, 3 tablespoons sugar, salt and margarine in a small saucepan. Heat over low heat, stirring, just until the margarine is melted. Cool to lukewarm.
3. Sprinkle the yeast and the ½ teaspoon sugar over very warm water in 1-cup glass measure. ("Very warm water" should feel comfortably warm when dropped on your

wrist.) Stir to dissolve the yeast. Let stand until bubbly, about 10 minutes.
4. Stir together the flour, cornmeal and dry milk powder in large bowl. Add the eggs, margarine mixture and yeast mixture; beat until well blended. Stir in the cheese and chilies. Turn the batter into the prepared pan. Cover with buttered wax paper and a towel. Let rise in a warm place, away from drafts, until doubled in bulk, about 1 hour. Preheat the oven to moderate (350°).
5. Bake in the preheated moderate oven (350°) for 35 minutes or until browned on top. Remove the bread from the pan; cool on wire rack. Serve warm or at room temperature.

Golden Coffee Bread

Bake at 350° for 50 to 60 minutes.
Makes one 7-inch round loaf (8 servings).

Nutrient Value Per Serving: 623 calories, 13 gm. protein, 22 gm. fat, 233 mg. sodium, 145 mg. cholesterol.

  1 envelope active dry yeast
  ¼ cup very warm water
  ½ cup sugar
  ¾ cup milk
  *¼ teaspoon saffron threads
      OR: 1½ teaspoons ground cinnamon*
  3 eggs
  4½ to 5 cups unsifted all-purpose flour
  10 tablespoons butter or margarine
  ½ cup golden raisins
  ½ cup coarsely chopped candied fruits
  *½ cup chopped blanched almonds
      Sliced almonds (optional)*

1. Sprinkle the yeast into the very warm water in a 1-cup glass measure. ("Very warm water" should feel comfortably warm when dropped on your wrist.) Add 1 teaspoon of the sugar. Stir until the yeast and sugar are

dissolved. Let stand until bubbly, about 10 minutes.

2. Heat the milk with the remaining sugar in a saucepan until lukewarm; pour into a large mixing bowl. Add the saffron, 2 eggs and one egg yolk (reserve the remaining egg white), yeast mixture and 3 cups of the flour. Beat until smooth and elastic, 4 minutes. Beat in the butter gradually, about 4 minutes. Add the remaining flour; beat 2 minutes. Stir in the raisins, fruits and almonds. Smooth the top.

3. Cover the bowl with wax paper, then a clean towel. Let rise in a warm place, away from drafts, for 1 hour or until doubled in bulk. Grease a straight-sided ovenproof bowl or soufflé dish, 7¼ x 3½-inches.

4. Stir the dough down; turn out onto a lightly floured surface. Knead lightly several times, using only enough flour to keep the dough from sticking; shape into a ball. Press gently into the prepared bowl. Cover. Let rise again in a warm place until double in bulk, about 1 hour. Brush with the slightly beaten reserved egg white; decorate the top with sliced almonds if you wish. Preheat the oven to moderate (350°).

5. Bake in the preheated moderate oven (350°) for 50 to 60 minutes or until the loaf sounds hollow when tapped on the bottom of the loaf. If the loaf browns too quickly, cover it loosely with foil. Cool in the bowl on a wire rack for 10 minutes. Turn out onto the wire rack; cool completely. To serve, cut into quarters; slice each quarter crosswise.

 *Pecan Corn Muffins*

Bake at 350° for 20 minutes.
Makes 18 muffins.

Nutrient Value Per Serving: 233 calories, 6 gm. protein, 11 gm. fat, 209 mg. sodium, 46 mg. cholesterol.

3½ cups unsifted whole-wheat flour
1 cup yellow cornmeal
1 envelope active dry yeast
1 teaspoon baking powder
1 teaspoon salt
1 cup milk
½ cup (1 stick) butter
½ cup water
⅓ cup honey
2 eggs
1 cup coarsely chopped pecans

1. Grease 18 medium-size muffin-pan cups. Sprinkle each with cornmeal.

2. Combine 1 cup of the flour, the cornmeal, yeast, baking powder and salt in a large bowl.

3. Heat the milk, butter, water and honey in a small saucepan until the butter melts; cool to lukewarm. Pour into the flour mixture. Beat at medium speed with an electric mixer for 2 minutes. Beat in the eggs. Stir in the remaining flour. Add the pecans.

4. Shape the dough in the prepared muffin cups, filling each three-quarter full. Smooth the tops slightly. Cover; let rise in a warm place, to top of muffin cups, about 45 minutes. Preheat the oven to moderate (350°).

5. Bake in the preheated moderate oven (350°) for 20 minutes or until golden. Turn onto a wire rack. Serve warm.

Fast-Rising Yeast Breads

The old-fashioned flavor of yeast breads hasn't changed—but the time you spend making them has! Use the new, quick-acting dry yeast that mixes directly with the dry ingredients and causes the dough to rise up to 50 percent faster.

TIPS FOR USING FAST-RISING DRY YEAST
Follow these pointers for using the new yeast in our delicious breads, as well as in your own favorite recipes.
● **Always include water in the ingredients. If your recipe calls for all milk or liquid other than water, decrease the amount of liquid by ¼ cup per envelope of fast-rising yeast used and substitute an equal amount of water.**
● **Combine the yeast with about two thirds of the flour and the other dry ingredients in a large bowl. No need to dissolve the yeast in a liquid first.**
● **Heat the liquids and solid or liquid fats, but not the eggs, in a saucepan until *hot* to the touch, 130°. This is hotter than the 110°-115° usually required if the yeast is being dissolved directly in a liquid.**
● **Stir the hot liquids into the dry ingredients; add the eggs, if using. Blend at low speed with an electric mixer; then beat at medium speed for 3 minutes. Stir in enough remaining flour to make a soft dough.**
● **Follow the recipe directions for kneading and rising (the rising time is reduced by one half to one third). Start checking the dough halfway through the suggested rising time in a recipe calling for regular yeast.**

▉ Greek Trinity Bread

Bake at 375° for 35 minutes.
Makes 1 loaf (18 slices).

Nutrient Value Per Slice: 193 calories, 4 gm. protein, 4 gm. fat, 101 mg. sodium, 40 mg. cholesterol.

3½ to 4 cups **unsifted all-purpose flour**
⅓ cup **granulated sugar**
¾ teaspoon **salt**
1 envelope **fast-rising dry yeast**
⅓ cup **milk**
⅓ cup **water**
⅓ cup **unsalted butter or margarine**
2 **eggs, at room temperature**
1 tablespoon **grated lemon rind**
⅓ cup **currants**
⅓ cup **chopped candied red cherries**
2 teaspoons **water**
1 teaspoon **lemon juice**
1 cup **sifted 10X (confectioners') sugar**

1. Combine 2 cups of the flour, the ⅓ cup granulated sugar, salt and yeast in a large bowl; stir to mix well.
2. Combine the milk, water and butter in a small saucepan. Heat to 130° (mixture should feel comfortably hot to the touch). Add to the flour mixture. Add the eggs and lemon rind. Blend at low speed with an electric mixer; then beat at medium speed for 3 minutes. Gradually stir in ½ cup of the remaining flour to make a soft dough.
3. Turn the dough out onto a well floured surface. Knead until smooth and elastic, 8 to 10 minutes, using up to 1 cup of the remaining flour to prevent sticking.
4. Place the dough in a buttered large bowl, turning the dough to bring the buttered side up. Cover; let rise in a warm place, away from drafts, until almost doubled in bulk, 30 to 40 minutes.
5. Punch the dough down. Knead in the currants and candied red cherries, a little at a time. Divide the dough into 3 equal parts;

shape each into a ball. Arrange, touching, like a clover leaf, on a greased large cookie sheet. Cover with buttered wax paper and a towel. Let rise in a warm place, away from drafts, until doubled in bulk and balls have joined, 20 to 30 minutes. Preheat the oven to moderate (375°).

6. Bake in the preheated moderate oven (375°) for 35 minutes or until the bread is nicely browned and sounds hollow when tapped on the bottom of the loaf. Transfer to a wire rack.

7. Gradually stir the water and lemon juice into the 10X (confectioners') sugar in a small bowl until smooth and a good spreading consistency. Spread over the top of the bread.

▲ **Swiss Easter Bread**

🍸 *Swiss Easter Bread*

Five pastel-colored eggs are nestled in the braid of this colorful Easter bread. The eggs are uncooked, so take care in tucking them in. After baking, frost and decorate the bread with colored sprinkles.

Bake at 350° for 35 minutes.
Makes 1 loaf (18 slices).

Nutrient Value Per Slice: 200 calories, 6 gm. protein, 6 gm. fat, 104 mg. sodium, 111 mg. cholesterol.

3 to 3½ cups unsifted all-purpose flour
¼ cup granulated sugar
1 envelope fast-rising dry yeast
½ teaspoon salt
⅓ cup milk
⅓ cup water
2 tablespoons unsalted butter or margarine
2 eggs, at room temperature
⅓ cup chopped mixed candied fruits
½ cup chopped blanched almonds
5 uncooked eggs, pastel colored
1 tablespoon milk
⅛ teaspoon vanilla
1 cup sifted 10X (confectioners') sugar Colored sprinkles

1. Combine 2 cups of the flour, the granulated sugar, yeast, and salt in a large bowl; stir to mix well.

2. Combine the ⅓ cup milk, water and butter in a small saucepan. Heat to 130° (mixture should feel comfortably hot to the touch). Add to the flour mixture. Add the 2 eggs. Blend at low speed with an electric mixer; then beat at medium speed for 3 minutes. Gradually stir in 1 cup of the remaining flour to make a soft dough.

3. Turn the dough out onto a well-floured surface. Knead until smooth and elastic, 8 to 10 minutes, using up to ½ cup of the remaining flour to prevent sticking.

4. Place the dough in an oiled large bowl, turning to bring the oiled side up. Cover; let rise in a warm place, away from drafts, until doubled in bulk, 30 to 35 minutes.

5. Punch the dough down. Turn out onto a floured surface. Knead in the candied fruits and almonds, a little at a time. Divide the dough into thirds. Roll each piece into a 20-inch rope. Loosely braid the ropes together. Shape into a circle, joining the ends securely together. Transfer to a greased large cookie sheet. Carefully tuck the pastel-colored eggs into the braid, spacing evenly around the bread. Cover with buttered wax paper and a towel. Let rise in a warm place, away from drafts, until doubled in bulk, 30 to 40 minutes. Preheat the oven to moderate (350°).

6. Bake in the preheated moderate oven (350°) for 35 minutes or until the bread is nicely browned and sounds hollow when tapped on the bottom of the loaf. Transfer the bread to a wire rack to cool.

7. Gradually stir the 1 tablespoon of milk and the vanilla into the 10X (confectioners') sugar in a small bowl until smooth and a good pouring consistency. Drizzle over the top of the bread. Decorate with colored sprinkles.

Basil Breads

Two unusual breads from one recipe—a coiled loaf and rolls.

Bake loaf at 375° for 30 to 35 minutes; bake rolls at 375° for 20 to 25 minutes.
Makes 1 loaf (8 servings) and 8 rolls.

Nutrient Value Per Serving: 239 calories, 7 gm. protein, 2 gm. fat, 283 mg. sodium, 18 mg. cholesterol.

7½ **cups unsifted all-purpose flour**
1 **tablespoon sugar**
2 **teaspoons salt**
1 **envelope fast-rising dry yeast**
2½ **cups water**
1 **cup finely chopped fresh basil leaves**
1 **tablespoon lemon juice**
3 **teaspoons sesame seeds (optional)**
2 **tablespoons finely chopped walnuts**
2 **tablespoons grated Parmesan cheese**
1 **egg yolk**
1 **teaspoon water**

1. Set aside 1 cup of the flour. Combine the remaining flour, sugar, salt and yeast in a large bowl; stir to mix well.

2. Heat the water in small saucepan to 130° (water should feel comfortably hot to the touch). Add to the flour mixture. Beat with a wooden spoon until smooth. Gradually stir in enough of the remaining flour to make a soft dough.

3. Turn out onto a lightly floured surface. Knead until smooth and elastic, 8 to 10 minutes, adding more flour as needed to prevent sticking. Form into a ball. Place in an oiled bowl. Turn dough, oiled side up. Cover with plastic wrap. Refrigerate 12 to 24 hours.

4. Punch the dough down; turn out onto a lightly floured surface. Knead a few times. Invert bowl over dough. Let rest for 10 minutes.

5. Combine ½ cup of the chopped basil, the lemon juice and 2 teaspoons of the sesame seeds, if you wish, in a small bowl. Combine the remaining basil, the walnuts and Parmesan cheese in another small bowl. Reserve 1 tablespoon of this mixture.

6. Divide the dough in half. Keep one half under the bowl. Roll the other half into a 16 x 12-inch rectangle. Spread with the basil-lemon mixture. Roll up from a long side, jelly-roll fashion, into a 16-inch long roll.

7. Lightly oil a solid 8-inch circle on a cookie sheet no larger than 15 x 12-inches. Coil the roll into a 6-inch circle on the oiled section. With the remaining section of the roll, coil a 4-inch circle on top. Tuck the end of the roll into the center of the top circle. The bread should look like a flattened cone. Cover; let rise in a warm place, away from drafts, until doubled in bulk, about 45 minutes.

8. Meanwhile, divide the remaining half of the dough into 8 equal pieces. Roll each piece into a 5-inch circle. Place about 1½ tablespoons of the basil-Parmesan mixture in the center of each. Pinch the dough together over the top of the filling. Arrange the rolls on a lightly oiled cookie sheet, three pairs in a row, all touching. Place 1 roll at each end of the row. Cover; let rise in a warm place, away from drafts, until doubled in bulk, about 45 minutes.

9. Preheat the oven to moderate (375°). Arrange one oven shelf in the bottom third of the oven, the second shelf in the top third; the shelves should be at least 7 inches apart.

10. Beat the egg yolk with 1 teaspoon of water. Brush the coiled loaf with the egg

wash. Sprinkle with the reserved 1 teaspoon sesame seeds, if you wish. Brush the rolls with plain water. Sprinkle with the reserved 1 tablespoon basil-Parmesan mixture.

11. Bake the loaf on the bottom shelf in the preheated moderate oven (375°) for 30 to 35 minutes, and the rolls on the top shelf for 20 to 25 minutes or until they sound hollow when tappped on the bottom of the loaf or rolls. Transfer to a wire rack. Let stand at least 10 minutes before cutting the loaf or tearing the rolls apart.

FASTER RISING BASIL BREADS
Overnight rising in the refrigerator produces a dough that is very easy to work with. If you would rather make these breads without the refrigerator rising time, cover the dough and let it rise in a warm place, away from drafts, for about 40 minutes or until doubled in volume. Also reduce the rising times 5 to 10 minutes in steps 7 and 8.

3. A Delicious Start:
Appetizers, Soups and Salads

*G*reat beginnings—that's what appetizers, soups and salads should bring to your meals. They should stimulate your appetite for the culinary delights yet to come. Some of the soups and salads in this chapter are more hearty and may be served as the main course for a lunch or light dinner.

Many of our appetizers are quick and easy to make. Others may be made ahead, then refrigerated or frozen. Serve them as party snacks, with cocktails before dinner or as a first course at the dinner table.

The soups range from cool and light to hot and hearty. The lighter soups make a great first course. Be sure the soup you serve has a flavor, color and texture that will complement the rest of your meal. Don't feel tied down by tradition when serving soup as a first course. Occasionally, a chilled soup in the fall or winter is a delightfully surprising contrast to a rich, hot main course. The hearty soups, like Monastery Lentil Soup, may be served in larger portions as a main course. They make a satisfying meal, when served with a green salad, crusty bread, cheese and fruit.

The salads you serve should be visual as well as flavorful treats that add color and texture to your meal. Light salads may be served at the beginning of a meal to stimulate the appetite or during the meal to complement the main course. Salad dressings are usually tangy or tart. Be sure the dressing you choose will enhance the rest of the meal, not conflict with it. Some salads, containing meat, poultry, fish or beans, are hearty enough to be served as the main course of a light meal.

Have a delicious start!

Appetizers

◀Clockwise from upper left: Beef Roulade to dip in tangy Mustard Sauce (page 67); Fruited Rice Squares (page 64); and Appetizer Cheesecake Fingers (page 65).

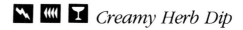 *Creamy Herb Dip*

Serve this with an assortment of fresh vegetables for dipping.

Makes about 1½ cups.

Nutrient Value Per Tablespoon: 56 calories, 1 gm. protein, 6 gm. fat, 82 mg. sodium, 13 mg. cholesterol.

2   **to 3 cloves garlic**
2   **tablespoons lemon juice**
1   **egg**
½   **cup grated Parmesan cheese**
½   **cup small parsley sprigs**
1   **teaspoon leaf basil, crumbled**
½   **teaspoon salt**
     Pinch of cayenne pepper
½   **cup olive or vegetable oil**
½   **cup plain yogurt**

1. Place the garlic, lemon juice, egg, cheese, parsley, basil, salt and cayenne in the container of an electric blender; cover. Whirl until smooth, scraping down the sides of the blender.
2. Remove the center of the blender cover. With the blender running, pour the oil in a thin stream into the mixture, stopping once or twice to scrape down the sides of the blender; the mixture should be thick. Stir in the yogurt. Scrape into a serving bowl. Cover; refrigerate for 2 hours.

Mango Chutney Cream Cheese

Simple and tasty.

Makes 1½ cups.

Nutrient Value Per Tablespoon: 47 calories, 1 gm. protein, 3 gm. fat, 39 mg. sodium, 10 mg. cholesterol.

½   **cup Indian mango chutney**
1   **package (8 ounces) cream cheese, softened**
¼   **cup chopped green onions**
     Pinch of curry powder
     Pinch of ground ginger
     Chopped green onion (optional)

1. Strain the chutney by forcing it through a wire mesh sieve, pushing gently with the back of a wooden spoon; reserve the juice; finely chop the fruit and stir back into the juice.
2. Beat the cream cheese, chutney, green onions, curry and ginger with a wooden spoon until smooth and spreadable. Use to fill store-bought hors d'oeuvre cups, home-made croustades or spread on crackers. Garnish with additional chopped green onions, if you wish.

Stuffed Edam Cheese with Crisp Vegetables

Makes about 3 cups (6 generous servings).

Nutrient Value Per Serving: 726 calories, 43 gm. protein, 52 gm. fat, 1786 mg. sodium, 154 mg. cholesterol.

6   **carrots, cut into thin diagonal pieces**
2   **sweet green peppers, cut into strips**
2   **celery stalks, cut into diagonal pieces**
1   **medium-size zucchini, thinly sliced**
¼   **pound mushrooms, thickly sliced**
1   **Dutch Edam cheese (about 2 pounds)**
2   **tablespoons prepared horseradish**
½   **cup undrained pickle relish**
1   **cup (8 ounces) dairy sour cream**
6   **slices bacon, crisp-fried and crumbled**
     Parsley and dill sprigs

1. Prepare the vegetables; wrap and chill.
2. Cut ½ inch off the top of the Edam; scoop out the center with a sharp knife and then a spoon, leaving a shell about ½ inch thick; wrap and chill. Shred the removed cheese; place in a medium-size bowl; stir in the horseradish, pickle relish, sour cream and bacon; beat until blended; chill.
3. To serve, allow the dip to warm to room temperature before filling the shell; garnish with parsley and dill. Serve with the vegetables. Refill the shell as needed.

✦ ⊤ *Salmon Spread*

With a can of salmon on hand you'll be ready to whip up this spread in minutes.

Makes 2½ cups.

Nutrient Value Per Tablespoon: 35 calories, 2 gm. protein, 3 gm. fat, 80 mg. sodium, 5 mg. cholesterol.

> 1 *can (16 ounces) salmon, drained and flaked*
> ½ *cup finely chopped onion*
> ⅓ *cup finely chopped celery*
> 3 *tablespoons sweet pickle relish*
> ⅓ *cup mayonnaise*
>   *Pimiento (optional)*
>   *Pickle relish (optional)*

Combine the salmon, onion, celery and relish in a medium-size bowl. Add the mayonnaise and stir to mix. Use this spread to fill store-bought hors d'oeuvre cups, homemade croustades or as a spread on crackers. Garnish with a pimiento diamond and pickle relish, if you wish.

✦ ⊤ *Fluffy Tuna Pâté*

Serve as an attractive centerpiece for a luncheon buffet.

Makes 12 servings.

Nutrient Value Per Serving: 187 calories, 11 gm. protein, 16 gm. fat, 359 mg. sodium, 61 mg. cholesterol.

> 5 *slices bacon*
> 2 *packages (8 ounces each) cream cheese, softened and cut into pieces*
> 2 *cans (7 ounces each) tuna packed in water, drained and flaked*
> 2 *tablespoons dry white wine*
> 2 *tablespoons lemon juice*
> 1 *tablespoon soy sauce*
> 1 *teaspoon dried dillweed*
> 2 *tablespoons parsley*
>   *Lettuce leaves*
>   *Olive slice*
>   *Crackers and/or raw vegetables for dipping*

1. Fry the bacon in a small skillet until it is crisp. Drain on paper toweling. Reserve 1 piece for garnish. Crumble the remaining 4 pieces.
2. Beat together the cream cheese, tuna, wine, lemon juice, soy sauce and dillweed in a medium-size bowl until smooth. Stir in the parsley and crumbled bacon.
3. Generously oil a 3-cup fish mold or 3-cup bowl. Allow a slight pool of oil to run to the bottom of the mold. Pack the fish mixture into the prepared mold; unmold immediately onto a lettuce-lined plate.
4. Use an olive slice for the eye; cut up the reserved bacon slice for scales. Serve with crackers and/or raw vegetables.

◀Fluffy Tuna Pâté

▓ 🍸 *Salmon-Cucumber Pâté*

A light and delicately flavored two-layered pâté. Serve as an appetizer or on a bed of lettuce or watercress as a light luncheon dish.

Makes 12 servings.

Nutrient Value Per Serving: 316 calories, 11 gm. protein, 29 gm. fat, 658 mg. sodium, 73 mg. cholesterol.

CUCUMBER LAYER
- 1 **package (8 ounces) cream cheese**
- ½ **cup dairy sour cream**
- 1 **teaspoon salt**
- 6 **to 8 drops liquid red pepper seasoning**
- 1 **medium-size cucumber, pared, seeded and shredded**
- 1 **small onion, finely chopped**
- 2 **tablespoons snipped fresh dill**

SALMON LAYER
- 1 **can (16 ounces) salmon, drained and skin and bones removed**
- ¾ **cup mayonnaise**
- ¼ **cup finely chopped onion**
- 2 **tablespoons lemon juice**
- 2 **tablespoons prepared horseradish**
- 2 **tablespoons chopped parsley**
- 1 **teaspoon salt**
- ½ **teaspoon paprika**
- 2 **envelopes unflavored gelatin**
- ½ **cup cold water**
- 1 **cup heavy cream, whipped**

    Salmon or red lumpfish caviar (about 2 tablespoons)
    Cucumber slices
    Lemon slices
    Dill sprigs
    Party rye bread and crackers

1. Prepare the Cucumber Layer: Beat the cream cheese in a medium-size bowl until softened and smooth; beat in the sour cream, salt and red pepper seasoning. Stir in the cucumber, onion and dill. Set aside.
2. Prepare the Salmon Layer: Flake or mash the salmon with a fork in a large bowl. Combine with the mayonnaise, onion, lemon juice, horseradish, parsley, salt and paprika. Set aside.
3. Sprinkle the gelatin over cold water in a 1-cup glass measure; let soften for 5 minutes. Set the cup in simmering water; stir to dissolve the gelatin. Remove from the heat.
4. Stir 3 tablespoons of the gelatin liquid into cucumber mixture. Pour into a 9 x 5 x 3-inch loaf pan, or 7- or 8-cup mold, rinsed with cold water. Chill while finishing the salmon.
5. Stir the remaining gelatin liquid into the salmon mixture. Fold in the whipped cream. Carefully spoon over the cucumber layer in the pan; cover. Chill for 6 hours or overnight.
6. To serve, run the tip of a thin-bladed knife around the top edge of the mold. Dip the mold quickly in and out of hot water. Cover with a chilled serving platter; invert; shake gently to release; lift off the pan. Garnish with caviar, cucumber slices, lemon slices and dill. Serve with party rye bread and crackers.

▓ 🍸 *Basil, Carrot and Chicken Pâté*

A spectacular make-ahead cold pâté, which, when cut, reveals layers of pale pink, green and orange. This could easily star as the centerpiece for a luncheon buffet.

Bake at 350° for 50 to 60 minutes.
Makes 10 servings.

Nutrient Value Per Serving: 194 calories, 19 gm. protein, 10 gm. fat, 251 mg. sodium, 96 mg. cholesterol.

- 2 **medium-size carrots, pared**
- 1½ **pounds boneless skinned chicken breasts, cut into chunks**

¾ **cup heavy cream**
½ **cup dry white wine**
½ **cup coarsely chopped onion**
4 **egg whites**
¾ **teaspoon salt**
2 **cups firmly packed fresh basil leaves**
1 **egg yolk**
1 **cup chopped parsley**
½ **cup dairy sour cream**
 Basil leaves
 Carrot curls

1. Cut each carrot lengthwise into ½-inch square strips. Trim the strips so they fit end to end down the length of the pan. Coarsely chop enough of the scraps to make ⅓ cup.

2. Cook the carrot strips and chopped carrots in enough simmering water to cover in a medium-sized saucepan until tender. Drain well. Separate the strips from the chopped carrots.

3. Place the chicken in the bowl of a food processor fitted with the metal blade. Process until finely chopped. Add the heavy cream, wine, onion, egg whites and salt. Process until the mixture is creamy and very smooth. (You should have about 5 cups.)

4. Preheat the oven to moderate (350°). Generously grease a 8½ x 4 x 2⅝-inch loaf pan.

5. Spoon 2 cups of the chicken mixture into the prepared pan. Spread evenly into a ½-inch-thick layer over the bottom and up both long sides, but not the ends. Spoon the remaining mixture into a large measuring cup.

6. Combine 1 cup of the basil leaves and 1¼ cups of the remaining chicken mixture in the bowl of a food processor. Process until the basil is finely chopped and evenly combined with the chicken. Reserve ¼ cup of the basil-chicken mixture. Spoon the remainder into the loaf pan; carefully spread evenly over the chicken layer

on the bottom and 1½ inches up the long sides.

7. Rinse out the processor bowl. Combine the chopped carrots, ½ cup of the chicken mixture without basil and the egg yolk in the processor bowl. Process until the carrots are puréed and the mixture is uniform in color. Spoon half of this mixture down the center of the pâté. Press the 2 carrot strips, end to end, down center of carrot-chicken mixture. Top with the remaining carrot-chicken mixture. Spread the reserved ¼ cup basil-chicken mixture over the carrot-chicken mixture to completely cover it; smooth the top. Top with the remaining chicken mixture without basil; spread evenly.

8. Bake in the preheated moderate oven (350°) for 50 to 60 minutes or until the top is firm to the touch. Cool on a rack to room temperature. Cover; refrigerate overnight.

9. Chop the remaining basil leaves. Mix with the chopped parsley in a small bowl. Cover; refrigerate.

10. To serve, carefully unmold the pâté onto a platter. Spread the sides and top lightly with sour cream. Coat the outside with the chopped basil-parsley mixture. Garnish with the basil leaves and carrot curls, if you wish.

MICROWAVE DIRECTIONS
650 Watt Variable Power Microwave Oven Directions: Cook carrots in ¼ cup water in a 8½ x 4½ x 2-inch microwave-safe loaf dish, tightly covered, at full power for 4 minutes. Remove the carrots. Dry the loaf dish; use for the pâté. Prepare the pâté according to the recipe above. Cover loosely with wax paper. Microwave at full power for 5 minutes. Turn the dish a half turn. Microwave at half power for 15 minutes. Let cool to room temperature. Refrigerate, unmold and cover with the sour cream and the basil-parsley mixture as directed above.

◼ ▮ *Fruited Rice Squares*

Marinate the fruit mixture a day ahead.

Makes 54 squares.

Nutrient Value Per Square: 114 calories, 1 gm. protein, 4 gm. fat, 67 mg. sodium, 32 mg. cholesterol.

½ *cup finely chopped candied orange* *(peel)*
¾ *cup finely chopped glacé cake mix* *(candied fruits for cakes and desserts)*
⅓ *cup rum*
 Graham Cracker Crust (recipe follows)
2 *cups water*
1 *cup long-grain white rice*
1½ *cups milk*
1 *tablespoon grated orange rind*
3 *envelopes unflavored gelatin*
⅔ *cup orange juice*
1 *cup sugar*
½ *cup milk*
4 *egg yolks, slightly beaten*
1 *cup heavy cream, whipped*
 Whipped cream for garnish (optional)
 Candied fruit for garnish (optional)

1. A day before making the rice squares, combine the finely chopped candied orange peel and glacé cake mix with the rum in a small bowl. Cover with plastic wrap and refrigerate overnight, stirring one or two times.
2. The next day, prepare the Graham Cracker Crust.
3. Bring 2 cups of water to boiling in a medium-size saucepan. Add the rice. Cover; lower the heat to medium; cook for 20 minutes or until the water is absorbed. Add the 1½ cups milk; cook, stirring occasionally, until all the milk is absorbed and the rice is tender. Stir in the grated orange rind.
4. Sprinkle the gelatin over the orange juice in a small bowl to soften.
5. Combine the sugar, ½ cup milk and egg yolks in a medium-size saucepan. Cook, stirring occasionally, until the mixture

thickens and coats the back of a metal spoon; do not let the mixture boil. Stir in the gelatin mixture until it is dissolved; pour into a large bowl. Stir in the rum and fruit mixture and the rice. Cool slightly.
6. Gently fold the whipped cream into the cooled rice mixture. Turn into the graham cracker crust. Chill until firm, for about 3 hours.
7. Cut into 54 (1-inch) squares. Top each with a whipped cream rosette and chopped mixed fruits, if you wish.

Graham Cracker Crust: Combine 2 cups graham cracker crumbs, ½ cup sugar and ½ cup (1 stick) melted butter or margarine in a 13 x 9 x 2-inch baking pan; blend well. Press evenly over the bottom of the pan; but not up the sides. Refrigerate until ready to fill.

◼ ◼ ▮ *Marinated Roquefort and Onion Hors d'Oeuvre Sandwiches*

No one will be able to stop at just one of these goodies.

Makes about 44 sandwiches.

Nutrient Value Per Sandwich: 45 calories, 2 gm. protein, 2 gm. fat, 130 mg. sodium, 3 mg. cholesterol.

½ *pound Roquefort or blue cheese*
1 *medium-size red onion, sliced*
⅓ *cup olive oil*
1 *tablespoon lemon juice*
1 *tablespoon red wine vinegar*
2 *cloves garlic, crushed*
½ *teaspoon dry mustard*
½ *teaspoon salt*
¼ *teaspoon pepper*
⅓ *cup finely chopped parsley*
1 *loaf (11 ounces) Westphalian or dark* *pumpernickel bread*

1. Finely crumble the cheese into a 9-inch pie plate. Top with the onion slices.
2. Combine the oil, lemon juice, vinegar, garlic, dry mustard, salt and pepper in a small bowl; blend well. Pour over the crumbled cheese and onion slices. Sprinkle with the parsley. Cover with plastic wrap; let stand for 2 to 3 hours.
3. To serve, cut the bread into triangles. Spoon a small amount of marinated cheese mixture onto each triangle.

> **MAKE-AHEAD TIP**
> **Prepare the cheese and let it marinate for 12 to 24 hours to develop flavor.**

Appetizer Cheesecake Fingers

One pan of this savory mixture cuts into many servings ready for your favorite garnish.

Bake crust at 450° for 8 minutes; then cheesecake at 350° for 35 minutes.
Makes 45 servings.

Nutrient Value Per Serving: 133 calories, 4 gm. protein, 11 gm. fat, 142 mg. sodium, 46 mg. cholesterol.

1 *package piecrust mix*
½ *cup toasted sesame seeds*
2 *packages (3 ounces each) cream cheese, softened*
4 *eggs*
¼ *cup brandy*
½ *teaspoon dry mustard*
½ *teaspoon salt*
1 *cup heavy cream*
1½ *cups shredded Swiss cheese (6 ounces)*
¼ *pound blue cheese, crumbled*
1 *pint dairy sour cream*

GARNISHES
  Smoked salmon, fresh dill, chopped green onion, cherry tomato halves, chopped ripe olives, sieved hard-cooked egg yolk, chopped pickle

1. Preheat the oven to very hot (450°).
2. Combine the piecrust mix and toasted sesame seeds in a medium-size bowl. Prepare the mix according to label directions. Press the dough evenly over the bottom of a 15 x 10 x 1-inch jelly-roll pan. Prick with a fork.
3. Bake in the preheated very hot oven (450°) for 8 minutes. Remove from the oven. Lower the oven temperature to 350°.
4. Beat the cream cheese in a large mixing bowl until light and fluffy. Gradually beat in the eggs, one at a time, beating well after each addition. Add the brandy, mustard, salt and heavy cream; blend well. Stir in the Swiss and blue cheeses. Turn into the partially baked crust.
5. Bake in the moderate oven (350°) for 25 minutes. Remove from the oven; let stand on a wire rack for 5 minutes.
6. Spread the sour cream over the top of the baked cheesecake. Return to the oven. Bake for 8 to 10 minutes or until the top is set. Cool on a wire rack to room temperature.
7. Cut the cheesecake into 45 (3 x 1-inch) strips. Decorate with the garnishes, as you wish.

> **MAKE-AHEAD TIP**
> **Prepare the cheesecake through step 6. Wrap in freezer paper or aluminum foil; freeze. To serve, remove from the freezer. Thaw at room temperature. Cut into 45 (3 x 1-inch) strips. Garnish as desired.**

▲**Barbecued Chicken Wing Appetizer**

2. To prepare the barbecue sauce, combine the catsup, Worcestershire sauce, vinegar, dry mustard, onion powder, garlic powder, pepper and liquid red pepper seasoning in a small bowl.
3. Brush the wings all over with half (about 6 tablespoons) of the barbecue sauce. Arrange the wings in one layer in an aluminum foil-lined baking dish.
4. Bake in the preheated moderate oven (375°) for 25 minutes. Brush the chicken with the remaining sauce. Continue to bake for another 20 minutes or until tender. Arrange chicken wings on a lettuce-lined platter. Garnish with orange slices.

⍗ *Barbecued Chicken Wing Appetizer*

Bake at 375° for 45 minutes.
Makes 6 servings.

Nutrient Value Per Serving: 291 calories, 24 gm. protein, 17 gm. fat, 454 mg. sodium, 72 mg. cholesterol.

> 3 **pounds chicken wings,**
>   **wing tips removed (about 20)**
> ¾ **cup catsup**
> 1 **tablespoon Worcestershire sauce**
> 1½ **teaspoons distilled white vinegar**
> ½ **teaspoon dry mustard**
> ½ **teaspoon onion powder**
> ½ **teaspoon garlic powder**
> ¼ **teaspoon pepper**
> 5 **to 6 drops liquid red pepper seasoning**
>   **Lettuce leaves**
>   **Orange slices**

1. Preheat the oven to moderate (375°). Line a 13 x 9 x 2-inch baking dish with aluminum foil. Pat the wings dry with paper toweling.

⊶ ⍗ *Beer Crêpes with Herring and Beet Filling*

Makes 10 servings.

Nutrient Value Per Serving: 180 calories, 7 gm. protein, 10 gm. fat, 356 mg. sodium, 137 mg. cholesterol.

> 1 **jar (1 pound) whole beets, drained**
> 1 **jar (8 ounces) herring in cream sauce**
> ¼ **cup chopped green onion**
> ½ **teaspoon Dijon-style mustard**
> ½ **cup dairy sour cream**

CRÊPES
> 2 **eggs**
> 2 **egg yolks**
> 1 **cup beer**
> 1 **cup sifted all-purpose flour**
> 1 **teaspoon salt**
> 2 **tablespoons melted butter**

1. Cut the drained beets into ½-inch pieces. Combine with the herring, green onion, mustard and sour cream in a small bowl. Stir to blend well. Refrigerate while preparing the beer crêpes.

2. Prepare the Crêpes: Combine the eggs, egg yolks and beer in a medium-size bowl. Stir in the flour, salt and melted butter until well blended.

3. Heat a small skillet or crêpe pan (6 inches) over medium-high heat; butter lightly. Pour in the batter, ¼ cup at a time, quickly rotating the pan to spread the batter evenly. Cook over medium heat to brown lightly, about 1 minute on each side. Cool. Stack the crêpes between sheets of wax paper.

4. Assemble the Crêpes: Fold each crêpe in half and in half again to form a cone shape. Fill with the prepared filling.

FREEZE CRÊPES FOR FUTURE USE
Make the crêpes a day or two ahead or make two batches, one to use right away and one to freeze for another time. Cool the crêpes thoroughly, stack using 2 pieces of wax paper to separate each crêpe, wrap in freezer wrap or aluminum foil and freeze. Remove from the freezer an hour before using.

◀◀◀ 🍸 *Beef Roulade*

Make a day or two ahead.

Bake at 350° for 50 minutes.
Makes 40 servings.

Nutrient Value Per Servings: 108 calories, 9 gm. protein, 7 gm. fat, 141 mg. sodium, 44 mg. cholesterol.

2 **eggs, slightly beaten**
¾ **cup fresh bread crumbs (2 slices)**
½ **cup catsup**
⅓ **cup chopped parsley**
½ **teaspoon leaf basil, crumbled**
¼ **teaspoon leaf oregano, crumbled**

¼ **teaspoon pepper**
1 **clove garlic, crushed**
2 **pounds ground round**
  Plain dry bread crumbs
3 **packages (4 ounces each)**
  boiled ham slices
3 **cups shredded Swiss cheese (¾ pound)**
  Mustard Sauce (recipe follows)

1. Preheat the oven to moderate (350°).
2. Combine the eggs, bread crumbs, catsup, parsley, basil, oregano, pepper, garlic and ground round in a large bowl; mix lightly until well blended. Divide into 2 equal portions.
3. Cut two 12 x 12-inch squares of aluminum foil. Sprinkle each with dry bread crumbs. Pat out each half of the meat mixture on the foil to a 9 x 12-inch rectangle. Arrange the ham slices on top of each to within ½ inch of the edges. Sprinkle each with Swiss cheese. Using the foil as an aid, roll up the meat from a long side, jelly-roll fashion. Seal the edges and ends. Place on a foil-lined jelly-roll pan.
4. Bake in the preheated moderate oven (350°) for 50 minutes. Cool to room temperature. Serve sliced with Mustard Sauce.

Mustard Sauce: Combine 1 cup dairy sour cream, ¼ cup mayonnaise, 2 tablespoons Dijon-style mustard, 1 to 3 teaspoons drained prepared horseradish and ¼ cup chopped green onion; mix until well blended.

Soups

Cool Avocado Soup

Makes 8 servings (about 5 cups).

Nutrient Value Per Serving: 150 calories, 4 gm. protein, 13 gm. fat, 407 mg. sodium, 6 mg. cholesterol.

> 2 **large ripe avocados**
> 1 **tablespoon lemon juice**
> 2 **cans (13¾ ounces each) chicken broth, chilled**
> ½ **cup dairy sour cream**
> ½ **cup buttermilk**
> 2 **green onions, white part only, sliced**
> ¼ **teaspoon salt**
> **Lemon slices for garnish**

1. Peel and pit the avocados. Slice the avocados, reserving several very thin slices for garnish. Brush the reserved slices with ½ teaspoon lemon juice to prevent discoloration; cover; refrigerate.
2. Working in batches, combine the chicken broth, sour cream, buttermilk, green onion, avocado, the remaining lemon juice and salt in the container of an electric blender. Cover; whirl until smooth. Pour into a soup tureen. Refrigerate for 15 minutes or until throughly chilled.
3. To serve, garnish with the reserved avocado slices and the lemon slices.

▲ Cool Avocado Soup

Cold Cucumber and Yogurt Soup

A refreshing soup that goes well with barbecued foods.

Makes 6 servings.

Nutrient Value Per Serving: 77 calories, 4 gm. protein, 4 gm. fat, 144 mg. sodium, 15 mg. cholesterol.

1   **large cucumber**
¼   **teaspoon salt**
2   **or 3 cloves garlic, finely chopped**
⅛   **teaspoon pepper**
3   **cups plain yogurt**
3   **tablespoons finely chopped fresh mint**
    OR: 1 tablespoon dried mint, crumbled

1. Pare the cucumber. Finely chop or shred the cucumber; place in a colander. Toss with the salt and set aside over a bowl or in the sink to drain for 30 minutes.
2. Mash the garlic with a mortar and pestle. Or, place in the container of an electric blender. Cover; whirl briefly until mashed. Add the pepper and 3 tablespoons of the yogurt to the mashed garlic in the mortar or the blender. Mash or whirl until the mixture is a smooth paste.
3. Combine the garlic paste with the remaining yogurt in a medium-size bowl until well blended. Add the cucumber and chopped mint; mix well. Cover; refrigerate until well chilled. If the soup seems too thick, thin it with a little cold water to the desired consistency. Serve in chilled soup bowls.

⁴⁴⁴ *Gazpacho*

This gazpacho is thickened with ground almonds, which give the soup a very rich taste.

Makes 8 servings.

Nutrient Value Per Serving: 229 calories, 8 gm. protein, 16 gm. fat, 512 mg. sodium, 0.1 mg. cholesterol.

4   **cloves garlic**
1   **cup blanched whole almonds**
¼   **cup olive oil**
3   **cups chicken broth**
3   **cups tomato juice**
½   **teaspoon pepper**

    Liquid red pepper seasoning
1½ **pounds ripe tomatoes**
2   **cucumbers**
½   **cup chopped onions**
1   **cup ¼-inch cubes white bread**

1. Combine 3 cloves of the garlic, the almonds, 2 tablespoons of the olive oil and 1 cup of the chicken broth in the container of an electric blender or food processor. Cover; whirl until smooth.
2. Combine the remaining chicken broth and the tomato juice in a medium-size saucepan. Bring to boiling. Lower the heat to medium. Stir in the almond mixture. Cook, stirring, until thickened.
3. Remove the gazpacho from the heat. Stir in pepper and liquid red pepper seasoning to taste. Transfer to a bowl. Refrigerate, covered, until very cold, several hours or overnight.
4. Peel and seed the tomatoes; finely chop. Pare and seed the cucumbers; finely chop. Place the tomato, cucumber and chopped onion in separate bowls. Cover; refrigerate.
5. Heat the remaining 2 tablespoons of oil in a medium-size skillet. Finely chop the remaining clove of garlic. Add to the skillet. Add the bread cubes; sauté until golden. Remove the bread cubes to paper toweling to drain and cool.
6. To serve, fold half the chopped tomato, half the chopped cucumber and half the chopped onion into the soup. Pass the remaining tomato, cucumber, onion and bread cubes.

◼ ◼ *Quick Gazpacho*

This Cuban rendition of a Spanish soup originally called for 1 cup of olive oil and 3 eggs. Even a small bowl was filling as a whole dinner. This scaled-down version is lighter and still delicious.

Makes 6 servings.

Nutrient Value Per Serving: 133 calories, 3 gm. protein, 10 gm. fat, 259 mg. sodium, 56 mg. cholesterol.

1   *clove garlic*
1   *large sweet green pepper, halved, seeded and coarsely chopped*
1   *large cucumber, pared, halved, seeded and cut into chunks*
2   *tablespoons red wine vinegar*
¼   *cup olive or vegetable oil*
1   *egg*
3   *cups tomato juice*
¼   *teaspoon pepper*
1   *medium-size ripe tomato, halved, seeded and finely chopped*
    Finely chopped parsley

1. Combine the garlic, green pepper, cucumber, vinegar, oil, egg and 1 cup of the tomato juice in the container of an electric blender or food processor. Cover; whirl until smooth. Pour into a bowl.
2. Stir the remaining 2 cups of tomato juice, pepper and chopped tomato into the puréed mixture. Cover; chill well.
3. Serve in individual chilled bowls with a sprinkling of chopped parsley.

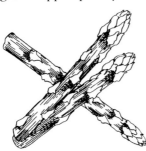

◼ *Asparagus Cream Soup*

This delicate soup may be served hot or chilled.

Makes 12 servings.
Nutrient Value Per Serving: 124 calories, 5 gm. protein, 7 gm. fat, 257 mg. sodium, 18 mg. cholesterol.

1   *large onion, chopped (1 cup)*
¼   *cup (½ stick) butter or margarine*
1   *pound all-purpose potatoes, pared and sliced*
2   *cans (13¾ ounces each) chicken broth*
2   *pounds fresh slender asparagus*
1   *cup half and half*
    Salt
    White Pepper

1. Sauté the onion in the butter in a large saucepan for 2 minutes. Stir in the potatoes and chicken broth. Bring the mixture to boiling. Cover; lower the heat; simmer for 20 minutes or until the potatoes are very tender.
2. Meanwhile, wash the asparagus; trim and discard the ends. Cut into 1-inch pieces. Add to the potato mixture. Cook for 5 minutes or just until the asparagus are tender. Remove from the heat. Remove some of the asparagus tips with a slotted spoon to use as garnish, if you wish. Stir the half and half into the soup.
3. Ladle about one quarter of the soup into the container of an electric blender or food processor. Cover; whirl until the mixture is smooth. Pour into a large bowl. Repeat with the remaining soup. Season with salt and pepper, if necessary. If serving the soup hot, return the soup to the saucepan and reheat. Or, cover the bowl and chill. Garnish the individual bowls of soup with asparagus tips, if you have set them aside.

◣ ⦅⦅ *Fresh Tomato-Basil Soup*

Serve this soup either cold or hot.

Makes 6 servings.

Nutrient Value Per Serving: 236 calories, 5 gm. protein, 18 gm. fat, 518 mg. sodium, 60 mg. cholesterol.

½ *cup chopped onion*
1 *tablespoon butter*
¼ *cup all-purpose flour*
1 *can (13¾ ounces) chicken broth*
2 *pounds ripe Italian plum tomatoes, peeled and coarsely chopped*
1½ *tablespoons lemon juice*
1½ *cups finely chopped fresh basil leaves*
¾ *teaspoon salt*
1 *cup heavy cream or milk*

1. Sauté the onion in the butter in a large saucepan until tender, about 5 minutes.
2. Stir the flour into the chicken broth in a small bowl. Add to the onions in the saucepan. Bring to boiling, stirring constantly, until slightly thickened. Stir in the chopped tomato, lemon juice, ½ cup of the chopped basil and the salt. Return to boiling. Lower the heat; simmer for 5 minutes.
3. Stir the cream into the soup. Return just to boiling. Remove from the heat. Stir in the remaining basil.

◣ ▢ *French Cabbage Soup*

Makes 4 servings.

Nutrient Value Per Serving: 168 calories, 8 gm. protein, 8 gm. fat, 775 mg. sodium, 15 mg. cholesterol.

4 *cups shredded green cabbage (1 small head)*
1 *cup sliced carrots*
2 *tablespoons butter or margarine*
2 *cups water*

1 *can (1 pound, 3 ounces) chunky steak and potato soup*

1. Sauté the cabbage and carrot in the butter in a large saucepan just until the cabbage is wilted but not brown, about 5 minutes.
2. Add 2 cups water and the chunky soup. Bring to boiling. Cover; lower the heat. Simmer for 20 minutes. Serve with crusty whole-wheat bread, if you wish.

SPEEDY SHREDDING
Use a food processor to shred this large amount of cabbage in seconds, then to slice the carrots.

⦅⦅ ▢ *Garden Vegetable Soup*

Makes 8 servings.

Nutrient Value Per Serving: 188 calories, 8 gm. protein, 7 gm. fat, 1090 mg. sodium, 0 mg. cholsterol.

4 *cups shredded Savoy or green cabbage (1 medium-size)*
4 *carrots, sliced (1½ cups)*
3 *celery stalks, sliced (1 cup)*
2 *parsnips, pared and diced (1 cup)*
3 *tablespoons vegetable oil*
4 *cans (13¾ ounces each) chicken broth*
3 *medium-size all-purpose potatoes, peeled and diced*
2 *zucchini, sliced (2 cups)*
2 *cups cauliflower flowerets*
1 *small sweet red pepper, halved, seeded and diced*
2 *tomatoes, cored and diced*
1½ *teaspoons salt*
1 *teaspoon leaf thyme, crumbled*
2 *teaspoons Worcestershire sauce*
¼ *to ½ teaspoon pepper*
¼ *cup chopped parsley*

1. Sauté the cabbage, carrots, celery and parsnips in the oil in a large kettle or Dutch oven over medium heat until the cabbage is wilted, 10 to 15 minutes.
2. Meanwhile, place the chicken broth in a medium-size saucepan. Bring to boiling. Add to the kettle. Add the potatoes, zucchini, cauliflower, sweet red pepper, tomatoes, salt, thyme, Worcestershire and pepper. Bring to boiling. Cover; lower the heat; simmer for 15 to 20 minutes or until the vegetables are just tender. Uncover; cool, stirring occasionally. Refrigerate until ready to serve.
3. To reheat and serve: Slowly bring the soup just to boiling, stirring often. Stir in the parsley. Ladle into large shallow soup bowls.

■ ▼ ◻ *Egg Drop Soup*

Makes 2 servings.

Nutrient Value Per Serving: 81 calories, 7 gm. protein, 4 gm. fat, 655 mg. sodium, 137 mg. cholesterol.

- *1   can (13¾ ounces) chicken broth*
- *1½ teaspoons cornstarch*
- *¼ cup water*
- *1   green onion, cut diagonally into ¼-inch slices*
- *1   egg, slightly beaten*
- *1   tablespoon dry sherry*

1. Bring the chicken broth to boiling in a medium-size saucepan. Mix the cornstarch with ¼ cup cold water in a cup. Stir the cornstarch mixture and green onion into the broth; cook, stirring constantly, for 1 minute.
2. Gently stir in the egg and sherry, just until the egg cooks and separates into shreds. Remove from the heat; ladle into soup cups.

▼ *Cream of Pumpkin Soup with Cinnamon Croutons*

Makes 8 servings (about 8 cups).

Nutrient Value Per Serving: 282 calories, 7 gm. protein, 21 gm. fat, 890 mg. sodium, 699 mg. cholesterol.

- *2   tablespoons butter or margarine*
- *1   large onion, chopped (1 cup)*
- *2   cans (13¾ ounces each) chicken broth*
- *1   can (1 pound) solid-pack pumpkin*
- *1   teaspoon salt*
- *¼ teaspoon ground cinnamon*
- *¼ teaspoon ground nutmeg*
- *⅛ teaspoon ground ginger*
- *⅛ teaspoon pepper*
- *2   cups milk*
- *1   cup heavy cream*
- *Cinnamon Croutons (recipe follows)*

1. Heat the butter in a large saucepan or Dutch oven; add the onion; sauté until tender but not brown, about 10 minutes. Add 1 can of chicken broth; bring to boiling; cover; lower the heat; simmer for 15 minutes.
2. Ladle the liquid and onion into the container of an electric blender; cover. Blend until the mixture is smooth, about 1 minute. Return to the saucepan.
3. Add the remaining chicken broth, pumpkin, salt, cinnamon, nutmeg, ginger and pepper. Stir until smooth. Bring to boiling; cover. Lower the heat; simmer for 10 minutes, stirring often.
4. Stir in the milk and cream; heat just to boiling, but do not boil. Taste for seasonings; add more if you wish.
5. Garnish each serving with Cinnamon Croutons.

Cinnamon Croutons: Blend 3 tablespoons softened butter or margarine with 1 tablespoon brown sugar and ¼ teaspoon ground cinnamon in a small bowl. Spread on 4 slices of whole-grain bread. Place in a single layer on a cookie sheet. Bake in a preheated hot oven (400°) for 8 to 10 minutes or until the toast is crisp and topping is bubbly. Cut into small triangles or squares.

Split Pea Soup

Dutch pea soup, a national favorite, thick with hearty ingredients, is a meal in itself.

Makes 12 servings.

Nutrient Value Per Serving: 284 calories, 19 gm. protein, 8 gm. fat, 775 mg. sodium, 24 mg. cholesterol.

- *1 package (1 pound) dried green split peas*
- *2 quarts water*
- *1 teaspoon salt*
- *1 teaspoon pepper*
- *1 bay leaf*
- *1 teaspoon leaf thyme, crumbled*
- *2 whole cloves*
- *1 large onion*
- *2 medium-size potatoes, pared and diced (3 cups)*
- *½ pound cooked ham, diced (1½ cups)*
- *½ pound smoked sausage, sliced (1 cup)*
- *2 large leeks, well washed and sliced*
- *2 large celery stalks, thinly sliced*
- *2 tablespoons chopped parsley*

1. Wash and sort the peas. Combine the peas, water, salt, pepper, bay leaf and thyme in a large kettle or Dutch oven. Press the cloves into the onion; add to the kettle.
2. Bring the pea mixture to boiling. Lower the heat; cover; simmer, stirring occasionally, until the peas are tender, about 1 hour.
3. Remove the onion and bay leaf. Purée the soup through a coarse sieve; return the mixture to the kettle.
4. Add the potatoes, ham, sausage, leeks and celery. Simmer, uncovered, until the potatoes are tender, about 45 minutes.
5. To serve, ladle the soup into a tureen or individual soup bowls; garnish with chopped parsley.

Monastery Lentil Soup

Makes 5 servings.

Nutrient Value Per Serving: 379 calories, 18 gm. protein, 19 gm. fat, 1235 mg. sodium, 24 mg. cholesterol.

- *2 large onions, chopped (2 cups)*
- *1 carrot, coarsely grated*
- *½ teaspoon leaf marjoram, crumbled*
- *½ teaspoon leaf thyme, crumbled*
- *¼ cup olive or vegetable oil*
- *1 can (1 pound) tomatoes*
- *5 cups water*
- *3 beef bouillon cubes*
- *1 cup dried lentils, rinsed*
- *1 teaspoon salt*
- *¼ teaspoon pepper*
- *¼ cup dry sherry or dry white wine*
- *¼ cup chopped parsley*
- *1 cup shredded Cheddar cheese (4 ounces)*

1. Sauté the onions, carrot, marjoram and thyme in the oil in a large kettle or Dutch oven, stirring often, until lightly browned, about 5 minutes.
2. Add the tomatoes, water, bouillon cubes, lentils, salt and pepper, stirring to dissolve the cubes; bring to boiling. Lower the heat; cover; simmer for about 1 hour or until the lentils are tender.
3. Add the sherry and parsley; simmer for 2 minutes. Serve in soup bowls; garnish with a sprinkling of cheese.

VARY THE GARNISH
Try topping this hearty soup with Swiss cheese, chopped green onions, or croutons sprinkled with Parmesan cheese.

◼️ ◻️ *Norwegian Fish Chowder*

Makes 6 servings.

Nutrient Value Per Serving: 362 calories, 31 gm. protein, 13 gm. fat, 1014 mg. sodium, 105 mg. cholesterol.

> 2 *leeks, well washed and sliced*
> 2 *carrots, sliced*
> 3 *tablespoons butter or margarine*
> 1½ *to 2 pounds fresh or frozen cod or haddock fillets*
> 2 *cups water*
> 1 *teaspoon salt*
> 1 *can condensed cream of celery soup*
> 3 *cups frozen O'Brien potatoes*
> 1 *small cucumber, peeled and halved lengthwise*
> 3 *cups hot milk*
> 1 *tablespoon chopped fresh dill*

1. Sauté the leeks and carrots in 2 tablespoons of the butter in a kettle for 4 to 5 minutes, or until tender but not browned. Cut the fish into serving-size pieces; place in the kettle. Add the water and salt. Bring to boiling. Lower the heat; cover and simmer for 15 minutes or until the fish flakes easily. Remove the fish from the kettle with a slotted spoon; set aside.
2. Add the celery soup and potatoes to the kettle. Bring to boiling. Cover; lower the heat; simmer 5 minutes.
3. Remove the seeds from the cucumber halves. Slice crosswise into ⅛-inch-thick slices. Sauté in a small skillet in the remaining tablespoon butter for 3 to 4 minutes. Add to the kettle with the milk, fish and dill. Bring just to boiling. Remove from the heat. Serve hot.

Salads

GREEN SALADS

The perfect addition to a summer meal—or a delicious entrée when made with chilled meats and cheeses.

MOST POPULAR SALAD GREENS

- *Iceberg,* the best known lettuce, has a nice crisp texture and stores well. After purchasing, wash, dry well, and store the lettuce in a large plastic bag or a tightly covered plastic container, with a drainage space, in the refrigerator.
- *Romaine lettuce,* has long, dark green outside leaves with lighter, almost yellow inside leaves. The darker green leaves have the higher vitamin content, so use as many of these leaves as possible, discarding only the bruised parts.
- *Boston or butterhead (cabbage) lettuce,* has tender, velvety leaves that separate easily and a delicate flavor. Wash just before serving, in a bowl of very cold water and blot dry on paper towels.
- *Leaf lettuce,* also known as *red tipped lettuce or oakleaf lettuce,* grows in large leafy bunches. The tender long leaves are delicate and should be washed just before serving.

> **FRUIT IN YOUR GREEN SALAD**
> **Add apple slices, orange or Mandarin orange sections, and cubed avocado to your next green salad and serve it with a blue cheese dressing.**

NICE SALAD ADDITIONS

• *Belgian endive,* an imported salad ingredient, is more expensive than other greens, and, therefore, used sparingly in salads. Sliced lengthwise, the long slender leaves add an elegant touch.

• *Curly endive or chicory* has long, narrow, curly dark green outer leaves and pale green inner leaves. A slightly bitter taste makes them a good choice to combine with other, milder greens.

• *Green and red cabbage,* shredded into a salad, add color and texture.

• *Spinach* has a crisp texture, slightly biting taste and lots of vitamins in its dark green leaves.

Garlic Vinaigrette: Mash 1 or 2 large chopped garlic cloves with ½ teaspoon of the salt. Add to the jar with the other ingredients.

Mustard Vinaigrette: Add 1 tablespoon Dijon-style mustard to the jar with the other ingredients.

DRESS UP YOUR DRESSING
Add crumbled blue cheese, fresh herbs, chopped walnuts, cubed avocado or freshly grated Parmesan cheese to your favorite vinaigrette or prepared dressing for a new and exciting flavor.

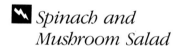 *Basic Vinaigrette and Variations*

Makes about 2 cups.

Nutrient Value Per Tablespoon: 90 calories, 0 gm. protein, 10 gm. fat, 135 mg. sodium, 0 mg. cholesterol.

1½ cups olive oil OR: ¾ cup olive oil and
*   ¾ cup vegetable oil*
⅓ cup wine vinegar OR: fresh lemon juice
2 teaspoons salt
½ teaspoon pepper

Combine the oil, vinegar, salt and pepper in a screw-top jar. Shake well to blend. Serve at room temperature.

Herb Vinaigrette: Crumble 1 tablespoon of leaf basil or oregano, or a mixture of half of each. Add to the jar with the remaining ingredients.

Spinach and Mushroom Salad

Makes 8 servings.

Nutrient Value Per Serving: 138 calories, 3 gm. protein, 13 gm. fat, 264 mg. sodium, 4 mg. cholesterol.

¼ cup mayonnaise
¼ cup vegetable oil
2 tablespoons wine vinegar
2 tablespoons Dijon-style mustard
½ teaspoon leaf tarragon, crumbled
¼ teaspoon salt
⅛ teaspoon pepper
1 pound spinach
½ pound mushrooms, sliced

1. Beat the mayonnaise, oil, vinegar, mustard, tarragon, salt and pepper in a small bowl until blended.
2. Wash and sort the spinach; pat dry; tear into bite-size pieces into a large salad bowl. Add the mushrooms.
3. Just before serving, pour the dressing over the salad and toss until the salad is well coated.

■▲ ◀◀◀ *Marinated Cauliflower Salad*

Piquant and crunchy, this salad is also good to tote to a picnic or a pot-luck supper.

Makes 8 servings.

Nutrient Value Per Serving: 300 calories, 4 gm. protein, 29 gm. fat, 600 mg. sodium, 0 mg. cholesterol.

> 1   *cup vegetable oil*
> ¼   *cup red wine vinegar*
> 2   *teaspoons salt*
> ½   *teaspoon pepper*
> ½   *teaspoon garlic powder*
> 1   *teaspoon leaf oregano, crumbled*
> 1   *head cauliflower (about 1½ pounds)*
> 3   *medium-size zucchini, sliced*
> 1   *medium-size red onion, sliced*
> 1   *head Romaine lettuce*
> ⅓   *cup sliced pitted black olives*

1. Combine the oil, vinegar, salt, pepper, garlic powder and oregano in a large plastic food bag. Place the bag, open end up, in a large bowl. Divide the cauliflower into flowerets; place in the bag; shake gently to coat; close the bag. Refrigerate overnight.

2. About 45 minutes before serving, pour the contents of the bag into a serving bowl. Add the zucchini and onion; toss to coat well. At serving time, tear the lettuce into bite-size pieces. Add the lettuce and olives to the marinated vegetables; toss again.

■▲ ◀◀◀ *Cucumber Salad*

Makes 8 side-dish servings.

Nutrient Value Per Serving: 24 calories, 1 gm. protein, 1 gm. fat, 145 mg. sodium, 1 mg. cholesterol.

> 4   *medium-size cucumbers, pared*
> 1   *medium-size onion*

> 3   *tablespoons chopped fresh dill*
> ½   *teaspoon salt*
> 3   *to 4 tablespoons plain yogurt*

Coarsely grate the cucumber and onion into a bowl. Drain off the excess liquid. Add the dill, salt and yogurt; mix well. Chill until serving time.

■ *Orange-Avocado Salad with Molasses Dressing*

The molasses adds an unusual accent to the dressing.

Makes 8 servings.

Nutrient Value Per Serving: 218 calories, 2 gm. protein, 18 gm. fat, 8 mg. sodium, 0 mg. cholesterol.

> ½   *cup peanut or vegetable oil*
> 5   *tablespoons lime juice or lemon juice*
> 2   *tablespoons molasses*
> 1   *teaspoon dry mustard*
> 4   *heads Bibb lettuce, washed and dried*
> 1   *avocado*
> 4   *navel oranges*
> 1   *medium-size red onion*
> 1   *Belgian endive*

1. Prepare the Molasses Dressing: Combine the oil, lime juice, molasses and mustard in a jar with a tight-fitting lid. Shake until well blended. Refrigerate until ready to use.

2. Arrange the lettuce on a platter or in a shallow bowl. Halve, peel and pit the avocado; slice lengthwise into wedges. Peel and slice the oranges crosswise. Arrange the avocado and orange slices in overlapping rows on the lettuce.

3. Peel the onion; cut it in half lengthwise, then cut the halves into thin wedges. Slice the endive into thin julienne strips. Mix the onion and endive; arrange over the orange slices in the center of the platter. Serve the Molasses Dressing separately.

Tuna and Orange Main-Dish Salad

Makes 6 servings.

Nutrient Value Per Serving: 371 calories, 20 gm. protein, 28 gm. fat, 759 mg. sodium, 20 mg. cholesterol.

2 medium-size heads Boston, Romaine, leaf, iceberg lettuce and/or chickory OR: 1½ pounds fresh spinach, trimmed and washed
2 cans (7 ounces each) solid white tuna packed in water, drained and broken into chunks
1½ cups peeled orange sections, drained and seeds removed (preferably 2 large navel oranges)
1 medium-size red onion, sliced and separated into rings (about 1 cup)
1 can (3.5 ounces) pitted black olives, drained and quartered Lemon-Rosemary Dressing (recipe follows)
½ cup slivered almonds, toasted

1. Tear the greens into bite-size pieces. Arrange them in a large salad bowl (you should have about 10 cups of salad greens). Arrange the tuna, oranges, onions and olives on top of the greens.
2. To serve, pour the Lemon-Rosemary Dressing over the salad. Top with slivered almonds. Toss to mix well.

Lemon-Rosemary Dressing: Combine 1 tablespoon fresh lemon juice, 1 tablespoon distilled white vinegar, 1 teaspoon grated lemon rind, 1 teaspoon salt, ½ teaspoon leaf rosemary, crumbled, ¼ teaspoon pepper and ½ cup vegetable oil in a large screw-top jar; shake until well blended. Pour over the salad just before serving. Makes ⅔ cup.

▲**Festive Layered Salad**

Festive Layered Salad

Layered salads are perfect for summer buffet tables. You can make them early in the day, and then put them out just before your guests arrive. Feel free to use any combination of vegetables, cheese, beans, fruit or whatever strikes your fancy. You might even want to try a layered fruit version for a stunning dessert.

Makes 8 servings.

Nutrient Value Per Serving: 535 calories, 15 gm. protein, 43 gm. fat, 555 mg. sodium, 125 mg. cholesterol.

1 cup small macaroni shells
4 cups shredded Romaine lettuce
4 carrots, pared and cut into 2-inch sticks
1 package (10 ounces) frozen green peas, thawed
1 small red onion, halved, sliced crosswise and separated into rings
½ pound piece cooked ham, cut into ½-inch cubes (2 cups)
½ cup shredded Swiss cheese (2 ounces)
1½ cups mayonnaise
2 tablespoons snipped fresh dill OR: 1½ teaspoons dried dillweed
2 hard-cooked eggs, cut into wedges

1. Cook the macaroni shells following label directions. Drain well in a colander. Cool to room temperature.
2. Place the lettuce in an even layer in the bottom of a 3-quart clear glass bowl. Arrange the carrot sticks in an even layer over the lettuce. Cover with a layer of macaroni, then the peas, onion and ham. Sprinkle the top with Swiss cheese.
3. Combine the mayonnaise and dill in a small bowl. Mound the dressing in the center of the salad. Arrange the egg wedges around the dressing. Cover with plastic wrap. Chill for several hours.
4. Just before serving, toss well to coat.

Jellied Chicken and Basil Salad

Perfect for a summer buffet table.

Makes 8 servings.

Nutrient Value Per Serving: 159 calories, 28 gm. protein, 3 gm. fat, 228 mg. sodium, 70 mg. cholesterol.

½ cup coarsely chopped onion
1 tablespoon butter
2 pounds boneless skinned chicken breasts
1 cup water
⅓ cup finely chopped fresh basil leaves
½ teaspoon salt
2 envelopes unflavored gelatin
1 cup dry white wine
1 tablespoon lemon juice
1½ teaspoons sugar
10 to 12 small basil leaves
¼ cup finely chopped parsley

1. Sauté the onion in the butter in a large skillet until golden. Add the chicken, water, 2 tablespoons of the chopped basil and salt. Bring to boiling. Lower the heat; simmer until the chicken is cooked through.
2. Remove the chicken breasts from the broth with a slotted spoon. Cut into ½-inch chunks. Spread out on a platter. Cover; refrigerate until cold, about 2 hours.
3. Strain the broth through a sieve into a 4-cup glass measure. Refrigerate.
4. When the chicken is cold, sprinkle the gelatin over the wine in a medium-size saucepan; let stand for 10 minutes to soften. Stir over very low heat until the gelatin is dissolved.
5. Skim the fat from the chilled cooking broth. Add the gelatin mixture. Stir in the lemon juice and sugar. Add enough water to make 3½ cups. Pour into a bowl. Place in the refrigerator, or set in a larger bowl of ice and water, stirring occasionally, until the mixture is as thick as unbeaten egg whites, about 1 hour in refrigerator, or about 30 minutes in ice water; remove from the refrigerator or ice water.
6. Spoon ¼ cup of the gelatin mixture into the bottom of 6-cup metal mold. Arrange the basil leaves in the gelatin. Chill until firm, about 5 minutes in the refrigerator, or 1 to 2 minutes in the freezer.
7. Fold the chicken, remaining chopped basil and the parsley into the remaining gelatin mixture. Pour into the mold. Refrigerate until set, 4 hours or overnight.
8. To unmold, dip briefly in warm water. Loosen the edge with the tip of a knife. Invert a serving plate over the mold; turn right side up; shake gently. Remove mold.

> **TO COOK CHICKEN BREAST**
> **Place the breast in a saucepan with 1 bay leaf, 1 celery stalk with leaves, cut in several pieces, half of a small onion, salt and pepper to taste and water to just cover the chicken. Bring to boiling, lower the heat and simmer, covered, for 20 minutes. Cool in the broth. Use the broth for soup or a sauce—if you will not be using it soon, freeze it in a plastic freezer container.**

◀◀◀ *Oriental-Style Chicken Salad*

A pleasing mix of flavors for a main-dish salad.

Makes 4 servings.

Nutrient Value Per Serving: 726 calories, 32 gm. protein, 31 gm. fat, 976 mg. sodium, 84 mg. cholesterol.

½ pound mezzani (macaroni)
1 can (20 ounces) pineapple chunks in pineapple juice
1 envelope instant chicken broth
2 tablespoons sesame seeds
1 whole chicken breast (about 12 ounces), cooked
1 package (10 ounces) frozen snow peas
1 can (8 ounces) water chestnuts, sliced
4 green onions, thinly sliced
1½ tablespoons soy sauce
1 cup dairy sour cream
⅓ cup mayonnaise

1. Cook the mezzani following label directions just until "al dente"; drain and put in a large bowl.
2. Drain the pineapple, reserving the juice. Combine the chicken broth with 2 tablespoons of the reserved pineapple juice in a cup; pour over the pasta; toss.
3. Toast the sesame seeds in a small skillet, about 5 minutes. Transfer to a small bowl. Skin and bone the chicken; cut into 2-inch strips. Blanch the snow peas in boiling water in a large saucepan for about 2 minutes; drain; cool.
4. Add the pineapple chunks, sesame seeds, water chestnuts, chicken, snow peas and green onions to the pasta.
5. Combine the soy sauce, sour cream, mayonnaise and 3 tablespoons of the reserved pineapple juice in a small bowl; beat until well mixed. Toss two thirds of the dressing with the salad. Cover; refrigerate for several hours. Add the remaining dressing; toss again just before serving.

◀◀◀ *Macaroni and Chicken Salad with Tuna Dressing*

Macaroni plus chicken and tuna make a filling main dish.

Makes 6 servings.

Nutrient Value Per Serving: 450 calories, 27 gm. protein, 23 gm. fat, 536 mg. sodium, 58 mg. cholesterol.

2 cups maruzzelle (small shells)
¼ cup cream or milk
1 envelope instant chicken broth
1 whole chicken breast (about 12 ounces), cooked
1 cup finely chopped celery
1 small onion, finely chopped (¼ cup)
½ cup minced parsley
1 can (7 ounces) tuna
¼ cup mayonnaise
¼ cup light cream or milk
⅓ cup vegetable oil
1 tablespoon red wine vinegar
1 clove garlic
¼ teaspoon leaf tarragon, crumbled
¼ teaspoon salt
⅛ teaspoon pepper

1. Cook the maruzzelle following label directions just until "al dente"; drain. Put in a large bowl.
2. Combine the ¼ cup cream and instant chicken broth in a cup; pour over the hot pasta; toss; let cool.
3. Skin and bone the chicken; shred or chop finely. Add the chicken, celery, onion and parsley to the pasta; toss lightly.
4. Combine the tuna, mayonnaise, remaining cream, oil, vinegar, garlic, tarragon, salt and pepper in the container of an electric blender. Whirl, stopping the blender often to scrape down the sides, until the dressing is smooth. Pour the dressing over the salad; toss until evenly coated. Serve, or cover and refrigerate for up to 24 hours.

◖◖◖ ▢ *Chicken-Macaroni Salad*

You can use light or dark meat or a combination of both for the salad, or leftover turkey, if you like. Roasting the peppers adds an extra special flavor.

Makes 12 servings.

Nutrient Value Per Serving: 558 calories, 23 gm. protein, 36 gm. fat, 639 mg. sodium, 161 mg. cholesterol.

 3 *large sweet red peppers, halved*
 1 *package (1 pound) small elbow macaroni*
1½ *cups mayonnaise*
1½ *cups dairy sour cream*
 4 *hard-cooked eggs, chopped*
 ¼ *cup lemon juice*
 3 *tablespoons prepared mustard*
 2 *tablespoons drained capers*
 1 *teaspoon salt*
 ¼ *teaspoon pepper*
 4 *cups cubed cooked chicken (about 2 pounds uncooked boneless chicken breast)*
 2 *cans (5.7 ounces each) pitted black colossal olives, drained*
 2 *medium-size onions, grated*
 2 *cups finely chopped celery*

1. Arrange the pepper halves, skin-side up, on a cookie sheet. Broil 6 inches from the heat, turning once, until charred and soft, 5 to 8 minutes. Peel and remove seeds. Slice the peppers into 1 x ¼-inch strips.
2. Cook the pasta following package directions. Drain and place in a large bowl.
3. Stir together the mayonnaise, sour cream, chopped eggs, lemon juice, mustard, capers, salt and pepper in a medium-size bowl. Spoon the dressing over the pasta. Add the chicken. Toss to blend well.
4. Reserve 8 red pepper strips for garnish. Chop the remaining strips and add to the salad. Reserve 8 olives for garnish. Chop the remaining olives and add to the salad along with the onion and celery. Toss well to mix. Cover; refrigerate until ready to serve, up to 3 hours. (Add more mayonnaise or sour cream just before serving if the salad is too dry.)
5. For garnish, fold each of the reserved pepper strips in half. Insert the ends of each into a pitted olive. Mound the salad into a salad bowl. Garnish with the stuffed olives.

◖◖◖ *Curried Macaroni and Bologna Salad*

A slightly sweet and sour combination heightened by a mild curry dressing.

Makes 4 servings.

Nutrient Value Per Serving: 698 calories, 16 gm. protein, 47 gm. fat, 1174 mg. sodium, 64 mg. cholesterol.

 ½ *pound farfalle (bow ties)*
 ½ *cup finely chopped dill pickle*
 2 *tablespoons dill pickle juice*
 ½ *pound bologna, sliced ¼ inch thick*
 1 *cup diced celery*
 1 *tart apple, quartered, cored and coarsely chopped*
 ¾ *cup dairy sour cream*
 ½ *cup mayonnaise*
 ¾ *teaspoon curry powder*

1. Cook the farfalle following label directions just until "al dente"; drain. Put in a large bowl. Add the dill pickle and juice; toss to mix; cool.
2. Cut the bologna into ¼-inch cubes. Add to the pasta along with the celery and apple.
3. Combine the sour cream, mayonnaise and curry powder in a small bowl, blending well. Add two thirds of the dressing to the salad; toss until the ingredients are well coated. Cover; refrigerate for at least 4 hours. Just before serving, add the remain-

ing dressing; toss again. The salad can be covered and refrigerated for up to 2 days.

Pasta Verde Salad

The zippy flavor of this green and white salad makes an attractive addition to a cold supper.

Makes 4 servings.

Nutrient Value Per Serving: 508 calories, 10 gm. protein, 31 gm. fat, 852 mg. sodium, 4 mg. cholesterol.

½ *cup olive or vegetable oil*
¼ *cup red wine vinegar*
½ *teaspoon salt*
¼ *teaspoon pepper*
2 *tablespoons grated Romano cheese*
2 *teaspoons anchovy paste*
   OR: 3 anchovy fillets, mashed
¼ *cup chopped parsley*
½ *pound farfalle (bow ties)*
2 *small zucchini, washed*
1 *large sweet green pepper*
½ *cup thinly sliced green onion*
½ *cup chopped pitted green olives*
2 *tablespoons drained capers*
2 *tablespoons chopped peperoncini*
   (small green peppers in jar; optional)

1. Combine the oil, vinegar, salt, pepper, cheese and anchovy paste in a small bowl. Beat until well blended; stir in the parsley.
2. Cook the farfalle following label directions just until "al dente"; drain. Toss with 3 tablespoons of the dressing in a large bowl; cool.
3. Cut the unpeeled zucchini into 2-inch strips. Blanch 1 minute in boiling water in a small saucepan; drain. Halve and seed the green pepper; cut into thin strips. Add the zucchini, pepper, onions, olives, capers and peperoncini, if you wish, to the pasta.
4. Pour the remaining dressing over the pasta; toss until well combined. The salad can be covered and refrigerated for up to 2 days.

Green Potato Salad

Makes 12 servings.

Nutrient Value Per Serving: 247 calories, 5 gm. protein, 9 gm. fat, 321 mg. sodium, 0 mg. cholesterol.

5 *pounds small new potatoes,*
   uniform in size
⅓ *cup dry white wine (optional)*
24 *medium-size green onions*
1 *medium-size cucumber*
2 *medium-size sweet green peppers,*
   halved, seeded and cut into ¼-inch dice
1 *cup chopped parsley*
⅓ *cup lemon juice*
1 *tablespoon Dijon-style mustard*
2 *teaspoons leaf tarragon, crumbled*
1½ *teaspoons salt*
½ *teaspoon pepper*
½ *cup olive oil*

1. Cook the potatoes in enough boiling salted water to cover in a kettle or Dutch oven until fork-tender, 15 to 20 minutes. Drain. When cool enough to handle, peel; cut into ¼-inch-thick slices. Place in a large bowl. Pour the wine, if you wish, over the warm potatoes.
2. Thinly slice the green onions, keeping the white part separated from the green; you should have about 1 cup of the white and about 1½ cups of the green. Add the white to the potatoes.
3. Pare, halve and seed the cucumber. Cut into ¼-inch dice. Add along with the green pepper to the potatoes.
4. Combine the green portions of the onions, the parsley, lemon juice, mustard, tarragon, salt and pepper in the container of an electric blender or food processor. Cover; whirl until puréed. With the machine running, pour in the olive oil. Process until well blended. Pour the dressing over the salad. Toss to coat. Cover; refrigerate.
5. Serve the salad chilled.

◀◀◀ ▢ *Herring Salad*

Makes 4 to 6 servings.

Nutrient Value Per Serving: 168 calories, 10 gm. protein, 5 gm. fat, 284 mg. sodium, 71 mg. cholesterol.

1 **jar (8 ounces) herring in wine sauce, drained and cut into ½-inch slices**
2 **medium-size potatoes cooked, peeled and diced (3 cups)**
2 **medium-size onions, minced (1 cup)**
1 **medium-size tart apple, pared, quartered, cored and diced (1 cup)**
1 **cup diced cooked beets**
¾ **cup finely chopped dill pickles**
¼ **cup red wine vinegar**
2 **tablespoons sugar**
2 **tablespoons water**
⅛ **teaspoon pepper**
    Lettuce leaves
1 **hard-cooked egg, sliced**

1. Combine the herring, potatoes, onion, apple, beets and pickle in a large bowl.
2. Combine the vinegar, sugar, water and pepper in a 1-cup glass measure; mix well. Pour over the salad and toss gently; cover. Refrigerate at least 4 hours to allow flavors to blend, tossing once.
3. To serve, mound the salad on lettuce leaves; garnish with egg slices.

◀◀◀ ▼ *Tuna-White Bean Salad*

This attractive salad, flecked with bits of purple and green, can be made 1 or 2 days ahead.

Makes 12 servings.

Nutrient Value Per Serving: 304 calories, 18 gm. protein, 13 gm. fat, 447 mg. sodium, 7 mg. cholesterol.

1 **package (1 pound) dried Great Northern beans**
2 **quarts water**
2 **cans (7 ounces each) solid white tuna packed in oil, drained and flaked**
2 **large red onions, finely chopped (3 cups)**
1 **package (10 ounces) frozen peas, thawed**
½ **cup olive oil**
⅓ **cup fresh lemon juice**
2 **teaspoons leaf oregano, crumbled**
1½ **teaspoons salt**
¾ **to 1 teaspoon pepper**
1 **lemon for garnish**

1. Pick over the beans; rinse under cold water. Soak the beans overnight in enough water to cover in a large bowl. Drain; rinse.
2. Combine the beans and the 2 quarts of water in a kettle or Dutch oven. Bring to boiling. Lower the heat; simmer for 35 to 45 minutes or just until tender. Drain; cool to room temperature.
3. Combine the beans, tuna and red onion in a large bowl. Reserve ⅓ cup peas for garnish. Add the remaining peas to the salad.
4. Combine the oil, lemon juice, oregano, salt and pepper in a screw-top jar; shake well to blend. Pour over the salad. Toss gently to coat. Cover; refrigerate until ready to serve.
5. Make a lemon basket for garnish: Draw a ½-inch-wide strip with a pencil down the center of one half of the lemon; this will form the handle. Cut down into the center of the lemon following the outlines of the handle. Starting at the ends of the lemon, cut horizontally in toward the center strip. Remove the wedges from the top half of the lemon. Cut out the lemon from the underside of the handle. Scoop out the pulp from the bottom half of the lemon. Fill the basket with the reserved peas.
6. To serve, mound the salad in a large serving bowl. Garnish with the lemon basket.

Tuna Salad-Stuffed Pita Breads Italiano

Makes 4 servings.

Nutrient Value Per Serving: 499 calories, 28 gm. protein, 28 gm. fat, 695 mg. sodium, 70 mg. cholesterol.

> 1 **package (8 ounces) mozzarella cheese, cut into ½-inch cubes**
> 1 **can (7 ounces) tuna packed in water, drained and flaked**
> 1 **cup cherry tomatoes, quartered**
> 1 **medium-size red onion, halved, thinly sliced and separated into rings**
> 2 **large celery stalks, diced**
> ¼ **cup olive oil**
> 3 **tablespoons red wine vinegar**
> 1 **tablespoon leaf basil, crumbled**
> ½ **teaspoon salt**
> ¼ **teaspoon crushed red pepper flakes**
> ⅛ **teaspoon black pepper**
> 4 **whole-wheat pita breads**

1. Combine the mozzarella, tuna, cherry tomatoes, red onion and celery in a large bowl.
2. Combine the olive oil, vinegar, basil, salt, red pepper flakes and black pepper in a small screw-top jar. Cover; shake well to blend. Pour the dressing over the tuna mixture; toss well to coat. Cover it with plastic wrap. Refrigerate for at least 1 hour.
3. To serve: Cut the top quarter from each pita bread to form a pocket. Spoon the marinated salad into each pita.

CHICKEN SALAD-STUFFED PITA BREADS
Substitute 1 cup cooked, cubed chicken for the tuna—a great way to use up that leftover chicken.

▼ **Tuna Salad-Stuffed Pita Breads Italiano**

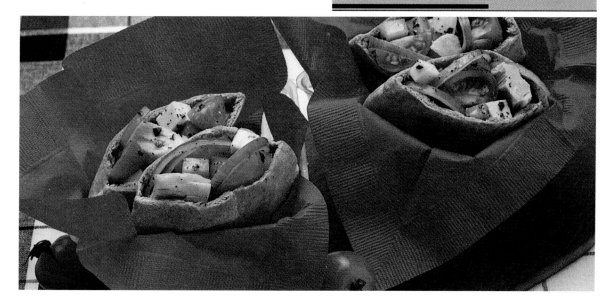

▨ ▼ *Marinated Tomato-Rice Salad*

Make several hours or a day ahead; then unmold just before serving.

Makes 12 servings.

Nutrient Value Per Serving: 279 calories, 5 gm. protein, 10 gm. fat, 190 mg. sodium, 0 mg. cholesterol.

> 7 *medium-size ripe tomatoes (about 2 pounds), cored*
> ½ *cup cider vinegar*
> 1 *tablespoon leaf basil, crumbled*
> 1 *tablespoon sugar*
> 3 *cups brown rice*
> 2 *small cucumbers, pared, halved, seeded and diced (about 1½ cups)*
> 1 *cup chopped parsley*
> ½ *cup olive oil*
> 9 *green onions, thinly sliced*
> 1 *teaspoon salt*
> ½ *teaspoon pepper*

1. Prepare a tomato rose for the garnish: Starting at the bottom of one of the tomatoes, cut the skin of the tomato with a vegetable peeler in one long continuous strip, about ¾ inch wide. Starting with the end you first removed, roll the strip, skin-side out, into a rose shape. Cover with damp paper toweling and refrigerate until needed.
2. Cut 5 of the remaining tomatoes, plus the peeled tomato, into ¾-inch cubes. Place in a medium-size bowl. Add the vinegar, basil and sugar; stir to mix well. Cover; marinate in the refrigerator for 1 hour.
3. Cook the rice following label directions. Drain; cool to room temperature.
4. Combine the rice, cucumber and parsley in a large bowl. Stir in the olive oil. Add the green onion, marinated tomatoes, salt and pepper; stir to mix well.
5. Pack 3 cups of the rice mixture into a

3½-quart bowl. Cut the remaining tomato into ¾-inch cubes. Arrange the cubes, skin-side out, in a ring around the outside of the bowl. Add the remaining rice mixture to the bowl; pack well. Cover; refrigerate for 1 hour.
6. To serve, gently run a thin spatula around the inside of the bowl. Invert the salad onto a large serving plate. Garnish the top with the tomato rose.

▢ *Brown Rice Salad*

The nutty flavor and chewiness of brown rice make it a perfect candidate for a cold salad.

Makes 6 servings.

Nutrient Value Per Serving: 187 calories, 4 gm. protein, 8 gm. fat, 153 mg. sodium, 0 mg. cholesterol.

> 1 *cup brown rice*
> 2 *tablespoons vegetable or peanut oil*
> 1½ *tablespoons white wine vinegar*
> 2 *teaspoons soy sauce*
> ½ *teaspoon ground coriander (optional) Dash of liquid red pepper seasoning*
> 8 *radishes, grated*
> 2 *green onions, thinly sliced Green leaf lettuce*
> ¼ *cup toasted slivered almonds Green Onion brushes (optional)*

1. Cook the rice according to label directions. Drain. Transfer to a bowl.
2. Meanwhile, beat together the oil, vinegar, soy sauce, coriander, if you wish, and red pepper seasoning in a small bowl.
3. Pour the dressing over the warm rice; toss gently to coat. Cool to room temperature.
4. Stir in the radishes and green onions. Spoon the rice into a lettuce-lined bowl. Sprinkle with almonds. Serve at room temperature or chilled. Garnish with green onion brushes, if you wish.

GREEN ONION BRUSHES
**Trim green onions and cut them into
4-inch lengths. Draw the tip of a very sharp
knife lengthwise through the green ends
several times to make the "bristles." To
make green onion frills, prepare green
onions as above; then drop them into a
bowl of ice water for 15 minutes to curl the
green ends.**

◀◀◀ ▢ *Billy's Coleslaw*

**An old-fashioned cooked dressing makes this
coleslaw special.**

Makes 10 servings.

Nutrient Value Per Serving: 253 calories, 2 gm.
protein, 87 gm. fat, 140 mg. sodium, 21 mg.
cholesterol.

1 *medium-size green cabbage (2 pounds)*
3 *large carrots, pared and grated*
1 *medium-size red onion, finely chopped*
½ *cup olive oil*
2 *tablespoons all-purpose flour*
2 *teaspoons dry mustard*
  Dash of liquid red pepper seasoning
½ *teaspoon salt*
6 *tablespoons sugar*
½ *cup white wine vinegar*
1 *cup heavy cream*
2 *egg yolks*

1. Trim the outer leaves from the cabbage; quarter
   and core. Shred; you should have about 10
   cups of cabbage. Place in a large bowl. Add
   the carrots and red onion; toss to mix well.
2. Heat the oil in a heavy medium-size skillet
   over medium heat. Stir in the flour just until
   blended. Add the mustard, liquid red
   pepper seasoning, salt, sugar and vinegar.
   Cook, stirring constantly, until thick.
3. Combine the heavy cream and egg yolks in
   a small bowl. Stir in some of the hot oil

mixture. Add the cream mixture to the oil
mixture in the skillet. Cook over medium
heat, stirring constantly, until thick.
4. Pour the hot dressing over the cabbage
   mixture; toss to coat. Let cool slightly.
   Cover; refrigerate several hours before
   serving. Toss again just before serving.

◀◀◀ *Pepper Coleslaw*

**Chopped sweet red and green pepper add
color to this coleslaw.**

Makes 10 servings.

Nutrient Value Per Serving: 220 calories, 1 gm.
protein, 22 gm. fat, 34 mg. sodium, 0 mg. cholesterol.

1 *medium-size green cabbage (2 pounds)*
1 *large sweet green pepper, halved, seeded
   and coarsely chopped*
1 *large sweet red pepper, halved, seeded
   and coarsely chopped*
1 *cup sliced celery*
⅔ *cup sliced green onion*
1 *cup vegetable oil*
6 *tablespoons white wine vinegar*
  Sweet red and green pepper rings (optional)

1. Trim the outer leaves from the cabbage;
   quarter and core. Shred; you should have
   about 10 cups of cabbage. Combine the
   cabbage, green and red pepper, celery and
   green onion in a large bowl.
2. Combine the oil and vinegar in a small
   bowl; blend well. Pour the dressing over the
   cabbage mixture; toss to coat. Cover;
   refrigerate for several hours before serving.
3. Garnish with red and green pepper rings, if
   you wish.

COLESLAW TIP
**If you have a food processor, use it to
shred your cabbage in seconds.**

4. The Main Course: Meats, Poultry and Fish and Shellfish

$\mathcal{T}$he main course is the most important part of every meal. It is enhanced by all the other courses. Because the main course is central to your planning, this chapter offers a large selection of meat, poultry and fish main-dish courses. They vary from quick and easy family favorites to special gourmet selections. Remember, each is keyed with our special symbols signifying quick, make-ahead, special and/or family recipes.

The meats section is comprised of beef, pork and lamb selections. Your dining can take on an international flavor with our Ginger-Beef Stir-Fry, Beef Bourguignonne and Curried Lamb Piroshki. You can also enjoy "all-American" favorites such as Oven Roasted Ribs with San Francisco Sweet and Sour Sauce.

Poultry, always an economical choice, is elevated to new heights of gastronomic achievement in the recipes of this chapter. No matter which part of the chicken your family prefers, breast, wing, thigh or leg, we've got a tempting new way to prepare it. All-time favorites such as Family Circle's Most Popular Fried Chicken are also represented.

Fish, whether fresh or frozen, offers variety for your menus. Broccoli-Stuffed Sole, with its rich, golden Hollandaise sauce, will make any meal an occasion. The Fillet of Flounder with Lobster can be made in minutes with the help of frozen food items.

At the end of this chapter we have included a special section on barbecues, with tips on barbecue equipment, starting the fire and cleaning the grill. Recipes for steak, burgers, pork, chicken, turkey breast and shrimp, among others, are offered.

Happy cooking!

◀Beef Teriyaki and Vegetables (page 94).

Beef

▥ ▯ ▢ *Roast Beef au Poivre*

Serve this roast beef sliced, either warm or cold, with the three zesty sauces. If served cold, the roast can be prepared a day ahead.

Heat oven to 450°, place roast in the oven and immediately lower oven temperature to 325° and roast for about 1¾ hours.
Makes 12 servings.

Nutrient Value Per Serving: 215 calories, 35 gm. protein, 7 gm. fat, 86 mg. sodium, 102 mg. cholesterol.

- **1 rolled eye-of-round roast (about 5 pounds)**
- **2 tablespoons cracked black pepper**
- **1 teaspoon garlic powder**
  Mustard Sauce (recipe follows)
  Spicy Horseradish-Caper Sauce (recipe follows)
  Choron Sauce (recipe follows)
  Parsley (optional)

1. About 2 hours before roasting, remove the roast from the refrigerator. Mix pepper and garlic powder on wax paper. Roll roast in seasonings to coat evenly; rub into surface. (Do not coat ends.) Let roast stand for about 2 hours at room temperature.
2. Preheat the oven to very hot (450°). Place roast on a rack in a roasting pan. Insert meat thermometer so it reaches center of meat.
3. Place roast in the preheated very hot oven (450°). Immediately lower the oven temperature to slow (325°). Roast the meat for 20 to 23 minutes per pound for medium-rare (140°) on a meat thermometer, or for 24 to 28 minutes per pound for medium (160°) on a meat thermometer.
4. Prepare the three sauces while the meat is roasting.
5. Remove the roast to a cutting board. Let stand 15 minutes before carving. Slice thinly; arrange on a platter; garnish with parsley, if you wish. Serve with the three sauces. To serve cold, refrigerate after standing for 15 minutes.

Mustard Sauce: Combine 1 cup dairy sour cream, 1 tablespoon cider vinegar and 2 tablespoons Dijon-style mustard (or to taste) in a small bowl until well blended. Makes 1 cup.

Spicy Horseradish-Caper Sauce: Combine ½ cup heavy cream, ½ cup mayonnaise, 2 tablespoons prepared horseradish and ⅓ cup drained and chopped capers in a small bowl; mix until well blended. Garnish with capers, if you wish. Makes 1⅓ cups.

Choron Sauce: Combine 4 egg yolks, 2 tablespoons lemon juice, ¼ teaspoon salt and 2 to 4 tablespoons tomato paste in the container of an electric blender. Cover; whirl until smooth. Gradually blend in ½ cup (1 stick) melted butter until thoroughly blended. Makes 1 cup.

MEAT SELECTION TIPS
- **The color of meat is an important indication of tenderness. For example, beef can vary from dark pink to dark red. The lighter the color, the younger the animal and more tender the meat.**
- **Watch out for liquid loss in a package. The drier the package, the fresher tasting the meat. The presence of liquid also indicates that the meat may have been frozen or is of a lower grade.**

BEEF ROASTING CHART

CUT	APPROX. WEIGHT	OVEN TEMP.	ROASTING TIME	INTERNAL TEMP.
Rib roast: Time based	4 lbs.	325°F	1¾ hours	140°F (R)
on short cut, 6 inches		325°F	2¼ hours	160°F (M)
from tip of the rib to the		325°F	3 hours	170°F (WD)
chine bone (back bone).				
If cut longer than 6	6 lbs.	325°F	3¼ hours	140°F (R)
inches, roast will take less		325°F	3¾ hours	160°F (M)
time per pound.		325°F	4¼ hours	170°F (WD)
Beef rib eye roast	4 to 6 lbs.	350°F	1¼ to 2 hours	140°F (R)
		350°F	1½ to 2¼ hours	160°F (M)
		350°F	2¼ to 2½ hours	170°F (WD)
Tenderloin	4 to 6 lbs.	425°F	¼ to 1 hour	140°F (R)

(R)-Rare   (M)-Medium   (WD)-Well Done

Beef Bourguignonne

Makes 6 servings.

Nutrient Value Per Serving: 386 calories, 33 gm. protein, 22 gm. fat, 699 mg. sodium, 103 mg. cholesterol.

2 pounds boneless beef, chuck or
*   top round, cut into 1-inch cubes*
*   Vegetable oil*
*   Pepper*
1 cup dry red wine
¾ cup water
12 small white onions
½ pound small or medium-size
*   mushrooms, halved*
1 envelope golden mushroom soup mix
*   Salt*

1. Brown the beef, part at a time, in its own fat in a Dutch oven or kettle. (Add a little vegetable oil, if necessary, to prevent sticking.) Season to taste with pepper. As the meat browns, remove it to a platter.

2. Add the wine and ¾ cup water to the Dutch oven, scraping up the browned bits from the bottom and sides. Return the meat to the Dutch oven. Add the onions, mushrooms and soup mix. Cover; simmer for 1½ to 2 hours or until the meat is tender. Season with salt to taste.

MONEY-SAVING TIPS
Buy meat in quantity when the price is right and the meat looks good; then freeze it.

   Keep track of the "regular" meat prices so you can determine if a sale is really a sale.

◼ ◖◖◖ ◻ *Old-Fashioned Beef Stew (Top of the Range Method)*

Makes 6 servings.

Nutrient Value Per Serving: 467 calories, 38 gm. protein, 19 gm. fat, 777 mg. sodium, 98 mg. cholesterol.

¼ *cup all-purpose flour*
1 *teaspoon salt*
½ *teaspoon pepper*
2 *pounds lean boneless chuck, cut into 1½-inch cubes*
3 *tablespoons vegetable oil*
3 *onions, each cut into 8 wedges*
1 *clove garlic, minced*
1 *can (12 ounces) beer*
1 *cup beef broth*
2 *tablespoons tomato paste*
1 *teaspoon leaf thyme, crumbled*
½ *teaspoon leaf marjoram, crumbled*
1 *bay leaf*
3 *medium-size potatoes, quartered*
4 *medium-size carrots, sliced*
½ *pound broccoli, cut into small pieces*
½ *cup sliced celery*
1 *can (4 ounces) mushrooms, drained OR: ½ pound mushrooms sautéed in 1 tablespoon butter*
¼ *cup chopped parsley*

1. Combine the flour, salt and pepper in a medium-size bowl. Add the beef; stir well to coat the cubes.
2. Heat 2 tablespoons of the oil in a large heavy saucepan or Dutch oven. Brown the beef, a few cubes at a time, on all sides; remove pieces as they brown. Add the remaining 1 tablespoon oil to the saucepan; sauté onion wedges and garlic for 3 minutes, stirring often. Add the beer, beef broth, tomato paste, thyme, marjoram and bay leaf; bring to boiling, stirring to mix well.
3. Return the beef cubes to the pot; cover tightly. Lower the heat; simmer about 1¼

BEEF STEW—FIVE WAYS
Make this hearty beef stew your way—on the range, in the oven, in a pressure cooker, a slow cooker or a microwave oven. The cooking chart will enable you to decide on the technique that suits your time and equipment.

hours or until the meat is almost done. Add the potatoes and carrots; cover; simmer for 15 minutes. Add the broccoli and celery; cover; simmer for 5 minutes longer. Stir in the mushrooms; sprinkle with the parsley.

Oven Method: Follow steps 1 and 2 above, using a Dutch oven or large flameproof casserole. Return the beef cubes to the Dutch oven; add the potatoes and carrots. Cover and bake in a preheated slow oven (325°) for 1 hour and 15 minutes or until the meat is tender. Add the broccoli and the celery; cover and bake for 15 minutes longer. Remove the casserole from the oven. Stir in the mushrooms; sprinkle with the chopped parsley.

Pressure Cooker Method: Follow steps 1 and 2 above, using a 6-quart pressure cooker. Return the beef cubes to the cooker; close cover securely; place the pressure control over the vent pipe and cook on high heat until the control starts to jiggle and rock. Lower the heat to medium so the control rocks gently. Pressure cook for 10 minutes. Remove from the heat; place closed cooker under cold running water for about 1 minute or until no steam hisses when you start to remove the control. Carefully remove the control, then the cover. Add the potatoes and carrots; close cover securely; place pressure control over the vent pipe and cook on high heat until control starts to jiggle and rock. Lower heat to medium so control rocks gently. Pressure cook for 5 minutes. Remove from heat; place closed cooker under cold running water for about 1 minute or until no steam hisses when you start to remove the control. Carefully remove control, then the cover. Add the broccoli and celery. Partially cover with lid; cook for 5 minutes with no pressure. Stir in the mushrooms; sprinkle with the parsley.

Slow Cooker Method: Follow steps 1 and 2 above, using a large skillet or saucepan, and using only 1 cup beer and ½ cup beef broth. Place the skillet mixture in a slow cooker. Add the carrots and beef cubes, then the potatoes, broccoli and celery. Cover and cook on low heat for 6 to 8 hours or until the meat and vegetables are tender. Stir in the mushrooms; sprinkle with chopped the parsley.

Note: To keep broccoli a bright green, you can add to slow cooker for last hour of cooking time.

Microwave Method: Follow steps 1 and 2 above, using a large skillet or saucepan. Place the skillet mixture and the beef cubes in a 3-quart microwave-safe casserole. Cover. Microwave on medium setting for 20 minutes, stirring once, or until the meat is almost tender. Add the potatoes and the carrots. Cover; microwave on high setting for 15 minutes, stirring every 5 minutes. Add the broccoli and celery. Cover; microwave on high setting for 5 minutes longer. Remove the casserole from microwave. Stir in the mushrooms; sprinkle with the chopped parsley. Cover and let stand for 5 minutes.

Top of Range	**1 hour 20 minutes**
Oven	**1 hour 30 minutes**
Pressure Cooker	**20 minutes**
Slow Cooker	**6 to 8 hours**
Microwave	**40 minutes**

SAVE BONES FOR SOUP
Don't throw away any fresh bones or trimmings. Freeze them until you have enough for a hearty pot of soup. (Dark-colored bones should not be used.)

Hotchpotch

An added bonus of this dish is the flavorful broth which can be used for soup.

Makes 4 servings.

Nutrient Value Per Serving: 450 calories, 41 gm. protein, 18 gm. fat, 186 mg. sodium, 108 mg. cholesterol.

> *1   beef brisket (about 2 pounds)*
> *3   medium-size potatoes, pared and cut in half*
> *3   medium-size carrots, pared*
> *3   medium-size onions*
> *1   leek, well washed*
> *4   slices cooked bacon, crumbled*

1. Place the brisket in a large kettle or Dutch oven with water to cover. Bring to boiling; lower the heat; cover; simmer for 2½ hours.
2. Add the potatoes, carrots, onions and leek. Simmer, covered, until the vegetables and meat are tender, about 30 minutes.
3. Remove the vegetables with a slotted spoon to a large bowl. With a potato masher, gently mash the vegetables adding just enough stock to moisten.
4. Mound the vegetables on a serving platter; sprinkle with the crumbled bacon. Slice the brisket and arrange on top of the vegetables.

Honey-Mustard-Glazed Corned Beef

The vegetables are cooked in the broth for this satisfying one-pot meal.

Makes 4 servings plus enough for 2 bonus meals.

Nutrient Value Per Serving: 955 calories, 45 gm. protein, 64 gm. fat, 1720 mg. sodium, 201 mg. cholesterol.

1 *corned beef brisket (about 5 pounds)*
1 *medium-size onion, quartered*
2 *celery tops*
4 *carrots, pared and halved crosswise*
12 *small new potatoes (about 1 pound)*
½ *head cabbage (about ¾ pound), cut into four wedges and cored*
¼ *cup honey*
1 *tablespoon spicy brown mustard*
 Chopped parsley (optional)
 Horseradish Cream (recipe follows)

1. Place the corned beef in a large kettle. Add enough water to cover. Heat slowly to boiling; skim the fat. Add the onion and celery; lower the heat; cover. Simmer for 3 hours.
2. Add the carrots, potatoes and cabbage wedges to the kettle; cover. Simmer for 30 minutes longer or until the meat and vegetables are tender.
3. Preheat the broiler.
4. Remove the vegetables with a slotted spoon to a large heated serving platter; cover. Keep warm. Lift the corned beef, draining over the kettle, onto a shallow roasting pan. Combine the honey and mustard in a small bowl; brush over the meat.
5. Broil the meat 6 inches from the heat for about 5 minutes or just until honey mixture bubbles and begins to brown.
6. Slice the corned beef thinly against the grain. Transfer to a serving platter with the vegetables. Garnish with chopped parsley, if you wish. Serve with Horseradish Cream.

Horseradish Cream: Whip ½ cup heavy cream with 1 to 2 tablespoons prepared horseradish until soft peaks form.

FOR BONUS MEALS
Wrap the remaining meat in plastic wrap or aluminum foil; refrigerate. When ready to use, slice the remaining meat into thin slices. Trim all fat. Use 12 slices for the Hot Reuben Sandwiches (recipe follows). Cut the remaining meat into thin strips for a main-dish salad. Combine with spinach, cauliflower flowerets, sliced mushrooms and hard-cooked eggs, and dress with your favorite vinaigrette.

Hot Reuben Sandwiches

Bake at 350° for 15 minutes.
Makes 4 servings.

Nutrient Value Per Serving: 889 calories, 36 gm. protein, 65 gm. fat, 2350 mg. sodium, 143 mg. cholesterol.

½ *cup mayonnaise or salad dressing*
¼ *cup chili sauce*
¼ *cup chopped dill pickle*
4 *round soft onion rolls, split*
12 *slices cooked corned beef*
1 *can (8 ounces) sauerkraut, rinsed and drained*
4 *slices caraway Muenster cheese, (from an 8-ounce package)*

1. To make the dressing: Combine the mayonnaise, chili sauce and dill pickle in small bowl.

2. Spread the top and bottom half of the rolls with the dressing. Place the corned beef on the bottom half of each roll, dividing evenly. Top each with sauerkraut (about 3 tablespoons) and 1 slice cheese, cut to fit. Cover with the top half of the roll.

3. Tear off 4 pieces of aluminum foil; wrap each sandwich securely. Heat in a toaster oven or preheated moderate oven (350°) for 15 minutes or until heated thoroughly.

Beef Sukiyaki

Use an electric wok or skillet and prepare Beef Sukiyaki at the table. If you don't want to cook the complete dish at the table, prepare the Beef Sukiyaki through step 5 in the kitchen and finish the cooking (starting with step 6) at the table.

Makes 4 servings.

Nutrient Value Per Serving: 851 calories, 29 gm. protein, 48 gm. fat, 2903 mg. sodium, 77 mg. cholesterol.

1   pound boneless sirloin steak
1   package (about 7¾ ounces) cellophane
*   noodles or bean threads**
3   to 4 tablespoons vegetable oil
2   teaspoons sesame oil
2   medium-size onions, sliced

3   celery stalks, sliced diagonally
*   ½ inch thick*
½   pound mushrooms, sliced ¼ inch thick
¾   pound fresh spinach, washed
*   and trimmed (6 cups)*
1   small eggplant (½ to ¾ pound),
*   sliced ¼ inch thick*
½   cup soy sauce
2   to 3 tablespoons sugar
1   can (8 ounces) sliced water chestnuts,
*   drained*
⅓   cup chicken broth
⅓   cup dry sherry
*   Sliced radishes for garnish*

1. Place the meat in the freezer 30 minutes for easier slicing; slice ⅛ inch thick.

2. Soak the cellophane noodles in boiling water for 10 minutes or until transparent; drain.*

3. Combine the vegetable oil and sesame oil in a cup.

4. Heat a wok or large skillet; add 1 tablespoon of the oil mixture. Stir-fry the onion and celery for 2 to 3 minutes; remove to a plate. Stir-fry the mushrooms 2 to 3 minutes; remove to a plate. Stir-fry the spinach quickly, until barely wilted; remove to a strainer. Stir-fry the eggplant for 3 minutes; remove to a plate. Add oil as needed.

5. Add about a third of the meat to the wok in one layer; sprinkle with 2 to 3 tablespoons of the soy sauce and 1 to 2 teaspoons of the sugar; cook for 1 minute; turn the meat over and push to one side or remove to a plate. Repeat with the remaining meat.

6. Arrange the meat, vegetables, water chestnuts and noodles in the wok in separate mounds. Combine the remaining soy sauce sugar, broth and sherry; pour over all. Cover, cook on high heat for 2 minutes or until heated. Garnish with radishes.

7. Serve right from the wok, with rice and additional soy sauce, if you wish.

*Or substitute 6 ounces cooked vermicelli.

◼️ 🍽️ ⬜ *Beef Teriyaki and Vegetables*

Makes 6 servings.

Nutrient Value Per Serving: 251 calories, 26 gm. protein, 8 gm. fat, 953 mg. sodium, 71 mg. cholesterol.

> 1 *flank steak (about 1½ pounds)*
> ⅓ *cup dry sherry*
> ⅓ *cup chicken broth*
> ½ *cup soy sauce*
> 1 *clove garlic, minced*
> 1 *teaspoon sugar*
> 1 *medium-size sweet potato*
> 12 *small mushrooms (about ¼ pound)*
> 1 *sweet green pepper, cored and seeded*
> 4 *green onions*
> 1 *tablespoon vegetable oil*
> 1 *cup fresh bean sprouts*

1. Place the steak in a shallow glass dish. To prepare the teriyaki sauce, stir together in a small bowl the sherry, chicken broth, soy sauce, garlic and sugar; pour about two thirds of this sauce over the steak; marinate for 15 minutes. Reserve the remaining teriyaki sauce.
2. Peel the potato; slice very thin. Cut the mushrooms in half. Cut the pepper into 1-inch squares. Cut the green onions into 1-inch lengths. Arrange the vegetables on a tray.
3. Drain the steak, pat dry and broil 4 inches from the heat, 2 to 3 minutes on each side for rare. Keep warm.
4. Heat the oil in a wok or skillet; add the sweet potato slices and stir-fry for 1 minute; add the mushrooms, green pepper and green onions. Stir-fry for 2 to 3 minutes until crisp-tender. Stir in bean sprouts; stir-fry for 1 minute to heat through.
5. Slice the steak crosswise, on the diagonal, into thin slices. Arrange with the vegetables on a heated platter. Serve with the reserved teriyaki sauce.

PREVENT SHRINKAGE
Avoid overcooking meat. This causes dry-tasting, less tender meat and makes for more shrinkage and, therefore, fewer servings.

◼️ ⬜ *Ginger-Beef Stir-Fry with Vegetables*

Makes 6 servings.

Nutrient Value Per Serving: 212 calories, 19 gm. protein, 11 gm. fat, 702 mg. sodium, 51 mg. cholesterol.

> 1 *egg white*
> 1 *tablespoon cornstarch*
> ½ *teaspoon salt*
> ½ *teaspoon sugar*
> ¼ *teaspoon ground ginger*
> ¼ *teaspoon red pepper flakes*
> 1 *flank steak (about 1 pound), cut into 2 x ½-inch strips*
> ½ *cup finely chopped green onion*
> 3 *tablespoons vegetable oil*
> 2 *tablespoons soy sauce*
> 2 *tablespoons dry sherry*
> 2 *medium-size carrots, thinly sliced*
> 1 *medium-size zucchini, thinly sliced*
> ¼ *pound fresh or frozen pea pods, thawed*

1. Whisk together the egg white, cornstarch, salt, sugar, ginger and red pepper flakes in a medium-size bowl. Add the steak; toss to coat. Reserve.
2. Sauté the green onion in oil in a 10-inch skillet for 1 minute. Add the steak; stir-fry until browned and tender; add more oil if necessary to prevent sticking. Stir in the soy sauce and sherry, scraping up the brown bits from the bottom of the skillet. Add the carrots, zucchini and pea pods. Stir-fry for several minutes until the vegetables are crisp-tender and heated through.

No-Fuss Meatloaf

Bake at 350° for 40 minutes.
Makes 8 servings.

Nutrient Value Per Serving: 321 calories, 23 gm. protein, 17 gm. fat, 520 mg. sodium, 77 mg. cholesterol.

> 2 **pounds ground beef, chuck or round, or a mixture**
> 2 **cups herb-seasoned stuffing mix**
> 1 **can (1 pound) stewed tomatoes**
> 2 **tablespoons Worchestershire sauce**
> ¼ **cup tomato catsup**
>   **Salt**
>   **Pepper**
>   **Fresh parsley (optional)**

1. Preheat the oven to moderate (350°). Oil an 8-cup ring mold.
2. Place the meat, stuffing mix and salt and pepper to taste in a large bowl. Combine the stewed tomatoes and Worcestershire in the container of an electric blender or food processor. Whirl just until the tomatoes are crushed. Add to the meat mixture. Mix lightly with your hands until well blended. Press into the prepared ring mold. Unmold onto a jelly-roll pan. Brush with catsup.
3. Bake in the preheated moderate oven (350°) for 40 minutes. Let stand for 10 minutes. Transfer to a serving platter. Fill the center with your favorite stir-fried vegetable mixture. (We like broccoli flowerets, snow peas, sweet red pepper and mushrooms.) Garnish with parsley, if you wish.

GROUND MEAT TIPS
● **Buy meat the day you plan to use it whenever possible. If ground meat must be saved until the next day, wrap it in wax paper and store it in the coldest part of your refrigerator.**
● **To freeze ground meat, wrap it in plastic wrap or aluminum foil soon after purchasing and place in the freezer.**

Skillet Cumin Meatloaf

Makes 6 servings.

Nutrient Value Per Serving: 335 calories, 23 gm. protein, 19 gm. fat, 610 mg. sodium, 79 mg. cholesterol.

> 1 **pound ground round**
> 1 **pound pork sausage meat**
> ¾ **cup coarsley chopped celery**
> ¾ **cup raisins**
> ¼ **teaspoon salt**
> ¼ **teaspoon pepper**
> ¼ **cup water**
> 1 **small tomato, peeled, seeded and diced**
> 1 **small onion, diced**
> 1 **small sweet green pepper, halved, seeded and diced**
> 1 **large clove garlic**
> ½ **teaspoon whole cumin seeds**
>   **Celery leaves**
>   **Cherry tomato**

1. Mix together lightly the beef and pork sausage in a large bowl. Add the celery, raisins, salt and pepper.
2. Combine the water, tomato, onion, green pepper, garlic and cumin in the container of an electric blender. Whirl until smooth. Pour over the meat. Mix well.
3. Pack the meat into an ungreased 10-inch

▲ **Skillet Cumin Meatloaf**

cast-iron skillet; smooth the top so it mounds.

4. Cook, covered, over low heat on top of the stove for 55 minutes or until the meat is done. Drain the fat. Turn the loaf out onto a celery leaf-lined board. Garnish with additional leaves and a cherry tomato, if you wish.

AN ALTERNATE BAKING DISH
This meatloaf can be baked in a round casserole in a preheated moderate oven (350°) for 1 hour.

Carrot and Meat Pie

Bake pastry at 400° for 15 minutes; bake pie at 375° for 30 minutes.
Makes 6 servings.

Nutrient Value Per Serving: 649 calories, 14 gm. protein, 50 gm. fat, 735 mg. sodium, 203 mg. cholesterol.

- **1 package (11 ounces) piecrust mix**
- **¼ cup chopped shallots or onion**
- **2 tablespoons butter**
- **½ pound carrots, pared and shredded**

½ **cup chicken broth**
½ **teaspoon salt**
¼ **teaspoon pepper**
½ **pound ground beef round**
½ **teaspoon leaf thyme, crumbled**
½ **teaspoon leaf marjoram, crumbled**
1¼ **cups heavy cream**
1 **egg**
1 **egg yolk**

1. Preheat the oven to hot (400°).
2. Prepare piecrust mix following the package directions. Press the pastry evenly over the bottom and sides of a 10-inch tart pan with removable bottom; trim pastry level with rim. Prick bottom all over with a fork. Chill for 20 minutes.
3. Fit a piece of aluminum foil in the pastry shell; add rice or dried beans for weight.
4. Bake in the preheated hot oven (400°) for 10 minutes. Remove the foil and rice or beans. Bake the pastry 5 minutes longer. Remove to a wire rack. Lower the oven temperature to moderate (375°).
5. Sauté the shallots in the butter in a large skillet over medium heat for 3 minutes or until softened. Stir in the carrots, chicken broth, mace, salt and pepper. Cook for 5 minutes or until the carrots are tender. Raise the heat to medium-high. Continue cooking, stirring constantly, until the cooking liquid has evaporated. Transfer the mixture to a medium-size bowl.
6. Add the ground round, thyme and marjoram to the same skillet. Sauté over medium-low heat, breaking up the meat with a wooden spoon, until no pink remains. Add the beef to the carrot mixture; mix well. Spoon evenly over the bottom of the pastry shell.
7. Beat the cream with the egg and egg yolk in a small bowl; pour over meat filling.
8. Bake in the moderate oven (375°) for 30

minutes or until the center is set and the top is puffed and golden. Let stand for 10 minutes before slicing.

Cottage Pie

Similar to a shepherd's pie, but made with only ½ pound of ground beef.

Bake at 375° for 45 minutes.
Makes 6 servings.

Nutrient Value Per Serving: 419 calories, 17 gm. protein, 20 gm. fat, 995 mg. sodium, 152 mg. cholesterol.

2 **pounds potatoes, pared and cut into eighths**
2 **teaspoons salt**
4 **tablespoons (½ stick) unsalted butter**
1 **tablespoon vegetable oil**
2 **cups chopped onion (2 large onions)**
1 **cup finely chopped carrots**
1 **clove garlic, finely chopped**
1 **teaspoon leaf sage, crumbled**
½ **pound lean ground beef**
2 **tablespoons all-purpose flour**
1 **cup beef broth**
½ **teaspoon pepper**
3 **tablespoons tomato paste**
1 **package (10 ounces) frozen peas, partially thawed**
¼ **cup heavy cream**
¼ **teaspoon freshly grated nutmeg OR: ½ teaspoon ground nutmeg**
2 **eggs**
Ground nutmeg (optional)

1. Cook the potatoes in boiling water with ½ teaspoon of the salt in a medium-size sauce-pan, for 15 to 20 minutes or until tender; drain well; keep warm.

2. Meanwhile, melt 1 tablespoon of the butter with the oil in a large heavy skillet over medium heat. Stir in the onion and carrot; sauté, stirring, until lightly browned, about 10 minutes. Add the garlic and sage; sauté 1 minute longer.

3. Crumble the beef into the skillet; cook until no longer pink. Drain off the excess fat. Stir in the flour until well combined. Add the broth, ¾ teaspoon of the salt, ¼ teaspoon of the pepper and the tomato paste; stir until well blended. Fold in the partially thawed peas; cook, stirring occasionally, until thickened. Pour into an ungreased 8 x 8 x 2-inch square baking dish, spreading evenly.

4. Preheat the oven to moderate (375°).

5. Mash the potatoes. Beat in the cream, nutmeg and the remaining butter, salt and pepper until smooth and fluffy. Beat in the eggs, one at a time. Spoon over the meat filling, spreading evenly; make sure the potato touches all sides of pan. If you wish, decorate the top by drawing the tines of a fork from the center to the edges.

6. Bake in the preheated moderate oven (375°) for 45 minutes or until the top is puffed and golden. Sprinkle with ground nutmeg, if you wish.

Quick Chili con Carne California Style

Makes 4 servings.

Nutrient Value Per Serving: 429 calories, 27 gm. protein, 29 gm. fat, 955 mg. sodium, 77 mg. cholesterol.

- **2 tablespoons vegetable oil**
- **1 pound ground round**
- **1 large onion, chopped (1 cup)**
- **1 tablespoon chili powder**
- **½ teaspoon ground cumin**
- **1 teaspoon salt**
- **⅓ cup dry red wine**
- **1 can (8 ounces) tomato sauce**
- **1 green pepper, seeded and diced**
- **4 cups shredded iceberg lettuce**
- **1 avocado, peeled, pitted and sliced**
- **4 green onions, sliced**

1. Heat the oil in a wok or large skillet; add the beef and onion; cook, stirring, until the meat browns slightly. Stir in the chili powder, cumin and salt.

2. Add the wine, tomato sauce and green pepper. Cover; cook, stirring often, for 5 minutes.

3. Arrange the lettuce and avocado on plates; spoon the hot chili over and sprinkle with the onions. Serve with hot tortillas or cornbread.

Beef Burgers Paprika with Noodles and Cabbage

Makes 4 servings.

Nutrient Value Per Serving: 711 calories, 40 gm. protein, 38 gm. fat, 1124 mg. sodium, 192 mg. cholesterol.

- **1¼ pounds ground round**
- **2 tablespoons butter or margarine**
- **8 ounces wide egg noodles**
- **3 cups shredded green cabbage (1 small)**
- **¼ pound small mushrooms, halved or sliced**
- **1 tablespoon paprika**
- **1 envelope onion soup mix**
- **1½ cups water**
- **2 tablespoons butter**
- **½ teaspoon poppy or caraway seeds**
- **½ cup dairy sour cream**
   Fresh dill sprigs

▲ **Beef Burgers Paprika with Noodles and Cabbage**

1. Bring 3 quarts lightly salted water to boiling in a large saucepan.
2. Shape the beef into 4 equal-size patties.
3. Heat 2 tablespoons butter in a large skillet. Cook the patties over medium heat, 4 to 6 minutes on each side.
4. Cook the noodles and cabbage in boiling water for 6 minutes or until tender.
5. Remove the patties from the skillet; keep warm. Sauté the mushrooms in the same skillet for 3 minutes. Stir in the paprika; cook for 1 minute. Stir in the soup mix and water. Bring to boiling, stirring often. Reduce the heat; cover; simmer for 5 minutes.
6. Drain the noodles and cabbage. Return to the saucepan. Stir in the remaining 2 tablespoons of butter and the poppy seeds. Arrange on a platter with the meat patties.

7. Stir the sour cream into the mushroom/ onion soup sauce. Heat, stirring, but do not boil. Spoon part of the sauce over the meat and noodles. Serve the remaining sauce separately. Garnish with sprigs of dill.

MAKE AND FREEZE GROUND BEEF PATTIES
To freeze a large number of ground beef patties, shape the patties, place them on wax paper on a cookie sheet, cover with wax paper and place in the freezer. When frozen, remove from the cookie sheet, store in a plastic bag or wrap in aluminum foil with 2 pieces of wax paper between the patties. Return to the freezer.

◻ *Mexican Beef and Corn Cakes*

Makes 6 servings.

Nutrient Value Per Serving: 573 calories, 28 gm. protein, 31 gm. fat, 830 mg. sodium, 123 mg. cholesterol.

MEXICAN BEEF
 1   *medium-size onion, sliced*
 1   *clove garlic, finely chopped*
 2   *tablespoons vegetable oil*
 1   *pound ground round*
 ¼   *teaspoon pepper*
 1   *can (15 ounces) tomato sauce*
 2   *teaspoons chili powder*
 1   *can (4 ounces) chopped green chilies, drained*
 ¼   *teaspoon leaf basil, crumbled*
 ¼   *teaspoon ground cinnamon*
 ¼   *teaspoon leaf marjoram, crumbled*

CORN CAKES
 1   *cup milk*
 1   *egg*
 3   *tablespoons vegetable oil*
 1½ *cups* sifted *all-purpose flour*
 3   *tablespoons sugar*
 3½ *teaspoons baking powder*
 ½   *cup shredded Cheddar cheese (2 ounces)*
 1   *package (10 ounces) frozen whole kernel corn, thawed*

TOPPINGS
     Shredded Cheddar cheese, chopped green onion, shredded iceberg lettuce and chopped tomato

1. Prepare the Mexican Beef: Sauté the onion and garlic in the oil in a large skillet until tender. Add the meat; cook, breaking up with a wooden spoon, until the meat is browned.
2. Add the pepper, tomato sauce, chili powder, green chilies, basil, cinnamon and marjoram. Cook over medium heat, stirring frequently, until the mixture thickens, about 15 minutes.
3. Prepare the Corn Cakes while the meat mixture is cooking: Combine the milk, egg and oil in a medium-size bowl. Stir in the flour, sugar and baking powder until well blended. Fold in the shredded cheese and thawed corn.
4. Heat a lightly greased griddle to medium-hot. Pour the batter, ½ cup at a time, onto the griddle to form 5-inch pancakes. Cook until the edges begin to brown and bubbles appear on top. Turn; cook until the other side is golden.
5. Serve the Corn Cakes with the hot Mexican Beef mixture. Top each with shredded cheese, chopped green onion, shredded lettuce and chopped tomato.

◻ *Beef Empanadas*

Serve these meat-filled pies for a Sunday night supper.

Bake at 400° for 15 minutes.
Makes 12 empanadas.

Nutrient Value Per Serving: 186 calories, 7 gm. protein, 9 gm. fat, 219 mg. sodium, 60 mg. cholesterol.

DOUGH
 2   *cups* unsifted *all-purpose flour*
 ¼   *teaspoon salt*
 3   *tablespoons bacon fat, melted*
     OR: vegetable shortening, melted
 1   *tablespoon vegetable oil*
 ⅓   *cup milk*
 ⅓   *cup warm water*

FILLING
 1   *cup finely chopped onion (large onion)*
 2   *cloves garlic, finely chopped*
 1   *teaspoon vegetable oil*
 2   *teaspoons chili powder*
 ¼   *teaspoon ground cumin*

½ **pound lean ground beef**
2 **hard-cooked eggs, chopped**
18 **medium-size pimiento-stuffed green olives, sliced**
Prepared hot chili sauce (optional)

1. Prepare the Dough: Combine the flour, salt, shortening and vegetable oil in a medium-size bowl; stir to blend. Heat the milk in a small saucepan over low heat until bubbles appear around the edges. Add to the flour mixture along with the warm water. Stir with a fork to form soft dough.
2. Turn the dough out onto a lightly floured board. Knead until smooth, about 3 minutes. Cover; let rest for 20 minutes.
3. Prepare the Filling: Sauté the onion and garlic in the 1 teaspoon oil in a medium-size skillet until tender and lightly browned, about 5 minutes. Stir in chili powder and cumin. Crumble the beef into the skillet. Sauté, stirring, 3 minutes or until the beef loses its pink color.
4. Form the dough into a 12-inch long roll on a lightly floured board. Slice into 12 equal pieces. Roll out each piece on a lightly floured board into a 5-inch round.
5. Preheat the oven to hot (400°). Lightly grease a cookie sheet.
6. Place about 1½ tablespoons of the filling in the center of each round and top with 1 tablespoon chopped egg and about 1 tablespoon sliced olives. Moisten the edges of several rounds with water. Fold in half and press edges firmly together to form half circle. (Empanadas should be very plump with the filling.) Trim with scissors to make a neat edge. Repeat with the remaining rounds. Place the empanadas on the prepared cookie sheet.
7. Bake in the preheated oven (400°) for 15 minutes. Serve hot with hot chili sauce, if you wish.

"Meatball" Pizza

Make this pizza with a thick homemade whole-wheat crust, or, for a quicker version, with a pizza crust mix.

Bake at 450° for 20 minutes.
Makes 6 servings.

Nutrient Value Per Serving: 573 calories, 27 gm. protein, 22 gm. fat, 865 mg. sodium, 104 mg. cholesterol.

PIZZA CRUST
2¼ **cups unsifted all-purpose flour**
1 **cup whole-wheat flour OR: 1 cup additional all-purpose flour**
1 **envelope fast-rising dry-yeast**
1 **tablespoon sugar**
½ **teaspoon salt**
1 **tablespoon olive or vegetable oil**
1 **cup water**

TOMATO SAUCE
1 **can (15 ounces) tomato sauce**
½ **teaspoon sugar**
½ **teaspoon leaf basil, crumbled**
¼ **leaf oregano, crumbled**
1 **clove garlic, finely chopped**

MEATBALLS
½ **pound lean ground beef**
⅓ **cup packaged unseasoned bread crumbs**
1 **egg**
½ **teaspoon leaf basil, crumbled**
½ **teaspoon leaf oregano, crumbled**
¼ **teaspoon pepper**
1 **sweet green pepper, halved and cut into ¼-inch-wide strips**
1 **medium-size onion, cut into eighths**
1 **tablespoon olive or vegetable oil**
1 **package (8 ounces) mozzarella cheese, shredded**
¼ **cup grated Parmesan cheese**

1. Prepare the Pizza Crust: Combine 1¼ cups flour, whole-wheat flour, yeast, sugar and salt in a large bowl.

2. Heat the oil and water in a saucepan to 130° (mixture should feel comfortably hot). Stir into the flour mixture until well combined. Gradually knead in ½ to ¾ cup all-purpose flour to form a soft dough. Turn out onto a lightly floured board. Knead until smooth and elastic, about 5 minutes, adding more flour as necessary to prevent sticking. Form the dough into a ball; place in a lightly oiled bowl; bring oiled side up. Cover; let rise in a warm place away from drafts, until doubled in volume, 35 to 40 minutes.

3. Prepare Tomato Sauce: Set aside ¼ cup of the canned tomato sauce. Combine the remaining sauce, sugar, basil, oregano and garlic in a small saucepan. Bring to boiling. Lower the heat; simmer for 5 minutes. Cool to room temperature. Reserve.

4. Prepare the Meatballs: Combine the ground beef, bread crumbs, egg, basil, oregano, pepper and reserved ¼ cup tomato sauce in a medium-size bowl. Shape the meat mixture into about 40 meatballs, using 1 rounded teaspoon for each. Place on wax paper. Pat each with moistened fingers into a 1¼-inch circle. Reserve.

5. Sauté the green pepper and onion in the oil in a medium-size skillet, for 6 minutes or until golden. Cool. Reserve.

6. Lightly grease a large cookie sheet. Punch the dough down. Roll out on the prepared cookie sheet to 15 x 11-inch rectangle. Pinch edges up to form 14 x 10-inch rectangle. Cover lightly; let rise 30 minutes or until doubled in volume.

7. Preheat the oven to very hot (450°).

8. Gently spread the Tomato Sauce over the dough. Top with the sautéed peppers and onion, half the mozzerella cheese, the meatballs and remaining mozzarella; sprinkle with the Parmesan.

9. Bake in the preheated very hot oven (450°) for 20 minutes or until the crust is crisp and golden brown and cheese is bubbly.

Note: To use active dry yeast, increase the rising time in step 2 to about 1 hour and in step 6 to 45 minutes.

▲*Clockwise from bottom:* **"Meatball" Pizza (page 101), Sloppy Joe Quiche (page 170) and Cottage Pie (page 97).**

Pork

▯ ▢ Pork Roast with Dumplings

Braising the pork in a covered Dutch oven with a little liquid keeps the meat moist.

Braise pork at 325° for 1¾ to 2 hours; bake dumplings at 325° for 20 minutes. Makes 8 servings.

Nutrient Value Per Serving: 613 calories, 32 gm. protein, 45 gm. fat, 1159 mg. sodium, 105 mg. cholesterol.

> 1 **boneless rolled loin of pork (about 3 pounds)**
> 2 **medium-size onions, sliced**
>   **Salt**
>   **Pepper**
>   **Water**
> 2 **pounds sauerkraut, rinsed and drained**
> 1 **cup buttermilk baking mix**
>   **Milk**
> 1 **red apple, cored and sliced**

1. Preheat the oven to slow (325°).
2. Brown the pork in its own fat in a Dutch oven or kettle. Add the onion near the end of browning; cook until browned, about 5 minutes. Season with salt and pepper to taste. Add 1½ cups water. Cover.
3. Braise in the preheated slow oven (325°) for 1 hour. Stir in the sauerkraut. Braise, covered, for 45 to 60 minutes or until the pork is tender.
4. About 15 minutes before the end of the cooking time, prepare the buttermilk baking mix with milk, following package directions.
5. Remove the pork to a platter; keep warm. Leave the oven on.
6. Add the apple to the sauerkraut. Drop baking mix batter by tablespoonfuls onto the top of the sauerkraut mixture.
7. Bake, uncovered, in a slow oven (325°) for 10 minutes. Cover; bake for 10 minutes.
8. To serve, slice pork. Arrange on a platter with the dumplings and sauerkraut mixture.

◤ ▢ Braised Pork Chops with Cabbage

Makes 4 servings.

Nutrient Value Per Serving: 361 calories, 23 gm. protein, 21 gm. fat, 651 mg. sodium, 83 mg. cholesterol.

> 4 **to 6 thin pork chops (about 1¼ pounds)**
> 1 **tablespoon butter**
> 1 **small red cabbage (about 1 pound), shredded**
> 1 **apple, red or green, halved, cored and sliced**
> 2 **tablespoons light brown sugar**
> 1 **teaspoon salt**
> ½ **teaspoon caraway seeds**
> ⅛ **teaspoon pepper**
> 3 **tablespoons cider vinegar**
>   **Frozen fried potato rounds, cooked according to label directions**
>   **Watercress (optional)**

1. Brown the pork chops on both sides in a large heavy skillet over medium-high heat. Remove the chops from the skillet.
2. Add the butter, cabbage, apple, sugar, salt, caraway seeds, pepper and vinegar to the skillet. Cook over low heat, stirring, until well mixed.
3. Return the chops to the skillet. Cover; cook over low heat for 15 to 20 minutes or until the pork and cabbage are tender. Arrange on a platter with the potato rounds. Garnish with watercress, if you wish.

▲Braised Pork Chops with Cabbage

■ ▢ *Thyme Pork Chops with Stuffing*

Makes 4 servings.

Nutrient Value Per Serving: 560 calories, 27 gm. protein, 27 gm. fat, 906 mg. sodium, 75 mg. cholesterol.

- 2 **tablespoons leaf thyme, crumbled**
- 4 **thin pork chops (5 ounces each)**
- 2 **tablespoons vegetable oil**
- 2 **tablespoons water**
- 1 **package (6¼ ounces) 15-minute stuffing mix for pork**
- 1¾ **cups unsweetened apple juice**
- ¼ **cup sliced celery**
- ¼ **cup golden raisins**

1. Press the thyme into both sides of the chops.
2. Sauté the chops in the oil in a large skillet for 2 minutes on each side or until browned. Add the water; cover; lower the heat; cook for 25 to 30 minutes or until the chops are tender.
3. Meanwhile, prepare the stuffing mix according to the package directions, substituting the apple juice for the water and adding the celery and raisins. Keep warm.
4. To serve, arrange the pork chops on a platter with the stuffing.

■ ◀◀ ▼ ▢ *Fruited Pork Stew (Top of the Range Method)*

Make this delicious stew your way—on the range, in the oven, in a pressure cooker, a slow cooker or a microwave oven. The cooking chart will enable you to decide on the technique that suits your time and equipment.

Makes 8 servings.

Nutrient Value Per Serving: 568 calories, 27 gm. protein, 21 gm. fat, 679 mg. sodium, 68 mg. cholesterol.

- ⅓ **cup unsifted all-purpose flour**
- 1 **teaspoon salt**
- ½ **teaspoon pepper**
- 2 **pounds boneless pork shoulder, trimmed and cut into 1-inch cubes**
- ¼ **cup vegetable oil**
- 2 **cloves garlic, crushed**
- 3 **leeks, washed well to remove any sand and cut into ½-inch pieces**
- 1 **package (8 ounces) mixed dried fruit**
- 1 **cup applejack (apple brandy) or apple juice**
- 1 **tablespoon caraway seeds**
- ½ **teaspoon ground ginger**
- 2 **cans (13¾ ounces each) beef broth**

FRESH PORK ROASTING CHART

CUT	APPROX. WEIGHT	OVEN TEMP.	ROASTING TIME	INTERNAL TEMP.
Leg (fresh ham)				
half, bone-in	7 to 8 lbs.	325°F	4 to 4½ hours	170°F
whole, bone-in	14 to 16 lbs.	325°F	5½ to 6 hours	170°F
Loin, center, bone-in	3 to 5 lbs.	325°F	1¾ to 2½ hours	170°F
boneless	3 to 5 lbs.	325°F	2 to 3 hours	170°F

2 packages (10 ounces each) frozen Brussels sprouts
1 butternut squash (1¼ pounds), pared, seeded and cut into ¼-inch-thick slices
1 cup raisins

1. Combine the flour, salt and pepper in a plastic bag; add the pork cubes; toss until well coated. Shake off excess flour mixture.

2. Heat the oil in a large heavy saucepan or Dutch oven. Brown pork, a few cubes at a time, on all sides; remove pieces as they brown. Add the garlic and leeks to the saucepan; cook until lightly browned.

3. Return the pork to the saucepan. Add the dried fruit, applejack, caraway seeds, ginger and broth. Bring to boiling; cover; simmer for 1 hour or until the meat is almost fork-tender. Add the Brussels sprouts and squash; mix well; cover; cook until the vegetables are tender, about 15 minutes. Stir in the raisins.

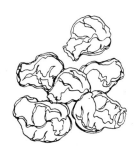

Oven Method: Follow steps 1 and 2 above, using a Dutch oven or large flameproof casserole. Return pork to Dutch oven. Add caraway seeds, ginger and beef broth; stir to mix well. Cover; bake in a preheated moderately slow oven (325°) for 1 hour. Add dried fruit, applejack, Brussels sprouts and squash; stir to mix well. Cover; bake 35 to 40 minutes or longer until vegetables are tender. Remove from the oven; stir in raisins.

Pressure Cooker Method: Follow steps 1 and 2 above, using a 6-quart pressure cooker. Return pork to pressure cooker. Add caraway seeds, ginger and broth; mix well. Close cover securely; place pressure control over the vent pipe. Cook on high heat until the control starts to jiggle and rock. Lower heat to medium so the control rocks gently. Pressure cook for 10 minutes. Remove from heat; place closed cooker under cold running water for about 1 minute or until no steam hisses when you start to remove the control. Carefully remove the control, then the cover. Stir in dried fruit, applejack, Brussels sprouts and squash; close the cover securely. Place pressure control over vent pipe. Cook over high

heat until control starts to jiggle and rock. Lower heat to medium so that the control rocks gently. Pressure cook for 5 minutes. Remove from heat; place closed cooker under cold running water for 1 minute or until no steam hisses when you start to remove the control. Carefully remove the control, then the cover. Stir in raisins.

Slow Cooker Method: Follow steps 1 and 2 above, using a large skillet. Place pork, garlic, leeks, caraway seeds, ginger, beef broth and only ½ cup applejack in a 6-quart slow cooker. Cover; cook on low heat for 6 hours. Add dried fruit, Brussels sprouts and squash; mix well. Cover; cook on low heat for 2 hours or until meat and vegetables are tender. Stir in raisins.

Microwave Method: Follow steps 1 and 2 above, using a large skillet. Place pork, garlic, applejack, caraway seeds, ginger, and beef broth in a 3-quart microwave-safe casserole. Cover; microwave on medium setting for 20 minutes, stirring once, or until meat is almost tender. Add dried fruit, Brussels sprouts and squash; stir to mix well. Cover; micro-wave on high setting 20 minutes or until vegetables are tender. Remove from oven. Stir in raisins.

Oven	**1 hour, 35 minutes**
Top of stove	**1 hour, 15 minutes**
Microwave	**40 minutes**
Slow cooker	**8 hours**
Pressure cooker	**18 minutes**

🍽 *Rice Pancakes with Sweet and Sour Pork*

Makes 6 servings.

Nutrient Value Per Serving: 860 calories, 28 gm. protein, 44 gm. fat, 1690 mg. sodium, 209 mg. cholesterol.

SWEET AND SOUR PORK
- ⅓ **cup soy sauce**
- ⅓ **cup sugar**
- 1½ **pounds boneless pork loin, cut into 1-inch cubes**
- ½ **cup cornstarch**
- ⅓ **cup vegetable oil**
- 2 **cloves garlic, crushed**
- 2 **sweet green peppers, halved, seeded and cut into 1-inch squares**
- 2 **carrots, pared and cut into ¼-inch-thick slices**
- 1 **can (20 ounces) pineapple chunks in their own juice**
- 1 **cup dry sherry**
- ½ **cup cider vinegar**
- ¼ **cup sugar**
- 2 **tablespoons cold water**

RICE CAKES
- ½ **cup** sifted **all-purpose flour**
- ¼ **cup sugar**
- 3 **teaspoons baking powder**
- ½ **teaspoon salt**
- 3 **eggs**
- ¼ **cup milk**
- 2 **cups cooked rice**
- 2 **green onions, thinly sliced**
- ½ **cup frozen peas, thawed**

1. Prepare the Sweet and Sour Pork: Combine the soy sauce and ⅓ cup sugar in a bowl; add the pork. Toss to coat. Let stand 2 hours. Drain the meat; reserve the marinade.
2. Place the cornstarch in a shallow bowl; add the marinated pork a few cubes at a time; toss to coat well; shake off excess. Reserve remaining cornstarch.
3. Sauté the meat in the oil in a skillet, until well browned. Add the garlic, green peppers and carrots; sauté until the vegetables are crisp-tender.
4. Drain the pineapple, reserving the juice. Add the juice, sherry, vinegar and ¼ cup sugar to the skillet. Cook over medium heat for 10 minutes. Add cold water to reserved cornstarch; stir until dissolved. Add the reserved soy sauce marinade. Add to skillet; cook, stirring constantly, until the sauce thickens and clears, about 5 minutes. Set aside.
5. Sift the flour, sugar, baking powder and salt onto a sheet of wax paper. Beat the eggs and milk in a bowl; blend in sifted dry ingredients. Fold in rice, green onions and peas until well blended.
6. Pour the batter, ½ cup at a time, onto a medium-hot, lightly greased griddle. Cook until the edges begin to brown and bubbles appear on top. Turn; cook until golden.
7. Serve hot with Sweet and Sour Pork.

BUYING RIBS
Pork ribs shrink slightly in cooking, so plan on ¾ to 1 pound per serving.

KNOW YOUR RIBS
Baby backs, cut from a porker's back, include the rib bone and meat from the eye of loin. They are generally meatier but more expensive.

Spareribs are the larger variety, and include the breast bone, rib bones and rib cartilage.

◻ *Oven-Roasted Ribs*

Use ¼ cup of the barbecue sauce of your choice for each pound of ribs.

Bake at 450° for 30 minutes; then at 300° for 45 minutes.
Makes 1 serving spareribs.
Makes 1 serving baby backs.

Nutrient Value Per Pound Ribs Without Sauce: 791 calories, 38 gm. protein, 70 gm. fat, 65 mg. sodium, 160 mg. cholesterol.

> 1 *pound spareribs OR: baby back ribs*
>   *Salt*
>   *Pepper*
>   *Barbecue Sauce (recipes follow)*

1. Preheat the oven to very hot (450°).
2. Rinse the ribs; drain them well. Sprinkle with salt and pepper. Place on a rack in a roasting pan. Pour 3 cups water into the roasting pan.
3. Bake in the preheated very hot oven (450°) for 30 minutes. Remove ribs to a platter. Drain the roasting pan; wipe dry. Lower the oven temperature to slow (300°).
4. Return ribs to rack in the pan. Use ¼ cup barbecue sauce per pound of ribs. Brush half the sauce over one side.
5. Bake ribs in the preheated slow oven (300°) for 25 minutes. Turn ribs over; brush with remaining sauce. Bake 20 minutes or until thoroughly cooked at thickest part.
6. Preheat the broiler. Brush the ribs with any sauce from the pan. Broil until crisp on both sides. Cut into serving-size pieces. Serve with additional sauce for dipping.

> **COOKING TIP**
> **Home-cooked ribs taste best if precooked, either by oven roasting or parboiling, before saucing and baking.**

◻ *Parboiled-Broiled Ribs*

Plan on ¾ to 1 pound of ribs per serving. Use ¼ cup barbecue sauce per pound of ribs.

Bake at 350° for 30 minutes.
Makes 1 serving spareribs.
Makes 1 serving baby backs.

Nutrient Value Per Pound Ribs Without Sauce: 804 calories, 38 gm. protein, 70 gm. fat, 1931 mg. sodium, 160 mg. cholesterol.

> 1   *pound spareribs OR: baby back ribs*
> 1   *onion*
> 2   *whole cloves*
> ¼   *cup soy sauce*
> 2   *teaspoon leaf marjoram, crumbled*
> 1   *teaspoon salt*
> ½   *teaspoon pepper*
>   *Barbecue Sauce (recipes follow)*

1. Rinse the ribs. Cut them into 3-inch sections. Place in a large saucepan; add water to cover.
2. Peel the onion; press the cloves into the onion. Add to the saucepan along with the soy sauce, marjoram, salt and pepper. Bring to boiling. Lower the heat; simmer for 50 minutes or until tender. Drain well.
3. Preheat the oven to moderate (350°).
4. Cut the ribs into single rib pieces, or leave in 3-inch sections. Arrange in single layers on a rack in a roasting pan.
5. Measure ¼ cup barbecue sauce per pound of ribs. Brush half the barbecue sauce on one side of the ribs.
6. Bake the ribs in the preheated moderate oven (350°) for 15 minutes. Turn the ribs over. Brush remaining sauce on the ribs. Bake for 15 minutes or until thoroughly cooked at the thickest part.
7. Preheat the broiler. Brush the ribs with any sauce in the bottom of the pan. Broil until crisp and well browned on both sides. Serve with additional sauce for dipping.

All-American "BBQ" Sauce

If we had to elect the "most typical" American barbecue sauce, it would be the following Texan sluice, seasoned with store-boughts plus a goodly pinch of kitchen thrift. It can be prepared in less than 30 minutes.

Makes about 1⅔ cups.

Nutrient Value Per ¼ Cup: 87 calories, 1 gm. protein, 2 gm. fat, 480 mg. sodium, 5 mg. cholesterol.

> 1   *medium-size onion, finely chopped*
> 1   *tablespoon unsalted butter*
> ¾   *cup catsup*
> 3   *tablespoons dark brown sugar*
> 3   *tablespoons Worchestershire sauce*
> 2   *tablespoons prepared steak sauce*
> 1   *tablespoon cider vinegar*
> ¼   *cup water*
>   *Dash of liquid red pepper seasoning*

Sauté the onion in the butter in a medium-size saucepan over medium-low heat for 5 minutes; do not allow the onion to brown. Stir in all the remaining ingredients. Bring to boiling. Lower the heat; simmer for 20 minutes, stirring occasionally. Refrigerate the cooled barbecue sauce in a tightly covered container for up to 2 weeks.

San Francisco Sweet and Sour Barbecue Sauce

This thick, golden apricot-tinged purée is similar to a Chinese duck sauce.

Makes about 1½ cups.

Nutrient Value Per ½ Cup: 137 calories, 1 gm. protein, 7 gm. fat, 336 mg. sodium, 0 mg. cholesterol.

> ⅓   *cup dried apricots*
> 1½ *cups water*
> 1   *shallot, finely chopped*
>   *OR: 1 green onion, finely chopped*
> ½   *cup tarragon vinegar*
> ¼   *cup honey*
> ¼   *cup catsup*
> 3   *tablespoons vegetable oil*
> ½   *teaspoon soy sauce*
> ½   *teaspoon leaf oregano, crumbled*
> ½   *teaspoon salt*
> ¼   *teaspoon pepper*

1. Combine the apricots and water in a saucepan. Bring to boiling. Lower the heat; simmer for 25 minutes, or until tender. Cool slightly.
2. Drain the apricots over a measuring cup. Place the apricots and ½ cup of the drained liquid (add water, if necessary to make ½ cup) in the container of an electric blender or food processor. Cover; blend until smooth.
3. Combine the apricot purée and all of the remaining ingredients in a medium-size saucepan. Bring to boiling. Remove from the heat. Refrigerate the cooled sauce in a tightly covered container for up to 2 weeks.

 Maple Country Barbecue Sauce

In the good old days, "sugaring-off time" (whether it occurred in Vermont, New York or Ohio) meant an excess of maple syrup that was converted into other farm-kitchen uses. After maple fudge and maple sugar, those resourceful country cooks came up with this excellent topping for ribs and such. Soothing as a syrup, it is perhaps a bit spicier than you would expect.

Makes about 2 cups.

Nutrient Value Per ¼ Cup: 135 calories, 1 gm. protein, 3 gm. fat, 769 mg. sodium, 8 mg. cholesterol.

2 tablespoons unsalted butter
1 cup prepared chili sauce
½ cup maple syrup
½ cup catsup
½ cup cider vinegar
1 tablespoon dry mustard
1 teaspoon celery seeds
1 teaspoon cayenne pepper
½ teaspoon salt

Combine the butter, chili sauce, maple syrup, catsup, cider vinegar, dry mustard, celery seeds, cayenne pepper and salt in a medium-size saucepan. Bring to boiling. Lower the heat; simmer 20 minutes, stirring occasionally. Refrigerate the cooled barbecue sauce in a tightly covered container for up to 2 weeks.

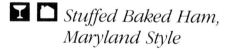 *Stuffed Baked Ham, Maryland Style*

Garden greens tucked down into little pockets add a marvelous flavor.

Bake at 325° for 2½ hours.
Makes 8 generous servings plus enough for another meal.

Nutrient Value Per Serving: 337 calories, 38 gm. protein, 10 gm. fat, 2282 mg. sodium, 90 mg. cholesterol.

1 fully cooked ham (about 10 pounds)
1 package (10 ounces) frozen
**   chopped kale**
1 cup finely chopped fresh spinach
1 large onion, finely chopped
**   (1 cup)**
¾ cup finely chopped watercress
½ cup finely chopped celery tops
½ teaspoon salt
¼ teaspoon pepper
½ cup honey
2 tablespoons cider vinegar
2 teaspoons dry mustard
**   Watercress, (optional)**

1. Trim the rind, if any, from the ham. Shave the ham fat covering to about ¼ inch. Make X-shaped cuts with a small paring knife, 2 inches deep and 1 inch apart, staggering all over the fat side.
2. Cook the kale in boiling salted water to cover, following label directions; drain; cool; squeeze out the excess water with your hands.
3. Combine the kale, spinach, onion, watercress, celery tops, salt and pepper in a medium-size bowl.
4. Press the greens mixture into the ham pockets, packing down well. Place the ham, fat-side up, in a large shallow baking pan.
5. Bake in a slow oven (325°) for 2 hours.
6. Stir the honey, vinegar and dry mustard together; brush part over the ham. Continue baking and brushing with the remaining honey mixture for 30 minutes or until the top is richly glazed. Remove the ham from the pan and let stand about 20 minutes for easier carving.
7. Carve the ham carefully, holding the slices to keep the filling in place. Garnish the platter with watercress, if you wish.

THE BEST HALF
Of a whole smoked ham is the shank half, or portion, weighing 7 to 10 pounds. Ask the butcher to slice one or two ham steaks and you will have several meals from your ham.

◻ *Scalloped Potatoes and Ham*

Stretch your leftover ham with potatoes and cheese in this hearty casserole.

Bake at 350° for 1½ hours.
Makes 6 servings.

Nutrient Value Per Serving: 485 calories, 20 gm. protein, 26 gm. fat, 1568 mg. sodium, 90 mg. cholesterol.

½ cup (1 stick) butter or margarine
½ cup all-purpose flour
2 teaspoons salt
¼ teaspoon pepper
3 cups milk
3 cups cubed cooked ham
*   (about ½ pound)*
1 large onion, chopped (1 cup)
1 large sweet green pepper, halved, seeded
*   and chopped (1 cup)*
½ cup shredded sharp or mild
*   Cheddar cheese (2 ounces)*
5 cups sliced, pared potatoes
*   (about 2 pounds)*

1. Heat the butter in a large saucepan over low heat; blend in the flour, salt and pepper. Cook, stirring constantly for 1 minute. Remove from the heat; gradually stir in the milk. Return to the heat; cook until thickened and bubbly.
2. Fold in the ham, onion, green pepper and cheese. Pour over the potatoes in a large bowl. Stir gently; then pour into a buttered 13 x 9 x 2-inch baking dish; cover with aluminum foil.
3. Bake in a moderate oven (350°) for 30 minutes. Uncover and continue baking for 1 hour or until browned and bubbly. Let stand for 10 minutes before serving.

▯ *Country Smoked Meats and Sausages with Apples*

Vary the sausages and meats, depending on the region where you live.

Bake at 350° for 20 minutes.
Makes 8 servings.

Nutrient Value Per Serving: 387 calories, 19 gm. protein, 25 gm. fat, 1290 mg. sodium, 78 mg. cholesterol.

1 fully cooked ham steak (about 6 ounces)
2 to 4 red and/or green apples,
*   cored and quartered*
½ cup maple syrup
½ pound spicy, bulk sausage meat,
*   cut into 4 patties*
1 pound cheese and parsley Italian
*   sausage in a coil (optional)*
½ pound hot Italian sausages
½ pound sliced Canadian bacon,
*   OR: thin smoked pork chops*
½ pound kielbasa sausage

1. Preheat the oven to moderate (350°). Place the ham and apples in a shallow baking dish in which they just fit. Drizzle syrup over.
2. Bake in the preheated moderate oven (350°) for 20 to 25 minutes, basting several times until the apples are tender and the ham is heated through. Lower the oven temperature to slow (250°).
3. Cook the sausage patties in a skillet following package directions. Remove to a jelly-roll pan; cover with aluminum foil. Keep warm.
4. Push 2 long skewers through the sausage coil to make an X for easy handling. Prick the coil and hot Italian sausages. Cook in the same skillet over medium heat, turning once, until browned and cooked through, about 15 minutes. Remove to the jelly-roll pan.

CURED AND SMOKED PORK ROASTING CHART

CUT	APPROX. WEIGHT	OVEN TEMP.	ROASTING TIME	INTERNAL TEMP.
Ham, cook before eating,				
bone-in half	5 to 7 lbs.	325°F	2½ to 3 hours	160°F
Ham, fully cooked,				
bone-in half	5 to 7 lbs.	325°F	1½ to 2¼ hours	140°F
boneless, half portion	3 to 4 lbs.	325°F	1¼ to 1¾ hours	140°F
Arm picnic shoulder,				
bone-in	5 to 8 lbs.	325°F	2½ to 4 hours	170°F
Boneless shoulder roll	2 to 3 lbs.	325°F	1½ to 1¾ hours	170°F

5. Cook the kielbasa in a medium-size saucepan in simmering water to cover, for 10 to 15 minutes. Remove to a cutting board; cut into 2½-inch pieces. Add to the jelly-roll pan. Keep warm in a slow oven (250°).

6. Brown the Canadian bacon in a skillet for 4 to 5 minutes on each side.

7. Arrange the meats, sausages and apples on a platter; drizzle with juice from the ham.

Note: Sausages and meat can be browned and cooked ahead of time and reheated on the jelly-roll pan at 350° for 10 minutes.

▼ *Fontina and Ham Crêpe Cake*

Bake at 350° for 25 minutes.
Makes 6 servings.

Nutrient Value Per Serving: 907 calories, 39 gm. protein, 73 gm. fat, 861 mg. sodium, 441 mg. cholesterol.

> *2   eggs*
> *2   egg yolks*
> *1   cup milk*
> *1¼ cups sifted all-purpose flour*
> *½   teaspoon salt*
> *1   tablespoon chopped parsley*
> *1   teaspoon leaf chervil, crumbled*
> *½   teaspoon leaf tarragon, crumbled*
> *2   tablespoons butter, melted*
> *1   pound boiled ham, thinly sliced*
> *¾   pound Fontina cheese, shredded*
> *2   cups heavy cream*

1. Combine the eggs, egg yolks, and milk in a bowl; stir in the flour, salt, parsley, chervil, tarragon and butter until well blended.

2. Heat a small (6-inch) skillet or crêpe pan over medium-high heat; butter lightly. Pour in the batter, 3 tablespoons at a time, quickly rotating the pan to spread the batter evenly. Cook over medium heat to brown lightly, about 1 minute on each side. Cool. Stack the crêpes between wax paper.

3. Assemble the crêpe cake: Lightly butter a 6-inch straight-sided soufflé dish or casserole. Place one crêpe on the bottom of the dish; top with ham slices and about 2 tablespoons shredded cheese; repeat layers until the dish is filled. Press down lightly.

4. Bake in a preheated moderate oven (350°) for 25 minutes.

5. Heat the cream in a saucepan; add the remaining cheese. Stir until melted and the sauce is smooth.

6. Remove the crêpe cake from the oven; let stand for 5 minutes. Unmold. Serve with the cheese sauce.

Lamb

🍸 Leg of Lamb Roulade

This boned roast, filled with an anchony-herb mixture, is easy to carve at the table.

Roast at 350° for 1¾ hours.
Makes about 12 servings.

Nutrient Value Per Serving: 328 calories, 42 gm. protein, 15 gm. fat, 162 mg. sodium, 156 mg. cholesterol.

　1　*large onion, finely chopped (1 cup)*
　2　*cloves garlic, minced*
　2　*tablespoons butter or margarine*
　2　*teaspoons leaf rosemary, crumbled*
　1　*can (2 ounces) flat anchovy fillets,*
　　　drained and chopped
　1　*cup minced fresh parsley*
　¼　*teaspoon pepper*
　1　*leg of lamb (7½ to 8 pounds)*
　　　Water OR: lamb stock (see step 3)
　3　*tablespoons all-purpose flour*
　　　Salt
　　　Pepper

1. Sauté the onion and garlic in the butter in a small saucepan until tender, about 5 minutes. Remove from the heat. Stir in the rosemary, anchovies, parsley and pepper. Reserve.
2. Preheat the oven to moderate (350°).
3. Trim all but a thin layer of fat from the lamb. To bone the lamb, place fat-side down on a cutting board. Cut through the meat alongside the bone. Scrape the meat from around the bones. Remove the bones. To prepare the lamb stock for gravy, simmer the bones in enough water to cover for 2 to 3 hours.
4. Cut the thicker sections of the meat almost in half and open like a book, as flat as possible. Spread evenly with the anchovy

mixture. Roll up from a long edge, tucking in the ends. Tie at 1-inch intervals with string to form an even roll. Place seam-side down on a rack in an open shallow roasting pan.
5. Roast for 1¾ hours or until a meat thermometer registers 140° for rare. Remove to a heated platter. Let stand for 15 minutes. Remove the strings; carve into thin slices.
6. To make gravy, pour the drippings from the pan into a 2-cup glass measure. Let stand until the fat rises to the top. Skim off 2 tablespoons fat and return to the pan; discard remaining fat. Add water or lamb stock to the drippings in the cup to make 2 cups. Blend the flour into the fat in the pan. Gradually stir the liquid into the flour mixture until smooth. Bring to boiling, stirring constantly. Season with salt and pepper. Pour into a gravy boat.

WHEN BUYING A HALF LEG OF LAMB
Choose a 4-pound or more shank half. A smaller one would have a higher proportion of bone and less meat.

⧼⧼⧼ ⬜ Curried Lamb Piroshki

Wrapped inside the whole-wheat pastry packages is a spicy lamb filling. These would make tasty picnic fare.

Bake at 375° for 30 minutes.
Reheat at 325° for 10 to 15 minutes.
Makes 6 servings. (12 piroshki)

Nutrient Value Per Serving: 607 calories, 24 gm. protein, 29 gm. fat, 678 mg. sodium, 117 mg. cholesterol.

1½ cups *unsifted whole-wheat flour*
1 *envelope active dry yeast*
½ *teaspoon salt*
1¼ *cups very warm water*
1 *tablespoon vegetable oil*
1 *egg, slightly beaten*
2 *to 2½ cups unsifted all-purpose flour*
½ *cup chopped onion (1 medium size)*
1 *clove garlic, finely chopped*
3 *tablespoons butter*
1 *pound ground lamb*
  OR: ground beef chuck
2 *to 2½ teaspoons curry powder*
1 *teaspoon salt*
1 *container (8 ounces) plain yogurt*
  Melted butter (optional)

1. Combine the whole-wheat flour, yeast and salt in a medium-size bowl; stir to blend. Add very warm water and oil all at once. ("Very warm water" should feel comfortably warm when dropped on your wrist.) Beat for 2 minutes, scraping down the side of the bowl. Stir in the egg and ½ cup of the all-purpose flour. Beat for 2 minutes. Stir in enough of the remaining all-purpose flour to make soft dough that leaves the side of the bowl clean.

2. Turn the dough out onto a lightly floured board. Knead until smooth and elastic, for 5 to 10 minutes. Shape into a ball. Place in a greased bowl; turn to coat. Cover. Let rise in a warm place, away from drafts, for 1 hour or until doubled in bulk.

3. While the dough is rising, prepare the filling. Sauté the onion and garlic in the butter in a skillet until softened, 4 minutes. Stir in the lamb, cook; stirring often, until no longer pink. Stir in the curry powder and salt; cook for 2 minutes. Blend in the yogurt. Cover; lower the heat; simmer for 10 to 15 minutes. Reserve.

4. After the dough has risen, punch down. Divide into quarters. Cut each into 3 equal pieces. Cover with plastic wrap.

5. Working in batches of three, roll out the pieces of dough into circles with 4-inch diameters. Place 2 tablespoons of filling in the center of each. Moisten edges of circles with water. Fold over to make half-moons. Press edges firmly together to seal. Transfer to a greased cookie sheet. Repeat with the remaining dough and filling. Let rise in a warm place, away from drafts, for 1 hour.

6. Preheat the oven to moderate (375°).

7. Bake the piroshki in the preheated moderate oven (375°) for 30 minutes or until golden. Brush the tops with melted butter, if you wish. Cool on wire racks. Wrap and store in the refrigerator 1 to 2 days.

8. To reheat: Place the piroshki on a cookie sheet in a preheated slow oven (325°) for 10 to 15 minutes or until heated through.

LAMB ROASTING CHART

CUT	APPROX. WEIGHT	OVEN TEMP.	ROASTING TIME	INTERNAL TEMP.
Leg, bone-in	5 to 9 lbs.	325°F	2¼ to 3¾ hours	140°F (R)
			2½ to 4 hours	170°F (WD)
Leg, boneless	3 to 5 lbs.	325-350°F	1½ to 2¼ hours	140°F (R)

(R)-Rare   (WD)-Well Done

◻ *Lamb Chops Provençal*

Bake at 350° for 40 minutes.
Makes 6 servings.

Nutrient Value Per Serving: 561 calories, 30 gm. protein, 42 gm. fat, 145 mg. sodium, 126 mg. cholesterol.

2 *packages (10 ounces each) frozen*
   ratatouille
6 *shoulder lamb chops (2½ to 3 pounds)*
¾ *cup dry white wine*
6 *pitted black olives*
   Fresh watercress (optional)
   Cooked rice (optional)

1. Preheat the oven to moderate (350°).
2. Place the pouches of ratatouille in hot water to thaw slightly.
3. Heat a large heavy skillet over medium-high heat. Rub a small piece of fat from the lamb over the bottom of the skillet. Brown the chops a few at a time, in the skillet in their own fat. Remove the chops as they brown to a shallow ovenproof casserole just large enough to hold the chops in a single layer.
4. Add the wine to the skillet. Cook, scraping up the browned bits from the bottom and side of the skillet, for about 2 minutes. Add the slightly thawed ratatouille. Bring to boiling. Spoon over the lamb chops. Cover the casserole with aluminum foil.
5. Bake in the preheated moderate oven (350°) for 30 minutes. Uncover; baste the chops. Add the olives. Bake, uncovered, for 10 minutes longer. Garnish with watercress and serve with rice, if you wish.

BUY A WHOLE LEG OF LAMB
When they are on sale, buy a whole leg of lamb and ask the butcher to cut it into 1-inch-thick chops. You will get about 10 tender chops for broiling and shank meat for braising.

Poultry

HOW TO BUY CHICKEN
Look for chicken that has moist skin without any dry spots. Avoid packages where blood or juice has accumulated in the bottom—a sign that the chicken has been out for too long, or may have been frozen. Chicken should smell fresh. This can mean no smell at all or a pleasant chicken aroma. If upon opening the package at home you find a slight chicken odor, rinse the chicken under cold water and rub with a lemon half or dip briefly in vinegar-water.

▼ *Chicken in Rum-Raisin Sauce*

Serve this rich chicken dish with hot buttered noodles.

Bake at 450° for 40 minutes.
Makes 4 servings.

Nutrient Value Per Serving: 454 calories, 34 gm. protein, 29 gm. fat, 112 mg. sodium, 148 mg. cholesterol.

3 *tablespoons raisins*
3 *tablespoons dark rum*
1 *broiler-fryer, cut up (3 pounds)*
   Salt
   Pepper
½ *cup heavy cream*
1 *tablespoon sliced almonds, toasted*
   Parsley (optional)

1. Soak the raisins in the rum in a small cup for 30 minutes.
2. Preheat the oven to very hot (450°).
3. Arrange the chicken, skin-side up, in a

13 x 9 x 2-inch baking dish. Season with salt and pepper to taste.

4. Bake, uncovered, in the preheated very hot oven (450°) for 20 minutes or until the chicken begins to brown. Add the heavy cream. Continue baking, basting several times with sauce, until the chicken is tender and the sauce is slightly thickened, about another 20 minutes. Stir in the rum-raisin mixture.

5. Arrange the chicken on a heated platter. Spoon the sauce over and sprinkle with the toasted almonds. Garnish with parsley, if you wish.

▲ *Clockwise from left:* **Strawberry Shortbread (page 241), No-Fuss Meatloaf (page 95), Chicken in Rum-Raisin Sauce (page 116) and Lamb Chops Provençal (page 116).**

◼ ◼ ◼ ◻ *Chicken and Sausage Italiano (Top of the Range Method)*

Make this delicious dish your way—on the range, in the oven, in a pressure cooker, a slow cooker or a microwave oven. The cooking chart will enable you to decide on the technique that suits your time and equipment.

Makes 8 servings.

Nutrient Value Per Serving: 672 calories, 34 gm. protein, 41 gm. fat, 974 mg. sodium, 103 mg. cholesterol.

⅓ cup unsifted all-purpose flour
1 teaspoon salt
¼ teaspoon pepper
1 broiler-fryer (3 pounds), cut into eighths
¼ cup vegetable oil
3 cloves garlic, crushed
½ pound hot Italian sausages
½ pound sweet Italian sausages
1 pound small white onions, peeled
1 pound (3 large) sweet red pepper, cored, seeded and cut into ½-inch strips
1 pound (3 large) sweet green peppers, cored, seeded and cut into ½-inch strips
1 pound yellow squash, cut into ¾-inch chunks
1 pound mushrooms, quartered
1 can (2 pounds, 3 ounces) Italian plum tomatoes
2 bay leaves
2 teaspoons leaf basil, crumbled
1 teaspoon leaf oregano, crumbled
1 cup dry vermouth
½ cup orzo (rice-shaped pasta)

1. Combine the flour, salt and pepper in a plastic bag; add the chicken; toss until well coated.
2. Heat the oil in a large heavy saucepan or Dutch oven. Brown the chicken, a few pieces at a time, on all sides; remove the pieces as they brown. Add the garlic, sausages and onions; cook, removing pieces as they brown. Add the peppers, squash and mushrooms to the saucepan; cook until browned.
3. Return the chicken, garlic, sausages and onions to the saucepan. Add the tomatoes, bay leaves, basil, oregano and vermouth; stir to mix well. Bring to boiling; cover; simmer for 1 hour or until the chicken is almost tender. Stir in the orzo; cover; simmer for 15 minutes longer.

Oven Method: Follow steps 1 and 2, using a Dutch oven or large flameproof casserole, and setting aside the sautéed peppers, squash and mushrooms. Return the chicken, garlic, sausages and onions to the Dutch oven. Add the tomatoes, bay leaves, basil, oregano and vermouth; stir to mix well; cover. Place in a preheated slow oven (325°) for 1 hour, or until the meat is tender. Add the sautéed peppers, squash and mushrooms and the orzo. Cover; bake for 20 minutes or until the vegetables are tender.

Pressure Cooker Method: Follow steps 1 and 2, using a 6-quart pressure cooker, and setting aside the sautéed peppers, squash and mushrooms. Return the chicken, garlic, sausages and onions to the pressure cooker. Add the tomatoes, bay leaves, basil, oregano and vermouth; stir to mix well. Close the cover securely; place the pressure control over the vent pipe. Cook on high heat until the control starts to jiggle and rock. Lower the heat to medium so the control rocks gently. Pressure cook for 10 minutes. Remove from the heat. Place closed cooker under cold running water for about 1 minute or until no steam hisses when you start to remove the control. Carefully remove the control; then remove the cover. Add sautéed peppers, squash, mushrooms and orzo. Close the cover securely. Place the pressure control over the vent pipe. Cook over high heat until the control starts to jiggle and rock. Lower heat to medium so that the control rocks gently. Pressure cook for 5 minutes. Remove from heat; place closed cooker under cold running water for about 1 minute, or until no steam hisses when you start to remove the control. Carefully remove the control; then the cover.

Slow Cooker Method: Follow steps 1 and 2, using a large skillet, cooking the mushrooms with the sausages and setting aside the sautéed peppers and squash. Place the chicken, garlic, sausages, onions, mushrooms, tomatoes, bay leaves, basil, oregano and only ½ cup vermouth in a 6-quart slow cooker. Cover; cook on low heat for 6 hours. Add the sautéed peppers, squash and the orzo. Stir to mix well. Cover; cook on low heat for 2 hours longer or until the meat and vegetables are tender.

Microwave Method: Follow steps 1 and 2, using a large skillet, and setting aside the sautéed peppers, squash and mushrooms. Place the chicken, garlic, sausages and onions in a 4-quart microwave-safe casserole. Add the tomatoes, bay leaves, basil, oregano and vermouth. Cover. Microwave on medium setting for 20 minutes, stirring once, or until the meat is almost tender. Add the squash, peppers, mushrooms and orzo. Cover; microwave on high setting for 20 minutes, stirring every 5 minutes, or until the vegetables are tender.

Oven	1 hour, 20 minutes
Top of stove	**1 hour, 15 minutes**
Microwave	**40 minutes**
Slow cooker	**8 hours**
Pressure cooker	**20 minutes**

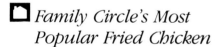

Family Circle's Most Popular Fried Chicken

Makes 4 servings.

Nutrient Value Per Serving: 622 calories, 47 gm. protein, 36 gm. fat, 1071 mg. sodium, 139 mg. cholesterol.

> 1 **broiler-fryer (3 to 3½ pounds), cut up**
> 1 **quart cold water**
> 1 **tablespoon salt**
> 1 **cup all-purpose flour**
> 1½ **teaspoons salt**
> 1½ **teaspoons pepper**
> 1 **quart vegetable oil**
> **Chicken Gravy (recipe follows)**

1. Soak the chicken in the water mixed with the 1 tablespoon salt in a large bowl for 2 hours or longer.

2. Combine the flour, 1½ teaspoons salt and pepper in a plastic or paper bag. Remove chicken from water and pat it dry with paper toweling. Add the chicken to the bag, a few pieces at a time, and shake to coat well. As the chicken is coated, place on a piece of wax paper.

3. Pour enough oil into a large deep skillet to fill half full. Heat the oil until very hot (370°) on a deep-fat frying thermometer). Add the chicken, skin-side down. (The oil must be deep enough to cover the chicken.) When the underside of chicken begins to brown, turn the heat down and partially cover with a lid.

4. Turn the chicken after about 15 minutes or when completely browned on the underside. Continue cooking, uncovered, until the second side is browned. Drain thoroughly on paper toweling before serving. Keep warm in a 250° oven while making the gravy.

Chicken Gravy

Makes about 1¼ cups.

Nutrient Value Per Serving: 144 calories, 2 gm. protein, 12 gm. fat, 30 mg. sodium, 13 mg. cholesterol.

> 3 **tablespoons fat from pan**
> 2 **tablespoons all-purpose flour**
> 1 **cup milk**
> **Salt**
> **Pepper**

1. Pour off the fat from the skillet, leaving the brown bits; return 3 tablespoons of the fat to the pan. Add the flour and cook, stirring and scraping the brown bits from the bottom, until lightly browned. Remove from the heat; gradually stir in the milk.

2. Return to the heat; cook and stir until thickened. If too thick, add more milk. Season with salt and pepper.

◼ ▢ *Quick Crispy Skillet Chicken*

A fast and easy pan-sautéed chicken, complete with vegetables and gravy.

Makes 6 servings.

Nutrient Value Per Serving: 385 calories, 38 gm. protein, 859 gm. fat, 17 mg. sodium, 179 mg. cholesterol.

 3 *whole boneless chicken breasts, skinned*
    and halved (about 1¾ pounds)
 3 *tablespoons all-purpose flour*
 1 *teaspoon salt*
 ¼ *teaspoon pepper*
 2 *eggs*
 1 *tablespoon milk*
 ⅔ *cup fine dry bread crumbs*
 ⅓ *cup finely chopped walnuts*
    Crisp-Cooked Vegetables (page 191)
 2 *tablespoons vegetable oil*
 2 *tablespoons butter or margarine*
    Sherry Pan Gravy (recipe follows)
    Watercress (optional)

1. Trim the chicken of all excess fat. Place the chicken in single layer on wax paper.
2. Mix the flour, salt and pepper in a small bowl; sprinkle over the chicken; turn to coat all sides.
3. Beat together the eggs and milk in a shallow bowl. Mix the bread crumbs and walnuts on wax paper. Dip each chicken breast in the egg mixture to coat, letting excess drip back into the bowl. Turn in the crumb mixture to coat evenly; pat lightly with your hand to help the crumbs stick. Place the breaded breasts in single layer on a small cookie sheet. Freeze briefly to set the coating, about 5 minutes.
4. Prepare Crisp-Cooked Vegetables.
5. Heat the oil and butter in large heavy skillet over medium-high heat until bubbly. Add the chicken breasts in single layer; brown 2 minutes on each side. Lower the heat;

continue cooking 4 to 5 minutes longer on each side or until the chicken is firm to the touch. Remove from the skillet. Keep warm.
6. Prepare the Sherry Pan Gravy.
7. Arrange the chicken on a warm platter with the vegetables. Garnish with watercress, if you wish. Serve with gravy and rice.

Sherry Pan Gravy: After the chicken has been removed from the skillet, add 3 to 4 tablespoons dry sherry and 1 can (13¾ ounces) chicken broth to the skillet. Bring to boiling, scraping up the browned bits from the bottom and side of the skillet. Stir together 3 tablespoons all-purpose flour and ⅓ cup cold water in a cup to make a smooth paste. Stir into the skillet; continue cooking and stirring until the sauce thickens. Lower the heat; simmer 2 minutes. Season to taste with salt and pepper. Pour into a gravy boat. Makes 1¾ cups.

▢ *Tunisian Baked Chicken*

Bake at 375° for 45 minutes.
Makes 8 servings.

Nutrient Value Per Serving: 266 calories, 29 gm. protein, 13 gm. fat, 524 mg. sodium, 77 mg. cholesterol.

 4   *whole chicken breasts*
     (about 12 ounces each), split
 3   *tablespoons all-purpose flour*
 1   *teaspoon salt*
 ¼   *teaspoon pepper*
 3   *tablespoons vegetable oil*
 1½ *cups coarsely chopped onion*
     (about 2 medium-size onions)
 2   *cloves garlic, minced*
 ¾   *teaspoon ground cumin*
 ½   *teaspoon paprika*
     Pinch of cayenne pepper
 ½   *cup chicken broth*
     Juice of 1 small lemon
 1   *small lemon, thinly sliced*
 ⅓   *cup halved pimiento-stuffed green olives*
 1   *tablespoon chopped parsley*

▲Tunisian Baked Chicken

1. Pat the chicken dry with paper toweling. Combine the flour, salt and pepper on wax paper. Turn the chicken in the flour mixture to coat evenly; shake off excess.
2. Sauté the chicken pieces a few at a time in the oil in a large skillet; remove the pieces to a 13 x 9 x 2-inch baking dish as they brown, arranging them in a single layer.
3. Preheat the oven to moderate (375°).
4. Add the onion, garlic, cumin, paprika and cayenne to the skillet; sauté until onion is slightly softened. Stir in the chicken broth and the juice of 1 small lemon, scraping up any browned bits from the bottom of the skillet. Bring to boiling; pour over the chicken. Arrange the lemon slices over chicken.
5. Bake, covered, in the preheated moderate oven (375°) for 40 minutes. Uncover; sprinkle with the olives. Bake, uncovered, for 5 minutes or until the chicken is tender. Sprinkle with parsley. Serve.

TYPES OF CHICKEN
● **Broiler-Fryers:** These weigh 1½ to 3½ pounds and are about 2 months old. The meat is tender, moist and perfect for broiling, grilling, sautéing, poaching and baking. Sold whole and in parts.
● **Roasters:** These weigh 3½ to 5 pounds and are 3 to 4 months old. Though not as juicy as the smaller birds, the roaster makes up for it in superior flavor. Sold whole and in parts.
● **Capons:** These birds are 1½ years old and weigh 5 to 7 pounds. They have a generous amount of white meat and are very flavorful. Sold whole.

◼ ▢ *Chicken Breasts with Yogurt Sauce*

Makes 4 servings.

Nutrient Value Per Serving: 515 calories, 35 gm. protein, 28 gm. fat, 721 mg. sodium, 110 mg. cholesterol.

- 2 **tablespoons butter or margarine**
- 2 **whole chicken breasts, split (about 12 ounces each)**
- ¾ **cup fresh or frozen diced onion**
- 1 **clove garlic, minced**
- 1 **teaspoon curry powder**
- ¼ **teaspoon ground cardamom**
- ¼ **teaspoon ground ginger**
- 2 **tablespoons tomato paste**
- 1 **cup plain yogurt**
- 1 **package (11 ounces) frozen French-style rice, cooked according to label directions**
  Avocado, halved, pitted, peeled and sliced
- 1 **lime, thinly sliced**
  Watercress (optional)

1. Heat the butter in a large skillet; add the chicken breasts, skin-side down; sauté until golden, 8 to 10 minutes per side. Push to the side of the skillet.
2. Stir the onion and garlic into the skillet. Sauté 5 minutes. Stir in the curry powder, cardamom and ginger; cook, stirring for 1 minute.
3. Mix together the tomato paste and yogurt; stir into the skillet. Heat to almost boiling but do not allow to boil. Spoon the sauce over the chicken; heat gently over low heat for 5 minutes.
4. Arrange the chicken breasts with sauce and rice on a platter. Garnish with avocado and lime slices, and watercress, if you wish.

FREEZING CHICKEN
When wrapping chicken for the freezer, be sure the package is airtight to prevent freezer burn. Do not rinse the chicken before freezing. For best results, wrap in freezer bags, wax-coated freezer paper or heavy duty aluminum foil, separating parts with wax paper to allow easy removal and quicker thawing.

The best way to thaw chicken to retain flavor and texture is to place the package in the refrigerator. Separated parts thaw in 7-8 hours; allow 12 hours for every 2 pounds of whole chicken.

▮ *Roast Chicken with Apple-Celery Stuffing and Cream Gravy*

Roast at 425° for 15 minutes; then at 375° for 2¼ hours.
Makes 6 servings.

Nutrient Value Per Serving: 548 calories, 48 gm. protein, 34 gm. fat, 725 mg. sodium, 165 mg. cholesterol.

Apple-Celery Stuffing (recipe follows)
1 roasting chicken (about 5 pounds)
1 teaspoon salt
¼ teaspoon pepper
3 tablespoons butter or margarine, melted
½ teaspoon paprika
Cream Gravy (recipe follows)

1. Prepare Apple-Celery Stuffing.
2. Preheat the oven to hot (425°).
3. Sprinkle the chicken inside and out with salt and pepper.
4. Stuff the neck and body cavities loosely with the Apple-Celery Stuffing. Skewer neck skin to back; close body cavity and tie legs to tail. Place chicken in a roasting pan.
5. Combine the melted butter and paprika in a small bowl. Brush part of the butter mixture over the chicken.
6. Roast the chicken in the preheated hot oven (425°) for 15 minutes; baste with the remaining melted butter mixture. Lower the oven temperature to moderate (375°). Roast the chicken for another 2¼ hours or until tender and a leg moves easily and juices are no longer pink. If the chicken browns too quickly, cover loosely with aluminum foil.
7. When the chicken is done, remove to a warm platter. Remove the skewers and string; keep warm while you make the gravy.

Cream Gravy: Drain off all but 2 tablespoons of fat from the roasting pan. Place the roasting pan over low heat. Stir in 2 tablespoons all-purpose flour; cook, stirring for 1 minute. Gradually stir in 1¼ cups chicken broth and ¼ cup half and half or heavy cream, scraping up any browned bits from the bottom of the pan. Bring to boiling, stirring constantly, until thickened and smooth. Add ⅛ teaspoon pepper. Serve with the chicken.

STUFFING POULTRY
Don't stuff poultry until you are ready to roast it. The stuffing can be made ahead and refrigerated until you are ready to use it. Always remove the stuffing from the bird immediately after the meal and store it in a separate container in the refrigerator.

Apple-Celery Stuffing

Toast at 350° for 10 minutes.

Nutrient Value Per Serving: 210 calories, 5 gm. protein, 10 gm. fat, 528 mg. sodium, 67 mg. cholesterol.

4 cups white bread cubes (8 slices day-old bread)
1 large onion, chopped (1 cup)
1 large carrot, pared and coarsely grated
1 cup diced celery
¼ cup (½ stick) butter or margarine
1 red Delicious apple, pared, cored and coarsely grated
¼ cup chopped parsley
½ cup chicken broth
1 egg, slightly beaten
½ teaspoon salt
½ teaspoon poultry seasoning
¼ teaspoon pepper

1. Place the bread cubes in single layer in a jelly-roll pan. Toast in a preheated moderate oven (350°) for 10 minutes or until browned; turn cubes occasionally.
2. Sauté the onion, carrot and celery in the butter in a large skillet until tender, 5 minutes. Remove to a large bowl. Add the bread cubes, apple, parsley, chicken broth, egg, salt, poultry seasoning and pepper; toss to thoroughly moisten the bread.

◀Russian Chicken

▯ ▯ *Russian Chicken*

Makes 4 servings.

Nutrient Value Per Serving: 655 calories, 46 gm. protein, 48 gm. fat, 814 mg. sodium, 205 mg. cholesterol.

1 broiler-fryer (3 pounds), cut into eighths
½ teaspoon salt
¼ teaspoon pepper
2 tablespoons butter
¾ cup water
¼ pound mushrooms, thinly sliced
1 large tomato, peeled, seeded and
 finely chopped
4 green onions, thinly sliced
½ teaspoon leaf thyme, crumbled
2 teaspoons all-purpose flour
1 chicken bouillon cube
½ cup dairy sour cream

1. Season the chicken with salt and pepper. Brown the chicken in the butter in a large skillet, about 10 minutes. Add ¼ cup of the water. Bring to boiling. Lower the heat; cover; simmer for 20 minutes or until tender. Transfer to a warmed platter; keep warm.
2. Scrape up any browned bits from the bottom of the skillet. Cook the mushrooms, tomato, green onion and thyme in the skillet for 3 minutes. Sprinkle the vegetables with the flour; stir to mix well and cook 1 minute.

3. Crumble the bouillon cube into the skillet; stir in the remaining ½ cup water. Continue stirring until the bouillon is dissolved and the mixture is smooth. Remove from the heat. Stir in the sour cream. Reduce the heat to very low. Cook until thickened and bubbly, about 3 minutes. Pour over the chicken and serve.

CHICKEN SAVINGS
You can save money by buying a whole frying chicken on sale and cutting it into parts yourself.

▰ ▯ ▯ *Chicken Provençal*

Makes 4 servings.

Nutrient Value Per Serving: 259 calories, 28 gm. protein, 13 gm. fat, 801 mg. sodium, 66 mg. cholesterol.

2 tablespoons olive oil
1 finely chopped clove garlic
1 pound boneless chicken breast,
 sliced, ½ inch thick
3 small zucchini (1 pound), sliced
1 teaspoon leaf basil, crumbled
¼ teaspoon leaf oregano, crumbled
1 teaspoon salt
⅛ teaspoon pepper
1 cup cherry tomatoes
1 can (3½ ounces) pitted black olives
2 tablespoons lemon juice
 French bread or garlic toast

1. Heat oil in a wok or large skillet. Stir fry the garlic, chicken and zucchini over high heat for 4 to 5 minutes. Add the basil, oregano, salt and pepper; cook for 1 more minute.
2. Add the tomatoes and olives. Cook and stir for 2 minutes. Stir in the lemon juice. Serve with French bread or garlic toast.

■■ *Lemon Chicken*

Serve with hot cooked rice.

Makes 4 servings.

Nutrient Value Per Serving: 481 calories, 40 gm. protein, 24 gm. fat, 1021 mg. sodium, 166 mg. cholesterol.

¼ cup sesame seeds
½ cup packaged seasoned bread crumbs
1 egg
4 boneless, skinless chicken breast halves, slightly flattened (1¼ pounds)
⅓ cup fresh lemon juice
4 teaspoons soy sauce
2 to 3 tablespoons sugar
1 tablespoon cornstarch
1 cup water
3 tablespoons vegetable oil
2 green onions, cut into 1-inch lengths
1 small sweet red pepper, cut into julienne strips
2 tablespoons butter
4 cups shredded crisp lettuce
½ lemon, sliced

◀Lemon Chicken

1. Combine the sesame seeds and crumbs on wax paper. Beat the egg with a fork in a saucer. Dip the chicken pieces, one at a time, in the egg, then in the crumb mixture. Pat lightly to help the coating stick. Set aside, uncovered, 10 minutes.
2. Combine the lemon juice, soy sauce, sugar, cornstarch and water in a 2-cup glass measure. Set aside. Heat 1 tablespoon of the oil in a small saucepan; cook the green onions and red pepper for 1 minute. Remove from the heat.
3. Heat the remaining oil and butter in a large skillet over medium-high heat; cook the chicken until golden brown, 4 to 5 minutes on each side. Remove from the skillet; cut crosswise into ½-inch strips. Arrange on lettuce on a serving plate.
4. Add the cornstarch mixture to the saucepan. Bring to boiling; stir until thickened and bubbly. Spoon over the chicken. Garnish with the sliced lemon.

■■■■ *Chicken Breasts with Lemon Parsley*

Prepare the breaded chicken breasts and refrigerate at least 30 minutes ahead of time. Then, quickly sauté and serve with a lemon sauce made in the same skillet.

Makes 6 servings.

Nutrient Value Per Serving: 318 calories, 35 gm. protein, 13 gm. fat, 424 mg. sodium, 179 mg. cholesterol.

6 **boneless chicken breast halves, skinned (about 1¾ pounds)**
½ **teaspoon salt**
¼ **teaspoon pepper**
2 **eggs**
3 **tablespoons water**
¼ **cup all-purpose flour**
¾ **cup packaged unseasoned bread crumbs**
2 **tablespoons butter or margarine**
2 **tablespoons vegetable oil**
2 **tablespoons lemon juice**
2 **tablespoons chopped parsley**
¼ **teaspoon grated lemon rind**

1. Flatten the chicken breasts between two sheets of wax paper with a rolling pin or the flat side of a meat mallet to ¼-inch thickness. Sprinkle with salt and pepper.

2. Beat the eggs with 1 tablespoon of the water in a shallow dish. Place the flour and the bread crumbs on two separate pieces of wax paper. Turn the chicken breasts in the flour to coat evenly; shake off excess. Dip the chicken in the egg mixture; then lightly coat with bread crumbs.

3. Refrigerate the chicken breasts for at least 30 minutes or place in the freezer for 15 minutes to firm up the coating.

4. Heat the butter and the oil in a large skillet over medium heat. Sauté the chicken breasts in batches, 2 to 3 minutes on each side or until they are golden and firm to the touch. Transfer to a serving platter; keep warm.

5. Add the remaining 2 tablespoons of water and the lemon juice to the skillet. Cook about 1 minute, scraping up any browned bits from the bottom of the skillet. Spoon the sauce over the warm chicken breasts. Sprinkle with chopped parsley and grated lemon rind.

Chinese Fried Rice with Chicken

Makes 6 servings.

Nutrient Value Per Serving: 421 calories, 31 gm. protein, 11 gm. fat, 985 mg. sodium, 146 mg. cholesterol.

1½ **cups long-grain white rice**
1¼ **pounds boneless chicken breasts OR: chicken thighs, skinned and cut into ½-inch chunks**
¼ **cup soy sauce**
¼ **teaspoon pepper**
3 **tablespoons vegetable oil**
2 **eggs, slightly beaten**
2 **cups fresh bean sprouts**
2 **cups small broccoli flowerets**
1 **large sweet red or green pepper, halved, seeded and cut into ¼-inch dice (1 cup)**
2 **green onions, thinly sliced**
2 **tablespoons dry sherry or water**

1. Cook the rice following label directions.

2. Meanwhile, place the chicken in a medium-size bowl. Mix the soy sauce and pepper in a cup. Add 1 tablespoon to chicken; toss to mix.

3. Heat 1 tablespoon of the oil in a wok or large skillet over high heat. Add the eggs; cook, stirring, until lightly set, about 15 seconds. Remove with a slotted spoon to a small plate; keep warm.

4. Add the remaining oil to the wok. Add the chicken pieces; stir-fry until cooked through, about 4 minutes. Remove with a slotted spoon to a bowl; keep warm.

5. Add the bean sprouts, broccoli, red pepper and green onion to the wok. Stir-fry for 1 minute. Add the sherry; cover; cook for 2 minutes.

6. Add the cooked hot rice, chicken and remaining soy mixture. Toss until the rice is evenly coated. Gently stir in the eggs, breaking them up. Serve at once.

Chicken-Sausage Risotto Pie

Bake at 350° for 30 minutes.
Makes 6 servings.

Nutrient Value Per Serving: 427 calories, 21 gm. protein, 21 gm. fat, 833 mg. sodium, 63 mg. cholesterol.

- 1 **cup long-grain white rice**
- ½ **pound shredded mozzarella cheese (2 cups)**
- ¼ **cup freshly grated Romano cheese**
- 1 **medium-size onion, chopped (½ cup)**
- 2 **cloves garlic, chopped**
- 2 **tablespoons olive oil**
- 2 **sweet Italian sausage links (4 ounces)**
- 1 **can (16 ounces) whole tomatoes, undrained**
- 2 **cans (8 ounces each) tomato sauce**
- 1 **teaspoon leaf basil, crumbled**
- ½ **teaspoon pepper**
- ½ **cup (4 ounces) cubed (¼ inch) cooked chicken (half of a medium-size boneless, skinless chicken breast)**
- 1 **tomato, cored, halved and sliced**

1. Cook the rice following label directions without adding butter. Drain; cool. Mix rice with mozzarella cheese and 2 tablespoons of the Romano cheese in a large bowl. Reserve.
2. Sauté the onion and garlic in oil in a large skillet until the onion is softened, about 3 minutes. Add the sausage; cook until the sausage is browned. Add the canned tomatoes and tomato sauce, breaking up the tomatoes with a wooden spoon. Stir in the basil and pepper. Bring to boiling. Lower the heat; cover; simmer for 10 minutes. Uncover; add the chicken; simmer 35 minutes or until reduced to about 3 cups. Transfer the sausage to a cutting board. Cut into ¼-inch slices.
3. Preheat the oven to moderate (350°). Grease a 9-inch pie plate.
4. Pack half the rice mixture into the bottom of the prepared pie plate. Spoon the chicken pieces and half the tomato sauce over the rice. Cover with the remaining rice mixture. Spoon the remaining tomato sauce over center. Garnish the center with the sliced sausage. Sprinkle with the remaining Romano cheese.
5. Bake in the preheated moderate oven (350°), uncovered, for 10 minutes. Remove from the oven. Arrange the tomato slices around the outer edge. Bake for 20 minutes or until bubbly.

Baked Chicken and Pork Loaf with Herbed Tomato Sauce

Bake at 350° for 1 hour.
Makes 8 servings.

Nutrient Value Per Serving: 276 calories, 25 gm. protein, 14 gm. fat, 624 mg. sodium, 108 mg. cholesterol.

- 3 **slices whole-wheat or white bread**
- ½ **cup milk**
- 1 **pound ground chicken (about 4 boned and skinned breast halves)**
- 1 **pound ground pork**
- 1 **egg, slightly beaten**
- 2 **green onions, thinly sliced**
- 2 **tablespoons chopped parsley**
- 1 **teaspoon salt**
- ½ **teaspoon leaf sage, crumbled**
- ¼ **teaspoon leaf marjoram, crumbled**
- ¼ **teaspoon pepper**
  Herbed Tomato Sauce (recipe follows)

1. Preheat the oven to moderate (350°).
2. Crumble the bread slices into the milk in a large bowl. Add the chicken, pork, egg, green onion, parsley, salt, sage, marjoram and pepper; stir until well blended. Shape into a loaf and place in a shallow baking dish or in a loaf pan.

3. Bake in the preheated moderate oven (350°) for 1 hour. Slice. Serve with Herbed Tomato Sauce spooned over.

Herbed Tomato Sauce: Sauté 1 small onion, chopped (¼ cup) in 1 tablespoon vegetable oil in a medium-size saucepan until tender. Stir in 1 can (2 pounds, 3 ounces) Italian-style tomatoes, drained and broken up, ¼ teaspoon salt, ¼ teaspoon sugar, ¼ teaspoon leaf basil, crumbled, ¼ teaspoon leaf marjoram, crumbled and ⅛ teaspoon pepper. Bring to boiling; lower the heat; simmer, stirring frequently, for 30 minutes or until the sauce has thickened. Makes about 1¾ cups sauce.

◻ *Sweet-and-Sour Apricot-Glazed Chicken Thighs*

Bake at 375° for 45 minutes.
Makes 4 servings.

Nutrient Value Per Serving: 487 calories, 37 gm. protein, 23 gm. fat, 893 mg. sodium, 137 mg. cholesterol.

▲ **Sweet-and-Sour Apricot-Glazed Chicken Thighs**

8 **chicken thighs (2½ pounds)**
1 **teaspoon salt**
¼ **teaspoon pepper**
½ **cup apricot jam**
2 **tablespoons bottled chili sauce**
1 **tablespoon Dijon-style mustard**
   Cooked rice (optional)
   Raisins (optional)
   Almond slivers (optional)
   Chopped parsley (optional)

1. Preheat the oven to moderate (375°).
2. Pat the chicken dry. Sprinkle with salt and pepper. Place the chicken, skin-side up, in a 13 x 9 x 2-inch baking dish.
3. Combine the apricot jam, chili sauce and mustard in a small bowl. Force the mixture through a small strainer with the back of a spoon.
4. Bake the chicken in the preheated moderate oven (375°) for 25 minutes. Brush the skin

1. Heat the oil in a large deep skillet or Dutch oven. Add the garlic, thyme and rosemary; sauté for 1 minute. Add the bay leaf, wine and chicken broth. Cover; simmer on low heat while preparing the vegetables.
2. Pare the carrots; cut on a diagonal into 1-inch lengths; add to the skillet. Scrub the potatoes; cut in half; add to the skillet. Cook, covered, until tender, about 25 minutes.
3. Meanwhile, cut the chicken into quarters. Add to the skillet 5 minutes before end of the cooking time.
4. Arrange the chicken and vegetables in a serving dish; garnish with parsley. To eat the garlic, press the purée from the skin with a fork; spread on toast.

side of the chicken with half the apricot glaze. Bake for 20 minutes more or until tender, brushing with the remaining glaze. Serve on a bed of hot cooked rice with raisins, almond slivers and chopped parsley, if you wish.

◼ ￼ ◻ *Ragout of Chicken with Garlic*

Makes 4 servings.

Nutrient Value Per Serving: 473 calories, 40 gm. protein, 25 gm. fat, 239 mg. sodium, 117 mg. cholesterol.

 2 *tablespoons olive or vegetable oil*
20 *cloves unpeeled garlic (1 large or 2 small bulbs)*
 ½ *teaspoon leaf thyme, crumbled*
 ½ *teaspoon leaf rosemary, crumbled*
 1 *bay leaf*
 ½ *cup dry white wine*
 ½ *cup chicken broth or water*
 4 *carrots (about ½ pound)*
 9 *small new red potatoes (about ½ pound)*
 1 *barbecued or roasted chicken from deli department (about 1½ to 2 pounds)*
 1 *tablespoon chopped fresh parsley French bread, sliced and toasted*

◼ ◻ *Chicken Livers and Peppers*

Serve with buttered noodles.

Makes 4 servings.

Nutrient Value Per Serving: 270 calories, 25 gm. protein, 14 gm. fat, 406 mg. sodium, 637 mg. cholesterol.

 1 *pound chicken livers*
 1 *tablespoon butter or margarine*
 2 *tablespoons vegetable oil*
 2 *teaspoons all-purpose flour*
 ½ *teaspoon salt*
 ¼ *teaspoon pepper*
 1 *large sweet green pepper, halved, seeded and cut into 1-inch pieces*
 ½ *pound medium-size mushrooms, sliced*
 1 *teaspoon Worcestershire sauce*
 2 *tablespoons Madeira wine*
 2 *tablespoons chopped parsley*

1. Wash the chicken livers; drain on paper toweling; trim and cut each in half.
2. Heat the butter and 1 tablespoon of the oil in a wok or large skillet; add livers. Combine the flour, salt and pepper in a cup; sprinkle over the livers. Stir-fry over high heat until browned, 4 minutes. Remove to a plate.
3. Add the remaining oil, green pepper and mushrooms to the wok; stir-fry 3 to 4 minutes. Stir in the green onions, Worcestershire sauce and Madeira; cook for 1 minute. Return the livers to the wok. Cook and stir for 2 minutes. Sprinkle with the parsley.

Roast Duck with Orange Sauce

Roast at 425° for 20 minutes; then at 350° for 1½ hours.
Makes 4 servings.

Nutrient Value Per Serving: 963 calories, 40 gm. protein, 65 gm. fat, 851 mg. sodium, 171 mg. cholesterol.

1 **frozen duckling (4 to 5 pounds), thawed**
1 **carrot, chopped**
1 **medium-size onion, chopped (½ cup)**
2 **tablespoons vegetable oil**
1 **can (10½ ounces) condensed beef broth**
1 **cup water**
1 **small bay leaf**
1 **sprig parsley**
⅛ **teaspoon salt**
⅛ **teaspoon leaf thyme, crumbled**
⅛ **teaspoon pepper**
3 **navel oranges**
3 **cups boiling water**
3 **tablespoons sugar**
¼ **cup red wine vinegar**
2 **tablespoons cornstarch**
1 **tablespoon butter**
3 **tablespoons orange-flavored liqueur**
¾ **cup port or Madeira wine**
   Rice Pilaf (page 192)

1. Remove the wing tips and giblets from the duckling. Cut up the giblets; sauté with carrot and onion in the oil in a medium-size saucepan for 10 minutes. Stir in the broth, water, bay leaf, parsley, salt, thyme and pepper. Simmer, partially covered, for 1 hour. Strain and reserve the broth (about 1 cup).
2. Pare the thin orange-colored rind from two of the oranges (no white) with a vegetable parer; cut into thin slivers, about 2 inches long. Simmer in 3 cups boiling water for 15 minutes to blanch. Drain and dry on paper toweling. Remove the white from the oranges; slice the oranges; reserve.
3. Preheat the oven to hot (425°). Remove the fat from the cavity of the duckling; sprinkle the cavity with salt and pepper. Stuff with half of the blanched orange rind. Prick the skin all over with a 2-tined fork. Truss and place in a roasting pan, breast-side up.
4. Roast in the preheated hot oven (425°) for 20 minutes. Lower the oven temperature to moderate (350°) and continue roasting for 1½ hours or until tender.
5. Combine the sugar and vinegar in a medium-size saucepan. Bring to boiling; lower the heat; simmer until the mixture turns a deep brown color. (Watch carefully so it doesn't burn.) Remove from the heat; add ¼ cup of the reserved broth to dissolve the syrup. Stir the remaining broth and cornstarch in a small cup; stir into the saucepan. Heat to boiling, stirring just until thick and clear. Add the butter, orange liqueur and remaining half of the reserved julienned rind.
6. Place the duckling on a cutting board. Skim the remaining fat from the pan. Add the wine to the drippings; stir over low heat, scraping up the brown bits in the pan. Strain into the duck sauce.
7. Remove the strings from the duckling; cut into quarters with poultry shears. Arrange on a warmed platter with the reserved orange sections. Serve with sauce and Rice Pilaf.

TO THAW FROZEN POULTRY
Thawing frozen poultry takes time, so be sure to plan ahead. Place the bird, in its freezer wrapping, on a tray or roasting pan in the refrigerator. Duckling, large roasters, capons and small turkeys (4 to 12 pounds) will take 1 to 2 days to thaw; turkeys (12 to 20 pounds) will take 2 to 3 days; and a large turkey weighing up to 24 pounds will take 3 to 4 days.

▌ *Apricot-Mustard Glazed-Turkey Breast*

Makes 10 servings.

Nutrient Value Per Serving (4 ounces) Sliced Turkey: 370 calories, 34 gm. protein, 4 gm. fat, 295 mg. sodium, 78 mg. cholesterol.

- 1 *frozen turkey breast (6 to 6¼ pounds), thawed*
- 10 *cups water*
- 2 *teaspoons salt*
- ¼ *teaspoon pepper*
- ⅓ *cup chopped celery with tops*
- 1 *large carrot, pared and sliced*
- 1 *large onion, coarsely chopped*
- 4 *sprigs parsley*
- 1 *jar (12 ounces) apricot preserves*
- 2 *to 3 teaspoons Dijon-style mustard*

1. Rinse the turkey breast. Place in a 4-quart kettle or Dutch oven. Add the water, salt, pepper, celery, carrot, onion and parsley.
2. Bring slowly to boiling. Lower the heat; cover; simmer for 2¼ hours or until a meat thermometer inserted in the turkey registers 180°.
3. Remove the turkey breast to a serving platter. Keep warm. Reserve the broth and vegetables for another use.

4. To prepare the glaze, gently heat the preserves in a small saucepan. Force through a sieve with the back of a spoon. Return to the saucepan. Stir in mustard to taste. Brush some of the glaze over the turkey.

TURKEY VALUE
Buy a turkey weighing between 14 and 16 pounds for the best value. It will have a more meaty breast than a bird of lower weight.

TO ROAST AN UNSTUFFED TURKEY
Place a 14- to 15-pound turkey, breast-side up, on a rack in a shallow roasting pan. Brush with melted butter. Roast in a slow oven (325°) for 4½ to 5½ hours. Baste occasionally. A stuffed turkey will take about 1 hour longer to be done. This turkey will serve 14 to 16 people with ample leftovers for seconds.

A TURKEY IS COOKED
●When a meat thermometer, inserted in the thickest part of the thigh, without touching bone, reads 185°.
●When the drumstick moves up and down freely. (Grasp, using several thicknesses of paper toweling to protect your fingers.)
●When the thick part of the thigh feels soft when pressed.
●When the juices are yellow or almost colorless. (Pierce the inner thigh with a fork tine.)

▲ Apricot-Mustard Glazed-Turkey Breast

Fish and Shellfish

▼ Crab-Stuffed Flounder

Bake at 350° for 18 to 20 minutes.
Makes 4 servings.

Nutrient Value Per Serving: 243 calories, 25 gm. protein, 13 gm. fat, 576 mg. sodium, 116 mg. cholesterol.

   1 small onion, chopped (¼ cup)
   ¼ cup chopped celery
   ¼ chopped sweet red pepper
   4 tablespoons (½ stick) butter or
       margarine
   ¼ pound crabmeat, picked over and flaked
   ½ cup soft bread crumbs (about 1 slice)
   3 teaspoons lemon juice
   ½ teaspoon salt
   ⅛ teaspoon pepper
       Few drops of liquid red pepper
       seasoning
   4 small flounder fillets (about
       4 ounces each)
       Paprika
       Lemon wedges and parsley (optional)

1. Preheat the oven to moderate (350°). Butter a small shallow baking dish.

2. Sauté the onion, celery and red pepper in 2 tablespoons of the butter in a saucepan until soft, about 2 minutes. Mix in the crabmeat, bread crumbs, 1 teaspoon lemon juice, salt, pepper and red pepper seasoning.

3. Place the fillets skin-side up. Mound the crab mixture in the center of the fillets. Overlap the ends of fillets over the top of the stuffing. Fasten with wooden picks. Place in the prepared dish.

4. Melt the remaining 2 tablespoons of butter in a small saucepan; stir in the lemon juice. Pour over the fish; sprinkle with paprika.

5. Bake in the preheated moderate oven (350°) for 18 to 20 minutes or until the fish flakes when pierced with a fork. Garnish with lemon wedges and parsley, if you wish.

MICROWAVE DIRECTIONS
650 Watt Variable Power Microwave Oven Directions: Combine the onion, celery, sweet red pepper and butter in a shallow microwave-safe baking dish large enough to hold 4 fish rolls. Cover tightly. Microwave at full power for 4 minutes. Add the crabmeat, bread crumbs, 1 teaspoon lemon juice, salt, pepper and red pepper seasoning; mix well. Assemble the rolls as directed above. Place in the same baking dish. Cover with the butter-lemon juice mixture; sprinkle with paprika. Cover tightly. Microwave at full power for 4 minutes.

FOR FRESH FISH, LOOK FOR
● **Firm flesh that springs back when pressed with your fingertip.**
● **Shiny scales that adhere firmly to the skin (they should not be slimy).**
● **Reddish-pink gills, free of odor or discoloration.**
● **Bulging, clean and clear eyes.**

⏳ Flounder and Salmon Roulade

Makes 8 servings.

Nutrient Value Per Serving: 380 calories, 35 gm. protein, 25 gm. fat, 567 mg. sodium, 160 mg. cholesterol.

> 1 *fresh or frozen salmon steak (about 1 pound)*
> 4 *fresh or frozen thawed flounder or sole fillets (about 8 ounces each)*
> 2 *teaspoons lemon juice*
> ¼ *teaspoon pepper*
> ½ *cup water*
> ½ *cup dry white wine*
> 2 *shallots, chopped*
> ½ *teaspoon salt*
> 1 *teaspoon leaf tarragon*
>   *Crab Sauce (recipe follows)*
>   *Fresh dill (optional)*

1. Skin and bone the salmon; halve crosswise; cut each half into 4 strips.
2. Halve each flounder fillet lengthwise; sprinkle with lemon juice and pepper. Place a strip of salmon on the thick end of each fillet. Roll up, jelly-roll fashion; secure with wooden picks.
3. Combine the water, wine, shallots and salt in a large skillet. Tie the tarragon in a small piece of cheesecloth; drop into the skillet. Stand the fish rolls in the skillet.
4. Bring to boiling; lower the heat; cover; simmer for 5 minutes or just until the fish becomes white and feels firm, not spongy, to the touch. Remove the rolls with a slotted spoon to a warm platter; keep warm.
5. Cook the pan liquid rapidly until reduced to ½ cup; reserve.
6. Prepare the Crab Sauce: spoon over the fish; garnish with fresh dill, if you wish.

Crab Sauce: Cook 1½ cups heavy cream rapidly in a large saucepan until reduced to 1 cup. Add the reserved fish liquid, ¼ teaspoon salt, ⅛ teaspoon paprika and 1 can (6½ ounces) drained crab with any cartilage removed. Heat, stirring constantly, until piping hot.

DON'T OVERCOOK FISH
Fish is cooked when it changes from a translucent off-white to a solid opaque-white and when the flesh just begins to separate easily when touched with a fork.

◩ ⏳ ▢ Fillet of Flounder with Lobster and Julienned Vegetables

Bake at 500° for 10 minutes.
Makes 4 servings.

Nutrient Value Per Serving: 228 calories, 30 gm. protein, 9 gm. fat, 588 mg. sodium, 78 mg. cholesterol.

▲**Fillets of Flounder with Lobster and Julienned Vegetables**

4 *flounder fillets (1¼ to 1½ pounds)*
1 *medium-size carrot, pared*
1 *medium-size leek*
1 *fennel or celery stalk*
  Vegetable oil
½ *teaspoon salt*
⅛ *teaspoon pepper*
¼ *teaspoon leaf tarragon, crumbled*
1 *package (6½ ounces) frozen lobster Newburg in boilable bag, partially thawed*

1. Cut out four 12-inch squares of aluminum foil.
2. Rinse the flounder fillets; dry on paper toweling.
3. Cut carrot, leek and fennel or celery into 2½ x ¼-inch julienne strips.
4. Brush the lower half of each aluminum foil square with a little oil. Place a flounder fillet on each, folding the fillet to fit. Spread the vegetables equally over each fillet. Sprinkle with salt, pepper and tarragon. Divide the lobster Newburg into 4 equal portions; spread over each fillet.
5. Fold the top half of the aluminum foil over to meet the lower edge. Fold the edges all around twice, to seal. Place the packages on a hot cookie sheet in the oven, 1 inch apart.
6. Bake in a preheated very hot oven (500°) for 10 minutes. Remove the packages to dinner plates; cut an X in top; open up and serve in the aluminum foil.

◼ 🍸 *Broccoli-Stuffed Sole*

Bake at 375° for 15 minutes.
Makes 4 servings.

Nutrient Value Per Serving: 351 calories, 44
gm. protein, 14 gm. fat, 745 mg. sodium, 198
mg. cholesterol.

1   **package (10 ounces) frozen chopped
     broccoli, thawed and drained**
1   **egg, slightly beaten**
2   **slices white bread, crumbled**
4   **sole or flounder fillets
     (about 8 ounces each)**
2   **tablespoons lemon juice**
¼   **teaspoon salt**
¼   **teaspoon pepper**
¼   **cup dry white wine**
2   **tablespoons butter**
1   **envelope (1.25 ounces) Hollandaise
     sauce mix**

1. Preheat the oven to moderate (375°).
2. To make the stuffing, purée the broccoli in
   a blender or food processor, or finely chop
   with a knife. Transfer to a small bowl. Add
   the egg and bread; mix well.
3. Slice each fillet in half lengthwise. Sprinkle
   with the lemon juice, salt and pepper. Place
   the broccoli stuffing in the center of each
   fillet strip, dividing evenly. Roll up jelly-roll
   fashion.
4. Place 2 stuffed rolls in each of 4 individual
   casseroles. Pour 1 tablespoon of wine into
   each. Dot the fish with butter; cover with
   foil.
5. Bake in the preheated moderate oven (375°)
   for 15 to 20 minutes or just until the fish
   becomes white and feels firm, not spongy to
   the touch.
6. Meanwhile, prepare the Hollandaise sauce
   following label directions. Pour over the
   stuffed fillets just before serving.

◼ ▭ *Salmon Timbales*

Bake at 325° for 30 minutes.
Makes 2 servings.

Nutrient Value Per Serving: 1258 calories, 57
gm. protein, 98 gm. fat, 1961 mg. sodium, 284
mg. cholesterol.

1   **can (15½ or 16 ounces) salmon, drained
      and flaked**
1   **medium-size onion, chopped (½ cup)**
1   **small sweet green pepper, halved,
      seeded and chopped (½ cup)**
½   **cup chopped celery**
½   **cup packaged unseasoned bread crumbs**
¼   **cup plain yogurt**
¼   **cup mayonnaise**
1   **egg, slightly beaten**
¼   **teaspoon pepper**
     Cucumber-Dill Sauce (recipe follows)
     Sprigs of dill (optional)

1. Preheat the oven to slow (325°). Generously
   grease four 6-ounce custard cups.
2. Combine the salmon, onion, green pepper,
   celery, bread crumbs, yogurt, mayonnaise,
   egg and pepper in bowl. Stir until well
   blended. Divide the mixture evenly among
   the prepared custard cups; pack well.
   Arrange on a small cookie sheet.
3. Bake in the preheated slow oven (325°) for
   30 minutes or until the salmon mixture
   begins to pull away from the sides of the
   cups.
4. Meanwhile, prepare the Cucumber-Dill
   Sauce.
5. To unmold the timbales, run a small knife
   around the inside edge of each cup. Invert
   onto a serving dish. Spoon Cucumber-Dill
   Sauce over the tops. Garnish with sprigs of
   dill, if you wish.

Cucumber-Dill Sauce: Stir together ½ cup
mayonnaise, ¼ cup dairy sour cream, ¼ cup plain
yogurt, ¾ cup finely chopped seeded cucumber,
¼ cup finely chopped onion and 1 tablespoon

▲**Salmon Timbales**

chopped fresh dill, or 1 teaspoon dried dillweed, in a saucepan. Heat over very low heat just until warmed through.

MICROWAVE DIRECTIONS
650 Watt Variable Power Microwave Oven Directions: Assemble the salmon mixture as directed in the recipe. Pack into 4 well-greased 6-ounce microwave-safe custard cups. Place on microwave-safe plate. Cover each with plastic wrap; cut slits for vents. Microwave at full power 2 minutes. Rotate plate a quarter turn. Microwave at full power 2 more minutes or until top feels firm to the touch. Let stand, covered, 5 minutes. Combine sauce ingredients in small microwave-safe bowl or 2-cup glass measure. Microwave at full power 2 minutes, stirring once. Unmold timbales and serve as directed in recipe.

◼ ▼ ◻ *Shrimp and Scallops in Mustard-Dill Sauce*

Serve this quick dish with brown rice or new potatoes.

Makes 4 servings.

Nutrient Value Per Serving: 338 calories, 22 gm. protein, 24 gm. fat, 427 mg. sodium, 174 mg. cholesterol.

1 *tablespoon vegetable oil*
1 *small cucumber, pared, halved, seeded and sliced ½ inch thick*
½ *pound thin asparagus or green beans, cut into 1-inch lengths*
1 *tablespoon butter or margarine*
½ *pound shrimp, shelled and deveined*
½ *pound sea scallops, split or sliced crosswise*
3 *tablespoons white wine vinegar*
4 *teaspoons Dijon-style mustard*
¾ *cup heavy cream, heated*
¼ *cup snipped fresh dill*
   Snipped fresh dill for garnish (optional)

1. Heat the oil in a wok or large skillet. Sauté the cucumber and asparagus or beans for 3 to 5 minutes. Remove to a bowl.
2. Add the butter, shrimp and scallops to the wok. Stir-fry until the shrimp turn pink and the scallops firm up, about 4 minutes. Remove to a bowl.
3. Swirl the vinegar in the wok over high heat until reduced by half. Stir in the mustard and cream; cook and stir until slightly thickened, 2 to 3 minutes. Add the dill and shrimp-vegetable mixture. Heat through. Garnish with dill.

◼ ◻ *Spanish Rice and Seafood Stew*

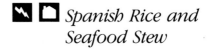

Makes 6 servings.

Nutrient Value Per Serving: 191 calories, 15 gm. protein, 2 gm. fat, 788 mg. sodium, 67 mg. cholesterol.

1 *can (13¾ ounces) chicken broth OR: 1½ cups water*
2 *packages (11 ounces each) frozen Spanish-style rice*
6 *to 8 ounces fresh or thawed frozen shrimp, peeled and deveined*
12 *small fresh clams (optional)*
1 *teaspoon grated orange rind Crusty bread (optional)*

1. Combine the chicken broth and contents of the flavor packets from the rice in a Dutch oven or kettle. Bring to boiling over medium heat. Add the rice mix; separate with a fork. Add the shrimp, and clams, if you wish. Bring to boiling. Cover tightly.
2. Cook, stirring occasionally, until the clams have opened and the shrimp are light pink, 6 to 10 minutes. Stir in the orange rind.
3. Spoon the stew into shallow bowls. Serve with crusty bread, if you wish.

TO FREEZE FISH
Freeze as soon as possible after catching (and cleaning) or purchasing. Freeze, wrapped in plastic wrap or aluminum foil, with 2 pieces of wax paper between the fillets for easy separation.

Thaw frozen fish in the refrigerator, but remember it is really better to cook the fish frozen. This takes a little longer, but there is less loss of liquid, which means better flavor and texture.

Barbecue

STEP-BY-STEP GUIDE TO A SUCCESSFUL BARBECUE
Follow our tips and you'll be grilling perfectly every time!
Equipment: Make sure you have the right tools—they'll make cooking outdoors easier and safer. Always choose long-handled equipment and protective mitts to shield your hands from heat and grease spatters. Check out the following suggestions for specific items.
• *Metal spatula:* Turning meats with a fork can pierce them, letting juices escape, so use a spatula. (For large pieces of meat, however, a fork gives you a firmer hold.)
• *Tongs:* For hard-to-grip pieces, such as chicken legs, potatoes and corn. The best ones open and close like scissors.
• *Large basting brush:* Use for putting sauces or butters on foods.
• *Skewers:* For kabobs. Best ones are 16-inch-long skewers with large, easy-to-grip handles. Avoid skewers which come in fours, attached at the handle; you can't turn these skewers individually on the grill.
• *Hinged grill basket:* Handy for cooking small items, such as vegetables, or foods that crumble when turned, such as fish fillets. Comes in many shapes.
Tip: To make it easier to remove grilled food from basket, heat basket over coals before putting food inside, brush lightly with oil.

Pork and Vegetable Kabobs

When grilling different foods on the same skewer, select or cut ingredients so they will cook in the same amount of time.

Makes 6 servings.

Nutrient Value Per Serving: 387 calories, 26 gm. protein, 23 gm. fat, 1434 mg. sodium, 76 mg. cholesterol.

½ *cup dry sherry*
6 *tablespoons soy sauce*
6 *tablespoons vegetable oil*
1 *teaspoon ground ginger*
8 *cloves garlic, finely chopped*
1 *piece trimmed boned pork shoulder (1½ pounds), cut into forty-two 1-inch cubes*
24 *medium-size mushrooms*
2 *large sweet red peppers, each halved, seeded and cut into 12 pieces*
2 *medium-size onions, each cut into 6 wedges*
1 *medium-size yellow squash, cut into 6 rounds*

1. Stir together the sherry, soy sauce, oil, ginger and garlic in a large bowl. Add the pork, mushrooms, red pepper, onion and yellow squash. Stir to mix well. Cover. Refrigerate for 24 hours, stirring once.
2. Thread 7 pork cubes onto each of 6 long skewers, alternating with 4 mushrooms, 4 red pepper pieces, 2 onion wedges and 1 piece of squash.
3. Grill the kabobs 6 inches from the coals, turning once and basting with the marinade, until the pork is no longer pink and the vegetables are tender, 15 to 25 minutes. Heat any remaining marinade and pass as a dipping sauce. Use a small fork to slide the pork and vegetables onto serving plates.

HOW TO START THE FIRE
● Stack coals in a pyramid in the center of the grill.
● Douse coals with liquid starter. (Caution: *Never use kerosene or gasoline.*) Wait 2 minutes for the starter to soak in before igniting.
● Wait 30 to 45 minutes. Coals are ready when they're ash-gray around the edges, red hot in their centers.
● Spread coals with a long fork in a tight, even layer. Food should be completely underlined with hot coals.
● Adjust the grill rack to the proper cooking height. This will be at the point at which you can place your palm, very carefully, over it for *1* second without discomfort.
● To give grilled foods a special taste, sprinkle a handful of soaked aromatic wood chips over the glowing coals. You can find chips at home centers, mail-order concerns and gourmet shops.
Hickory: Gives a pronounced smoky taste to all foods. Use sparingly—it's strong!
Apple, cherry and alder: These add a mild, fruity flavor.
Mesquite: Derived from a shrub from the Southwest. Has a pungent taste. Use in small quantities for pork, beef and lamb or stronger-flavored fish, such as salmon.
CLEAN-UP
● To clean the grill, once it has cooled down: Use a stiff, narrow wire or special grill brush to scrape the rack and inside of the grill—no water needed!

Loin of Pork with Apple Glaze

Cooking the pork first in a microwave oven before grilling reduces the overall cooking time by half.

Makes 6 servings.

Nutrient Value Per Serving: 786 calories, 38 gm. protein, 44 gm. fat, 465 mg. sodium, 137 mg. cholesterol.

3 **pound rolled boned loin of pork, (about 5 pounds with bone)**
1 **tablespoon leaf sage, crumbled**
1 **teaspoon salt**
¼ **teaspoon pepper**
1 **medium-size onion, cut into small wedges**
1½ **cups apple jelly**
2 **tablespoons apple jack brandy**

1. Rub the pork with the sage, salt and pepper. Tuck the onion wedges into the loin.
2. Boil the apple jelly in a saucepan for 3 minutes. Stir in the apple jack. Remove from the heat.
3. Place the meat on the spit. Attach the spit to the electric rotisserie. Grill over hot coals, basting frequently with the apple glaze, for 2 to 3 hours or until a meat thermometer registers 170°.
4. Let stand for 15 minutes before carving. Serve with any remaining glaze.

MICROWAVE DIRECTIONS
650 Watt Variable Power Microwave Oven Directions: Prepare the loin of pork as directed in the above recipe. Place fat-side up in a shallow microwave-safe baking dish. Cover with wax paper. Microwave at half power for 15 minutes. Grill as directed in the recipe, 1 hour or until a meat thermometer registers 170°.

Pork Sausage Patties

Makes 20 patties.

Nutrient Value Per Pattie: 138 calories, 9 gm. protein, 11 gm. fat, 511 mg. sodium, 39 mg. cholesterol.

2 **pounds boneless fatty pork shoulder,**
   trimmed of connective tissue
½ **pound boneless pork loin**
1½ **tablespoons coarse salt**
1 **teaspoon leaf sage, crumbled**
½ **teaspoon anise seeds**
½ **teaspoon pepper**
3 **large cloves garlic, finely chopped**
¼ **cup ice water**

1. Cut the shoulder and loin into cubes. Grind the meats together in a food grinder fitted with a medium disc, or in a food processor, using an on-and-off motion.
2. Combine the ground meats, salt, sage, anise seeds, pepper, garlic and ice water in large bowl; mix until well blended.
3. Shape 1 tablespoon of the meat mixture into a small pattie. Sauté in a small skillet over medium heat for 3 to 4 minutes or until browned and cooked throughout. Taste the cooked sausage for seasoning. Add more seasoning to the remaining sausage mixture, if you wish; blend well. Shape sausage meat into 2½-inch patties.
4. Grill over moderately hot coals, turning once, for 8 to 10 minutes or until browned and cooked throughout.

◰ ▯ ◻ *Onion-Marinated Flank Steak*

Makes 8 servings.

Nutrient Value Per Serving: 238 calories, 27 gm. protein, 13 gm. fat, 593 mg. sodium, 81 mg. cholesterol.

1 **medium-size onion, coarsely chopped**
¼ **cup vegetable oil**
¼ **cup buttermilk OR: dairy sour cream**
2 **teaspoons salt**
2 **teaspoons ground ginger**
1½ **teaspoons ground cumin**

½ **teaspoon pepper**
1 **flank steak (about 2¼ pounds)**

1. Combine the onion and vegetable oil in the container of an electric blender. Cover; whirl until the onion is finely chopped. With the motor running, gradually pour in the buttermilk. Add the salt, ginger, cumin and pepper; whirl until blended.
2. Place the steak in a deep glass baking dish. Pour the marinade over; brush both sides of the meat. Cover; refrigerate, turning once, for 24 to 48 hours.
3. Grill the steak 6 inches from the coals, turning once and basting with the marinade, for 15 to 20 minutes for medium-rare. Transfer to a carving board. Let stand for 5 minutes.
4. Slice diagonally against the grain into thin slices.

▯ ◻ *Marinated Steak Sandwiches*

Makes 8 servings.

Nutrient Value Per Serving: 221 calories, 24 gm. protein, 12 gm. fat, 700 mg. sodium, 71 mg. cholesterol.

1 **skirt or flank steak (2 pounds), trimmed**
½ **cup soy sauce**
½ **cup vegetable oil**
¼ **cup dry sherry**
2 **cloves garlic, finely chopped**
2 **tablespoons grated fresh gingerroot**
   OR: 1 teaspoon ground ginger
1 **tablespoon grated orange rind**
   Assorted sliced breads, toasted
   Sliced onion and tomato (optional)

1. Place the skirt steak in a large glass baking dish.
2. Combine the soy sauce, oil, sherry, garlic, gingerroot and grated orange rind in a

small bowl; blend well. Pour over the steak. Let marinate, covered, for 3 hours, at room temperature, turning occasionally.

3. Grill the steak over hot coals, basting frequently with the marinade, for 3 to 5 minutes per side for medium-rare. Remove to a cutting board and let stand for 5 minutes.

4. Slice the steak thinly on the diagonal. Place slices of steak on toasted bread. Serve with sliced onion and tomato, if you wish.

BARBECUE SAFETY TIPS
● **Never cook food on a charcoal grill in your home or garage.**
● **Never use liquid starters once the fire is started. Flare-ups are dangerous.**
● **Keep a spray bottle filled with water near the barbecue to douse flare-ups. Never pour water on a charcoal fire.**

◼ *Barbecued Hamburgers*

Makes 8 servings.

Nutrient Value Per Serving: 173 calories, 17 gm. protein, 9 gm. fat, 178 mg. sodium, 55 mg. cholesterol.

2½ pounds ground round or chuck
⅓ cup Sherried Barbecue Sauce (recipe follows)
1 tablespoon Worcestershire sauce Pepper

1. Lightly combine the beef, Sherried Barbecue Sauce and Worcestershire in a large bowl. Shape into 8 equal patties. Press pepper into both sides of the patties.

2. Grill over hot coals, turning once, 8 to 10 minutes for rare.

◼◼ ◼ ◼ *Sherried Barbecue Sauce*

An easy barbecue sauce that takes just minutes to prepare. Try with chicken or other grilled meats.

Makes about 2 cups.

Nutrient Value Per ¼ Cup: 102 calories, 1 gm. protein, 1 gm. fat, 695 mg. sodium, 0 mg. cholesterol.

1 bottle (16 ounces) barbecue sauce with mushrooms
½ cup dry sherry
3 cloves garlic, finely chopped

Combine the barbecue sauce, sherry and garlic in a jar with a tight-fitting lid. Cover; shake well. Can be stored in the refrigerator for up to 1 month.

◼ *Marinated Boned Shoulder of Lamb*

If you can't find a boned lamb shoulder in the meat case in your supermarket, ask the butcher to prepare one for you.

Makes 12 servings.

Nutrient Value Per Serving: 156 calories, 20 gm. protein, 8 gm. fat, 139 mg. sodium, 75 mg. cholesterol.

1 3-pound boned shoulder of lamb (about 4½ pounds with bone), fat trimmed
1 cup dry white wine
3 cloves garlic, finely chopped
1 tablespoon leaf tarragon, crumbled
1 teaspoon salt
¼ teaspoon pepper

1. Starting with a long side, roll shoulder up. Tie securely at 1-inch intervals across the width; once or twice across the length.
2. Combine the wine, garlic, tarragon, salt and pepper in double plastic bags. Add the lamb. Fasten the bags securely. Place in a medium-size bowl. Marinate at room temperature for 3 hours, turning the bags once or twice.
3. Remove the lamb from the bags. Skewer on a spit. Place the spit in the electric rotisserie. Grill over hot coals for about 1½ hours or until a meat thermometer registers 130° for rare. Let stand for 15 minutes before carving.

MICROWAVE DIRECTIONS
650 Watt Variable Power Microwave Oven Directions: Trim, roll and marinate the lamb as directed in the above recipe. Place the lamb, fat-side up, on microwave-safe trivet in a microwave-safe baking dish. Cover loosely with wax paper. Microwave at half power for 15 minutes or until internal temperature reaches 100° to 110°. Grill as directed above for about 30 minutes or until a meat thermometer registers 130° for rare.

BE CHARCOAL WISE
● **If you barbecue often, save money by purchasing the largest bag of charcoal available.**
● **Store the charcoal tightly closed in a cool, dry place. Charcoal is difficult to light if it gets wet or absorbs a lot of moisture from the air.**

Barbecued Chicken

This recipe contains a quick and easy all-purpose barbecue sauce, which can be used on ribs, hamburgers or chops.

Makes 4 servings.

Nutrient Value Per Serving: 353 calories, 31 gm. protein, 19 gm. fat, 539 mg. sodium, 104 mg. cholesterol.

BARBECUE SAUCE
- **2   medium-size onions, sliced**
- **3   cloves garlic, finely chopped**
- **2   tablespoons vegetable oil**
- **¼   cup red wine vinegar**
- **¼   cup light brown sugar**
- **2   tablespoons spicy prepared mustard**
- **1   can (28 ounces) whole tomatoes**
- **1   teaspoon salt**
- **¼ to ½ teaspoon cayenne pepper**

- **4   chicken legs with thighs (about 2 pounds)**

1. Prepare the Barbecue Sauce: Sauté the onion and garlic in oil in a large heavy saucepan for 3 minutes or until the onion is softened. Stir in the vinegar, brown sugar and mustard. Bring to boiling. Stir in the tomatoes, salt and cayenne pepper. Boil, uncovered, stirring frequently, for 20 minutes. Cool.
2. Working in batches, spoon the sauce into the container of an electric blender. Cover; whirl until smooth.*
3. Combine 3 cups of the Barbecue Sauce with the chicken in a large bowl; mix well to coat the chicken. Carefully lift up the skin from the chicken; spread the sauce underneath the skin. Cover the bowl with plastic wrap. Refrigerate for 24 hours, turning the chicken occasionally.
4. Grill the chicken 8 inches from the coals, turning frequently with tongs and basting often with the sauce, until the chicken is browned and is no longer pink near the bone, about 45 to 60 minutes. Heat the remaining Barbecue Sauce and serve with the chicken.

*Note: This recipe makes about 4 cups of Barbecue Sauce. Kept refrigerated, the flavor will intensify after 2 to 3 days.

Chicken Legs with Lemon and Herbs

A piquantly flavored chicken for those who prefer a change-of-pace from its barbecue sauce cousin.

Makes 6 servings.

Nutrient Value Per Serving: 435 calories, 30 gm. protein, 33 gm. fat, 816 mg. sodium, 104 mg. cholesterol.

4   lemons, halved
½ cup vegetable oil
8   cloves garlic, finely chopped
4   teaspoons leaf basil, crumbled
2   teaspoons leaf thyme, crumbled
2   teaspoons salt
½ teaspoons crushed red pepper flakes
*   (optional)*
6   chicken legs with thighs
*   (about 3 pounds)*

1. Squeeze the juice from the lemons into a large bowl; reserve the lemon halves. Beat in the oil, garlic, basil, thyme, salt and red pepper flakes, if using. Add the lemon halves.
2. Cut each chicken leg at the joint. Add to the marinade; toss to coat. Lift up the skin from chicken; spread the marinade underneath. Refrigerate, covered, 24 hours, turning pieces once.
3. Grill the chicken 8 inches from the coals. turning frequently with tongs and basting with the marinade until the chicken is brown and is no longer pink near the bone, about 45 to 60 minutes. Transfer the chicken to a serving platter. Heat any remaining marinade and serve with the chicken.

Chicken Wings with Mustard Glaze

Makes 6 servings.

Nutrient Value Per Serving: 325 calories, 24 gm. protein, 23 gm. fat, 1544 mg. sodium, 72 mg. cholesterol.

½ cup Dijon-style mustard
¼ cup soy sauce
2   tablespoons olive oil
½ teaspoon ground ginger
4   cloves garlic, finely chopped
3   pounds chicken wings

1. Combine the mustard, soy sauce, oil, ginger and garlic in a large bowl. Add the chicken wings; mix to coat well. Cover; let stand at room temperature for 45 minutes.
2. Place the chicken wings in an oiled, hinged grill basket, or directly on the grill. Brush with the remaining mustard mixture. Grill over moderately hot coals, turning once, about 15 to 20 minutes or until no longer pink near the bone and the outside is crispy.

Chopped Chicken Cakes

Makes 6 servings.

Nutrient Value Per Serving: 204 calories, 27 gm. protein, 10 gm. fat, 297 mg. sodium, 94 mg. cholesterol.

3   whole chicken breasts (about 2 pounds),
*   boned and skinned*
⅓ cup heavy cream
½ teaspoon salt
¼ teaspoon pepper
2   tablespoons melted butter
*   Lemon wedges*

1. Coarsely chop the chicken breasts with a sharp knife, or in a food processor fitted with a metal chopping blade, with several quick on and off turns. Do not chop the meat too finely.
2. Combine the chicken, heavy cream, salt and pepper in a bowl. Form into 6 equal patties. Brush one side with butter.
3. Place the patties on the grill, buttered-side down, over moderately hot coals. Grill for 6 minutes. Brush with butter. Turn with a spatula; grill for 6 to 8 minutes longer. Serve with lemon wedges.

Stuffed Turkey Breast

A thin layer of savory mushroom stuffing coats the turkey under the skin. The collected pan drippings can be used to make a rich, delicious gravy.

Makes 8 servings.

Nutrient Value Per Serving: 449 calories, 66 gm. protein, 16 gm. fat, 359 mg. sodium, 197 mg. cholesterol.

1 whole turkey breast (6 pounds), thawed if frozen

MUSHROOM STUFFING
1 pound mushrooms
1 clove garlic, finely chopped
½ teaspoon salt
⅛ teaspoon pepper
½ cup (1 stick) unsalted butter
5 small onions
2 slices white bread, toasted
1 teapoon leaf thyme, crumbled
½ teaspoon liquid red pepper seasoning

1. Prepare a covered kettle barbecue grill with equal amounts of charcoal briquettes on two sides of the grill for indirect grilling.

Position a drip pan in the center under the grill rack.
2. Rinse the turkey breast under cold water; set aside to drain well.
3. Prepare the Mushroom Stuffing: Rinse the mushrooms under cold water; drain well. Chop finely. Heat the butter in a large skillet over low heat. Add the mushrooms, garlic, salt and pepper; sauté over low heat, stirring occasionally, 20 minutes or until the mixture becomes a thick paste.
4. Meanwhile, peel and quarter the onions. Place in the bowl of a food processor fitted with the metal chopping blade. Chop finely. Crumble the toasted bread into the processor bowl. Add the thyme and liquid red pepper seasoning. Reserve in the processor bowl.
5. When the mushroom mixture is thick, add to the other ingredients in the processor bowl. Process until the mixture is smooth and well blended.
6. Carefully spread a layer of stuffing under the skin to cover the turkey breast. Place the remaining stuffing in the neck cavity. Cover with the neck skin.
7. Place the breast, skin-side up, on the grill, in a roast holder over the drip pan. Cover the grill. Cook the turkey for 1½ to 2 hours or until the flesh is no longer pink and a meat thermomcter inserted in the thickest part registers 160°. Let stand 15 minutes before slicing.

Note: The juices and pan drippings in the drip pan can be used to make gravy.

◻ *Grilled Fish with Olive Sauce*

Makes 4 servings.

Nutrient Value Per Serving: 381 calories, 48 gm. protein, 20 gm. fat, 251 mg. sodium, 113 mg. cholesterol.

> 1 *teaspoon pepper*
> 1 *large or 2 small firm-fleshed fish steaks, such as halibut or haddock (about 2 pounds)*
> ¼ *cup olive oil*
> ½ *cup pitted black olives, coarsely chopped*
> 2 *teaspoons lemon juice*
> 1 *teaspoon finely chopped garlic*

1. Press the pepper into both sides of the fish. Brush with the oil.
2. Place the fish in an oiled, hinged grill basket or on a grill. Grill over moderately hot coals, turning once, for 10 minutes per measured 1 inch of thickness or until the fish flakes when pierced with a fork.
3. Meanwhile, combine the olives, lemon juice and garlic in a small bowl; stir to mix well.
4. Transfer the fish to a serving platter. Sprinkle with the olive mixture.

◻ *Fish Fillets Grilled in Lettuce*

Grilling a lean fish, such as sole, cod or flounder, wrapped in lettuce keeps the fish moist and lends a subtle flavor.

Makes 6 servings.

Nutrient Value Per Serving: 273 calories, 33 gm. protein, 13 gm. fat, 340 mg. sodium, 125 mg. cholesterol.

> 6 *tablespoons unsalted butter*
> 2 *tablespoons lemon juice*
> 2 *tablespoons chopped fresh dill*
>   *OR: 2 tablespoons chopped parsley*
> ½ *teaspoon salt*

> ¼ *teaspoon pepper*
> 1 *large head Romaine lettuce*
> 6 *thick fish fillets, such as sole, cod or flounder (2½ pounds), fresh or frozen, thawed*
>   *Lemon wedges (optional)*

1. Melt the butter in a small saucepan. Stir in the lemon juice, dill, salt and pepper.
2. Oil two hinged grill baskets. Line one side of each grill basket with overlapping Romaine leaves. Place 3 fillets in single layer over the leaves in each basket. Drizzle the fish with about one third of the seasoned butter. Cover the fillets completely with the leaves; make sure none of the fish is exposed. Close the baskets.
3. Grill the fish about 8 inches from the coals, turning the baskets once, until the fish is opaque-white at its thickest part, about 10 minutes.
4. Carefully open the baskets and remove the top layer of leaves. Transfer the fillets to a serving platter. Drizzle the fish with the remaining seasoned butter. Garnish with lemon wedges, if you wish.

▼ ◻ *Skewered Shrimp with Vegetables*

Makes 6 servings.

Nutrient Value Per Serving: 272 calories, 22 gm. protein, 13 gm. fat, 270 mg. sodium, 171 mg. cholesterol.

> 1 *large zucchini, halved lengthwise*
> 18 *large shrimp (about 1½ pounds), peeled and deveined*
> 18 *cherry tomatoes*
> 12 *strips bacon*
> ¼ *cup honey*
> 4 *teaspoons grated orange rind*

1. Slice each zucchini half into 6 equal pieces.

▶***Clockwise from bottom:*** **Skewered Shrimp with Vegetables (page 146), Brown Rice Salad (page 84) and Citrus Ice (page 268).**

2. Thread 3 shrimp onto each of 6 long skewers, alternating with 2 zucchini pieces, 3 cherry tomatoes and 2 strips of bacon; spiral the bacon around the shrimp and vegetables as you thread it.
3. Combine the honey and orange rind in a bowl. Brush over the skewers.
4. Grill 6 inches from the coals, turning often and basting frequently with the honey mixture, for 8 to 10 minutes or until the shrimp is bright pink, the bacon is golden and the vegetables are tender. Use a small fork to slide the shrimp and vegetables onto serving plates.

Butterfly Shrimp

Makes 6 servings.

Nutrient Value Per Serving: 156 calories, 22 gm. protein, 6 gm. fat, 175 mg. sodium, 194 mg. cholesterol.

2 pounds large shrimp, shelled, but with the tails left on, and deveined
1/3 cup lemon juice
2 tablespoons vegetable oil
3 cloves garlic, finely chopped

1. Split the shrimp almost in half, lengthwise; open like a book and gently flatten.
2. Combine the lemon juice, oil and garlic in a large bowl. Add the shrimp; toss to coat. Let stand for 15 minutes.
3. Thread 4 shrimp on each of 6 skewers, or place in an oiled hinged grill basket.
4. Grill over moderately hot coals, turning, for 3 to 5 minutes or until pinkish in color and lightly browned.

5. The Main Course: Pasta, Dried Beans, Eggs and Cheese and Vegetables

Sausage and
Linguine Torte
March 1984

*M*ore great main-course meals! Pasta, beans, eggs, cheese and vegetables are the main ingredients in these nutritious, money-saving dishes. Although these recipes are basically meatless, some of them use small amounts of meat.

Pasta is a firmly established mainstay of our diet, evolving from an unimaginative side dish of spaghetti to a cornucopia of exciting main dishes. Pasta is available in so many shapes and sizes that only imagination limits its uses. We have included delicious noodle casseroles, made two at a time so you may have one for dinner and freeze one for a make-ahead meal. So quick and easy are some of these dishes that the sauce can be prepared in the short time it takes to boil the water and cook the pasta.

Serve up top-of-the-line main dishes created with beans, eggs and cheese at bargain basement prices. When combined with fresh vegetables, tomatoes and sometimes meat, these are some of the tastiest and most economical dishes you'll ever make. They're nutritious too!

As interest in physical fitness and healthful eating grows, people are consuming more vegetable main dishes with small amounts of meat or no meat at all. The year-round availability of many fresh vegetables and the new varieties now available, provide the ingredients for great vegetable main-dishes like Stir-Fried Vegetables with Tofu and Spaghetti Squash with Picadillo.

Good appetite!

Pasta

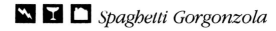

◀Sausage and Linguini Torte (page 154)

◼ 🍷 ▭ *Spaghetti Gorgonzola*

Makes 6 first-course or side-dish servings.

Nutrient Value Per Serving: 462 calories, 18 gm. protein, 16 gm. fat, 465 mg. sodium, 43 mg. cholesterol.

1   **medium-size sweet red pepper,
    cored, seeded and cut into thin strips**
3   **tablespoons butter or margarine**
4   **ounces Gorgonzola cheese, crumbled**
½   **cup milk**
⅓   **cup half and half**
1   **pound spaghetti, cooked following
    label directions and drained**
½   **cup freshly grated Parmesan cheese**

1. Sauté the red pepper in 1 tablespoon of the butter until crisp-tender. Reserve.

2. Combine the remaining 2 tablespoons butter, Gorgonzola cheese and milk in a small saucepan. Cook over low heat, stirring constantly, until the cheese melts and the sauce is smooth. Add the half and half; cook until the mixture is hot.

3. Pour over the hot, freshly cooked spaghetti in a warmed serving bowl; top with the reserved red pepper strips and Parmesan cheese. Toss gently to mix well. Pass extra Parmesan cheese and pepper, if you wish.

▼**Spaghetti Gorgonzola**

▲ Fettuccine with Fresh Tomato and Basil Sauce

Fettuccine with Fresh Tomato and Basil Sauce

Makes 6 first-course or side-dish servings.

Nutrient Value Per Serving: 358 calories, 11 gm. protein, 8 gm. fat, 7 mg. sodium, 71 mg. cholesterol.

4   *large ripe tomatoes, peeled, seeded*
    and coarsely chopped
1   *clove garlic, crushed*
1   *bunch fresh basil, stems removed*
    and leaves coarsely chopped
2   *tablespoons olive oil*
    Salt
    Pepper
1   *pound fettuccine, cooked following*
    label directions and drained
    Freshly grated Parmesan cheese
    (optional)

1. Combine the tomatoes, garlic, basil, olive oil, and salt and pepper to taste, in a large bowl. Stir to mix well.
2. Serve over the hot, freshly cooked fettuccine in a warmed serving bowl. Pass the Parmesan cheese and pepper, if you wish.

PASTA COOKING TIPS
● To cook pasta properly, at least 6 quarts of water should be used for each pound of pasta.
● Bring the water to boiling; then add 2 tablespoons of salt.
● Add the pasta gradually—in small amounts—to keep the water boiling. Stir frequently to keep the strands or pieces of pasta separate.
● Fresh pasta will cook much faster than dried pasta, in approximately 1 minute. For the proper cooking times for dried pasta, check the label directions.
● Do not rinse cooked hot pasta in cold water unless it is to be served cool in a pasta salad.

▲ **Rita's Carbonara**

◼◼◼ *Rita's Carbonara*

Makes 4 main-dish servings.

Nutrient Value Per Serving: 1176 calories, 35 gm. protein, 74 gm. fat, 852 mg. sodium, 412 gm. cholesterol.

- **½ pound bacon, diced**
- **3 cloves garlic, finely chopped**
- **4 eggs**
- **1 cup heavy cream**
- **1 cup freshly grated Parmesan cheese**
- **1 pound linguine, cooked following label directions and drained**

1. Cook the bacon in a large skillet, stirring often, until limp. Add the garlic; cook until the bacon is lightly browned (do not let bacon become too brown). Beat the eggs and cream together in a medium-size bowl until blended; pour into the skillet. Cook over medium heat, stirring constantly, until hot (do not overcook or the eggs will scramble). Remove from the heat; stir in the cheese.
2. Toss with the hot, freshly cooked linguine in a warmed serving bowl. Pass extra Parmesan cheese and pepper, if you wish.

◼◼ *Rotelle with Cheesy Pesto Sauce*

Makes 4 main-dish servings.

Nutrient Value Per Serving: 783 calories, 26 gm. protein, 36 gm. fat, 545 mg. sodium, 46 mg. cholesterol.

- **1 package (3 ounces) cream cheese, softened**
- **2 ounces blue cheese**
- **⅓ cup olive oil**
- **⅓ cup chopped fresh basil**
- **⅓ cup chopped fresh parsley**
- **2 cloves garlic, minced**
- **1 pound rotelle, cooked following label directions and drained**
- **¾ cup freshly grated Parmesan cheese**

1. Mix together the cream cheese and blue cheese in a small bowl until smooth. Gradually mix in the oil. Stir in the basil, parsley and garlic.
2. Spoon over the hot, freshly cooked rotelle in a warmed serving bowl; add the Parmesan cheese. Toss gently to mix well. Pass extra Parmesan cheese and pepper, if you wish.

▲ **Rotelle with Cheesy Pesto Sauce**

▲ **Elbow Twists with Vegetables**

Elbow Twists with Vegetables

Makes 6 first-course or side-dish servings.

Nutrient Value Per Serving: 543 calories, 19 gm. protein, 22 gm. fat, 419 mg. sodium, 37 mg. cholesterol.

- ¼ **cup (½ stick) butter or margarine**
- ¼ **cup vegetable oil**
- 4 **green onions, chopped**
- 2 **ounces thinly slice prosciutto, chopped**
- ¾ **pound zucchini, halved lengthwise and sliced**
- 6 **ounces mushrooms, halved or quartered**
- ⅓ **cup chicken broth**
- ⅓ **cup dry white wine**
- ½ **cup frozen peas**
- 1 **pound elbow twists, cooked following label directions and drained**
- 2 **small tomatoes, peeled and cut into wedges**
- ¾ **cup freshly grated Parmesan cheese**

1. Heat the butter and oil in a large skillet until the butter melts. Add the green onions and prosciutto; sauté for 2 minutes. Add the zucchini and mushrooms; sauté, stirring often, for 3 minutes. Add the chicken broth,

wine and peas; bring to boiling. Lower the heat; simmer for 5 minutes.
2. Pour over the hot, freshly cooked elbow twists in a warmed serving bowl; add the tomatoes and Parmesan cheese. Toss gently to mix well. Pass extra Parmesan cheese and pepper, if you wish.

Ziti with Fresh Broccoli Sauce

Makes 6 first-course or side-dish servings.

Nutrient Value Per Serving: 480 calories, 13 gm. protein, 20 gm. fat, 554 mg. sodium, 0 mg. cholesterol.

- 8 **cloves garlic, peeled and halved**
- ½ **cup vegetable oil, or as needed**
- 1 **bunch broccoli (about 1¼ pounds), trimmed and ends of stalks removed**
- 1½ **teaspoons salt**
- ¼ **teaspoon pepper**
- 1 **pound ziti, cooked following label directions and drained**
  Freshly grated Parmesan cheese (optional)

1. Place the garlic in a small heavy skillet; pour in enough of the oil to cover the garlic. Cook over medium heat until the garlic begins to brown.
2. Cook the broccoli in a small quantity of boiling water until tender; drain; cool slightly. Purée the broccoli in a blender or food processor. Add the garlic and cooking oil; whirl until the garlic is puréed. With the motor running, slowly pour in enough of the remaining oil until the broccoli mixture reaches a mayonnaise-like consistency. Stir in the salt and pepper.
3. Pour over the hot, freshly cooked ziti in a warmed serving bowl. Toss gently to mix well. Pass the Parmesan cheese and pepper, if you wish.

◼◼ 🍸 *Sausage and Linguine Torte*

Bake at 375° for 50 minutes.
Makes 8 servings.

Nutrient Value Per Serving: 590 calories, 29
gm. protein, 29 gm. fat, 831 mg. sodium, 175
mg. cholesterol.

1   pound linguine
2   tablespoons butter
1   pound Italian sausage, half sweet
*   and half hot*
1   tablespoon olive oil
1   medium-size onion, finely chopped
*   (½ cup)*
1   sweet green pepper, halved, seeded
*   and coarsely chopped*
3   teaspoons leaf oregano, crumbled
1   can (3.5 ounces) pitted ripe black olives,
*   sliced*
¼   cup finely chopped parsley
½   teaspoon salt
½   teaspoon pepper
3   eggs, slightly beaten
1   container (15 ounces) ricotta cheese
¼   cup grated Romano cheese
3   tomatoes (about 1¼ pounds),
*   thinly sliced*
1   cup shredded mozzarella cheese
*   (4 ounces)*
1   cup shredded Gruyère or Swiss cheese
*   (4 ounces)*
1   tablespoon grated Parmesan cheese
*   Tomato rose (optional)*
*   Fresh parsley (optional)*
*   Cream Sauce, optional (recipe follows)*

1. Cook the linguine in salted boiling water
   until just *al dente*, almost tender. Drain.
   Toss the hot linguine with the butter in a
   large bowl. Cover.
2. Preheat the oven to moderate (375°). Lightly
   grease and flour a 10-inch springform pan.
3. Remove and discard the sausage casings.
   Finely chop the sausage. Brown in the oil in

a large skillet, stirring, about 10 minutes.
Pour off the excess fat. Add the onion,
green pepper and 1 teaspoon oregano;
sauté for 5 minutes.

4. Combine the sausage mixture, olives,
   parsley, salt and pepper with the linguine;
   toss gently to combine. Whisk together the
   eggs, ricotta, remaining 2 teaspoons
   oregano and Romano cheese in a medium-
   size bowl until light and fluffy. Stir into the
   linguine mixture; toss gently to combine.
5. To assemble the torte for baking
   immediately: Press half the linguine mixture
   into the bottom of the prepared pan.
   Arrange half the sliced tomatoes over the
   linguine. Sprinkle with half the mozzarella
   and Gruyère cheese. Repeat the layers.
   Sprinkle the top with Parmesan. Cover the
   pan tightly with aluminum foil. (The torte
   can be refrigerated at this point for up to
   2 days.)
6. Bake in the preheated moderate oven (375°)
   for 50 minutes or until set. Remove the
   aluminum foil; bake for 5 minutes. Let stand
   for 10 minutes. Remove the pan and slice
   into wedges. Garnish with tomato rose and
   parsley, and serve with Cream Sauce, if
   you wish.

Cream Sauce

¼   cup (½ stick) butter or margarine
¼   cup all-purpose flour
1   cup milk
1   cup heavy cream
*   Pinch of ground nutmeg*
1   teaspoon salt
⅛   teaspoon white pepper
½   cup freshly grated Parmesan cheese

1. Melt the butter in a medium-size saucepan.
   Whisk in the flour. Gradually add the milk
   and cream, whisking constantly. Cook over

medium-high heat, stirring constantly until the sauce comes to a boil and is thick and smooth. Lower the heat; simmer, still stirring, for 2 to 3 minutes.

2. Remove the pan from the heat. Stir in nutmeg, salt and white pepper. Stir in the grated cheese until smooth. Keep warm until ready to serve.

MAKE TWO TORTES

You may double this recipe and make two tortes, one for now and one to freeze.

To Assemble the Torte for Freezing: **Omit the fresh tomato slices when layering; omit the sprinkling of Parmesan. Seal tightly with aluminum foil, date and freeze. When frozen, remove from the pan and wrap in aluminum foil.**

To Prepare for Serving: **Unwrap the torte and return to the original pan. Cover; let stand overnight in refrigerator. Uncover; arrange tomato slices on top (use only half the tomato slices); sprinkle with the Parmesan cheese. Cover tightly with aluminum foil. Bake in a preheated moderate oven (375°) for 1 hour and 45 minutes. Remove aluminum foil; bake for 15 minutes longer. Let stand for 10 minutes before slicing into wedges. Serve with Cream Sauce, if you wish.**

Sausage, Cheese and Noodle Pie

Bake at 375° for 30 minutes.
Makes 2 casseroles, 4 servings each.

Nutrient Value Per Serving: 672 calories, 31 gm. protein, 34 gm. fat, 1504 mg. sodium, 196 mg. cholesterol.

> 1 *package (16 ounces) lasagne noodles*
> 1 *large onion, finely chopped (1 cup)*
> 2 *carrots, pared and finely chopped (1 cup)*
> 2 *celery stalks, finely chopped (¾ cup)*
> 2 *cloves garlic, finely chopped*
> 2 *tablespoons butter or margarine*
> 5 *cups bottled home-style tomato or meatless spaghetti sauce*
> *OR: Homemade Tomato Sauce (recipe follows)*
> 1 *pound Italian sausage, half sweet, half hot, casings removed*
> 1 *container (15 ounces) ricotta cheese*
> ¾ *cup freshly grated Parmesan cheese*
> 2 *eggs, slightly beaten*
> 1 *teaspoon leaf oregano, crumbled*
> ½ *teaspoon leaf basil, crumbled*
> ½ *teaspoon salt*
> ¼ *teaspoon pepper*
> 1 *package (8 ounces) mozzarella cheese, thinly sliced*

1. Cook the lasagne in a large pot of lightly salted boiling water just until *al dente*, almost tender. Drain.

2. Line a 8 x 8 x 2-inch baking dish with heavy-duty aluminum foil, allowing enough overhang to cover the top of the filled casserole and tightly seal. Lightly grease a second similar size dish.

3. Preheat the oven to moderate (375°).

4. Sauté the onion, carrot, celery and garlic in butter in a large saucepan until crisp-tender, 5 to 10 minutes. Stir in the tomato sauce. Lower the heat; cook for 20 minutes, stirring occasionally.

5. Meanwhile, sauté the sausage meat in a large skillet over medium heat, stirring occasionally, until browned, about 15 minutes. Remove with a slotted spoon to paper toweling to drain; reserve.

6. Whisk together the ricotta cheese, ½ cup of the Parmesan cheese, eggs, oregano, basil, salt and pepper in a large bowl until the mixture is smooth and well blended.

7. Assemble the casseroles: Set aside 1 cup of the tomato sauce mixture. Spoon a few tablespoons of tomato sauce mixture into each casserole. Cutting noodles to fit, arrange a single layer of noodles over the bottom of each dish. Spread one quarter of the ricotta mixture over the noodles in each dish. Sprinkle each with one quarter of the sausage mixture. Arrange one quarter of the mozzarella slices over each. Spoon a few tablespoons of the tomato sauce mixture over all. Sprinkle each with 2 teaspoons of the remaining ¼ cup Parmesan. Repeat layers, ending with a top layer of noodles. Spoon ½ cup of the reserved tomato sauce over the top of each casserole. Sprinkle each with remaining Parmesan.

8. Bake the unlined casserole in the preheated moderate oven (375°) for 30 minutes. Let stand for 10 minutes before cutting into serving-size squares.

9. *To freeze foil-lined casserole:* Cover top with overhanging foil; seal tightly. Label, date and freeze. When frozen, remove the dish and return the foil package to the freezer. *To prepare for serving:* Remove the foil. Return the frozen noodle pie to the original baking dish. Cover; let stand in the refrigerator overnight. Bake, covered, in a preheated moderate oven (375°) for 1 hour and 15 minutes. Uncover; bake for 15 minutes longer. Let stand for 10 minutes before cutting into serving-size squares.

> **THIS RECIPE MAKES TWO CASSEROLES**
> Serve one casserole now and freeze the other.

Homemade Tomato Sauce

A quick and easy tomato sauce that can be easily doubled or tripled—it's great to make ahead and freeze. Use leftover sauce to spice up a meatloaf or stew, or to give an Italian flair to sautéed vegetables.

Makes about 5 cups.

Nutrient Value Per Cup: 180 calories, 4 gm. protein, 11 gm. fat, 960 mg. sodium, 0 mg. cholesterol.

1 large onion, chopped (1 cup)
1 clove garlic, finely chopped
¼ cup olive or vegetable oil
1 can (2 pounds, 3 ounces) Italian-style whole tomatoes with their liquid
1 can (6 ounces) tomato paste
2 teaspoons leaf basil, crumbled
1 teaspoon salt
Pinch of sugar
1 cup water

Sauté the onion and garlic in the oil in a large saucepan until tender. Stir in the tomatoes with their liquid, breaking up the tomatoes with a spoon, tomato paste, basil, salt, sugar and water. Bring to boiling; lower the heat; simmer, uncovered, stirring frequently, for 30 minutes or until the sauce has thickened.

Eggplant and Pork Casserole

THIS RECIPE MAKES TWO CASSEROLES
Serve one casserole now and freeze the other.

Bake at 400° for 25 minutes.
Makes 2 casseroles, 4 servings each.

Nutrient Value Per Serving: 442 calories, 20 gm. protein, 22 gm. fat, 1052 mg. sodium, 39 mg. cholesterol.

1 **package (8 ounces) elbow macaroni**
2 **eggplants (2 pounds), pared and cut lengthwise into ½-inch slices**
¼ **cup olive oil**
1 **medium-size onion, finely chopped**
2 **cloves garlic, finely chopped**
1 **pound lean ground pork**
2 **teaspoons leaf oregano, crumbled**
1 **teaspoon leaf basil, crumbled**
¾ **teaspoon salt**
¼ **teaspoon pepper**
5 **cups bottled home-style tomato or meatless spaghetti sauce OR: Homemade Tomato Sauce (page 156)**
⅓ **cup freshly grated Parmesan cheese**
1 **cup shredded Provolone**

1. Cook the macaroni in a large pot of lightly salted boiling water just until *al dente*, almost tender. Drain.
2. Line an 8 x 8 x 2-inch baking dish with heavy-duty aluminum foil, allowing enough overhang to cover the top of the filled casserole and tightly seal. Lightly grease a similar size dish.
3. Brush both sides of the eggplant slices lightly with oil. Place on an aluminum foil-lined broiler pan in a single layer. Broil until browned on each side. Lower the oven temperature to hot (400°).
4. Sauté the onion and garlic in 1 tablespoon of the olive oil in a large skillet for 3 minutes. Add the pork, oregano, basil, salt and pepper. Cook, stirring to break up the meat, until the pork is browned, for about 15 minutes. Drain off any excess fat. Reserve the pork mixture.
5. Combine 4 cups of the tomato sauce and the cooked macaroni in a large bowl; reserve the remaining cup of tomato sauce.
6. Assemble the casseroles: Spoon one quarter of the macaroni mixture into each prepared dish. Arrange one quarter of the eggplant slices on top. Sprinkle each with one quarter of the cooked pork mixture and one quarter of the Parmesan cheese. Repeat the layers. Spread the remaining 1 cup tomato sauce over the top of each casserole, dividing evenly. Sprinkle each with ½ cup shredded Provolone.
7. Bake the unlined casserole in the preheated hot oven (400°) for 25 minutes or until browned and bubbly. Let stand 10 minutes.
8. *To freeze foil-lined casserole:* Cover the top with the overhanging foil; seal tightly. Label, date and freeze. When frozen, remove the dish and return the foil package to the freezer. *To prepare for serving:* Remove the foil. Return the casserole to the original baking dish. Cover; let stand in the refrigerator overnight. Bake, covered, in a preheated moderate oven (375°) for 1 hour. Uncover, bake for 15 minutes longer. Let stand for 10 minutes.

◀◀◀ *Green Noodle and Beef Casserole*

Bake at 350° for 25 minutes.
Makes 6 individual casseroles.

Nutrient Value Per Serving: 973 calories, 40 gm. protein, 59 gm. fat, 1234 mg. sodium, 250 mg. cholesterol.

> *1   package (16 ounces) green fettuccine*
> *½   pound mushrooms, thinly sliced*
> *8   tablespoons (1 stick) butter*
> *1   pound lean ground beef*
> *1   medium-size onion, finely chopped*
> *2   cloves garlic, finely chopped*
> *3   cups bottled home-style tomato or meatless spaghetti sauce OR: Homemade Tomato Sauce (page 156)*
> *1   cup beef broth*
> *2   teaspoons leaf oregano, crumbled*
> *1   teaspoon leaf basil, crumbled*
> *½   teaspoon salt*
> *¼   teaspoon pepper*
> *1   container (15 ounces) ricotta cheese*
> *1   cup heavy cream*
> *½   cup freshly grated Romano cheese*
> *¼   cup freshly grated Parmesan cheese*

1. Cook the fettuccine in a large pot of lightly salted boiling water just until *al dente,* almost tender. Drain.
2. Preheat the oven to moderate (350°). Lightly grease 6 individual (about 2 cups each) ovenproof casseroles.
3. Sauté the mushrooms in 4 tablespoons of the butter in a large skillet for about 5 minutes or until golden. Remove with a slotted spoon; reserve.
4. Sauté the beef, onion and garlic in the same skillet, stirring to break up the meat, until the beef is browned, 10 to 15 minutes. Add the tomato sauce, broth, oregano, basil, salt and pepper. Bring to boiling; lower the heat; simmer gently, stirring occasionally, for 10 minutes.

5. Melt the remaining 4 tablespoons butter in a small saucepan. Whisk together the melted butter, ricotta, heavy cream, ¼ cup of the Romano cheese and the Parmesan cheese in a large bowl; fold in the cooked fettuccine. Add the beef mixture and the reserved sautéed mushrooms; toss gently to combine.
6. Divide the fettuccine mixture evenly among the 6 prepared casseroles. Sprinkle each with the remaining ¼ cup Romano cheese, dividing it evenly. Cover tightly with aluminum foil.
7. To serve immediately: Bake the covered casseroles in the preheated moderate oven (350°) for 20 minutes. Uncover; bake for 5 minutes longer.
8. *To freeze:* Label, date and freeze the unbaked tightly covered casseroles. *To prepare for serving:* Bake the covered frozen casseroles in a preheated moderate oven (375°) for 1 hour and 15 minutes or until hot and bubbly. Remove the foil; bake 5 minutes longer.

◥ ☐ *Pasta Niçoise*

Makes 4 servings.

Nutrient Value Per Serving: 612 calories, 28 gm. protein, 23 gm. fat, 639 mg. sodium, 60 mg. cholesterol.

> *8   cups cooked spaghetti twists or other pasta shapes*
> *½   cup Lemon Vinaigrette Dressing (recipe follows)*
> *2   cloves garlic, finely chopped*
> *1   small zucchini, sliced*
> *¼   pound green beans, trimmed*
> *1   can (4⅜ ounces) sardines*
> *1   can (7 ounces) solid white tuna packed in water, drained and flaked*
> *1   can (3.5 ounces) pitted black olives, drained*
> *1   basket cherry tomatoes*

1. Place the pasta in a large serving platter. Combine the dressing and garlic in a small bowl. Pour half of the dressing over the pasta; toss gently to coat.
2. Arrange zucchini, beans, sardines, tuna, olives and tomatoes on the pasta. Drizzle the remaining dressing over all. Serve.

FOR COOKED VEGETABLES
If you prefer less crunchy zucchini and green beans, cook them in boiling water, until they are crisp-tender. Drain; then rinse under cold water.

Lemon Vinaigrette Dressing

Makes 3 cups.

Nutrient Value Per 2 Tablespoons: 123 calories, 0 gm. protein, 14 gm. fat, 70 mg. sodium, 0 mg. cholesterol.

1½ cups lemon juice
1½ cups vegetable oil
¾ teaspoon salt
½ teaspoon sugar
¼ teaspoon pepper

Combine the lemon juice, oil, salt, sugar and pepper in a 1-quart screw-top jar. Cover tightly; shake well to blend. Refrigerate until ready to use.

Dried Beans

Special Baked Beans

Small bowls of these beans, cold, make a wonderful snack. Refrigerate for up to 4 days, or freeze.

Bake at 300° for 3 hours.
Makes 12 large servings.

Nutrient Value Per Serving: 445 calories, 17 gm. protein, 1 gm. fat, 790 mg. sodium, 0 mg. cholesterol.

2 pounds dry navy beans (4 cups)
*   Water*
*   Ham bone*
2 cups sugar
½ cup molasses
1 tablespoon salt
1 teaspoon dry mustard
½ teaspoon ground ginger
¼ teaspoon pepper
1 cup catsup

1. Pick over the beans and rinse them under running water. Combine the beans and enough water to cover in a large saucepan or kettle. Cover the pan and bring to boiling over medium heat; boil gently for 2 minutes. Remove from the heat; let stand, covered, for 1 hour.
2. Add the ham bone to the saucepan; add additional water to cover the beans completely, if necessary. Return the beans to the heat; bring to boiling; lower the heat; cover and simmer for about 1½ hours or until the beans are tender but before the skins burst. Add more water as needed to keep the beans covered.
3. Preheat the oven to slow (300°).
4. Drain the beans, reserving the liquid. Turn the beans into a 4-quart bean pot or baking dish. Combine the sugar, molasses, salt,

mustard, ginger, pepper, catsup and 1 cup hot bean liquid. Stir into the beans. If necessary, add just enough hot bean liquid to cover the beans; cover.
5. Bake in the preheated slow oven (300°) for 2 hours. Uncover; bake 1 hour longer to brown the top.

Baked Beans and Apples

Serve with baked ham, brown bread, green salad and dessert.

Bake at 400° for 45 minutes.
Makes 6 servings.

Nutrient Value Per Serving: 305 calories, 11 gm. protein, 5 gm. fat, 678 mg. sodium, 10 mg. cholesterol.

1   medium-size apple, pared, halved, cored and coarsely chopped
1   large onion, coarsely chopped
2   tablespoons butter or margarine
2   jars (18 ounces each) brick-oven baked beans
¼ cup molasses
2   tablespoons catsup
1   teaspoon dry mustard

1. Preheat the oven to hot (400°).
2. Sauté the apple and onion in the butter in a medium-size skillet until tender, 5 minutes. Turn into a large bowl. Add the beans, molasses, catsup and mustard; mix lightly. Spoon the bean mixture into 6-cup casserole.
3. Bake in the preheated hot oven (400°) for 45 minutes or until bubbly.

BAKED BEANS AND APPLES MAIN DISH
Add 8 ounces cooked ham to the bean
mixture for a delicious main-dish variation.

Cassoulet Alsace

Bake at 425° for 10 minutes.
Makes 4 servings.

Nutrient Value Per Serving: 659 calories, 34 gm. protein, 36 gm. fat, 1542 mg. sodium, 81 mg. cholesterol.

4   thin pork chops, cut from the loin or center (¾ pound)
½ pound smoked sausage, sliced (kielbasa)
1   teaspoon minced garlic
1   small sweet green pepper, cored, seeded and cut into strips
1   teaspoon leaf thyme, crumbled
½ cup dry white wine
1   can (1 pound) pork and beans in tomato sauce
1   can (1 pound, 4 ounces) white kidney beans, drained
1   can (8 ounces) sliced carrots, drained

1. Preheat the oven to hot (425°).
2. Brown the pork chops and sausage in a large skillet in their own fat. Remove to a plate.
3. Add the garlic and pepper to the skillet; sauté over medium heat for 2 to 3 minutes; stir in the thyme and wine. Cook, stirring to lift up the browned-on pieces. Stir in the pork and beans, kidney beans and carrots. Bring to boiling. Remove from the heat.
4. Arrange the meat, beans, pepper strips and carrots in a shallow 6½ x 10-inch ovenproof casserole.
5. Bake in the preheated hot oven (425°) for 10 minutes or until bubbly.

▲ **Cassoulet Alsace**

◻ *Nacho Gigante*

A Mexican pizza!

Bake tortillas at 375° for 5 minutes; broil for 2 minutes.
Makes 8 servings.

Nutrient Value Per Serving: 386 calories, 16 gm. protein, 17 gm. fat, 494 mg. sodium, 30 mg. (estimated value) cholesterol.

½ **pound dried kidney beans**
6 **cups water**
4 **tablespoons vegetable oil**
1 **teaspoon salt**
1 **can (4 ounces) green chilies, drained, seeded and chopped**
6 **(8-inch) flour tortillas**
1 **can (4 ounces) taco sauce (½ cup)**
½ **pound Monterey Jack cheese, shredded (2 cups)**

1. Wash and sort the beans. Soak overnight in cold water to cover in a large bowl. Or, use the Quick Method: Bring the beans to boiling; boil 2 minutes; cover; let stand for 1 hour. Continue with step 2 of the recipe.

2. Drain the beans; combine with the 6 cups water in a large kettle or Dutch oven. Bring to boiling; lower the heat; simmer for 1 hour or until beans are tender. Drain the beans, reserving ¼ cup of the cooking water.

3. Heat 2 tablespoons of the oil in a skillet over medium heat. Add the beans; mash with a potato masher or fork. Add the reserved liquid and salt. Continue cooking until the liquid is absorbed. Remove the beans from the heat. Blend in half of the chopped chilies.

4. Brush the tortillas with the remaining 2 tablespoons of oil. Prick all over with a fork. Place directly on the oven rack.

5. Bake in the moderate oven (375°) for 5 minutes or until tortillas begin to crisp. Arrange tortillas, overlapping, in a 14-inch pizza pan or rectangular baking pan.

6. Spread the beans over the tortillas. Pour the taco sauce on top of beans. Sprinkle the cheese on top; sprinkle with the remaining chilies. Broil for 2 minutes or until the cheese has melted.

▲ Marinated Black-Eyed Peas

◀◀◀ ⬠ *Marinated Black-Eyed Peas*

To turn this side dish into a main dish, add 1½ cups cubed cooked ham and 1½ cups cubed cheese.

Makes 12 side-dish servings.

Nutrient Value Per Serving: 247 calories, 9 gm. protein, 13 gm. fat, 18 mg. sodium, 0 mg. cholesterol.

- ⅔ *cup vegetable oil*
- 5 *tablespoons red wine vinegar*
- 2 *medium-size onions, chopped (1 cup)*
- 1 *cup chopped parsley*
- 2 *large cloves garlic, crushed*
- 2 *teaspoons leaf basil, crumbled*
- 1 *teaspoon leaf oregano, crumbled*
- ½ *teaspoon dry mustard*
- ½ *teaspoon black pepper*
  Pinch of red pepper flakes
- 1 *package (1 pound) black-eyed peas, picked over and rinsed*
  Sweet green pepper rings for garnish (½ inch thick)

1. Combine the vegetable oil, red wine vinegar, onion, parsley, garlic, basil, oregano, mustard, black pepper and red pepper flakes in a 4-cup measure. Reserve.
2. Cook the peas following label directions. Drain the peas in a colander. Place the peas in a large bowl. Mix the dressing; pour over the warm peas. Toss gently to mix. Cover with plastic wrap; refrigerate. Marinate overnight, tossing the peas once.
3. Line a large platter or serving bowl with green pepper rings. Mound the marinated peas in the center.

TO CLEAN BLACK-EYED PEAS
Spread the peas on a tray or a large plate. Remove and discard bits of foreign matter or broken and discolored peas. Place the peas in a large bowl of water. Immature beans will have shrunk within their skins and may float to the surface. Remove these along with any loose skins. Rinse the peas in a large colander.

Top-of-the-Stove Beans with Italian Sausage

Makes 8 servings.

Nutrient Value Per Serving: 500 calories, 21 gm. protein, 18 gm. fat, 1375 mg. sodium, 35 mg. cholesterol.

- ½ **pound sweet Italian sausage**
- ½ **pound hot Italian sausage**
- 1 **tablespoon vegetable oil**
- 1¾ **cups chopped onion**
- ¾ **pound mushrooms, sliced (3 cups)**
- 3 **cans (16 ounces each) pork and beans in tomato sauce**
- ⅓ **cup tomato juice**
- 1 **teaspoon leaf oregano, crumbled**
- 1 **teaspoon salt**
- ⅛ **teaspoon red pepper flakes**
- 4 **cups hot cooked rice**

1. Cook the sausages in the oil in a large skillet until the sausages are brown and no pink remains, about 20 minutes. Remove with a slotted spoon to a Dutch oven or a large heavy saucepan.
2. Pour off the fat from the skillet. Return 2 tablespoons of fat to the skillet. Sauté the onions and mushrooms until tender, about 3 minutes. Add the onion mixture to the sausages.
3. Add the beans, tomato juice, oregano, salt and pepper to the sausages. Bring to boiling; lower the heat; cover; simmer for 15 minutes. Serve over hot cooked rice.

Eggs and Cheese

ABOUT OMELET SKILLETS

- Any skillet with a rounded bottom, whether it's heavy aluminum, cast iron or stainless steel, can be used to make omelets. If it is your everyday skillet you plan to use, *do* clean it thoroughly with a soapy steel-wool pad, then rinse and dry. To season (which you must do each time), heat a ¼-inch depth of vegetable oil in the skillet over low heat for 10 minutes; pour off the oil, and wipe out the skillet.
- You can skip the cleaning process if you use a skillet solely for making omelets or a skillet with a nonstick surface. You need to season only the first time you use the skillet. Simply wipe off—not wash—after each use and it'll be ready for the next omelet.
- Omelets will stick to the skillet if you let the butter brown. If this happens, pour off the browned butter, wipe out the skillet with paper toweling and start again.

EGG STORAGE

- Store eggs in the refrigerator as soon as you get them home—large ends up. This keeps the yolk centered.
- Keep them away from strong-smelling foods, as the eggshell is porous and will absorb odors.
- If you're in doubt about an egg's freshness, break it into a saucer. A super-fresh egg has a cloudy white and a high-standing yolk. Older eggs will have less cloudy whites and flatter yolks. A "bad" egg will have a definite odor or "chemical" smell when sniffed.

▨ ▼ ▢ *Basic French Omelet*

Makes 1 serving.

Nutrient Value Per Serving: 238 calories, 18 gm. protein, 17 gm. fat, 744 mg. sodium, 822 mg. cholesterol.

> *3 eggs*
> *1 tablespoon water*
> *¼ teaspoon salt*
> *⅛ teaspoon white pepper*
> *Omelet filling (recipes follow)*
> *Parsley or celery leaves (optional)*

1. Beat the eggs, water, salt and pepper together in a medium-size bowl, using a fork.

2. Heat a 9- or 10-inch heavy seasoned skillet with a rounded bottom and sloping sides, or a heavy aluminum pan, with or without a nonstick surface. Swirl a tablespoon of butter over the entire surface of the pan.

3. When the butter stops foaming, pour the egg mixture into the skillet.

4. Cook over moderately high heat until the bottom is set. Using a heatproof spatula, move the cooked mixture to the center and allow the uncooked mixture to flow into the bottom of the pan. When cooked, the omelet should be barely brown on the bottom, soft and moist in the center.

5. Spoon the filling down the center of the omelet.

6. Using the spatula, and starting from the handle side, fold one third of the omelet over the center.

7. With a heated serving plate in one hand, grasp the skillet in the other, palm up and tilt so the omelet rolls over onto the plate. Garnish with parsley or celery leaves, if you wish.

▲ **Sausage and Pepper Omelet**

⚡ *Sausage and Pepper Filling*

Makes 1½ cups filling (enough for 2 French Omelets).

Nutrient Value Per Serving: 290 calories, 7 gm. protein, 24 gm. fat, 532 mg. sodium, 43 mg. cholesterol.

> 2 *hot or sweet Italian sausages or a combination (about 6 ounces)*
> 1 *small sweet green pepper, halved, seeded and thinly sliced (½ cup)*
> 1 *small sweet red pepper, halved, seeded and thinly sliced (½ cup)*
> 1 *medium-size onion, cut into thin wedges*
> ¼ *teaspoon leaf oregano, crumbled*
> ¼ *teaspoon leaf basil, crumbled*

1. Remove the casings from the sausages. Crumble into a large skillet. Cook slowly until the sausage is lightly browned; remove the sausage with a slotted spoon to paper toweling. Pour the sausage fat into a small cup; return 2 tablespoons to the skillet.
2. Sauté the peppers and onion in the fat in the skillet just until tender, for about 5 minutes. Add the cooked sausage, oregano and basil; toss gently to mix. Lower the heat; cover; keep warm.
3. Fill as directed in the French Omelet recipe.

▨ *Potato and Bacon Filling*

Makes 2 cups filling (enough for 2 French Omelets).

Nutrient Value Per Serving: 378 calories, 9 gm. protein, 28 gm. fat, 21 mg. sodium, 37 mg. cholesterol.

- **4 slices bacon**
- **2 medium-size cooked potatoes, peeled and diced**
- **2 tablespoons chopped green onion**
- **2 tablespoons chopped parsley**
- **2 tablespoons shredded Cheddar cheese**

1. Cook the bacon in a large skillet until crisp; drain on paper toweling; crumble and reserve.
2. Pour the bacon fat into a small cup; return 3 tablespoons fat to the skillet.
3. Sauté the potatoes and green onion in the fat until heated throughly. Lower the heat; cover; keep warm.
4. Spoon half the filling onto each French Omelet; sprinkle each with half the parsley and cheese just before folding.

▨ *Vegetable Filling*

Makes 2 cups filling (enough for 2 French Omelets).

Nutrient Value Per Serving: 254 calories, 4 gm. protein, 22 mg. fat, 701 mg. sodium, 0 mg. cholesterol.

- **1 large carrot, pared and cut into thin strips (1 cup)**
- **1 teaspoon chopped fresh gingerroot OR: ½ teaspoon ground ginger**
- **3 tablespoons sunflower or vegetable oil**
- **1 medium-size zucchini, cut into thin strips (1 cup)**
- **¼ pound mushrooms, sliced (1 cup)**
- **½ cup fresh bean sprouts OR: drained canned**
- **1 tablespoon soy sauce**
- **¼ teaspoon cornstarch**

1. Sauté the carrots and fresh gingerroot (ground, if you are using it, is added later) in oil in a large skillet for 3 minutes; add the zucchini and mushrooms. Stir-fry until the vegetables are tender, about 5 minutes. Add the bean sprouts; cook for 1 minute.
2. Combine the soy sauce, cornstarch and ground ginger, if using, in a small cup. Pour over the vegetable mixture, tossing with the vegetables until coated. Lower the heat; cover; keep warm.
3. Fill as directed in the French Omelet recipe.

▯ ▢ *Puffy Spanish Omelet*

Bake at 350° for 10 minutes.
Makes 4 servings.

Nutrient Value Per Serving: 373 calories, 13 gm. protein, 31 gm. fat, 804 mg. sodium, 466 mg. cholesterol.

- **6 eggs, separated**
- **6 tablespoons milk or water**
- **1 tablespoon salt**
- **¼ teaspoon pepper**
- **2 tablespoons butter or margarine**
- **1 medium-size onion, sliced**
- **1 small sweet green pepper, seeded and diced (½ cup)**
- **2 tablespoons butter**
- **¾ teaspoon leaf marjoram, crumbled**
- **⅛ teaspoon cayenne**
- **3 medium-size tomatoes, peeled and coarsely chopped**
- **1 cup dairy sour cream**
- **2 tablespoons snipped fresh chives**

1. Beat the egg whites until stiff in a large bowl with an electric mixer.
2. Beat the egg yolks slightly in a medium-size bowl with the same mixer. Add the milk, ½ teaspoon of the salt and pepper, beating until thick. Fold into the egg white mixture thoroughly.
3. Preheat the oven to moderate (350°). Heat a 10-inch skillet or omelet pan with an ovenproof handle. Swirl 2 tablespoons of the butter over the bottom and sides of the skillet.
4. Pour in the egg mixture. Cook over low heat for 5 minutes or until the mixture is set on the bottom and is golden brown.
5. Bake in the preheated moderate oven (350°) for 10 minutes or until puffy and golden on the top.
6. While the omelet is baking, sauté the onion and green pepper in the remaining 2 tablespoons butter in a large skillet until soft, about 5 minutes. Add the marjoram, remaining salt, cayenne and tomatoes; cook just until hot.
7. Remove the omelet from the oven. Loosen around the edge with a knife; cut a gash with a knife down the center of the omelet; place the tomato mixture down one side of omelet; fold over with a pancake turner or large spatula; turn onto a heated serving platter. Top with sour cream and chives. Serve at once.

◤ Onion-Tomato Frittata

Bake at 350° for 10 minutes.
Makes 6 servings.

Nutrient Value Per Serving: 325 calories, 18 gm. protein, 23 gm. fat, 655 mg. sodium, 475 mg. cholesterol.

  2 large onions, sliced
  3 tablespoons plus 1 teaspoon olive oil
  ½ cup diced fresh or frozen sweet green pepper
 10 eggs, at room temperature
  ⅓ cup grated Parmesan cheese
  1 teaspoon salt
  ¼ teaspoon pepper
  ½ cup fresh bread crumbs
  ½ teaspoon leaf oregano, crumbled
  1 clove garlic, finely chopped
  3 to 4 ripe tomatoes, thinly sliced
  4 ounces thinly sliced mozzarella or Provolone cheese

1. Sauté the onions in the 3 tablespoons oil in a 10-inch skillet with a heat-resistant handle until tender but not brown, 5 minutes; sauté the green pepper for 1 minute.
2. Meanwhile, beat the eggs, ¼ cup of the Parmesan cheese, salt and pepper in a large bowl just until blended. Add to the skillet. Cook over medium-low heat, lifting the bottom with a spatula as eggs set, for about 3 minutes.
3. Bake in a preheated moderate oven (350°), uncovered for 10 minutes or until the top is almost set.
4. Mix the crumbs, remaining Parmesan, oregano, garlic and 1 teaspoon oil.
5. Remove the skillet from the oven. Turn the oven to broil. Arrange the tomato and cheese slices overlapping on top of the frittata. Sprinkle with the crumb mixture.
6. Broil 4 inches from the heat until the cheese melts and the crumbs are golden brown, 2 to 4 minutes. Cut into wedges to serve.

▲ Potato and Chorizo Frittata

⚡ ▱ *Potato and Chorizo Frittata*

Bake at 350° for 10 minutes.
Makes 6 servings.

Nutrient Value Per Serving: 324 calories, 16 gm. protein, 26 gm. fat, 900 mg. sodium, 321 mg. cholesterol.

- **½ pound chorizo (Spanish sausage) or smoked garlic sausage, sliced (1 cup)**
- **1 can (8¼ ounces) whole potatoes, drained and sliced**
- **1 medium-size sweet green pepper, halved, seeded and chopped (½ cup)**
- **1 medium-size onion, chopped (½ cup)**
- **6 eggs**
- **3 tablespoons milk**
- **½ teaspoon salt**
- **¼ teaspoon pepper**
- **¼ teaspoon leaf basil, crumbled**
- **¼ cup (½ stick) butter**
- **1 tablespoon chopped parsley**

1. Preheat the oven to moderate (350°). Reserve ½ cup sliced sausage and ½ cup sliced potatoes for garnish; chop the remaining sausage and potatoes separately.

2. Sauté the chopped sausage in an 8-inch skillet with a heatproof handle over very low heat until some of the fat is rendered, about 1 minute. Add the green pepper and onion; cook until the vegetables are soft, about 5 minutes. Remove sausage mixture with slotted spoon to a small bowl; set aside.

3. Beat the eggs with the milk, salt, pepper and basil in a medium-size bowl until foamy.

4. Swirl the butter over the bottom and side of skillet over very low heat. Pour in the egg mixture. Cook over very low heat, stirring with the flat side of a fork and shaking the pan back and forth, until the frittata is firm on the bottom and almost set on top. Remove from the heat. Spread the reserved chopped sausage mixture and chopped potatoes over the top. Arrange the reserved slices of sausage and potato over all.

5. Bake in the preheated moderate oven (350°) for 10 minutes or until the eggs are set and the chorizo slices are heated through. Sprinkle with parsley just before serving. Cut into wedges.

⬛ ⬜ *Tomato-Broccoli Quiche*

Bake at 375° for 60 minutes.
Makes 8 main dish servings or 20 appetizer servings.

Nutrient Value Per Main-Dish Serving: 371 calories, 16 gm. protein, 24 gm. fat, 740 mg. sodium, 114 mg. cholesterol.

½   **package piecrust mix**
4   **cups chopped fresh broccoli**

1   **medium-size onion, chopped (½ cup)**
2   **tablespoons butter**
2   **tablespoons water**
1   **cup light cream**
2   **eggs**
½   **cup shredded Swiss cheese (2 ounces)**
1   **teaspoon salt**
⅛   **teaspoon pepper**
¼   **teaspoon ground nutmeg**
1   **cup freshly grated Parmesan cheese**
½   **cup packaged unseasoned bread crumbs**
3   **medium-size firm tomatoes, thinly sliced**

1. Prepare the piecrust mix following label directions, or make your own single-crust pastry recipe. Roll out to a 15 x 11-inch rectangle on a lightly floured surface; fit into an 11 x 7-inch baking dish. Turn edges under and press to sides.

2. Cook broccoli and onion, covered, in a large skillet over medium heat with the butter and water just until tender, about 5 minutes. Remove from the heat.

3. Beat the cream and eggs together in a medium-size bowl; stir in the Swiss cheese, salt, pepper and nutmeg. Add the broccoli mixture.

4. Combine the Parmesan cheese and bread crumbs in a small bowl. Preheat the oven to moderate (375°).

5. To assemble quiche: Sprinkle ⅓ cup of the Parmesan mixture on the bottom of the crust. Dip the tomato slices on both sides in the Parmesan cheese mixture and arrange half in a layer in the crust. Pour the broccoli mixture over the tomatoes. Arrange the remaining tomatoes, overlapping, along the long edges of the quiche. Sprinkle any remaining cheese mixture on top.

6. Bake in the preheated moderate oven (375°) for 60 minutes or until the top is puffy and a knife comes out clean when inserted near the center. Cool 20 minutes before cutting.

◘ *Sloppy Joe Quiche*

A tangy yogurt and cream custard tops the juicy Sloppy Joe filling. The filling and the pastry can be made the day ahead.

Bake crust at 400° for 15 minutes; bake pie at 375° for 30 to 40 minutes.
Makes 6 servings.

Nutrient Value Per Serving: 542 calories, 19 gm. protein, 39 gm. fat, 765 mg. sodium, 201 mg. cholesterol.

1   *Pastry Shell (recipe follows)**
1   *cup finely chopped onion (1 large onion)*
1   *cup finely chopped celery*
1   *tablespoon vegetable oil*
2   *cloves garlic, finely chopped*
3   *teaspoons paprika*
1   *teaspoon leaf basil, crumbled*
½   *teaspoon leaf thyme, crumbled*
½   *pound lean ground beef*
1   *can (8 ounces) tomato sauce*
1   *tablespoon cider vinegar*
½   *teaspoon salt*
½   *teaspoon pepper*
1   *cup coarsely shredded Cheddar cheese (4 ounces)*
2   *eggs*
¾   *cup heavy cream*
½   *cup plain yogurt*

1. Prepare the Pastry Shell dough at least 1 hour ahead or the day before.
2. Preheat the oven to hot (400°).
3. Roll out the chilled dough on a lightly floured surface to a 12-inch round. Fit into a 9-inch pie plate. Fold the edge under to make a stand-up edge; flute. Line the crust with aluminum foil. Fill with pie weights or dried beans.
4. Bake in the preheated hot oven (400°) for 10 minutes. Remove the foil and weights. Bake for 5 minutes longer. Remove from the oven. If any bubbles have formed, flatten them gently with a wooden spoon.

Lower the oven temperature to moderate (375°).

5. Sauté the onion and celery in oil in a medium-size skillet, stirring, 5 minutes. Add the garlic, 2 teaspoons of the paprika, basil and thyme. Cook for 1 minute. Crumble the ground beef into the skillet; cook until no longer pink. Drain off the excess fat. Add the tomato sauce. Simmer, stirring occasionally, for 10 minutes. Stir in the vinegar, salt and pepper.
6. Sprinkle the cheese over the bottom crust. Spoon the meat mixture over evenly.
7. Combine the eggs, cream and yogurt in a medium-size bowl. Beat with a wire whisk until smooth. Pour gently over the meat filling in the crust.
8. Bake the quiche on a cookie sheet in the preheated moderate oven (375°) for 30 to 40 minutes or until set and golden.
9. Cool on a wire rack 30 minutes before cutting. Sprinkle the top with the remaining paprika. Or, if you wish, cut a wax paper stencil and sprinkle paprika over it to make a design on the quiche; do not let the wax paper touch the surface of the quiche.

*Note: A piecrust mix may be substituted for the Pastry Shell. Follow package directions for a single crust 9-inch pie.

Pastry Shell: Stir together 1¼ cups *un*sifted all-purpose flour and ½ teaspoon salt in a medium-size bowl. Cut in ¼ cup chilled unsalted butter and 2 tablespoons chilled vegetable shortening with pastry blender until the mixture resembles coarse crumbs. Drizzle 3 tablespoons ice water over the mixture, tossing lightly with a fork just until dough forms a ball. Flatten into a 5-inch round. Wrap tightly. Refrigerate 1 hour or overnight.

MICROWAVE DIRECTIONS
650 Watt Variable Power Microwave Oven
Ingredient Changes: Reduce vegetable oil from 1 tablespoon to 1 teaspoon, tomato sauce from 1 can to ⅔ cup and vinegar from 1 tablespoon to 2 teaspoons.

Directions: Prepare a 9-inch pastry shell in a microwave-safe pie plate, from half of an 11-ounce box piecrust mix, following label directions. Chill. Prick bottom and sides with fork. Microwave, uncovered, at full power for 4 minutes. Combine the 1 teaspoon oil, onion, celery, garlic and crumbled beef in an 11¾ x 7½ x 1¾-inch microwave-safe baking dish. Cover. Microwave at full power 6 minutes, rotating a half turn after 3 minutes. Drain the meat mixture well. Stir in 2 teaspoons paprika, basil, thyme, the ⅔ cup tomato sauce, the 2 teaspoons vinegar and salt and pepper. Assemble the quiche as directed in steps above. Microwave, uncovered, at full power about 14 minutes, rotating a quarter turn twice. The center should be almost set. Let stand at room temperature 15 minutes to set center of quiche.

Nutrient Value Per Serving: 487 calories, 18 gm. protein, 36 gm. fat, 709 mg. sodium, 185 mg. cholesterol.

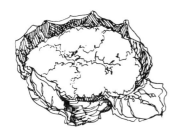

🍸 *Cheese and Wine Fondue*

One of the simplest of the wine recipes to serve at a small, informal gathering.

Makes 6 servings.

Nutrient Value Per Serving: 389 calories, 27 gm. protein, 26 gm. fat, 296 mg. sodium, 87 mg. cholesterol.

1¼ pounds Jarlsberg or Swiss cheese, shredded (5 cups)
1 tablespoon cornstarch
½ teaspoon dry mustard
½ teaspoon ground coriander
½ teaspoon caraway seeds, crushed
⅛ teaspoon salt
2 cups dry white wine
1 clove garlic
2 whole cloves
2 tablespoons aquavit, kirsch or vodka
1 loaf Italian or rye bread
   Blanched vegetables, such as firm broccoli and cauliflower flowerets
   Cubed cooked chicken breast, ham, frankfurters, etc.

1. Toss the shredded cheese with the cornstarch, mustard, coriander, caraway seeds and salt in a large bowl.
2. Heat the wine with the garlic and cloves in a fondue dish or flameproof casserole until bubbles start to rise from the bottom. Remove the garlic and cloves with a slotted spoon.
3. Gradually add the cheese mixture, stirring constantly with a wooden spoon after each addition, until the cheese melts. Do not boil. Stir in the aquavit, kirsch or vodka. Set the dish over an alcohol burner to keep hot while serving.
4. Cut the bread into bite-size pieces. (Mix 2 or 3 different kinds of breads.) Place in a basket or on serving plates. Arrange the blanched vegetables and cooked meat on plates. Set out fondue or regular forks so everyone can spear a piece of bread, vegetable or meat, then twirl it into hot cheese sauce.

SAVE LEFTOVER WINE
When you have leftover wine, cork it tightly and store it in the refrigerator to be used in cooking within a week or two. Any wine that has turned to vinegar is great for marinades and salad dressings, so don't throw it out!

◩ *Cheese Waffles with Ratatouille*

Bake ratatouille at 400° for 35 minutes.
Makes 7 servings.

Nutrient Value Per Serving: 533 calories, 15 gm.
protein, 34 gm. fat, 669 mg. sodium, 107 mg.
cholesterol.

RATATOUILLE

- 1 *medium-size onion, sliced*
- 1 *clove garlic, crushed*
- 1 *eggplant (1¼ pounds), pared and cubed*
- 6 *tablespoons vegetable oil*
- 1 *medium-size sweet green pepper, halved, seeded and cut into strips*
- 1 *medium-size sweet red pepper, halved, seeded and cut into strips*
- 1 *medium-size zucchini, cut into ½-inch pieces*
- 1 *medium-size yellow squash, cut into ½-inch pieces*
- ½ *pound mushrooms, sliced (2 cups)*
- 4 *medium-size tomatoes, cored and chopped*
- 1 *bay leaf*
- ½ *teaspoon leaf thyme, crumbled*
- ¼ *teaspoon pepper*

WAFFLES

- 2 cups sifted *all-purpose flour*
- 3 *teaspoons baking powder*
- ½ *teaspoon salt*
- 1½ *cups milk*
- 6 *tablespoons vegetable oil*
- 2 *eggs, separated*
- 1¼ *cups shredded Cheddar cheese (5 ounces)*

1. Preheat the oven to hot (400°).
2. Prepare the Ratatouille: Sauté the onion, garlic and eggplant in 4 tablespoons of the oil in a large ovenproof skillet or Dutch oven over low heat, stirring constantly, for 5 minutes or until the eggplant softens.
3. Add the remaining 2 tablespoons oil. Stir in the green pepper, red pepper, zucchini, yellow squash and mushrooms; sauté 5 minutes longer. Stir in the tomatoes, bay leaf, thyme, salt and pepper. Cover.
4. Bake in the preheated hot oven (400°) for 15 minutes; stir well; bake for 10 minutes longer. Uncover; bake for 10 minutes or until the vegetables are tender and some liquid has evaporated. Set aside. Keep warm.
5. Prepare the Waffles: Sift together the flour, baking powder and salt onto wax paper. Beat together the milk, oil and egg yolks in a bowl until blended. Gradually beat in the sifted dry ingredients; stir in the cheese.
6. Beat the egg whites until stiff but not dry; gently fold into the batter.
7. Heat a waffle maker to medium-hot. Pour the batter, a heaping ½ cup for 2 waffles, onto the waffle maker. Spread the batter to the edges. Cook until the waffles stop steaming; waffles should be cooked through and light brown. If not, close the waffle maker and cook a little longer.
8. Top each waffle with the heated ratatouille mixture. Serve at once.

Note: This recipe uses a double-waffle maker.

Vegetables

▨ ⓨ *Turkey Alfredo- Stuffed Artichokes*

Makes 4 servings.

Nutrient Value Per Serving: 422 calories, 27 gm. protein, 23 gm. fat, 299 mg. sodium, 113 mg. cholesterol.

4   large artichokes (about 2½ pounds)
½   lemon, sliced
2   cups cooked spaghetti twists or other
**   shaped pasta, cooked according to**
**   label directions**
1½ cups cooked cubed turkey
**   (about ½ pound)**
½   cup freshly grated Parmesan cheese
¾   cup heavy cream
¼   teaspoon coarsely ground pepper

1. Bring 3 quarts of water to boiling in a large saucepan.
2. Meanwhile, wash the artichokes well under cold water, making sure to clean the dirt from between the leaves. Cut about a ¾ inch piece from the top of each artichoke. With kitchen shears, trim ½ inch from the top of each leaf. Trim the stem even with the base so the artichoke stands upright.
3. Add the artichokes and the lemon slices to the boiling water. Cook for 5 to 20 minutes or until the center of the base feels just tender when pierced with a fork.
4. Remove the artichokes from the water with a slotted spoon. Drain upside down.
5. When cool enough to handle, gently spread out the center leaves and pull out the inner leaves with your fingers. With a teaspoon, scrape out fuzzy inner choke at the cavity's bottom. Cool completely. Refrigerate overnight.
6. Combine the cooked spaghetti twists, turkey and Parmesan cheese in a small bowl. Refrigerate overnight.
7. To serve: Heat the cream just to boiling in a medium-size saucepan. Stir in the turkey mixture. Cook, stirring, until very hot. Spoon into the artichokes. Sprinkle with pepper and serve.

WARM THE ARTICHOKES
If you wish to heat the artichokes themselves in this recipe, dip them into boiling water and drain them well before filling.

MICROWAVE DIRECTIONS
650 Watt Variable Power Microwave Oven

Ingredient Changes: Do not slice lemon half and increase heavy cream to 1 cup.
Directions: The day before serving, prepare the artichokes for cooking as directed above. Rub the cut surfaces with a lemon half. Place the artichokes in a microwave-safe baking dish. Cover. Microwave at full power for 12 to 14 minutes or until lower leaves can be easily pulled off, turning the dish a quarter turn. Drain off liquid. Prepare the filling as above, but with 1 cup heavy cream. Fill artichokes. Return the artichokes to the microwave-safe dish. Cover; refrigerate overnight. To heat, microwave, covered, at full power for 12 to 14 minutes or until heated through, turning a quarter turn.
Nutrient Value Per Serving: 473 calories, 28 gm. protein, 29 gm. fat, 305 mg. sodium, 134 mg. cholesterol.

◀Turkey Alfredo-Stuffed Artichokes

◼◪ ▢ *Sweet And Sour Cabbage with Pork*

This classic combination goes together faster in a wok.

Makes 4 servings.

Nutrient Value Per Serving: 340 calories, 21 gm. protein, 20 gm. fat, 815 mg. sodium, 79 mg. cholesterol.

¾ pound boneless lean pork
¼ pound brown-and-serve sausages
1 tablespoon butter or margarine
1 teaspoon salt
¼ teaspoon pepper
3 carrots, thinly sliced (1 cup)
2 tablespoons sugar
1 small savoy or green cabbage, shredded (8 cups)
3 tablespoons cider vinegar
¾ teaspoon anise seeds, crushed
Dark pumpernickel bread (optional)

1. Slice the pork ⅛ inch thick; cut into 1-inch wide strips. Cut the sausages in half.
2. Swirl the butter in a hot wok or large skillet to coat the bottom. Add the pork; stir-fry over medium to high heat for 3 to 4 minutes. Remove to a plate. Sprinkle with ½ teaspoon of the salt and the pepper.
3. Add the sausage and carrots to the wok; stir-fry for 2 minutes. Sprinkle with the sugar. Cook until the sugar melts. Stir in the cabbage until coated, 2 to 3 minutes.
4. Sprinkle with the vinegar, anise seeds and the remaining salt. Cook, stirring and tossing the cabbage occasionally, for 5 minutes. Return the pork to the wok; cook and stir for 1 minute. Serve with dark pumpernickel bread, if you wish.

◼◪ ▢ *Green Beans with Beef Sauce*

A new way to serve green beans as a main dish—and it takes less than 15 minutes to prepare. Serve with rice and a vegetable, such as summer squash.

Makes 4 servings.

Nutrient Value Per Serving: 188 calories, 13 gm. protein, 10 gm. fat, 431 mg. sodium, 39 mg. cholesterol.

1 pound green beans
⅓ cup beef or chicken broth
1 tablespoon soy sauce
1 tablespoon dry sherry
1 teaspoon cider vinegar
1 tablespoon Chinese oyster sauce (optional)
2 teaspoons cornstarch
1 tablespoon vegetable oil
1 tablespoon finely chopped fresh gingerroot OR: ½ teaspoon ground ginger
1 clove garlic, finely chopped
½ pound lean ground beef

1. Wash the beans; trim ends. Slice diagonally into 1-inch pieces.
2. Combine the broth, soy sauce, dry sherry, vinegar, oyster sauce, if you wish, and cornstarch in a small bowl; stir to dissolve the cornstarch. Reserve.
3. Heat the oil in a large skillet or wok over high heat. Add the green beans; stir-fry for 4 to 5 minutes or just until crisp-tender and golden brown in spots. Remove with a slotted spoon; reserve.
4. Add the ginger and garlic to the skillet; cook for 30 seconds. Crumble the beef into the skillet; cook just until no longer pink. Drain off the excess fat.
5. Stir the reserved sauce; add to the meat in the skillet. Cook, stirring, until thickened. Fold in the beans; reheat; serve immediately.

MICROWAVE DIRECTIONS
650 Watt Variable Power Microwave Oven

Ingredient Changes: Reduce vegetable oil from 1 tablespoon to 1 teaspoon.
Directions: Place sliced beans in an 11¾ x 7½ x 1¾-inch microwave-safe baking dish with the 1 teaspoon oil. Cover. Microwave at full power for 8 minutes, stirring once. Turn into a bowl. Cover; set aside. Crumble the beef into the same microwave baking dish. Add the ginger and garlic; mix together. Microwave, uncovered, at full power for 4 minutes. Meanwhile, stir together the broth, soy sauce, sherry, vinegar, oyster sauce, if you wish, and cornstarch in small bowl until smooth. Drain the meat, if necessary. Stir the cornstarch mixture into the meat until well blended. Microwave, uncovered, at full power for 2 minutes or until the sauce thickens, stirring once. Fold the beans into the sauce. Microwave, uncovered, at full power or 1 minute. Serve immediately.
Nutrient Value Per Serving: 163 calories, 13 gm. protein, 8 gm. fat, 430 mg. sodium, 39 mg. cholesterol.

Roasted Red and Green Pepper Platter

Makes 6 servings.

Nutrient Value Per Serving: 763 calories, 27 gm. fat, 1588 mg. sodium, 335 mg. cholesterol.

5 *sweet red peppers (1½ pounds)*
3 *sweet green peppers (1 pound)*
¾ *cup olive oil*
⅓ *cup red wine vinegar*
2 *tablespoons lemon juice*
1 *tablespoon chopped fresh basil*
2 *tablespoons drained capers*
2 *cloves garlic, minced*
½ *teaspoon salt*
¼ *teaspoon pepper*
   Escarole or romaine lettuce leaves
1 *package (8 ounces) sliced hard salami*
1 *package (8 ounces) sliced provolone cheese*
   Quick Deviled Eggs (recipe follows)

1 *can (4 ounces) pitted black olives, drained*

1. Preheat the broiler. Lay peppers in single layer on a broiler pan.
2. Broil 2 inches from heat, turning frequently, until blackened all over, 15 minutes.
3. Cool each pepper under cold water. Remove blackened skin with a sharp knife. Core; seed. Cut peppers into 2-inch wide strips. Pat dry on paper toweling. Place in a large bowl.
4. Combine oil, vinegar, lemon juice, basil, capers, garlic, salt and pepper in large jar with screw-top; cover. Shake well. Pour over peppers; toss to coat. Cover; refrigerate several hours or overnight to mellow flavors. Toss occasionally.
5. Prepare Quick Deviled Eggs.
6. To serve, line a large round platter with escarole leaves. Roll salami and provolone into cones. Place around the edge of the platter. Lift pepper strips from marinade with a slotted spoon, draining well. Spoon into center of the plate. Surround with deviled eggs and olives. Pour the remaining marinade into a serving bowl; pass as additional dressing.

Quick Deviled Eggs: Halve 6 hard-cooked eggs. Remove yolks from whites. Press yolks through a fine sieve into a small bowl. Stir in ¼ cup mayonnaise, 1 teaspoon prepared mustard, and salt and pepper to taste. Pipe or spoon into hollows of egg whites. Garnish with parsley.

TO HARD-COOK EGGS
Place the eggs in a saucepan and add cold water to cover the eggs by about 1 inch. Bring rapidly to boiling, cover, remove from the heat and let stand for 15 minutes. Drain and rinse under cold running water until the eggs are cold. Crack the shells on the counter top for easy peeling.

◼◻ Spaghetti Squash with Picadillo

Makes 4 servings.

Nutrient Value Per Serving: 525 calories, 28 gm. protein, 35 gm. fat, 635 mg. sodium, 77 mg. cholesterol.

- 1 **spaghetti squash**
- 1 **pound ground chuck**
- 1 **cup chopped onion (1 large)**
- 1 **sweet green pepper, cored, seeded and diced**
- 1 **large clove garlic, minced**
- 1 **cup bottled home-style tomato sauce**
- 1 **tablespoon red wine vinegar**
- ½ **teaspoon ground cinnamon**
- ¼ **teaspoon ground cumin**
- ⅛ **teaspoon ground cayenne**
- ¼ **cup raisins**
- 1 **jar (2¼ ounces) pitted Spanish olives**
- ½ **cup plus 2 tablespoons slivered almonds Salt**

1. Heat about 1½ inches of water in a large saucepan. Cut the squash in quarters with a large heavy knife. Remove the seeds. Place in the saucepan, rind-side down. Cover tightly; steam over a medium-high heat for 25 minutes.
2. Place a large skillet over high heat. Add the beef and brown in its own fat, breaking it up with a wooden spoon until all pink has disappeared, about 5 minutes. Add the onion, green pepper and garlic. Cook for 5 minutes, stirring often.
3. Stir in the tomato sauce, vinegar, cinnamon, cumin, cayenne, raisins and olives. Cover; cook for 10 minutes. Add the ½ cup almonds. (Add a little water if the mixture is too thick.) Add salt to taste.
4. Remove the squash from the saucepan to dinner plates. Scrape pulp into "spaghetti" with a fork and pile it back into the shells. Spoon the picadillo mixture over the squash. Sprinkle it with the remaining almonds.

◻ Swiss Chard Pancakes

Makes 4 servings (12 pancakes).

Nutrient Value Per Serving: 805 calories, 30 gm. protein, 54 gm. fat, 1124 mg. sodium, 259 mg. cholesterol.

- 2 **eggs**
- 1¼ **cups milk**
- 1½ **cups sifted all-purpose flour**
- 1 **teaspoon baking powder**
- ¼ **teaspoon salt**
- 3 **tablespoons vegetable oil**
- 1 **package (10 ounces) frozen chopped Swiss chard, kale or spinach, thawed and squeezed dry**
- 3 **to 4 tablespoons unsalted butter**
- 16 **tomato slices (2 tomatoes)**
- 20 **slices salami (4 ounces)**
  Mustard-Cheese Sauce (recipe follows)

1. To prepare the pancakes: Combine the eggs and milk in a bowl; beat with a rotary beater. Add the flour, baking powder and salt; beat until smooth. Stir in the oil and Swiss chard.
2. Melt 1 tablespoon of butter on a griddle or in a heavy skillet. Pour ¼ cup of the batter onto the griddle for each 5-inch pancake. Cook over a medium-low heat until the edges begin to brown, about 3 minutes. Turn; cook until golden. Continue with the remaining batter to make 12 pancakes; add butter as needed to prevent sticking. Keep pancakes warm in the oven in a single layer on a cookie sheet.
3. For each serving, prepare the following stack: one pancake, 2 slices tomato, 2 slices salami, one pancake; repeat layering. Garnish each stack with folded salami; secure with a wooden pick. Pour Mustard-Cheese Sauce over each.

Mustard-Cheese Sauce: Melt 2 tablespoons butter in a saucepan. Stir in 2 tablespoons flour; cook, stirring for 1 minute. Gradually stir in 1½ cups milk. Cook, stirring until thickened and bubbly.

▲ Swiss Chard Pancakes

Remove from the heat. Stir in 1 cup shredded Fontina cheese and 2 teaspoons Dijon-style mustard. Cover the surface with plastic wrap. Reheat over a very low heat just before serving.

USE FRESH SWISS CHARD
To use fresh Swiss chard, place 1 pound washed in a saucepan with the water that clings to the leaves. Cover; cook just until wilted. Drain; squeeze dry. Chop.

 *Stir-Fried Vegetables and Tofu*

A great vegetarian main dish for all seasons.

Makes 4 servings.

Nutrient Value Per Serving: 241 calories, 14 gm. protein, 15 gm. fat, 790 mg. sodium, 0 mg. cholesterol.

3   tablespoons vegetable oil
2   small cloves garlic, finely chopped

2   tablespoons chopped fresh gingerroot
1/8 to 1/4 teaspoon red pepper flakes
3   celery stalks, sliced diagonally
1   sweet red pepper, halved, seeded and
     cut in 1/2-inch wide strips
2   zucchini, cut in julienne strips (2 cups)
3   cups broccoli flowerets
     (about 2/3 bunch)
1   bunch green onions, sliced diagonally
     into 1-inch pieces
3/4 to 1 pound fresh tofu (bean curd), cut
     into 1-inch cubes
2   tablespoons soy sauce
1/4 cup chicken broth or water
1   teaspoon cornstarch
     Hot cooked rice

1. Heat the oil in a wok or skillet. Stir in garlic, ginger and red pepper flakes.
2. Add the celery, pepper, zucchini, broccoli and green onions. Stir-fry over high heat until oil coats the vegetables, 3 to 4 minutes. Add tofu.
3. Mix the soy sauce, broth and cornstarch until smooth. Add to the wok. Cook, stirring for 8 to 10 minutes or until the vegetables are crisp-tender. Serve with hot cooked rice and additional soy sauce.

6. Vegetables and Other Accompaniments

$\mathcal{S}$ummer is the time to enjoy versatile fresh vegetables at their very best—and at their lowest prices. Stir-frying, steaming or cooking in a small amount of water in a tightly covered saucepan are the best cooking methods to retain a vegetable's bright colors and nutrients. Vegetables lose nutrients when cooked with water. After cooking, reserve the liquid to add to your sauces and soups.

Vegetables should never be boring. The large selection available, whether fresh, frozen or canned, may be prepared and served in infinite ways. Try Acorn Squash Flan or Broccoli Soufflé for an exciting new side dish.

Accent your main dish or vegetable side dish with a flavorful accompaniment, such as Orange-Cranberry Relish, Basil Butter or Tomato-Apple Chutney and . . . enjoy!

Vegetables

FRESH VEGETABLE BASICS
- Buy the freshest vegetables you can find.
- Select vegetables that are of characteristic shape, color and size.
- Use the vegetables as soon as possible. Avoid buying too much at one time.
- Buy vegetables in season for better flavor and lower price.
- Wash all vegetables before cooking or eating.
- Don't overcook! Vegetables should be cooked only until they are crisp-tender.

◀Overnight Pickled Vegetables (page 192)

⏳ *Acorn Squash Flan*

Delicious as a vegetable accompaniment or as an unusual dessert.

Bake in a ring mold at 350° for 40 minutes; or bake in a bowl at 350° for 1 hour and 10 minutes.
Makes 8 servings.

Nutrient Value Per Serving: 210 calories, 5 gm. protein, 12 gm. fat, 212 mg. sodium, 229 mg. cholesterol.

> 1 *medium-size acorn squash (about 1 pound)*
> ½ *cup sugar*
> ¼ *teaspoon ground cinnamon*
> 2 *tablespoons butter, melted*
> ½ *teaspoon salt*
> ½ *teaspoon ground ginger*
> ¼ *teaspoon ground nutmeg*
> ⅛ *teaspoon ground cloves*
> ⅛ *teaspoon red pepper flakes, crushed*
> 1½ *cups half and half*
> 3 *eggs*
> 3 *egg yolks*
> 1 *tablespoon brandy*

1. Preheat the oven to moderate (350°). Grease a cookie sheet.
2. Slice the squash in half, lengthwise. Scoop out and discard the seeds. Place the squash halves, cut-side down, on the prepared cookie sheet.
3. Bake for 45 minutes or until tender. Cool. Scoop out the pulp; reserve. Leave the oven on.
4. Heat a 5-cup ring mold or 1½-quart oven-proof glass bowl in the moderate oven (350°) for 5 minutes. Grease a large piece of aluminum foil.
5. Combine the sugar and cinnamon in a small heavy saucepan. Heat over high heat until the sugar melts. Continue cooking, stirring constantly until the sugar is completely melted and the caramel is a deep golden color. Remove the heated ring mold from the oven. Leave the oven on. Carefully pour the caramel into mold, turning the mold to coat the bottom and sides evenly. Invert the mold onto a greased sheet of foil. Set aside.
6. Place the squash pulp in an electric blender or food processor. Add the melted butter, salt, ginger, nutmeg, cloves and crushed red pepper flakes. Cover; whirl until smooth.
7. Warm the half and half in a small saucepan over low heat; do not boil. Beat together the eggs and egg yolks in a large bowl. Beat the puréed squash mixture into the eggs. Slowly stir in the warmed half and half. Add the brandy. Pour the mixture into the prepared ring mold or bowl. Set the mold in a large pan; place on the oven shelf. Pour boiling water into the pan until it comes halfway up the sides of the mold.
8. Bake for 40 minutes for the ring mold, or 1 hour and 10 minutes for the bowl, or until a knife inserted in the center comes out clean. Remove the ring mold from the water bath. Let it stand for 10 minutes.
9. Run a sharp knife around the inside and outside edges of the mold. Carefully invert onto a shallow serving platter; the caramel sauce will run over the flan. Serve warm or chilled as a vegetable accompaniment or a dessert.

⏳ *Scalloped Asparagus*

Here is an elegant way to serve asparagus as a side dish.

Bake at 400° for 15 minutes; then 2 minutes to brown.
Makes 4 servings.

Nutrient Value Per Serving: 321 calories, 16 gm. protein, 23 gm. fat, 548 mg. sodium, 327 mg. cholesterol.

1 **pound fresh asparagus**
4 **tablespoons (½ stick) butter**
1 **tablespoon all-purpose flour**
1 **cup milk**
4 **hard-cooked eggs, finely chopped**
½ **teaspoon salt**
¼ **teaspoon cayenne pepper**
2 **tablespoons fine dry bread crumbs**
½ **cup grated Swiss cheese (2 ounces)**

1. Preheat the oven to hot (400°). Bring a large saucepan of salted water to boiling. Grease a 1½-quart shallow baking dish.

2. Snap off the tough ends of the asparagus; trim off any sandy scales; wash.

3. Add the asparagus to the boiling water. Cover; lower the heat; simmer for 10 minutes or until the lower parts of the stalks are fork-tender. Drain; transfer to paper toweling to drain further.

4. To prepare the cream sauce, melt 1 tablespoon of the butter in a small saucepan. Stir in the flour; cook for 1 minute. Gradually stir in the milk. Cook, stirring constantly, until the sauce thickens, about 3 minutes. Remove from the heat; reserve.

5. Arrange half the asparagus in a layer in the prepared baking dish. Sprinkle with half the chopped egg; dot with 1 tablespoon of the butter; season with salt and cayenne pepper. Arrange another layer with the remaining asparagus. Sprinkle the center portion of asparagus with the remaining chopped egg. Pour the reserved cream sauce down the middle of the casserole. Sprinkle the sauce with bread crumbs and cheese. Dot uncovered portions of asparagus with the remaining 2 tablespoons of butter to prevent drying out during baking.

6. Bake, covered, in the preheated hot oven (400°) for 15 minutes. Uncover; bake 2 to 3 minutes or until the top is browned.

▼ **Scalloped Asparagus**

Brussels Sprouts Soufflé

Preheat oven to 400°; bake soufflé at 375° for
35 minutes.
Makes 6 servings.

Nutrient Value Per Serving: 167 calories, 7 gm.
protein, 12 gm. fat, 277 mg. sodium, 168 mg.
cholesterol.

2 **teaspoons butter**
2 **tablespoons grated Parmesan cheese**
1 **container (10 ounces) Brussels sprouts,**
 trimmed
1 **medium-size potato, pared and cubed**
½ **cup heavy cream**
3 **egg yolks**
½ **teaspoon salt**
¼ **teaspoon pepper**
⅛ **teaspoon ground nutmeg**
 Dash of liquid red pepper seasoning
4 **egg whites**

1. Butter a 1-quart soufflé dish with the butter.
 Sprinkle 1 tablespoon of the Parmesan over
 bottom and sides of dish. To make a collar
 for the soufflé, tear off a length of aluminum foil long enough to encircle the dish.
 Fold in half lengthwise. Fasten the collar to
 the dish with a string or tape so the collar is
 2 inches higher than the rim.
2. Preheat the oven to hot (400°).
3. Cook the Brussels sprouts and potatoes in
 boiling salted water to cover until tender,
 about 15 minutes. Drain.
4. Place half the Brussels sprouts and half the
 potatoes in an electric blender or food
 processor. Add ¼ cup of the cream. Whirl
 until smooth. Transfer to a large bowl.
 Repeat with the remaining Brussels sprouts,
 potatoes and cream. Transfer to the bowl.
 Stir in the remaining Parmesan cheese.
5. Beat the egg yolks into the Brussels sprouts
 mixture one at a time, beating well after
 each addition. Stir in the salt, pepper,
 nutmeg and hot pepper sauce.

6. Beat the egg whites in a medium-size bowl
 until soft peaks form. Fold into the Brussels
 sprouts mixture until no streaks of white
 remain. Pour into the prepared soufflé dish.
7. Place the dish in the preheated hot oven
 (400°). Immediately lower the oven
 temperature to moderate (375°). Bake for
 35 to 40 minutes or until the soufflé is
 puffed and golden. Serve immediately.

Brussels Sprouts and Carrots Sauté

**Serve as a flavorful accompaniment with a
roast or baked ham.**

Makes 4 servings.

Nutrient Value Per Serving: 130 calories, 4 gm.
protein, 9 gm. fat, 254 mg. sodium, 23 mg.
cholesterol.

3 **tablespoons butter**
2 **cups Brussels sprouts (½ pound), halved**
1 **leek, cut into ½-inch thick slices**
2 **large carrots, cut into ½-inch thick slices**
1 **tablespoon water**
¼ **teaspoon caraway seeds**
¼ **teaspoon salt**
⅛ **teaspoon pepper**
 Sour cream (optional)

1. Melt the butter in a large skillet over
 medium heat. Sauté the Brussels sprouts for
 3 minutes. Stir in the leek and carrots;
 sauté for 2 minutes. Add the water; cover;
 steam for 5 minutes or until the Brussels
 sprouts are crisp-tender. (Add additional
 water if necessary.)
2. Sprinkle with the caraway seeds, salt and
 pepper. Serve with a dollop of sour cream,
 if you wish.

▲**Brussels Sprouts and Carrot Sauté**

⬛ *Red Cabbage with Apples*

Serve this as an accompaniment with pan-fried or grilled pork chops.

Makes 8 servings.

Nutrient Value Per Serving: 94 calories, 2 gm. protein, 2 gm. fat, 45 mg. sodium, 4 mg. cholesterol.

> 1 *medium-size red cabbage*
>   *(about 2 pounds)*
> 3 *medium-size tart apples, pared,*
>   *quartered, cored and sliced*
> 3 *tablespoons light brown sugar*
> 3 *tablespoons red wine vinegar*
> 1 *tablespoon butter*
> ½ *teaspoon pepper*

1. Trim the outer leaves from the cabbage; quarter and core; slice thinly to make about 12 cups.
2. Add enough water to a large kettle or Dutch oven to cover the bottom by 1 inch. Cover; bring to boiling. Add the cabbage; cover and return to boiling. Lower the heat; simmer,

covered, stirring occasionally, until the cabbage is tender, about 30 minutes.
3. Uncover the kettle. Add the apples; cook for 10 minutes longer.
4. Stir in the sugar, vinegar, butter and pepper until well blended.

⬛ *Corn Grilled in Husk*

Makes 8 servings.

Nutrient Value Per Serving: 120 calories, 3 gm. protein, 6 gm. fat, 135 mg. sodium, 15 mg. cholesterol.

> 8 *ears of fresh corn in husks*
> ¼ *cup (½ stick) unsalted butter, softened*
> ½ *teaspoon salt*
> ¼ *teaspoon pepper*

1. Gently pull back the corn husks, leaving them attached at the base. Discard all the corn silk.
2. Beat together the butter, salt and pepper in a small bowl. Brush over the corn. Bend back husks around corn, covering the ears completely. Tightly wrap each ear in a double thickness of aluminum foil.
3. Grill the foil-wrapped corn 6 inches from the coals, turning occasionally with tongs, for 20 to 30 minutes or until tender. Cool for 5 minutes before unwrapping. Remove the aluminum foil; pull back the husks. Serve with additional butter, if you wish.

FRESH CORN
Corn on the cob, yellow, white, or mixed, should have fresh green husks and plump and bright, firm kernels. Prepare immediately after purchase or, if necessary, store wrapped in plastic wrap for up to 2 days.

⊠ ⊡ *Creamy Corn Pudding*

Bake at 350° for 50 minutes.
Makes 8 servings.

Nutrient Value Per Serving: 303 calories, 14 gm. protein, 18 gm. fat, 458 mg. sodium, 220 mg. cholesterol.

4   *tablespoons butter*
4   *tablespoons all-purpose flour*
1   *teaspoon salt*
¼   *teaspoon white pepper*
¼   *teaspoon ground nutmeg*
4   *cups milk*
5   *eggs*
1   *cup ricotta cheese*
2   *packages (10-ounces each) frozen corn,
    thawed*

1. Preheat the oven to moderate (350°).
2. Melt the butter in a large saucepan. Stir in the flour, salt, pepper and nutmeg. Cook, stirring constantly, until bubbly, about 1 minute. Remove from the heat and gradually stir in the milk. Cook over medium heat, stirring until the sauce thickens and bubbles, about 1 minute.
3. Beat the eggs in a large bowl, just until blended; beat in the ricotta cheese. Gradually add the hot sauce while beating with a wire whisk. Stir in the corn.
4. Pour the corn mixture into a greased shallow 8- to 10-cup casserole. Set the casserole in a pan; place on the oven shelf. Pour boiling water to a 1-inch depth around the casserole.
5. Bake in the preheated moderate oven (350°) for 50 to 60 minutes or until the pudding is barely set in the center. Cool in the water bath for 20 minutes. Serve hot or warm.

⊠ ⊡ *Fresh Corn Fritters*

Fresh sweet corn, cut from the cob, then blended into a light batter and pan-fried. Delicious drizzled with maple syrup and served with baked ham for a hearty breakfast.

Makes 6 servings (about 2 dozen fritters).

Nutrient Value Per Serving: 215 calories, 5 gm. protein, 14 gm. fat, 351 mg. sodium, 113 mg. cholesterol.

3   *to 4 large ears corn on the cob, shucked*
⅔   *cup sifted all-purpose flour*
1   *teaspoon baking powder*
½   *teaspoon salt*
¼   *teaspoon ground nutmeg*
2   *eggs, separated*
2   *tablespoons milk*
¼   *cup (½ stick) butter or margarine,
    melted and slightly cooled*
¼   *cup sliced green onion
    Vegetable oil for frying*

1. Cut the corn from the cobs with a knife into a bowl. Press out the pulp and milk with the back of the knife. (You should have about 2 cups.)
2. Sift the flour, baking powder, salt and nutmeg onto wax paper.
3. Beat the egg whites in a small bowl until soft peaks form.
4. Beat the egg yolks with milk in a bowl; stir in melted butter, corn and green onion. Fold in the flour mixture; fold in the beaten whites until no streaks of white remain.
5. Pour oil into a large deep skillet to a depth of ½ inch; heat until a small amount of batter cooks quickly at the edges.
6. Drop slightly rounded tablespoons of batter into the hot oil; cook, turning once, 3 to 4 minutes or until golden on both sides. Remove with a slotted spoon; drain on paper toweling. Keep hot until all are cooked.

▮▯ Corn and Peppers with Cream

A quick and easy vegetable side dish prepared in foil packets on the grill. Let diners open their own packet of vegetables.

Makes 12 servings.

Nutrient Value Per Serving: 120 calories, 2 gm. protein, 8 gm. fat, 55 mg. sodium, 27 mg. cholesterol.

> **8** **ears corn on the cob**
> **1** **sweet green pepper, halved, seeded and finely chopped**
> **1** **sweet red pepper, halved, seeded and finely chopped**
> **1** **cup heavy cream**
>   **Dash of liquid red pepper seasoning**
> **¼** **teaspoon salt**
> **⅛** **teaspoon pepper**

1. Cut the kernels from each ear of corn into a large bowl. Add the green and red peppers, cream, liquid red pepper seasoning, salt and pepper; mix well.
2. Divide the corn mixture among 12 square (9 x 9-inch) pieces of heavy-duty aluminum foil; form each into a packet, sealing tightly so steam will not escape.
3. Place the packets on a grill over moderately hot coals. Grill for 10 to 15 minutes or until the corn is tender. Serve in the packets.

▮▯ French-Fried Eggplant Strips

Delicious with grilled steaks.

Makes 6 servings.

Nutrient Value Per Serving: 198 calories, 5 gm. protein, 5 gm. fat, 723 mg. sodium, 0 mg. cholesterol.

> **1** **large eggplant (2 pounds), pared and cut into 2½ x 3-inch "fingers"**
> **2** **teaspoons salt**
> **1½** **cups** sifted **all-purpose flour**
> **1** **bottle (12 ounces) beer**
>   **Vegetable oil for frying**

1. Place the eggplant in a large colander; sprinkle with salt; toss. Drain 1 hour.
2. Whisk the flour and beer together in a medium-size bowl. Let stand at room temperature for 1 hour.
3. Preheat the oven to very slow (250°). Place large brown paper bags on a jelly-roll pan.
4. Pour vegetable oil into a 2-quart saucepan to a depth of 2 inches. Heat to 370° on a deep-fat frying thermometer, or until a 1-inch cube of bread turns golden brown in 50 seconds.
5. Rinse the eggplant under cold running water. Pat dry on a towel. Stir beer batter.
6. Drop several eggplant "fingers" into the batter; turn to coat. Lift out with a fork, draining excess batter. Carefully place in the fat; do not crowd the pan. Fry, turning once or twice until lightly golden, about 3 minutes. Transfer with a slotted spoon to the paper-lined pan. Keep warm in a very slow oven (250°). Fry remainder. Serve immediately.

> **FRESH EGGPLANT**
> **Really a fruit, an eggplant should be firm and heavy in relation to size, with a uniformly dark, rich purple color. Use as quickly as possible after purchasing or, if necessary, store in a plastic bag in the refrigerator for a day or two.**

▲ *Clockwise from bottom:* **Fresh Corn Fritters (page 184), Green Beans with Water Chestnuts (page 186) and Roasted Red and Green Pepper Platter (page 175).**

Green Beans with Water Chestnuts

Makes 6 servings.

Nutrient Value Per Serving: 88 calories, 2 gm. protein, 5 gm. fat, 222 mg. sodium, 0 mg. cholesterol.

1½ **pounds fresh green beans, trimmed**
 2 **tablespoons vegetable oil**
 2 **slices fresh gingerroot, about ¼ inch thick**
 2 **cloves garlic, halved**
 1 **cup sliced celery**
 1 **can (8 ounces) water chestnuts, drained and halved**

½ **teaspoon salt**
⅛ **to ¼ teaspoon red pepper flakes**
¼ **cup water**

1. Slice the beans in half lengthwise.
2. Heat the oil in a large deep skillet; add the ginger and garlic; stir-fry for 1 minute. Add the celery and water chestnuts; stir-fry for 2 to 3 minutes or until crisp-tender. Remove the celery and water chestnuts to small bowl (leave the ginger and the garlic in skillet).

3. Add the beans, salt, pepper flakes and water to the skillet. Cover; steam for 15 minutes or until crisp-tender. Discard the ginger and garlic. Add the celery and water chestnuts. Heat for 1 minute. Spoon into a serving dish.

▲ **Green Beans in Garlic-Tomato Sauce**

FRESH GREEN BEANS
Look for clean, firm, but tender beans that are well-shaped and free of scars. Store in a plastic bag in the refrigerator.

 *Green Beans in Garlic-Tomato Sauce*

Makes 4 servings.

Nutrient Value Per Serving: 139 calories, 4 gm. protein, 6 gm. fat, 223 mg. sodium, 15 mg. cholesterol.

 1 *pound green beans, trimmed and*
      halved lengthwise
 1 *large onion, chopped (1 cup)*
 2 *large cloves garlic, finely chopped*
 2 *tablespoons butter*
 1 *tablespoon all-purpose flour*
 1 *teaspoon paprika*
 2 *cans (8¼ ounces each) whole tomatoes,*
      drained and liquid reserved

1. Drop the green beans in a large saucepan of boiling salted water. Cook for 2 minutes or just until crisp-tender. Drain; run under cold water to stop cooking. Drain.
2. Sauté the onion and garlic in the butter in a medium-size saucepan for 3 minutes or until the onion is softened. Stir in the flour and paprika until well blended. Cook for 1 minute. Stir in the reserved liquid from the tomatoes. Cook, stirring constantly until the sauce is slightly thickened, about 2 minutes.
3. Add the tomatoes and green beans; mix well, breaking up the tomatoes with the back of a wooden spoon. Cook, stirring constantly over low heat for 5 minutes or until the beans are tender and the mixture is thoroughly heated.

Mushrooms in Foil

Just the plain good flavor of mushrooms, lightly seasoned with tarragon, ideal with grilled meats.

Makes 4 servings.

Nutrient Value Per Serving: 133 calories, 3 gm. protein, 12 gm. fat, 287 mg. sodium, 31 mg. cholesterol.

 1 *pound mushrooms, stems removed*
 ¼ *cup (½ stick) unsalted butter, melted*
 ½ *teaspoon leaf tarragon, crumbled*
 ½ *teaspoon salt*
 ½ *teaspoon pepper*

1. Wipe the mushrooms with a damp cloth. Cut into ¼-inch slices. Divide evenly among four 9 x 9-inch pieces of heavy-duty aluminum foil.
2. Combine the melted butter, tarragon, salt and pepper in a small bowl. Drizzle over the mushrooms. Form into packets, sealing tightly.
3. Place the packets on a grill over moderately hot coals. Grill for 10 to 15 minutes or until tender. Serve in the packets.

Onion Cake

Serve this rich savory cake with its sour cream topping for brunch, supper or as a side dish.

Bake at 375° for 40 minutes.
Makes 6 servings.

Nutrient Value Per Serving: 332 calories, 8 gm. protein, 21 gm. fat, 523 mg. sodium, 128 mg. cholesterol.

- 4 **medium-size onions, sliced**
- 3 **tablespoons butter or margarine**
- 1 **package (10 ounces) refrigerated buttermilk biscuits**
- 1½ **cups dairy sour cream**
- 2 **eggs, slightly beaten**
  Salt
  Pepper

1. Preheat the oven to moderate (375°).
2. Sauté the onions in butter in a skillet until browned and softened, about 10 minutes.
3. Separate the biscuits. Press into the bottom and slightly up the side of an 8-inch springform pan. Spoon the sautéed onions over the top.
4. Whisk the sour cream and eggs in a bowl until blended. Season to taste with salt and pepper. Spoon evenly over the onions.
5. Bake in the preheated moderate oven (375°)

for 40 minutes or until the topping is set. Remove the pan from the oven; remove the sides of the pan. Serve warm.

Potato Pancake

Makes 4 servings.

Nutrient Value Per Serving: 314 calories, 12 gm. protein, 21 gm. fat, 518 mg. sodium, 56 mg. cholesterol.

- 2 **to 3 tablespoons vegetable oil**
- 1 **tablespoon butter**
- 3 **medium-size baking potatoes, pared and shredded (about 2 cups)**
- 1 **medium-size onion, shredded (about 1 cup)**
- ¼ **teaspoon salt**
- ⅛ **teaspoon pepper**
- 1½ **cups shredded Gouda cheese (6 ounces)**
  Chopped parsley (optional)

1. Heat 2 tablespoons of the oil and the butter in an 8-inch cast-iron skillet. Add the potatoes, spreading evenly over the bottom of the skillet. Sprinkle the onion over the potato. Press down firmly with a spatula. Sprinkle with salt and pepper.
2. Cook, uncovered, over medium-high heat for 5 minutes or until the underside is golden brown. Run a thin, flexible spatula around the edge of the skillet; loosen the pancake carefully with the spatula from the bottom of the pan before turning over. Turn the pancake over onto a cookie sheet or saucepan lid; slide the pancake back into the skillet, browned side up.
3. Cook for 5 minutes or until the underside is golden brown and the potatoes are cooked through. If necessary, add the additional 1 tablespoon oil to the skillet to prevent sticking.

4. Sprinkle the pancake with the cheese; cover; cook until the cheese melts, about 1 minute. Garnish with chopped parsley, if you wish. Cut into wedges to serve.

◼◼ Ratatouille

You can make this a day or two ahead; serve cold or warm.

Makes 4 servings.

Nutrient Value Per Serving: 94 calories, 3 gm. protein, 4 gm. fat, 369 mg. sodium, 0 mg. cholesterol.

3 cloves garlic, finely chopped
1 medium-size onion, sliced
4 large mushrooms, sliced
1 tablespoon olive oil
1 small eggplant (about ½ pound), with peel, cut into ½-inch cubes
1 medium-size zucchini, sliced
1 small sweet red pepper, cored, seeded and sliced
¾ cup tomato sauce
2 tablespoons lemon juice
½ teaspoon leaf oregano, crumbled
¼ teaspoon salt

1. Sauté the garlic, onion and mushrooms in the oil in a large heavy skillet until golden, for about 3 minutes. Add the eggplant; cover. Lower the heat; cook gently for 5 minutes.
2. Stir in the zucchini, red pepper, tomato sauce, lemon juice, oregano and salt. Cover; cook 5 minutes longer or until the zucchini and peppers are crisp-tender.

MICROWAVE DIRECTIONS
650 Watt Variable Power Microwave Oven
Directions: Stir together all ingredients in a 2-quart microwave-safe casserole with lid. Cover. Microwave at full power for 5 minutes. Stir; microwave, covered, at full power 5 minutes longer.

◼ Rutabaga Purée

Makes 6 servings.

Nutrient Value Per Serving: 155 calories, 2 gm. protein, 9 gm. fat, 151 mg. sodium, 22 mg. cholesterol.

2½ pounds rutabaga (yellow turnip), pared and cut into 2-inch cubes
⅔ cup finely diced slab or sliced bacon (3 ounces)
1 tablespoon butter
¼ cup heavy cream
¼ teaspoon ground sage
¼ teaspoon salt
⅛ teaspoon pepper

1. Cook the rutabaga in boiling salted water in a saucepan for 30 minutes or until tender. Drain. Reserve.
2. Sauté the bacon until crisp. Remove to paper toweling to drain.
3. Working in batches, combine the rutabaga with the butter and cream in the container of an electric blender or food processor. Cover; whirl until puréed. Return the purée to the saucepan. Add the sage, salt and pepper. Gently heat through. Garnish with the bacon.

◫ *Scalloped Tomato and Cheese Bake*

Bake at 350° for 30 minutes.
Makes 8 servings.

Nutrient Value Per Serving: 168 calories, 3 gm. protein, 13 gm. fat, 468 mg. sodium, 35 mg. cholesterol.

> 4   *large ripe tomatoes*
> 1   *medium-size onion, chopped (½ cup)*
> ¼   *cup (½ stick) butter or margarine*
> 2   *cups soft bread crumbs (4 slices)*
> 1   *teaspoon salt*
> ½   *teaspoon pepper*
> 1   *teaspoon sugar*
> ½   *teaspoon leaf marjoram, crumbled*
> ¼   *cup (½ stick) butter or margarine, melted*
> ¼   *cup shredded Cheddar cheese*

1. Core the tomatoes; cut each into 8 even-size wedges.
2. Sauté the onion in the butter in a large skillet until soft, for about 5 minutes. Add the bread crumbs, salt, pepper, sugar and marjoram; toss lightly. Preheat the oven to moderate (350°).
3. Line a 1½-quart shallow baking dish (7⅜ x 3⅝ x 2¼- inches) with half the tomatoes; sprinkle with half the bread mixture. Repeat with the remaining tomato wedges and crumb mixture. Drizzle melted butter over the top.
4. Bake in the preheated moderate oven (350°) for 25 minutes or until the tomatoes are soft and the crumb mixture is lightly browned. Sprinkle the cheese over the top and return to the oven until the cheese melts, for about 5 minutes.

MAKE-AHEAD TIP
This recipe can be made through step 3, covered and refrigerated. Remove from the refrigerator 30 minutes before baking. To bake, remove the cover and continue with step 4.

◫ *Sautéed Cherry Tomatoes*

Peel the tomatoes ahead, but sauté them just before serving.

Makes 8 servings.

Nutrient Value Per Serving: 47 calories, 1 gm. protein, 3 gm. fat, 286 mg. sodium, 4 mg. cholesterol.

> 3   *pints cherry tomatoes*
> 1   *tablespoon butter or margarine*
> 1   *tablespoon olive or vegetable oil*
> 1   *teaspoon salt*
> 1   *teaspoon sugar*
> ¼   *teaspoon white pepper*
> 1   *tablespoon chopped chives*

1. Pour water into a large saucepan to a depth of 3 to 4 inches. Bring to boiling. Add 1 pint of the tomatoes. Quickly remove with a slotted spoon to a bowl of cold water. Repeat with the remaining tomatoes. Drain the tomatoes; slip skins off each.
2. Just before serving, heat the butter and oil in a large skillet. Add the tomatoes, salt, sugar and pepper. Sauté just to heat the tomatoes. Sprinkle with chives and serve.

▼ ☐ Grilled Mixed Vegetables

A hinged grill basket is the ideal piece of equipment for grilling vegetables. They can be turned over easily without risk of breaking. If cooking several different kinds of vegetables at one time, carefully remove each as they are done.

Makes 6 servings.

Nutrient Value Per Serving: 105 calories, 2 gm. protein, 7 gm. fat, 7 mg. sodium, 0 mg. cholesterol.

- *3   tablespoons olive oil*
- *2   tablespoons lemon juice*
- *2   tablespoons finely chopped fresh basil*
- *1   small eggplant (¹⁄₂ pound), cut into ³⁄₄-inch slices*
- *3   medium-size tomatoes, cored and halved*
- *2   bunches large green onions, trimmed*

1. Beat the oil, lemon juice and basil in a small bowl until well blended. Oil two hinged grill baskets, or use one and work in batches.*
2. Arrange the eggplant, tomatoes and green onions in the grilling baskets. Brush with the seasoned oil. Close and secure the baskets.
3. Grill about 8 inches from the coals, turning over once, for 3 minutes per side; baste occasionally with the seasoned oil. Carefully open the baskets. Remove the tomatoes and green onions; keep warm.
4. Close the baskets. Continue to cook the eggplant 4 minutes longer. Drizzle any remaining oil over the vegetables just before serving.

Note: Vegetables can be grilled without the basket, on top of the grill.

▼ ☐ Crisp-Cooked Vegetables

Makes 6 servings.

Nutrient Value Per Serving: 109 calories, 4.6 gm. protein, 0.4 gm. fat, 32 mg. sodium, 0 mg. cholesterol.

- *6   red new potatoes, scrubbed*
- *10 small baby carrots, pared*
- *¹⁄₂ pound green beans*
- *1   pint fresh Brussels sprouts OR: 1 package (10 ounces) frozen Brussels sprouts*
- *1   small sweet yellow, red or green pepper, halved, cored, seeded and cut into ¹⁄₂-inch strips*
- *1   tablespoon butter*
- *¹⁄₂ pint cherry tomatoes, stemmed and washed*
    Chopped parsley (optional)

1. Pare a strip around the center of each potato with a swivel-bladed vegetable peeler.
2. Cook the potatoes and carrots in a large saucepan of salted boiling water for 5 minutes. Add the beans; cook for another 15 minutes or until the vegetables are tender. Drain; keep warm.
3. Meanwhile, cook the fresh Brussels sprouts in a second large saucepan of lightly salted boiling water for 10 minutes or until tender. Drain; keep warm. If using frozen Brussels sprouts, cook following label directions.
4. Sauté the sweet pepper in the butter in a medium-size skillet for 1 minute. Add the tomatoes; sauté for 2 to 3 minutes longer. Arrange the vegetables on a platter. Sprinkle the vegetables with parsley, if you wish.

Other Accompaniments

Rice Pilaf

Bake at 350° for 25 minutes.
Makes 4 servings.

Nutrient Value Per Serving: 311 calories, 5 gm. protein, 7 gm. fat, 709 mg. sodium, 0 mg. cholesterol.

1 **medium-size onion, chopped (½ cup)**
2 **tablespoons vegetable oil**
1⅓ **cups uncooked long-grain white rice**
1 **can (10½ ounces) condensed beef broth**
1½ **cups water**
⅛ **teaspoon pepper**

1. Preheat the oven to moderate (350°).
2. Sauté the onion in the oil in a small saucepan until tender, about 2 minutes. Add the rice; stir to coat with the oil. Transfer to a 1½-quart baking dish. Add the broth, water, salt and pepper, mixing well. Cover.
3. Bake in the preheated moderate oven (350°) for 25 minutes. Fluff up the rice with a fork to serve.

Orange-Cranberry Relish

Makes 2½ cups.

Nutrient Value Per Tablespoon: 20 calories, 1 gm. protein, 1 gm. fat, 2 mg. sodium, 0 mg. cholesterol.

2 **cups coarsely chopped orange sections (3 large oranges), seeds removed**
1 **cup whole berry cranberry sauce**
1 **tablespoon finely chopped candied ginger**
3 **tablespoons coarsely chopped blanched almonds, toasted**

Combine the oranges, cranberry sauce, ginger and almonds in a medium-size bowl; mix well. Cover; chill for several hours.

Overnight Pickled Vegetables

Serve with grilled hamburgers, roast meats or an afternoon sandwich.

Makes about 1 quart, 8 servings.

Nutrient Value Per Serving: 129 calories, 1 gm. protein, 1 gm. fat, 19 mg. sodium, 0 mg. cholesterol.

1 **cup water**
1 **cup sugar**
2 **teaspoons pickling spice**
⅔ **cup white vinegar**
2 **medium-size zucchini**
3 **medium-size carrots**
2 **medium-size sweet red peppers**
1 **small yellow squash**

1. Stir together the water, sugar and pickling spice in a medium-size saucepan. Bring to boiling. Lower the heat; simmer, uncovered, without stirring, for 5 minutes. Cool to

room temperature. Pour in the vinegar.

2. Slice the zucchini into ½-inch thick rounds. Pare the carrots. Halve and seed the red peppers. Cut the carrots and peppers into 1½ x ½-inch sticks. Slice the yellow squash into ½-inch thick rounds. You should have a total of about 4 cups of vegetables.

3. Pack the zucchini tightly, with round cut-sides facing outward, in the bottom of a 1-quart glass or clear plastic container with a tight-fitting lid.

4. Mix together the carrot and red pepper sticks. Arrange, standing upright, on top of the zucchini; pack tightly.

5. Pack the yellow squash, round cut-sides facing outward on top of the carrot and red pepper sticks. Make sure all the vegetables are tightly packed in the container or they will float to the top when the pickling liquid is added.

6. Slowly pour enough of the pickling liquid into the container to cover the vegetables. Gently move the vegetables so some of the spices fall between the vegetables. Cover tightly; refrigerate overnight. The vegetables can be stored in the refrigerator for up to 3 days.

◀◀◀ *Tomato-Apple Chutney*

Makes 7 pints.

Nutrient Value Per Serving: 18 calories, 0 gm. protein, 0 gm. fat, 11 mg. sodium, 0 mg. cholesterol.

15 *large ripe tomatoes, peeled, cored and chopped (2½ quarts)*
4 *large apples, pared, cored and chopped (1 quart)*
2 *large cucumbers, pared, seeded and chopped*
3 *medium-size onions, chopped*
3 *medium-size sweet red peppers, halved, seeded and chopped (2 cups)*
1 *cup raisins*
3 *cups firmly packed light brown sugar*
1 *hot red pepper (optional)*
1 *clove garlic, finely chopped*
1 *tablespoon ground ginger*
1 *teaspoon salt*
1 *teaspoon ground cinnamon*
3 *cups white vinegar*

1. Combine the tomatoes, apples, cucumbers, onions, sweet red peppers, raisins, brown sugar, hot red peppers, if you wish, garlic, ginger, salt, cinnamon and vinegar in a large heavy enamel or stainless steel kettle.

2. Bring slowly to boiling, stirring occasionally. Adjust the heat so the mixture bubbles gently. Cook, uncovered, for 1½ hours or until very thick and glossy. Watch the kettle toward the end of the cooking time, stirring frequently, to prevent mixture from sticking and burning.

3. About 30 minutes before the chutney is done, wash and rinse 7 pint canning jars and their lids. Immerse the jars and lids in separate kettles of hot water until ready to use them.

4. Ladle the chutney into the hot canning jars, leaving a ¼-inch headspace. Run a long, thin, non-metallic spatula around the inside of the jars to release the bubbles. Wipe the jar rims and threads clean with a damp cloth. Cover with the hot lids; screw on the bands firmly.

5. Process the jars in a boiling water bath for 10 minutes (water should cover jars by 1 to 2 inches). Remove the jars from the water bath; cool on wire racks. Check the seals. Label, date and store in a cool dark place.

TWO WAYS TO PEEL TOMATOES
1. Add tomatoes, a few at a time, to a large pot of boiling water. When the water returns to boiling, boil 10 seconds for very ripe tomatoes, and 20 seconds for firmer tomatoes. Remove with a slotted spoon. (If the skin splits, remove the tomato immediately.) Rinse under cold water to stop the cooking. Working from the bottom to the stem end, peel off the skin with a paring knife.
2. If peeling a few tomatoes, stick a long, two-tined fork into the stem end of the tomato. Hold the tomato directly in a gas burner flame. Slowly rotate the tomato so all sides begin to show a speckled brown color. Set aside to cool. Peel as above.

◀◀◀ *Red Chili Sauce*

Makes 5 pints.

Nutrient Value Per Tablespoon: 12 calories, 0 gm. protein, 0 gm. fat, 42 mg. sodium, 0 mg. cholesterol.

18 *medium-size tomatoes, cored and chopped (about 7 pounds)*
3 *large onions, coarsely chopped*
3 *large sweet red peppers, cored, seeded and coarsely chopped*
¾ *cup sugar*
1 *tablespoon salt*
2 *cups cider vinegar*
1 *tablespoon celery seeds*
1 *tablespoon mustard seeds*
¼ *cup finely chopped preserved ginger*
3 *tablespoons mixed pickling spice*

1. Combine the tomatoes, onions, red peppers, sugar and salt in a large enamel or stainless steel kettle. Simmer for 30 minutes, stirring frequently.

2. Stir in the vinegar, celery seeds, mustard seeds and ginger. Tie the pickling spices in cheesecloth; push down into the vegetables. Cook, stirring frequently, until thickened, for about 40 minutes.

3. Meanwhile, wash 5 pint canning jars and lids and bands in hot soapy water. Rinse. Leave the jars in hot water until needed. Place the lids and bands in the saucepan of simmering water until ready to use.

4. Remove the spice bag. Ladle the sauce into the clean, hot pint canning jars, leaving a ½-inch headspace. Run a long, thin, non-metallic spatula around the inside of the jars to release trapped bubbles. Wipe the jar rims and threads clean with a damp cloth. Cover the jars with the hot lids; screw on the bands firmly.

5. Process the jars in a boiling water bath for 15 minutes (water should cover jars by 1 to 2 inches). Remove the jars from the boiling water. Cool on wire racks. Test the seals. Label, date and store in a cool, dark place.

◥ ◀◀◀ *Pesto Sauce*

Serve over pasta, or just a tablespoon or two over chicken, fish or vegetables. Double or triple the recipe and freeze the extra so you can enjoy the rest throughout the winter.

Makes 6 servings (enough for 1 pound of pasta).

Nutrient Value Per ¼ Cup: 234 calories, 6 gm. protein, 22 gm. fat, 258 mg. sodium, 7 mg. cholesterol.

½ *cup olive oil*
3 *cloves garlic*
¼ *teaspoon salt*
2 *cups firmly packed fresh basil leaves*
2 *tablespoons pignoli (pine nuts)*
    OR: 2 tablespoons walnuts
⅔ *cup freshly grated Parmesan cheese*

1. Place the oil, garlic and salt in the container of an electric blender or food processor. Cover; whirl until smooth.
2. Add the basil and nuts. Blend until smooth. Transfer to a bowl. Fold in Parmesan cheese.
3. Spoon the pesto over 1 pound of hot cooked, drained pasta. Toss until evenly blended. Serve immediately with additional Parmesan and nuts, if you wish.

MAKE PESTO SAUCE AHEAD
Store pesto in the refrigerator in a jar covered with a layer of olive oil for several weeks. For longer storage, place in a 1-pint freezer container or ice cube cups and freeze. Transfer cubes to plastic bag.

▲ **Spaghetti with Pesto Sauce**

Basil-Marinara Sauce

Serve with pasta, over cooked fish, boneless chicken breasts or vegetables.

Makes about 5 cups (enough sauce for 1 pound of pasta).

Nutrient Value Per ½-Cup Serving: 53 calories, 2 gm. protein, 2 gm. fat, 305 mg. sodium, 0 mg. cholesterol.

1 cup coarsely chopped onion
2 cloves garlic, finely chopped
1 tablespoon olive oil
1 can (2 pounds, 3 ounces) whole Italian-style tomatoes
1 can (8 ounces) tomato sauce
2 cups firmly packed fresh basil leaves, finely chopped
¼ teaspoon salt

1. Sauté the onion and garlic in the oil in a saucepan until tender. Stir in the tomatoes with their liquid, breaking them up, the tomato sauce, ¼ cup of the chopped basil and the salt. Bring to boiling. Lower the heat; simmer uncovered, stirring frequently, until thickened, about 20 minutes.
2. Stir the remaining basil into the sauce. Serve immediately over hot cooked pasta. Or cool, then freeze in freezer containers.

BASIL STORAGE
Bunches of basil will store best for 2 to 3 days in the refrigerator, upright, with the stems or roots in a cup of water and the leaves loosely covered with a plastic bag. Do not wash until ready to use. If you wish to keep basil longer, then wash and drain very well on paper toweling. Remove the leaves from the stems. Freeze in plastic bags, either whole or chopped. Scoop out or break off the frozen amount needed, and add frozen to the dish while it is cooking.

Fresh Tomato-Basil Sauce

A no-effort, uncooked tomato sauce that can be made ahead and refrigerated. Be sure to return it to room temperature before using as a sauce for pasta or as a salad dressing.

Makes 6 servings (enough for 1 pound of pasta).

Nutrient Value Per ½ Cup Sauce: 55 calories, 3 gm. protein, 1 gm. fat, 276 mg. sodium, 0 mg. cholesterol.

> **2 pounds ripe Italian plum tomatoes, peeled and chopped**
> **½ cup sliced green onions**
> **3 cloves garlic, finely chopped**
> **¾ teaspoon salt**
> **¼ teaspoon coarse black pepper**
> **2 tablespoons tarragon vinegar**
> **2 cups firmly packed fresh basil leaves, finely chopped**

1. Combine the tomatoes, green onions, garlic, salt, pepper, vinegar and basil in a bowl; toss to mix well. Cover tightly. Set aside at room temperature for 2 hours before serving so the flavors can blend.
2. To serve: Stir to remix. Toss with 1 pound of hot cooked, drained pasta, or spoon over a salad as a dressing.

Tomato Marmalade

Makes 5 half-pint jars.

Nutrient Value Per Tablespoon: 50 calories, 0 gm. protein, 0 gm. fat, 1 mg. sodium, 1 mg. cholesterol.

> **1 lemon**
> **5 medium-size ripe tomatoes**
> **1 box (1¾ ounces) powdered pectin**
> **4½ cups sugar**
> **2 tablespoons chopped preserved ginger**

1. Wash and sterilize 5 half-pint canning jars in boiling water for 20 minutes. Leave the jars in the water while preparing the tomatoes. Place the two-piece jar lids in simmering water in a separate pan.
2. Pare thin strips of rind (yellow only) from the lemon; cut the rind into slivers. Simmer in water in a saucepan for 15 minutes; drain.
3. With a sharp knife, slice off the white membrane from the lemon; remove the seeds; cut the pulp into small pieces.
4. Peel the tomatoes. Core and cut them into eighths; you should have about 5 cups. Place in a 6-quart stainless steel or enamel pan or kettle with the lemon rind and pulp. Cover and bring to boiling. Lower the heat; simmer for 10 minutes. Measure. If necessary, add water to make 4 cups. Return to the pan. Stir in the pectin.
5. Place over high heat; stir until the mixture comes to a hard boil. Stir in the sugar and ginger. Bring to a full rolling boil. Boil for 1 minute. Remove from the heat. Skim off the foam with a metal spoon. Stir and skim for 7 minutes to prevent the fruit from floating.
6. Ladle the marmalade into the hot, clean jars, leaving a ¼-inch headspace. Wipe the rims and threads with a damp cloth. Cover the

◀Fresh Tomato-Basil Sauce

jars with the hot lids; screw on bands firmly. As each jar is sealed, invert. Turn upright after 5 minutes.

7. Let stand for 30 minutes. Shake gently. Check the seals. Label, date and store in a cool, dark place. If there is leftover sauce, refrigerate it in a covered container.

*From left: **Basil Butter** and **Basil Jelly**.*

🗟 Basil Jelly

Makes 4 half-pint jars.

Nutrient Value Per Tablespoon: 46 calories, 0 gm. protein, 0 gm. fat, 0.3 mg. sodium, 0 mg. cholesterol.

1½ cups firmly packed fresh basil leaves, finely chopped
1¾ cups water
3½ cups sugar
2 tablespoons lemon juice
1 packet (3 ounces) fruit pectin

1. Place the chopped basil in a saucepan. Add water. Bring to boiling. Remove from the heat. Set aside covered, for 15 minutes.
2. Wash 4 half-pint canning jars. Sterilize in boiling water for 10 minutes. Keep hot.
3. Strain the basil mixture into a 2-cup glass measure. Add water to measure 1¾ cups, if necessary. Return the mixture to the saucepan. Stir in sugar and lemon juice.
4. Bring the basil mixture to full boil over high heat, stirring constantly. When the mixture reaches boiling, immediately stir in the pectin. Return to a full boil; boil for 1 minute, stirring constantly. Remove from the heat.
5. Skim the foam from the top of the jelly. Pour the jelly into the prepared jars, leaving at least a ¼-inch headspace. Wipe the rims and threads clean. Cover the jars with the hot lids; screw on the bands firmly. Let the jelly stand until completely cool. Tighten the bands, if necessary.

6. Store in a cool, dry place for several months. After opening, store in the refrigerator for up to several weeks.

◤ Basil Butter

Spread on bread or place a pat on grilled steak, grilled chicken or hot vegetables.

Makes ½ cup.

Nutrient Value Per Serving: 101 calories, 1 gm. protein, 11 gm. fat, 2 mg. sodium, 31 mg. cholesterol.

1 tablespoon finely chopped fresh basil
2 teaspoons lemon juice
½ cup unsalted butter, softened

Stir the basil and lemon juice into the softened butter in a small bowl. Spoon into a serving container. Store, tightly covered, in the refrigerator.

7. The Best Course: Dessert Cakes and Cookies

A sumptuous array of dessert cakes and cookies to tempt any sweet tooth await you in this chapter. Family and friends will appreciate the time you took to make these special treats.

Cake, a rich, moist, irresistible dessert is the grandest finale to your meal. Best results will be achieved when care is taken to:

• Have the ingredients at room temperature.
• Use the proper measuring utensils for liquid and dry ingredients.
• Follow the recipe instructions carefully.

Butter cake, pound cake, fruitcake, sponge cake, cheesecake and even a quick-but-special company torte that you make from a mix, are included in our repertoire. Try Prunella Cake, a delicious, old-fashioned cake richly flavored with spices, bursting with fruit and frosted with a creamy icing. A special occasion will be even more memorable when celebrated with a sinfully rich Chocolate Fudge Layer Cake.

Cookies, as a dessert, a special treat or a gift, add to the festiveness of holidays and make regular days special. The beauty of cookies is that you can bake them ahead, then store them in an airtight container or freezer so they will be available whenever you want them. Delicious desserts made with cookies, such as Mocha Lace Roll-Ups and Strawberry Shortbread, are also included for your enjoyment.

Cakes

◄Chocolate-Chestnut Roll (page 208)

🍸 Lane Cake

Bake at 375° for 20 to 25 minutes.
Makes 12 serings.

Nutrient Value Per Serving: 762 calories, 9 gm. protein, 37 gm. fat, 404 mg. sodium, 246 mg. cholesterol.

3¼ cups sifted cake flour
3½ teaspoons baking powder
  1 cup (2 sticks) butter, at room temperature
  2 cups sugar
  1 teaspoon vanilla
  1 cup milk
  8 egg whites
     Lane Filling (recipe follows)

1. Preheat the oven to moderate (375°). Grease and flour three 9-inch round layer-cake pans.
2. Sift together the flour and baking powder.
3. Beat the butter and sugar in a large bowl until very light and creamy. Beat in the vanilla.
4. Stir the flour mixture alternately with the milk into the butter mixture; mix until smooth.
5. Beat the egg whites until stiff but not dry. Stir one fourth of the egg whites into the batter. Fold in the remaining whites just until mixed. Divide the batter equally among the prepared pans
6. Bake in the preheated oven (375°) for 20 to 25 minutes or until a cake tester inserted in the center comes out clean. Cool in the pans on wire racks for 10 minutes. Turn out onto the racks. Cool to room temperature.
7. Place a cake layer on a platter. Spread with one third of the Lane Filling. Repeat, stacking the layers with remaining filling. Garnish with the reserved pecan halves, cherries and coconut from the filling recipe.

Lane Filling

8 *egg yolks*
1¼ *cups sugar*
⅓ *cup bourbon*
1 *cup pecan halves*
1 *cup flaked coconut*
1 *cup glacé cherries*
½ *cup (1 stick) butter, at room temperature*
1 *cup raisins*

1. Mix the egg yolks and sugar in the top of a double boiler. Cook over hot water, stirring constantly, until the sugar dissolves and the mixture thickens to coat the back of a spoon. Remove from the heat, stir in the bourbon. Cool to room temperature.
2. Reserve some pecan halves, coconut and

cherries for garnishing the top of the cake. Coarsley chop the remaining pecans; quarter the remaining cherries.
3. Beat the butter in a bowl until light and creamy. Mix in the egg yolk mixture. Fold in the chopped pecans, quartered cherries, coconut and raisins.

BAKING TIPS
● Remember to preheat the oven to the proper temperature 10 minutes before baking.
● Don't open the oven door to check the cake until the minimum baking time is up. The cake will fall if the baking process is interrupted too early.

Chocolate Velvet Cake

To slightly sweeten the bitter chocolate filling, add extra sugar as indicated in step 8.

Bake cake at 400° for 8 to 10 minutes.
Makes 24 servings.

Nutrient Value Per Serving: 355 calories, 5 gm. protein, 25 gm. fat, 64 mg. sodium, 128 mg. cholesterol.

1 *recipe Sponge Cake (see Raspberry Roll, page 210)*
3 *boxes (8 ounces each) semisweet chocolate*
½ *cup strong coffee*
3 *egg yolks*
½ *cup Grand Marnier*
1 *cup egg whites (5 or 6 whites)*
½ *to 1 cup granulated sugar*
3½ *cups heavy cream*
2 *tablespoons 10X (confectioners') sugar*
2 *teaspoons vanilla*
Candied Violets (optional)

1. Preheat the oven to hot (400°). Line the bottoms of a 15 x 10 x 1-inch jelly-roll pan and an 8-inch round layer-cake pan with aluminum foil; lightly grease the aluminum foil.
2. Prepare the Sponge Cake batter, steps 3 and 4 for Raspberry Roll (page 210).
3. Spread 1 cup of the batter in the round layer-cake pan, and the remaining batter in the jelly-roll pan.
4. Bake in the preheated hot oven (400°) for 8 to 10 minutes or until golden brown.
5. Loosen the cakes around edges with a knife. Invert onto pieces of lightly oiled aluminum foil on wire racks. Peel the aluminum foil from the bottoms of the cakes. Cool to room temperature.
6. Combine the chocolate and coffee in the top of a double boiler. Heat over hot, not boiling, water until the chocolate is melted. Remove from the heat. Reserve.
7. Beat the egg yolks in a large bowl until frothy. Add the chocolate mixture and Grand Marnier. Beat until well combined. Set aside.
8. Beat the egg whites in a medium-size bowl until foamy. Gradually beat in ½ cup of the granulated sugar until the mixture forms firm peaks. (This amount of sugar will result in a European-style bitter chocolate flavor. For a sweeter filling, add up to an additional ½ cup of sugar.)
9. In a small bowl with the same beaters, beat the 1 cup of heavy cream until stiff.
10. Fold about one third of the whipped cream and one third of the beaten egg whites into the melted chocolate mixture. Fold in the remaining whipped cream and egg white until no streaks of white remain. Reserve.
11. Lightly oil a 2½-quart glass casserole or bowl. Measure and cut off a 15 x 6½-inch strip from the sponge cake baked in the jelly-roll pan. Fit strip, top surface up, into the center and up the sides of the casserole; ends should extend above rim. Cut

the remaining 15 x 3½-inch strip in half crosswise. Place each half on either side of center strip in the casserole; trim as necessary so pieces fit neatly into the casserole. Save scraps.
12. Set aside ½ cup of the chocolate filling. Spoon the remaining filling into the cake-lined casserole. Place an 8-inch round of cake on top of the chocolate filling. Turn the edges of the cake strips over to meet the cake round. Fill in any open spaces with bits of reserved cake scraps. Cover very tightly with plastic wrap to keep bottom pieces in place. Place in the freezer for 1½ hours or in the refrigerator for 3 to 4 hours.
13. Beat 1 cup of the heavy cream in a small bowl until stiff. Fold in the reserved ½ cup of chocolate filling. Cover; refrigerate.
14. Loosen the cake around the edges and turn out onto a platter. Frost completely with the whipped cream-chocolate mixture.
15. Beat together the remaining heavy cream, the 10X (confectioners') sugar and vanilla until stiff. Spoon into a large pastry bag fitted with large star tip. Decorate the cake with cream and candied violets, if you wish.
16. To serve, cut in wedges with a moistened knife, wiping the blade with a damp cloth after each cut. Store in the refrigerator.

A CAKE IS DONE
- When the cake shrinks slightly from the sides of the pan.
- When a fingertip is lightly pressed on the top of the cake and the top springs back to shape.
- When a cake tester or wooden pick inserted near the center of the cake comes out clean, with no batter or moist particles clinging to it.

Sour Cream-Walnut Cake

A delicate old-fashioned layer cake that will please the whole family.

Bake at 350° for 30 minutes.
Makes 8 servings.

Nutrient Value Per Serving: 890 calories, 9 gm. protein, 45 gm. fat, 352 mg. sodium, 173 mg. cholesterol.

2½ **cups** sifted *cake flour*
  1 **teaspoon baking soda**
  1 **teaspoon baking powder**
 ½ **cup (1 stick) butter or margarine**
 ¼ **cup vegetable shortening**
1¼ **cups sugar**
  3 **eggs**
  2 **teaspoons grated orange rind**
 ¾ **cup dairy sour cream**
 ¼ **cup milk**
  1 **cup finely chopped walnuts**
     Rum Butter Frosting (recipe follows)
     Coarsely chopped walnuts
     Kumquats and leaves (optional)

1. Preheat the oven to moderate (350°). Grease two 9 x 1½-inch round layer-cake pans; dust the pans lightly with flour; tap out the excess flour.
2. Sift together the flour, baking soda and baking powder onto wax paper.
3. Combine the butter, shortening, sugar and eggs in a large bowl. Beat with an electric mixer at high speed for 3 minutes or until the mixture is light and fluffy. Beat in the orange rind.
4. Combine the sour cream and milk. Stir the flour mixture into the batter, alternating with the sour cream mixture, beginning and ending with the flour. Stir in the finely chopped nuts. Scrape the batter into the prepared pans, dividing evenly.
5. Bake in the preheated moderate oven (350°) for 30 minutes or until the tops spring back when lightly pressed with a fingertip.

6. Cool the layers in the pans on wire racks for 10 minutes; loosen around the edges with a small spatula; turn out onto the wire racks; cool completely.
7. Prepare the Rum Butter Frosting.
8. Fill and frost the layers with Rum Butter Frosting. Cover the side with coarsely chopped walnuts; garnish with kumquats and leaves, if you wish.

Rum Butter Frosting: Beat ½ cup (1 stick) butter or margarine in a medium-size bowl until soft. Beat in 1 package (1 pound) 10X (confectioners') sugar alternately with 3 tablespoons rum and 1 tablespoon milk until the mixture is smooth and spreadable.

Prunella Cake

Bake at 350° for 25 minutes.
Makes 12 servings (one 8-inch layer cake).

Nutrient Value Per Serving: 302 calories, 3 gm. protein, 11 gm. fat, 150 mg. sodium, 72 mg. cholesterol.

 ⅔ **cup prunes**
1⅓ **cups** sifted *all-purpose flour*
 ½ **teaspoon baking powder**
 ½ **teaspoon baking soda**
 ½ **teaspoon ground allspice**
 ½ **teaspoon ground cinnamon**
 ½ **teaspoon ground nutmeg**
 ½ **cup (1 stick) butter or margarine**
  1 **cup sugar**
  2 **eggs**
 ⅔ **cup buttermilk**
     Creamy Icing (recipe follows)

1. Place the prunes in a saucepan with enough water to cover. Bring to boiling. Lower the heat; simmer gently for 15 minutes or until the prunes are almost tender. Drain, reserving prune juice for the Creamy Icing. Cool the prunes slightly. Pit; chop coarsely.

2. Preheat the oven to moderate (350°). Grease two 8-inch round layer-cake pans. Line each pan bottom with a circle of wax paper; grease and flour the wax paper.

3. Sift together the flour, baking powder, baking soda, allspice, cinnamon and nutmeg onto a sheet of wax paper; set aside.

4. Beat together the butter and sugar in a large bowl with an electric mixer at high speed until light and fluffy. Beat in eggs, one at a time, until well blended.

5. Add the sifted dry ingredients alternately with the buttermilk to the butter mixture, beginning and ending with the dry ingredients; beat until well blended. Stir in the chopped prunes. Divide the batter evenly into the prepared pans.

6. Bake in the preheated moderate oven (350°) for 25 minutes or until a wooden pick inserted near the center of each cake comes out clean.

7. Let the cakes cool in the pans on wire racks for 10 minutes. Turn out the cakes onto the racks; cool completely.

8. Fill the layers with Creamy Icing; spread top with icing.

Creamy Icing: Beat 2 cups *sifted* 10X (confectioners') sugar, ½ teaspoon ground cinnamon and 2 table-spoons softened butter until light and fluffy. Add 2 tablespoons of the reserved prune juice and 1 table-spoon lemon juice; beat until well blended.

Chocolate Fudge Layer Cake

Bake cake layers at 350° for 35 minutes.
Makes 12 servings.

Nutrient Value Per Serving: 509 calories, 5 gm. protein, 24 gm. fat, 330 mg. sodium, 105 mg. cholesterol.

2	**cups** sifted *cake flour*
2	**teaspoons baking powder**
½	**teaspoon baking soda**
½	**teaspoon salt**
3	**squares unsweetened chocolate**
⅔	**cup water**
1½	**cups sugar**
1	**teaspoon vanilla**
⅔	**cup butter or margarine, softened**
3	**eggs**
⅓	**cup buttermilk**
	Chocolate Fudge Filling (recipe follows)

1. Sift the flour, baking powder, baking soda and salt onto wax paper. Set aside.

2. Cook the chocolate, water and ¼ cup sugar in a saucepan, stirring constantly over low heat until thick and smooth. Transfer to a bowl; chill over ice water, stirring often. Add the vanilla. Preheat the oven to moderate (350°).

3. Beat the butter and remaining sugar in a large bowl until fluffy. Beat in eggs, one at a time. Add the chilled chocolate mixture; blend.

4. Add the sifted ingredients alternately with the buttermilk, beating well after each addition, until smooth. Pour into two greased and floured 8-inch round layer-cake pans.

5. Bake in the preheated moderate oven (350°) for 35 minutes or until the centers spring back when lightly pressed with a fingertip.

6. Remove the layers from the pans; cool on a wire rack. Split in half. Fill and frost with Chocolate Fudge Filling. Decorate with whipped cream and fresh raspberries, if you wish.

Chocolate Fudge Filling: Combine 6 squares semi-sweet chocolate and 3 tablespoons butter in a small saucepan. Place over very low heat just until melted. Transfer to a bowl; beat in 7 tablespoons milk, 1 teaspoon vanilla until blended. Gradually beat in 3 cups of *sifted* 10X (confectioners') sugar until smooth and spreadable.

▣ ☐ *Spiced Crumb Sheet Cake*

Bake at 350° for 25 to 30 minutes.
Makes 24 servings.

Nutrient Value Per Serving: 227 calories, 3 gm.
protein, 8 gm. fat, 56 mg. sodium, 44 mg.
cholesterol.

```
 2   cups firmly packed brown sugar
 5   cups sifted cake flour
 1   cup (2 sticks) unsalted butter
 2   teaspoons baking soda
 2   teaspoons ground cinnamon
 1   teaspoon ground cloves
 2   eggs, slightly beaten
2¼   cups buttermilk
 2   teaspoons vanilla
 ½   cup chopped walnuts (optional)
     Fruit Preserve Lattice Topping
       (optional, recipe follows)
     Walnut halves (optional)
```

1. Preheat the oven to moderate (350°).
   Generously grease a 15 x 10 x 1-inch jelly-roll
   pan.
2. Stir together the brown sugar and cake flour
   in a medium-size bowl until well combined.
   Slice the butter into the flour mixture. Work
   the butter into the flour mixture with a
   pastry blender or fingertips until the
   mixture resembles coarse crumbs.
3. Remove and reserve ¾ cup of the flour
   mixture. Stir the baking soda, cinnamon and
   cloves into the remaining flour mixture in
   the bowl. Make a well in the center; add the
   eggs, buttermilk and vanilla. Stir just until
   the mixture is evenly combined.
4. Spread the batter evenly in the prepared
   pan. Sprinkle with the reserved ¾ cup flour
   mixture or ½ cup chopped walnuts, if you
   wish.
5. Bake in the preheated moderate oven (350°)
   for 25 to 30 minutes or until the center
   springs back when lightly pressed with a
   fingertip. Cool completely on a wire rack.

6. Top with Fruit Preserve Lattice Topping, or
   serve plain, garnished with walnut halves.
   Cut into 24 pieces.

Fruit Preserve Lattice Topping

Makes 24 servings.

Nutrient Value Per Serving: 36 calories, 0 gm.
protein, 0 gm. fat, 2 mg. sodium, 0 mg.
cholesterol.

```
⅓   cup raspberry preserves
⅓   cup apricot preserves
```

Spoon the raspberry preserves in thin diagonal
strips, about 2 inches apart, across the top of
the cooled cake. Spoon the apricot preserves
in the opposite direction.

▣ ☐ *Banana Cake*

Bake at 350° for 25 to 30 minutes.
Makes 24 servings.

Nutrient Value Per Serving: 201 calories, 2 gm.
protein, 9 gm. fat, 117 mg. sodium, 56 mg.
cholesterol.

```
3¾   cups sifted cake flour
 3   teaspoons baking powder
 1   teaspoon baking soda
 ½   teaspoon salt
 ¼   cup dairy sour cream
 2   cups mashed ripe bananas
 1   cup (2 sticks) unsalted butter, softened
1½   cups sugar
 3   eggs
     Chocolate Frosting or Lemon Frosting
       (recipes follow)
```

1. Preheat the oven to moderate (350°). Generously grease a 15 x 10 x 1-inch jelly-roll pan.

2. Sift together the flour, baking powder, baking soda and salt onto a piece of wax paper. Stir the sour cream into the mashed bananas in a small bowl.

3. Beat together the butter, sugar and eggs in a large bowl with an electric mixer at high speed, for 3 minutes, or until light and fluffy.

4. Stir the flour mixture alternately with the banana mixture into the butter mixture, beating by hand after each addition, until the batter is smooth. Pour the batter into the prepared pan. Smooth the top with a spatula.

5. Bake in the preheated moderate oven (350°) for 25 to 30 minutes or until the center springs back when lightly pressed with a fingertip. Cool completely on a wire rack.

6. Top with your choice of frosting. Cut into 24 pieces.

Chocolate Frosting

Makes 24 servings.

Nutrient Value Per Serving: 110 calories, 0 gm. protein, 4 gm. fat, 2 mg. sodium, 11 mg. cholesterol.

½ **cup (1 stick) unsalted butter, softened**
1 **box (1 pound) 10X (confectioners') sugar**
3 **tablespoons unsweetened cocoa powder**
¼ **cup milk**
   Nuts and quartered orange slices (optional)

Beat the butter in a medium-size bowl with an electric mixer until fluffy. Beat in the 10X sugar and cocoa powder alternately with the milk until smooth and spreadable. Add a little more milk, if necessary. Spread evenly over the top of the cake. Garnish with nuts and orange slices, if you wish.

Lemon or Orange Frosting

Makes 24 servings.

Nutrient Value Per Serving: 107 calories, 0 gm. protein, 4 gm. fat, 1 mg. sodium, 10 mg. cholesterol.

½ **cup (1 stick) unsalted butter, softened**
1 **box (1 pound) 10X (confectioners') sugar**
¼ **cup lemon or orange juice, strained**
2 **tablespoons grated lemon or orange rind**
   Shredded lemon or orange rind for garnish (optional)
   Chopped pistachios or walnuts (optional)

Beat the butter in a medium-size bowl until fluffy. Beat in the 10X sugar alternately with the lemon or orange juice until smooth and spreadable. Fold in the grated orange or lemon rind. Spread evenly over the top of the cake. Garnish with shredded rind and nuts, if you wish.

TO STORE CAKES
Cover the cut surface of the cake with plastic wrap and place it in a cake keeper or invert a large bowl over the cake plate. The cake will keep for 2 or 3 days this way. Cakes with a cream frosting or filling should be refrigerated, with plastic wrap over the cut part.

▮▯ Yellow Sheet Cake

Bake at 350° for 25 to 30 minutes.
Makes 24 servings.

Nutrient Value Per Serving: 219 calories, 3 gm. protein, 11 gm. fat, 92 mg. sodium, 62 mg. cholesterol.

4½ **cups sifted *cake flour***
3 **teaspoons baking powder**
¼ **teaspoon salt**
1¼ **cups (2½ sticks) unsalted butter, softened**
1½ **cups sugar**
3 **eggs**
3 **teaspoons vanilla**
1½ **cups milk**
    Glazed Strawberry Topping or Blueberries and Cream Topping (recipes follow)

1. Preheat the oven to moderate (350°). Generously grease a 15 x 10 x 1-inch jelly-roll pan.
2. Sift together the flour, baking powder and salt onto a piece of wax paper.
3. Beat together the butter, sugar, eggs and vanilla in a large bowl with an electric mixer at high speed until light and fluffy, about 3 minutes.
4. Add the flour mixture and milk. Beat at medium speed, scraping down the sides frequently, until the mixture is smooth. Spread the batter evenly in the prepared pan.
5. Bake in the preheated moderate oven (350°) for 25 to 30 minutes or until the center springs back when lightly pressed with a fingertip. Cool completely on a wire rack.
6. Top with your choice of topping. Cut into 24 pieces.

Glazed Strawberry Topping

Makes 24 servings.

Nutrient Value Per Serving: 22 calories, 0 gm. protein, 0 gm. fat, 0 mg. sodium, 0 mg. cholesterol.

2 **tablespoons cornstarch**
1 **tablespoon sugar**
1 **package (10 ounces) frozen raspberries, thawed OR: frozen strawberries, thawed**
3 **pints fresh strawberries, hulled and halved**

1. Combine the cornstarch and sugar in a medium-size saucepan. Stir in the raspberries with their liquid well blended. Bring to boiling; simmer for 1 minute. Strain through a sieve into a medium-size bowl; discard the seeds. Spread half the glaze evenly over the top of the cake.
2. Arrange the strawberries, cut-side down in rows. Brush gently with the remaining glaze.

Blueberries and Cream Topping

Makes 24 servings.

Nutrient Value Per Serving: 63 calories, 1 gm. protein, 4 gm. fat, 6 mg. sodium, 14 mg. cholesterol.

2 **tablespoons cornstarch**
1 **tablespoon granulated sugar**
1 **package (10 ounces) frozen raspberries, thawed**
2 **bags (12 ounces each) dry-pack frozen blueberries**
1 **cup heavy cream**
2 **tablespoons 10X (confectioners') sugar**
½ **teaspoon vanilla**

1. Combine the cornstarch and sugar in a medium-size saucepan. Stir in the

raspberries with their liquid until well combined. Bring to boiling; simmer for 1 minute. Strain through a sieve into a large bowl; discard the seeds. Fold in the frozen blueberries.

2. Spoon the berries onto the top of the cake in 1-inch wide diagonal strips. Chill until set.

3. Beat together the cream, 10X sugar and vanilla in a small bowl until stiff peaks form. Spoon into a pastry bag fitted with a star tip. Pipe rows of stars between the rows of topping; refrigerate until ready to serve.

NO CHANGES PLEASE
If you want your cake to have the best volume, shape and texture possible, use the ingredients, measurements and pan size called for in the recipe. Follow the directions carefully.

Cranberry-Apple-Filled Walnut Cake Roll

Bake at 375° for 12 minutes.
Makes 10 servings.

Nutrient Value Per Serving: 280 calories, 4 gm. protein, 13 gm. fat, 125 mg. sodium, 115 mg. cholesterol.

2   large apples, such as McIntosh, Cortland or Rome Beauty, pared, cored and cut into ¼-inch pieces
1   cup whole fresh cranberries
¼   cup sugar
¼   cup water
2   tablespoons apple brandy
1   teaspoon lemon juice

½   teaspoon ground cinnamon
¼   teaspoon ground nutmeg

WALNUT CAKE ROLL
⅔   cup sifted all-purpose flour
1   teaspoon baking powder
¼   teaspoon salt
3   eggs, at room temperature
¾   cup sugar
⅓   cup water
1   teaspoon vanilla
⅓   cup finely ground walnuts
     10X (confectioners') sugar
1   cup heavy cream
1   teaspoon vanilla
½   teaspoon ground cinnamon
     Coarsely chopped walnuts
     Apple slices

1. Preheat the oven to moderate (375°). Grease a 15 x 10 x 1-inch jelly-roll pan; line with wax paper; grease paper.

2. Combine the apples, cranberries, sugar, water, apple brandy, lemon juice, cinnamon and nutmeg in a medium-size non-aluminum saucepan. Cook over medium heat, stirring until the cranberries pop and the mixture thickens, about 6 minutes. Let cool. Set aside.

3. Prepare the Walnut Cake Roll: Sift together the flour, baking powder and salt onto a piece of wax paper. Set aside.

4. Beat the eggs in a medium-size bowl for 3 minutes. Gradually beat in the sugar until very thick and pale, 5 minutes. Stir in the water and vanilla. Fold in the flour mixture and ground walnuts. Pour into the prepared pan, spreading evenly.

5. Bake in the preheated moderate oven (375°) for 12 minutes or until the cake is golden and the center springs back when lightly touched with a fingertip.

6. Loosen the cake around the edges with a knife. Invert the pan onto a clean towel dusted generously with 10X (confectioners') sugar. Remove the pan. Carefully peel off the wax paper. Starting at a short end, roll up the cake and towel together. Cool on a

wire rack for about 30 minutes.

7. When the cake is cool, unroll carefully. Spread the roll evenly with the fruit filling, leaving a 2-inch border along the short side which will be the outside seam. Reroll the cake from the short end, using the towel as an aid. Place the roll seam-side down on a serving plate.

8. Beat the heavy cream with the vanilla and cinnamon in a small bowl until stiff.

9. Pipe the whipped cream down the top of roll. Garnish with the coarsely chopped walnuts and apple slices. Serve with the remaining cream.

LEFTOVER YOLKS
Store leftover uncooked egg yolks, covered with water, in an airtight container for 2 or 3 days in the refrigerator. Drain the water from the yolks before using them in custards or sauces.

LEFTOVER WHITES
Store leftover egg whites in an airtight container in the refrigerator for up to 4 days. Use in soufflés and meringues.

▼ *Chocolate-Chestnut Roll*

Bake at 375° for 12 minutes.
Makes 10 servings.

Nutrient Value Per Serving: 504 calories, 13 gm. protein, 26 gm. fat, 85 mg. sodium, 167 mg. cholesterol.

- *½ cup* sifted *cake flour*
- *¼ cup* sifted *unsweetened cocoa powder*
- *1 teaspoon baking powder*
- *4 eggs, separated*
- *¾ cup sugar*
- *1 teaspoon vanilla*
- *2 tablespoons water*
  Chestnut Filling (recipe follows)
  Cocoa Cream (recipe follows)
  Dark Cocoa Cream (recipe follows)

1. Grease a 15 x 10 x 1-inch jelly-roll pan; line the bottom with wax paper; grease the paper. Sift together the flour, cocoa and baking powder. Preheat the oven to moderate (375°).

2. Beat the yolks in a medium bowl until fluffy. Gradually add the sugar, beating until very thick. Add the vanilla; stir in the water. Fold in the flour mixture.

3. Beat the egg whites until stiff and glossy peaks form. Gently fold into the reserved yolk mixture. Spread evenly in the prepared pan.

4. Bake in the preheated moderate oven (375°) for 12 minutes or until the center springs back when lightly pressed with a fingertip.

5. Dust the cake with 10X (confectioners') sugar; cover with a towel. Invert. Remove the pan and paper. Trim ¼ inch from the sides. Roll up the cake and towel from a short end. Place seam-side down on a wire rack; cool.

6. Unroll. Spread Chestnut Filling over the cake. Reroll the cake. Frost the roll with Cocoa Cream. Decorate with Dark Cocoa Cream.

Chestnut Filling: Beat 1 can (15½ ounces) chestnut purée until smooth and spreadable. Beat ¼ cup heavy cream, ¼ cup 10X (confectioners') sugar and 1 tablespoon rum until stiff. Fold into the purée.

Cocoa Cream: Beat 1 cup heavy cream, 2 tablespoons unsweetened cocoa powder and 1 tablespoon 10X (confectioners') sugar until stiff.

Dark Cocoa Cream: Beat ½ cup heavy cream, 5 tablespoons unsweetened cocoa powder, and 1 tablespoon 10X (confectioners') sugar until stiff.

▶ **Fudge-Mint Torte**

Fudge-Mint Torte

Bake at 375° for 15 to 20 minutes.
Makes 12 servings.

Nutrient Value Per Serving: 618 calories, 6 gm. protein, 42 gm. fat, 202 mg. sodium, 187 mg. cholesterol.

1 package (12 ounces) semisweet chocolate pieces
1 cup (2 sticks) butter or margarine
1½ cups firmly packed light brown sugar
4 eggs
1½ cups sifted all-purpose flour
Crème de Menthe Filling (recipe follows)

1. Grease three 9 x 1½-inch round layer-cake pans; line the bottoms with wax paper; grease the paper. Preheat the oven to moderate (375°).
2. Combine the chocolate pieces and butter in a small saucepan. Place over very low heat just until melted; remove from heat.
3. Transfer the chocolate mixture to a large bowl. Beat in the sugar. Beat in eggs, one at a time. Beat in the flour until well blended. Pour into the prepared pans, dividing evenly.
4. Bake in the preheated moderate oven (375°) for 15 to 20 minutes or until the tops spring back when lightly touched with a fingertip. Cool the cakes in the pans on wire racks for 10 minutes. Invert; peel off the paper; cool completely.
5. Stack and fill the layers with the Crème de Menthe Filling, using one-third between each layer and over the top. Garnish the top with chocolate shavings, if you wish.

Crème de Menthe Filling: Whip 2 cups heavy cream, ¼ to ⅓ cup green Crème de Menthe and 2 tablespoons 10X (confectioners') sugar until stiff.

◀◀◀ 🍸 *Raspberry Roll*

Bake cake at 400° for 10 to 12 minutes.
Makes 10 servings.

Nutrient Value Per Serving: 219 calories, 4 gm.
protein, 12 gm. fat, 91 mg. sodium, 142 mg.
cholesterol.

SPONGE CAKE
 4 eggs, separated
 ¼ teaspoon salt
 ⅓ cup granulated sugar
 2 teaspoons vanilla
 ⅔ cup sifted all-purpose flour

FILLING
**1½ cups fresh raspberries OR: small fresh
       strawberries**
 1 cup heavy cream
 2 tablespoons 10X (confectioners') sugar
 **2 tablespoons Framboise
       (raspberry-flavored liqueur)
       OR: 2 teaspoons vanilla**

SAUCE
 **2 packages (10 ounces each) frozen
       raspberries, slightly thawed**
 2 tablespoons Framboise (optional)
 1 tablespoon 10X (confectioners') sugar
 **6 to 8 large fresh raspberries
       OR: small strawberries for garnish**

1. Preheat the oven to hot (400°).
2. Grease a 15 x 10 x 1-inch jelly-roll pan. Line
   the bottom with aluminum foil; lightly
   grease aluminum foil.
3. Prepare the Sponge Cake: Beat together
   the egg whites and salt in a bowl until
   fluffy. Gradually beat in the sugar until the
   mixture forms firm peaks.
4. Beat together the egg yolks and vanilla in
   a small bowl. Fold in about ½ cup of the
   beaten egg whites. Fold in the remaining
   whites along with the flour. Spread the
   batter evenly in the prepared pan.
5. Bake in the preheated hot oven (400°)
   for 10 to 12 minutes or until golden

brown on top.
6. Loosen the cake around the edges with a
   knife. Invert onto a piece of lightly oiled
   aluminum foil on a wire rack. Peel the
   aluminum foil from the bottom of the
   cake. Cool to room temperature.
7. Prepare the Filling; Wash and thoroughly
   dry berries. If using strawberries, slice into
   quarters. Combine the heavy cream with
   the 10X (confectioners') sugar and
   Framboise or vanilla in a small bowl. Beat
   until stiff. Fold the berries into the cream.
   Spread the mixture evenly over the cooled
   sponge layer.
8. Using the foil as an aid, roll up the cake
   starting with a long side. Place on a serving
   plate, seam-side down. Cover tightly with
   plastic wrap. Chill. (The roll will slice
   better if chilled for at least 2 hours.)
9. Prepare the Sauce: Place the raspberries in
   the container of an electric blender or
   food processor. Cover; whirl until puréed.
   Strain into a bowl. Stir in the Framboise, if
   you wish.
10. To serve, sift 1 tablespoon 10X (confectioners')
    sugar over the roll. Spoon some of the
    raspberry sauce around the roll. Garnish
    the top of the roll with whole raspberries.
    Slice, serving with the remaining sauce.

🍸 ⬜ *Mimosa Cake*

Bake at 375° for 35 minutes.
Makes 16 servings.

Nutrient Value Per Serving: 126 calories, 3 gm.
protein, 1 gm. fat, 67 mg. sodium, 68 mg.
cholesterol.

1¼ cups sifted cake flour
1½ cups sugar
 10 egg whites
1½ teaspoons cream of tartar
 ¼ teaspoon salt

4 **egg yolks**
1 **teaspoon grated lemon rind**
1 **teaspoon vanilla**
  10X (confectioners') sugar

1. Preheat the oven to moderate (375°).
2. Sift the flour and ½ cup of the sugar onto wax paper; set aside.
3. Beat the egg whites, cream of tartar and salt in a large bowl with an electric mixer at high speed until foamy. Beat in the remaining 1 cup sugar, 1 tablespoon at a time, until the meringue forms soft peaks.
4. Fold the flour mixture into the meringue, one-third at a time, until completely blended.
5. Beat the egg yolks in a small bowl with an electric mixer at high speed until thick and lemon-colored. Beat in the lemon rind and vanilla.
6. Fold half of the meringue batter into the beaten egg yolks until no streaks of white remain.
7. Spoon the batters by tablespoonfuls, alternating colors, into an ungreased 10-inch tube pan. (Do not stir the batters in the pan.)
8. Bake in the preheated moderate oven (375°) for 35 minutes or until the top springs back when lightly pressed with a fingertip.
9. Invert the pan, placing the tube over a large funnel or a bottle; let the cake cool completely. Loosen the cake around the edge and the tube with a spatula. Cover the pan with a serving plate; turn upside down; shake gently; remove the pan. Sift 10X (confectioners') sugar over the top, if you wish.

▮ ◻ *Orange Chiffon Cake*

Bake at 325° for 55 minutes; then at 350° for 15 minutes.
Makes 12 servings.

Nutrient Value Per Serving: 451 calories, 6 gm. protein, 19 gm. fat, 370 mg. sodium, 127 mg. cholesterol.

2¼ **cups sifted *cake flour***
1½ **cups sugar**
 1 **tablespoon baking powder**
 1 **teaspoon salt**
 ½ **cup vegetable oil**
 5 **egg yolks, slightly beaten**
 ¾ **cup cold water**
 3 **tablespoons grated orange rind**
 8 **egg whites (1 cup)**
 ½ **teaspoon cream of tartar**
   Orange Buttercream Frosting (recipe follows)
 ⅓ **cup chopped pistachios**

1. Preheat the oven to moderate (325°). Sift together the sifted cake flour, sugar, baking powder and salt into a large bowl. Make a well in the center. Add the oil, yolks, water and rind; stir until well blended.
2. Beat the egg whites with the cream of tartar in a bowl until stiff peaks form. Fold gently into the flour mixture until no white streaks remain. Turn the batter into an ungreased 10-inch tube pan with a removable bottom.
3. Bake in the preheated moderate oven (325°) for 55 minutes. Raise the oven temperature to 350°. Bake 10 to 15 minutes, or until golden brown and the top springs back when lightly touched with a fingertip.
4. Invert the cake on a large funnel or a bottle; hang until completely cooled.
5. Loosen the cake from the edge of the pan and the center tube with a spatula. Remove the sides of the pan. Transfer the cake to a serving plate.
6. Frost the sides and top of the cake with Orange Buttercream Frosting. Sprinkle pistachios over the top.

Orange Buttercream Frosting: Beat together 3 cups sifted 10X (confectioners') sugar, ⅓ cup softened butter and 1½ tablespoons grated orange rind until well blended. Add 3 tablespoons orange juice. Beat until smooth and well blended.

ANGEL, CHIFFON AND SPONGE CAKES
● **Should always be baked in ungreased pans so these light, airy cakes can cling to the sides of the pan and rise to their full height.**
● **To cool these delicate cakes, suspend them, inverted, over the neck of a bottle or over an inverted funnel.**

Upside-Down Cake

Bake at 350° for 30 minutes.
Makes 8 servings (one 10-inch cake).

Nutrient Value Per Serving: 421 calories, 5 gm. protein, 10 gm. fat, 185 mg. sodium, 123 mg. cholesterol.

⅓   cup butter or margarine
½   cup firmly packed light brown sugar
1   can (20 ounces) pineapple rings in their own juice, drained
1½ cups sifted all-purpose flour
1½ teaspoons baking powder
3   eggs, well beaten
1½ cups granulated sugar
¾   cup pineapple juice
1½ teaspoons vanilla
    Ice cream (optional)

1. Preheat the oven to moderate (350°).
2. Melt the butter in a 10-inch cast-iron skillet in the oven. Stir in the brown sugar until melted; spread the mixture evenly over the bottom of the pan. Arrange the pineapple rings in the bottom of the pan over the sugar mixture. Set aside.
3. Sift together the flour and baking powder onto a sheet of wax paper. Set aside.
4. Combine the beaten eggs, granulated sugar, pineapple juice and vanilla in a large bowl; mix well with a wooden spoon. Stir in the sifted dry ingredients until well blended. Pour the cake batter over the pineapple

rings in the skillet.
5. Bake in the preheated moderate oven (350°) for 30 minutes or until a wooden pick inserted in the center comes out clean. Remove from the oven; let stand for 3 minutes. Invert onto a serving plate; remove the skillet. Serve warm with ice cream, if you wish.

Rhubarb Upside-Down Cake

Serve this cake warm with vanilla ice cream for a special treat.

Bake at 350° for 35 minutes.
Makes 9 servings.

Nutrient Value Per Serving: 278 calories, 3 gm. protein, 9 gm. fat, 85 mg. sodium, 32 mg. cholesterol.

1¼ cups sifted all-purpose flour
1½ teaspoons baking powder
1½ cups sugar
1   pound fresh rhubarb, leaves discarded, ends trimmed, and stalks cut into ½-inch slices (3 cups)
⅓   cup vegetable shortening
1   egg
1   teaspoon vanilla
½   cup milk

1. Preheat the oven to moderate (350°). Grease an 8 x 8 x 2-inch square baking pan.

▲**Rhubarb Upside-Down Cake**

2. Sift together the flour and baking powder onto wax paper.

3. Combine 1 cup of the sugar and the rhubarb in a large saucepan. Cook over medium-low heat, stirring constantly, until the sugar is completely melted and rhubarb just begins to soften, 5 to 8 minutes. Scrape into the prepared baking pan, spreading evenly.

4. Beat the shortening with the remaining ½ cup sugar in a large bowl until fluffy. Beat in the egg and vanilla. Beat in the flour mixture, alternately with the milk, starting and ending with dry ingredients, until well blended. Spoon the batter into mounds over the rhubarb; spread out as evenly as possible.

5. Bake in the preheated moderate oven (350°) for 35 minutes or until a wooden pick inserted in the center comes out clean. Cool the cake in the pan on a wire rack for 5 minutes.

6. Loosen the edges of the cake from the pan with a small knife. Cover the pan with an inverted high rimmed serving dish. Invert the pan and dish; shake gently. Lift off the pan. Cut into 9 squares. Spoon any syrup that runs onto the dish over the cake. Serve with ice cream.

Note: The cake can also be served directly from the pan, if you wish.

Chocolate Pound Cake

Bake at 350° for 1 hour and 20 minutes. Makes 12 servings.

Nutrient Value Per Serving: 559 calories, 7 gm. protein, 21 gm. fat, 338 mg. sodium, 114 mg. cholesterol.

3   cups sifted **all-purpose flour**
1   tablespoon baking powder
¼   teaspoon salt
1   cup (2 sticks) butter, softened
3   cups sugar
1½ tablespoons vanilla

▲ **Chocolate Pound Cake**

3   eggs
1   cup unsweetened cocoa powder
1¾ cups milk
      Confectioners' Frosting (recipe follows)
      Allegretti Glaze (recipe follows)
      Green grapes (optional)

1. Preheat the oven to moderate (350°). Sift the flour, baking powder and salt together onto wax paper.

2. Beat the butter and sugar together in a medium-size bowl until fluffy. Add the vanilla. Add the eggs one at a time, beating well after each addition. Add the cocoa. Add the milk alternately with the sifted dry ingredients in 3 additions, beating well after each addition. Pour into a greased and floured 10-inch (12 cup) Bundt® pan.

3. Bake in the preheated moderate oven (350°) for 1 hour and 20 minutes or until a cake tester inserted in the center comes out clean. Invert onto a wire rack; cool.

4. Drizzle the Confectioners' Frosting over the top. Drizzle the Allegretti Glaze over the Confectioners' Frosting. Garnish with green grapes dipped in Confectioners' Frosting, if you wish.

Confectioners' Frosting: Blend 1½ cups *sifted* 10X (confectioners') sugar with about 5 teaspoons water until smooth and well blended.

Allegretti Glaze: Melt 1 square unsweetened chocolate with ¼ teaspoon vegetable shortening in the top of a double boiler over hot water.

SIFT BEFORE MEASURING
When *sifted* flour is called for, sift the flour onto a piece of wax paper. Gently spoon the flour into a measuring cup; then, holding the cup over the wax paper, sweep the flat edge of a cake spreader or a knife across the top of the cup for an accurate measure. Pour the excess flour back into the flour container.

Chocolate-Pecan Yeast Cake with Creamy Butter Filling

Bake at 350° for 50 minutes.
Makes 16 servings.

Nutrient Value Per Serving: 486 calories, 6 gm. protein, 22 gm. fat, 295 mg. sodium, 69 mg. cholesterol.

- ¾ **cup milk**
- 1 **envelope active dry yeast**
- ¼ **cup very warm water**
- 1 **tablespoon granulated sugar**
- 3½ **cups sifted all-purpose flour**
- ¾ **cup (1½ sticks) margarine, softened**
- 2 **cups granulated sugar**
- ⅔ **cup cocoa powder**
- ½ **cup hot water**
- 3 **eggs, slightly beaten**
- 1 **teaspoon baking soda**
- ½ **teaspoon salt**
- ¼ **teaspoon ground nutmeg**
- ¼ **teaspoon ground cinnamon**
- ½ **teaspoon vanilla**
- 1 **cup finely chopped pecans**
  Creamy Butter Filling (recipe follows)
  10X (confectioners') sugar

1. Grease a 10-inch tube pan with a solid bottom.
2. Heat the milk in a small saucepan until bubbles appear around the edge; cool to lukewarm.
3. Sprinkle the yeast over very warm water in a large mixing bowl. ("Very warm water" should feel comfortably warm when dropped on your wrist.) Stir to dissolve the yeast. Add the lukewarm milk, the 1 tablespoon sugar and 1½ cups of the flour. Beat until smooth; cover. Let stand in a warm place, away from drafts, until the mixture is light and spongy, about 45 minutes.
4. Meanwhile, beat together the margarine and the 2 cups sugar in a small mixing bowl until light and fluffy; set aside.
5. Combine the cocoa powder and hot water in a small bowl; stir until smooth and well blended. Cool to lukewarm.
6. Add the cocoa and margarine to the yeast mixture. Add the eggs, the remaining 2 cups of flour, the baking soda, salt, nutmeg, cinnamon and vanilla. Beat at low speed for 6 minutes, scraping down the sides of the bowl occasionally. Stir in the chopped pecans.
7. Pour the batter into the prepared tube pan. Let stand uncovered in a warm place, away from drafts until doubled in volume, 2 to 2½ hours.
8. Preheat the oven to moderate (350°).
9. Bake in the preheated moderate oven (350°) for 45 to 50 minutes or until a wooden pick inserted in the top comes out clean. Remove the cake from the pan; cool on a wire rack.
10. Prepare the Creamy Butter Filling.
11. Carefully split the cooled cake horizontally into 3 equal layers. Spread the Creamy Butter Filling between the layers. Sprinkle the top of the cake with 10X (confectioners') sugar.

Creamy Butter Filling: Heat ½ cup (1 stick) butter in a heavy medium-size saucepan over low heat until golden brown; do not allow the butter to burn. Remove from the heat. Blend in 2½ tablespoons all-purpose flour and ¼ teaspoon salt. Slowly stir in ½ cup milk. Bring the mixture to boiling, stirring constantly. Boil for 1 minute. (The mixture will have a curdled appearance.) Remove from the heat. Place the saucepan in a large bowl of ice and water. Stir in 3 cups *sifted* 10X (confectioners') sugar and ½ teaspoon vanilla; stir until the filling is smooth and thick enough to spread, adding more 10X sugar if necessary. The consistency of the filling will depend on the amount of sugar used and the coolness of the filling.

Norwegian Honey Cake

Bake at 325° for 1 hour and 15 minutes.
Makes 12 servings.

Nutrient Value Per Serving: 405 calories, 7 gm. protein, 7 gm. fat, 52 mg. sodium, 79 mg. cholesterol.

 4 **cups** sifted ***all-purpose flour***
 1 **cup raisins**
 1 **teaspoon baking soda**
 ½ **teaspoon ground cloves**
 ½ **teaspoon ground cinnamon**
 3 **eggs**
 2⅓ **cups sugar**
 1½ **cups dairy sour cream**
 2 **tablespoons honey**
 3 **tablespoons grated orange rind**

1. Sprinkle 1 tablespoon of the flour over the raisins in a bowl; toss to coat. Sift together the remaining flour, baking soda, cloves and cinnamon. Preheat the oven to slow (325°). Grease and flour a 10-inch angel-cake tube pan.
2. Beat the eggs and sugar in a bowl until fluffy. Beat in the sour cream and honey. Stir in the flour mixture just until blended. Add the raisins and orange rind. Pour into the prepared pan.
3. Bake in the preheated slow oven (325°) for 1 hour and 15 minutes or until the cake pulls away from the sides of the pan and the top springs back when lightly pressed. Cool in the pan on a wire rack 5 minutes. Run a knife around the inner and outer edges of the cake. Turn out onto a wire rack; cool completely.
4. Store covered at room temperature overnight before cutting. Sprinkle the top with 10X (confectioners') sugar, if you wish.

▼Norwegian Honey Cake

Orange Ring Cake

Bake at 350° for 55 minutes.
Makes 12 servings.

Nutrient Value Per Serving: 314 calories, 4 gm. protein, 12 gm. fat, 113 mg. sodium, 46 mg. cholesterol.

- *1 cup chopped pitted dates*
- *1 teaspoon baking soda*
- *½ cup boiling water*
- *½ cup (1 stick) butter or margarine*
- *1 cup sugar*
- *1 egg*
- *2 cups sifted all-purpose flour*
- *1 cup milk*
- *Grated rind of 1 large orange*
- *½ cup chopped walnuts*
- *Orange Syrup (recipe follows)*

1. Preheat the oven to moderate (350°). Spray a 6-cup Bundt® pan or other decorative 6-cup pan with non-stick vegetable cooking spray.
2. Combine the dates, baking soda and boiling water in a small bowl; mix well.
3. Beat the butter and sugar in a large bowl with an electric mixer at high speed until light and fluffy. Beat in the egg until blended.
4. Add the sifted flour alternately with the milk to the butter mixture, beginning and ending with flour. Stir in the orange rind, walnuts and date mixture. Pour into the prepared pan.
5. Bake in the preheated moderate oven (350°) for 55 minutes or until a wooden pick inserted in the cake comes out clean. Let the cake cool in the pan on a wire rack for 10 minutes. Invert the cake onto a serving plate. If the cake rises unevenly, trim even with the sides of the pan with a serrated knife.
6. Slowly pour the Orange Syrup over the cake while it is still warm, allowing the syrup to soak in.

Orange Syrup: Combine ¼ cup sugar and ½ cup orange juice in small pan. Boil gently for 5 minutes.

White Fruitcake

Bake at 300° for 1 hour and 20 minutes.
Makes 3 small loaves.

Nutrient Value Per Loaf: 3279 calories, 41 gm. protein, 150 gm. fat, 1409 mg. sodium, 540 mg. cholesterol.

- *3 cups sifted all-purpose flour*
- *3 teaspoons baking powder*
- *1 cup (2 sticks) butter or margarine*
- *2 cups sugar*
- *4 eggs, separated*
- *1 cup milk*
- *2 cans (3½ ounces each) flaked coconut*
- *2 cups golden raisins*
- *2 cups walnuts, coarsely chopped*
- *½ pound candied red cherries, cut in half*
- *½ pound candied pineapple, cut into ½-inch pieces*

1. Preheat the oven to slow (300°). Grease three 8½ x 4½ x 2⅝-inch loaf pans. Line the bottoms with wax paper.
2. Sift together the flour and baking powder onto a sheet of wax paper.
3. Beat together the butter and sugar in a large bowl until light and fluffy. Beat in the egg yolks, one at a time, until well blended.
4. Add the sifted dry ingredients to the butter mixture, alternately with the milk, beginning and ending with the dry ingredients. Beat until well blended.
5. Beat the egg whites until they form soft peaks; gently fold into the cake batter.
6. Finely chop 1 can of the coconut. Fold the chopped coconut, the remaining can of coconut, raisins, walnuts, cherries and pineapple into the batter until blended. Divide evenly into the prepared pans.
7. Bake in the preheated slow oven (300°) for 1 hour and 20 minutes or until a wooden pick inserted near the center of each loaf comes out clean. Let the cakes cool in the pans on a wire rack for 10 minutes. Invert

the cakes on the rack. Remove the pans; peel off the wax paper. Cool the cakes completely. Wrap the cakes tightly in plastic wrap.

A HOLIDAY GIFT
These fruitcakes make great holiday gifts. Wrap 2 to give away and keep 1 to serve when unexpected holiday guests arrive.

Chocolate-Orange Marble Cheesecake

Bake at 350° for 1 hour.
Makes 16 servings.

Nutrient Value Per Serving: 413 calories, 7 gm. protein, 32 gm. fat, 208 mg. sodium, 140 mg. cholesterol.

½ cup graham cracker crumbs
1 tablespoon granulated sugar
2 tablespoons butter or margarine, melted
1 square unsweetened chocolate, melted
3 packages (8 ounces each) cream cheese, softened
¾ cup firmly packed light brown sugar
¼ cup granulated sugar
4 eggs
2 pints (4 cups) sour cream
1 tablespoon grated orange rind
6 squares semisweet chocolate, melted and cooled
   Orange slices (optional)
   Chocolate leaves (optional)

1. Combine the crumbs, the 1 tablespoon sugar, butter and unsweetened chocolate in a small bowl. Press into the bottom of a lightly buttered 9 x 3-inch springform pan.

Refrigerate. Preheat the oven to moderate (350°). Lightly butter a 9 x 3-inch springform pan.
2. Beat the cream cheese in a large bowl until smooth. Gradually beat in the sugars until they are well mixed. Beat in the eggs, one at a time, until fluffy. Beat in the sour cream and orange rind. Measure 3 cups of the cream cheese mixture into another bowl.
3. Beat the cooled chocolate into the 3 cups of cream cheese mixture until it is well mixed.
4. Spoon 1 cup of the plain cheese mixture over the crust in the prepared pan. Spoon half of the chocolate-cheese mixture in 4 separate mounds over the plain cheese layer. Cover with another cup of the reserved plain cheese mixture. Repeat the layers. Gently cut through the batter with a zigzag motion to marble, if you wish.
5. Bake in the preheated moderate oven (350°) for 1 hour. Turn off the oven; leave the cheesecake in the oven for 1 hour. Cool on a wire rack. Refrigerate overnight.

▲ Chocolate-Orange Marble Cheesecake

6. Remove from the pan. Decorate with orange slices and chocolate leaves, if you wish.

Note: If you like a less bitter chocolate flavor, you may wish to add 1 teaspoon vanilla along with the sour cream and orange rind in step 2.

TO MAKE CHOCOLATE LEAVES
Melt semisweet chocolate over hot water. Brush on the backs of small, non-poisonous leaves and refrigerate for about 5 minutes to harden the chocolate. Remove the leaf from the chocolate by pulling carefully down from the stem end. Use chocolate leaves to decorate any dessert.

Chocolate Pastry Cake

Bake at 425° for 5 minutes.
Makes 12 servings.

Nutrient Value Per Serving: 434 calories, 3 gm. protein, 32 gm. fat, 207 mg. sodium, 59 mg. cholesterol.

> 2 **packages (4 ounces each) sweet cooking chocolate**
> ½ **cup sugar**
> ½ **cup water**
> 2 **teaspoons vanilla**
> 1 **package (11 ounces) piecrust mix**
> 2 **cups heavy cream**
> **10X (confectioners') sugar**
> **Chocolate curls**

1. Preheat the oven to hot (425°).
2. Combine the chocolate, sugar and water in a small saucepan. Cook over low heat, stirring constantly, until smooth. Add the vanilla. Cool to room temperature.
3. Combine ¾ cup of the cooled chocolate sauce with the piecrust mix in a small bowl. Toss to evenly moisten dry ingredients. Gather the dough into a ball.
4. Divide the dough into 6 equal portions. Press each portion with floured fingers, over the bottom of an inverted 8-inch round layer-cake pan, to within ¼ inch of the edge; be sure the thickness is uniform. Prepare 2 or 3 at a time, depending on the number of pans you have.
5. Bake in the preheated hot oven (425°) for 4 to 5 minutes or until done; be careful the edges do not burn. Cool slightly. Remove with a long spatula to wire racks to cool completely.
6. Beat the cream in a medium-size bowl just until it forms soft peaks. Fold in the remaining chocolate sauce.
7. Stack the baked pastry rounds, spreading the chocolate cream between layers and around the sides.
8. Chill at least 6 hours or overnight.
9. To serve, sprinkle the top with 10X (confectioners') sugar. Garnish with chocolate curls.

TO MAKE CHOCOLATE CURLS
Let a square of semisweet chocolate or a thick milk chocolate bar soften slightly in a warm place. Do not melt the chocolate. Carefully draw a vegetable peeler across the chocolate to form curls. Use a wooden pick to lift the curls and place them on your dessert.

▲From left to right: **Double Mocha-Walnut Cookie (page 226), Pecan Cup Cookies (page 230), Merry Christmas Wreath (page 229), Chocolate-Pecan Refrigerator Cookie (page 234), Noel Star (page 225), Amaretto Cream Strawberries (page 224), Almond Butter Fingers (page 224), Stella (page 228), German Honey-Spice Cookie (page 223), Swiss Lemon Strips (page 228), Log Jam Cookies (page 227) and Neapolitan Cookies (page 232).**

Cookies and Cookie Desserts

▼ ▢ Chocolate Sandwich Cookies

Bake at 350° for 10 minutes.
Makes 2½ dozen cookies.

Nutrient Value Per Cookie: 135 calories, 2 gm. protein, 9 gm. fat, 1 mg. sodium, 10 mg. cholesterol.

1¾ cups sifted **all-purpose flour**
 3 tablespoons **unsweetened cocoa powder**
 ¼ teaspoon **ground cinnamon**
 ⅓ cup **ground walnuts (about ⅓ cup walnut pieces)**
 ½ cup plus 2 tablespoons (1¼ sticks) **unsalted butter, softened**
 ⅓ cup **superfine sugar**
 ½ teaspoon **vanilla**
 ½ teaspoon **grated lemon rind**
 ⅓ cup **currant jelly**
 2 squares **semisweet chocolate, melted**
 ¾ cup **chopped pistachio nuts**
    Candied red cherries, halved

1. Combine the flour, cocoa, cinnamon and

walnuts on wax paper. Beat the butter, sugar, vanilla and lemon rind in a medium-size bowl until fluffy. Stir in the flour mixture until well blended. Cover; refrigerate for about 1 hour or until the dough is cold and firm enough to handle easily.

2. Preheat the oven to moderate (350°). Grease cookie sheets.

3. Roll the dough, one-fourth at a time, on a lightly floured surface until slightly less than ⅛ inch thick. Cut into rounds with a floured 1½-inch scalloped or plain cookie cutter. Place 1 inch apart on the cookie sheets.

4. Bake in the preheated moderate oven (350°) for 10 minutes or until the cookies are just set. Remove and cool on wire racks. Spread the flat bottoms of the cookies with currant jelly; sandwich cookies in pairs. Spread the melted chocolate over tops; sprinkle with pistachio nuts; decorate with a cherry half.

COOKIE TIPS
• **Use a cold cookie sheet to prevent the cookies from losing their shape.**
• **Cookies should be of a uniform thickness and size so they will bake in the same amount of time.**
• **Bake one sheet at a time and be sure that the cookie sheet has at least 1 inch of space around its edges.**
• **Watch the cookies closely. Because oven temperatures vary, they may bake a little faster or slower than the regular baking time.**
• **Always remove the cookies from the cookie sheet to a wire rack immediately. The cookies will continue to bake if left on the sheet.**

sugar with an electric mixer until fluffy. Stir in the orange and lemon juices. Stir in the dry ingredients until blended. Chill for several hours or overnight until firm.
3. Preheat the oven to moderate (375°).
4. Roll out dough one-third at a time on a floured surface to ⅛-inch thickness. Cut out with a floured cookie cutter. Arrange 1 inch apart on ungreased cookie sheets.
5. Bake in the preheated moderate oven (375°) for 8 minutes or until set and lightly golden. Cool on wire racks.
6. If you wish, brush tops of the cookies with corn syrup and sprinkle with colored sugar and silver dragees. Decorate with white or colored Decorator Frosting.

Decorator Frosting: Combine 1 egg white, ½ teaspoon cream of tartar and 1 cup 10X (confectioners') sugar in a small bowl. Beat with an electric mixer until stiff but a good spreading consistency. Cover with a damp towel until ready to use. If you wish, stir food coloring into small amounts of the frosting before using. Pipe or spread onto the cookies.

🔲 *Orangy Sugar Cookies*

Bake at 375° for 8 minutes.
Makes 3 dozen large cookies.

Nutrient Value Per Cookie: 84 calories, 1 gm. protein, 3 gm. fat, 54 mg. sodium, 7 mg. cholesterol.

2¼ cups sifted all-purpose flour
1 teaspoon baking powder
¼ teaspoon salt
½ cup (1 stick) butter, softened
2 tablespoons grated orange rind
1 cup sugar
¼ cup orange juice
2 tablespoons lemon juice
 Corn syrup for garnish (optional)
 Colored decorating sugar and silver dragees for garnish (optional)
 Decorator Frosting (recipe follows)

1. Sift together the flour, baking powder and salt onto wax paper.
2. Beat together the butter, orange rind and

🔲 *Brown Molasses Cookies*

Bake at 375° for 10 to 12 minutes.
Makes 6 dozen cookies.

Nutrient Value Per Cookie: 78 calories, 1 gm. protein, 1 gm. fat, 34 mg. sodium, 6 mg. cholesterol.

4 cups sifted all-purpose flour
1 teaspoon baking soda
1 teaspoon baking powder
⅓ cup butter, softened
2 tablespoons grated orange rind
1 cup sugar
1 egg
1 cup light molasses
 Vanilla Decorating Icing (recipe follows)
 Silver dragees for garnish

1. Sift together the flour, baking soda and baking powder onto wax paper.
2. Beat together the butter and orange rind in a large bowl with an electric mixer until creamy. Add the sugar and egg. Beat until light and fluffy. Beat in the molasses. Add the flour mixture and beat on low speed just until well blended.
3. Divide the dough in half, wrap it in wax paper and refrigerate it overnight.
4. When ready to make the cookies, preheat the oven to moderate (375°). Lightly grease cookie sheets with vegetable shortening.
5. Roll out the dough on a lightly floured board to a ⅛-inch thickness. Cut out the cookies with floured cookie cutters. Arrange 1½ inches apart on the prepared cookie sheets.
6. Bake in the preheated moderate oven (375°) for 10 to 12 minutes or until firm. Remove the cookies from the cookie sheets to wire racks; cool completely.
7. Spoon Vanilla Decorating Icing into a pastry bag fitted with a writing tip. Pipe decorations onto the cooled cookies. Decorate with silver dragees.

Vanilla Decorating Icing: Blend 1 box (1 pound) 10X (confectioners') sugar with ½ teaspoon salt, 1 teaspoon vanilla and 3 to 4 tablespoons milk in a small bowl to make a smooth, firm frosting.

Christmas Tree Cookies

Bake at 350° for 15 minutes.
Makes about 5½ dozen cookies.

Nutrient Value Per Cookie: 56 calories, 1 gm. protein, 2 gm. fat, 22 mg. sodium, 12 mg. cholesterol. (Decorations not included.)

2¼ cups* sifted *all-purpose flour
½ teaspoon baking soda
½ teaspoon ground cinnamon
¼ teaspoon ground allspice
¼ teaspoon ground cloves
½ cup ground unblanched almonds (about ⅓ cup whole almonds)
½ cup (1 stick) butter, softened
¾ cup sugar
2 eggs
½ teaspoon vanilla
⅓ cup finely chopped candied citron
Lemon Glaze (recipe follows)
Candied citron
Cinnamon red hots

1. Combine the flour, baking soda, cinnamon, allspice, cloves and almonds on wax paper. Beat the butter, sugar, eggs and vanilla in a large bowl until fluffy. Blend in the flour mixture and citron. Cover; refrigerate about 1 hour or until the dough is cold and firm enough to handle easily.
2. Preheat the oven to moderate (350°). Grease cookie sheets.
3. Roll the dough, one-fourth at a time, on a lightly floured surface to a ⅛-inch thickness. Cut out with a medium-size tree-shaped cookie cutter. Place 1 inch apart on the prepared cookie sheets.
4. Bake in the preheated moderate oven (350°) for 15 minutes or until lightly browned. Remove from the cookie sheets; cool on wire racks. Spread the tops of the cooled cookies with Lemon Glaze; decorate with candied citron and cinnamon red hots.

Lemon Glaze: Gradually stir 2 tablespoons lemon juice into 1½ cups *sifted* 10X (confectioners') sugar in a bowl, until glaze is smooth and of a good spreading consistency.

⬛ *Small Sand Cookies*

Bake at 375° for 8 to 10 minutes.
Makes 4 dozen cookies.

Nutrient Value Per Cookie: 85 calories, 1 gm. protein, 5 gm. fat, 41 mg. sodium, 22 mg. cholesterol.

1⅓ cups firmly packed dark brown sugar
 1 cup (2 sticks) butter, softened
 2 egg yolks
 2 cups sifted all-purpose flour
 3 squares (1 ounce each) semisweet chocolate, melted
    Candy decorations for garnish (optional)

1. Beat together the brown sugar, butter and egg yolks in a large bowl with an electric mixer until fluffy. Gradually beat in the flour until smooth. Chill for several hours or overnight until firm.
2. Preheat the oven to moderate (375°). Grease cookie sheets with vegetable shortening.
3. Roll out the dough on a floured surface to ⅛-inch thickness. Cut out with a floured 2-inch round cookie cutter. Arrange cookies 1½ inches apart on the prepared cookie sheets.
4. Bake in the preheated moderate oven (375°) for 8 to 10 minutes. Transfer from the cookie sheets to wire racks to cool.
5. When completely cool, drizzle the cookies with melted chocolate. Sprinkle with candy decorations, if you wish.

🍸 *Spiced Almond Cookie Houses*

Bake at 350° for 12 minutes.
Makes about 3 dozen cookies.

Nutrient Value Per Cookie: 90 calories, 2 gm. protein, 6 gm. fat, 17 mg. sodium, 19 mg. cholesterol. (Decorations not included.)

1¼ cups sifted all-purpose flour
 ⅔ cup ground unblanched almonds (about ½ cup whole almonds)
 ½ teaspoon ground cinnamon
 ¼ teaspoon ground cloves
 ¼ cup (½ stick) butter, softened
 ¾ cup sugar
 2 eggs
 ½ teaspoon grated lemon rind
    Whole blanched almonds
 1 tablespoon milk
    Packaged frosting mix and sprinkles (optional)

1. Combine the flour, ground almonds, cinnamon and cloves on wax paper. Beat the butter, sugar, 1 of the eggs and lemon rind in a large bowl until fluffy. Stir in the flour mixture until well blended. Cover; refrigerate about 1 hour or until the dough is cold and firm enough to handle easily.
2. Preheat the oven to moderate (350°). Grease cookie sheets.
3. Roll the dough, one-fourth at a time, on a lightly floured surface to a ⅛-inch thickness. Cut out with a house-shaped cookie cutter, or make a paper pattern and trace by hand. Place 1 inch apart on the prepared cookie sheets. Press whole almonds into the cookies for the windows and door. Beat the remaining egg and milk in a small bowl until blended; brush over the cookies.
4. Bake in the preheated moderate oven (350°) for 12 minutes or until lightly browned. Remove from the cookie sheets; cool on a wire rack. Decorate the roof with packaged frosting mix and sprinkles, if you wish.

▨ ⬙ ☐ *Nutmeg Leaves*

Bake at 350° for 8 minutes.
Makes 8 dozen cookies.

Nutrient Value Per Cookie: 30 calories, 1 gm.
protein, 2 gm. fat, 16 mg. sodium, 5 mg.
cholesterol.

1½ **cups** sifted ***all-purpose flour***
 1 **teaspoon baking powder**
 ½ **teaspoon baking soda**
 ½ **teaspoon ground nutmeg**
 ½ **cup (1 stick) butter or margarine,**
      softened
 1 **egg**
 ½ **cup sugar**
1½ **tablespoons milk**
 1 **teaspoon vanilla**
 4 **squares (1 ounce each) semisweet**
      chocolate, melted
 ½ **cup chopped pistachio nuts**

1. Sift the flour, baking powder, baking soda
and nutmeg onto wax paper.
2. Beat the butter, egg and sugar in a large
bowl with an electric mixer until fluffy,
about 3 minutes. Stir in the milk and vanilla.
Stir in the flour mixture until blended and
smooth. Chill for several hours or overnight.
3. Preheat the oven to moderate (350°).
4. Roll out a quarter of the dough on a lightly
floured surface to a ¼-inch thickness.
Cut out the dough with a small floured
leaf-shape cookie cutter. Reroll the scraps
of dough and cut out as many leaves as you
can. Arrange on an ungreased cookie
sheet, 1 inch apart. Repeat with the
remaining dough.
5. Bake in the preheated moderate oven (350°)
for 8 minutes or until the cookies are set
and lightly browned. Cool on wire racks.
Decorate with the melted chocolate and
chopped pistachios.

▨ ⬙ ☐ *German Honey-Spice Cookies*

Bake at 400° for 10 minutes.
Makes about 3¼ dozen cookies.

Nutrient Value Per Cookie: 128 calories, 2 gm.
protein, 2 gm. fat, 16 mg. sodium, 7 mg. cholesterol.

 1 **cup honey**
 3 **cups** sifted ***all-purpose flour***
 ½ **teaspoon baking soda**
1½ **teaspoons ground cinnamon**
 ½ **teaspoon ground nutmeg**
 ¼ **teaspoon ground cloves**
 ⅔ **cup firmly packed light brown sugar**
 1 **egg**
 2 **teaspoons grated lemon rind**
 1 **tablespoon lemon juice**
 ½ **cup finely chopped candied citron**
 ½ **cup finely chopped blanched almonds**
 ⅓ **cup whole blanched almonds, split**
 1 **container (3 ounces) candied red**
      cherries, halved
      Clear Sugar Glaze (recipe follows)

1. Heat the honey in a medium-size saucepan
just to boiling; cool.
2. Sift together the flour, baking soda,
cinnamon, nutmeg and cloves onto wax
paper. Reserve.
3. Combine the cooled honey, brown sugar,
egg, lemon rind and juice in a large bowl.
Beat with a wooden spoon until smooth.
4. Stir in the flour mixture until well blended.
Stir in the citron and chopped almonds.
Form the dough into a ball; flatten. Wrap in
aluminum foil or plastic wrap. Chill at least
6 hours or overnight.
5. Preheat the oven to hot (400°). Grease 2
large cookie sheets.
6. Divide the dough in half. Roll half at a time
on a floured surface to a ¼-inch thickness.
Cut into rounds with a well-floured 2½-inch
cutter. Transfer to the prepared cookie

sheets, ½-inch apart. Decorate with the almond and cherry halves.

7. Bake in the preheated hot oven (400°) for 10 minutes or until the edges are slightly browned. Transfer to racks over wax paper.

8. While the cookies bake, prepare the Clear Sugar Glaze.

9. Brush warm cookies with the hot glaze. Cool completely. Store in a tightly covered container at least 1 or 2 weeks.

Clear Sugar Glaze: Heat 1 cup granulated sugar and ½ cup water to boiling. Boil gently 4 minutes or until a candy thermometer registers 230°. Remove from the heat; let bubbling subside. Stir in ¼ cup *sifted* 10X (confectioners') sugar. If the syrup becomes cloudy, stir in a teaspoon of water; reheat until clear again.

hour or until firm enough to handle.

4. Preheat the oven to moderate (350°). Beat the egg white in a small bowl until frothy.

5. Divide the dough in half. Roll each half on a floured surface to a rectangle ¼-inch thick and about 3 inches wide. Even edges with a ruler to measure 2½ inches wide. Cut crosswise into bars ¾ inch wide. Brush the tops with egg white. Sprinkle evenly with the almond-sugar mixture. Lift the bars with a spatula to ungreased cookie sheets, spacing ¼ inch apart.

6. Bake in the preheated moderate oven (350°) for 15 minutes or until golden brown. Transfer the cookies to wire racks; cool. Store in a tightly covered container for up to 2 weeks. Sprinkle with 10X (confectioners') sugar through a fine sieve, if you wish.

▦ 🍸 ⬜ *Almond Butter Fingers*

Bake at 350° for 15 minutes.
Makes about 4 dozen cookies.

Nutrient Value Per Cookie: 57 calories, 0.8 gm. protein, 4 gm. fat, 30 mg. sodium, 8 mg. cholesterol.

   ½ **cup chopped blanched almonds**
1½ **tablepoons granulated sugar**
   ¾ **cup (1½ sticks) butter or margarine, softened**
   ⅓ **cup granulated sugar**
   1 **teaspoon almond extract**
   2 **cups sifted all-purpose flour**
   1 **egg white**
      10X (confectioners') sugar (optional)

1. Combine the almonds with the 1½ tablespoons sugar. Reserve.

2. Beat the butter, ⅓ cup sugar and almond extract in a medium-size bowl until smooth. Stir in the flour until well blended.

3. Gather the dough into a ball; flatten. Wrap in aluminum foil or plastic wrap. Chill for 1

▦ 🍸 *Amaretto Cream Strawberries*

Bake at 350° for 10 minutes.
Makes about 6 dozen cookies.

Nutrient Value Per Cookie: 64 calories, 0.6 gm. protein, 4 gm. fat, 32 mg. sodium, 9 mg. cholesterol.

   1 **cup (2 sticks) butter or margarine, softened**
   ½ **cup sifted 10X (confectioners') sugar**
   1 **teaspoon amaretto (almond-flavored liqueur)**
2¼ **cups sifted all-purpose flour**
   ⅔ **cup ground blanched almonds**
      Amaretto Butter Cream (recipe follows)
      Green food coloring
      Red sugar crystals

1. Beat together the butter, 10X (confectioners') sugar and amaretto until smooth.

2. Stir in the flour and almonds until well blended. Chill for 1 hour.

3. Preheat the oven to moderate (350°). Grease 2 large cookie sheets.

4. Roll the dough, half at a time, on a floured surface, to a ¼-inch thickness. Cut out with a small floured spade- or heart-shaped cutter. Transfer with a spatula to the prepared cookie sheets, spacing ½ inch apart.

5. Bake in the preheated moderate oven (350°) for 10 minutes or until lightly browned around the edges. Transfer to wire racks; cool. Store in a tightly covered container for up to 2 weeks.

6. Prepare Amaretto Butter Cream. Reserve ½ cup plain. Tint remainder pale green with food coloring. Reserve.

7. Frost the cookies with plain butter cream. Dip in red sugar crystals or sprinkle crystals heavily over frosting, pressing in slightly.

8. Make a wax paper cone or use a cake decorator with a small round tip. Cut tip off cone to make a small opening. Fill with green-tinted butter cream. Pipe a green stem and long points to resemble a strawberry hull on top of each cookie.

Amaretto Butter Cream: Combine ¼ cup (½ stick) softened butter or margarine, 2 tablespoons almond-flavored liqueur, 1 tablespoon heavy cream and 2 cups *sifted* 10X (confectioners') sugar in a small bowl. Beat until well blended.

⌷ *Noel Stars*

Bake at 375° for 10 minutes.
Makes about 3 dozen cookies.

Nutrient Value Per Cookie: 73 calories, 1 gm. protein, 4 gm. fat, 41 mg. sodium, 15 mg. cholesterol.

1   cup *sifted all-purpose flour*
½   teaspoon ground cinnamon
¼   teaspoon salt
½   cup almond paste
1   egg yolk
½   cup (1 stick) butter or margarine, softened
¼   cup sugar
½   teaspoon vanilla
¼   cup toasted blanched almonds, finely chopped
   Confectioners' Icing (recipe follows)
   Green food coloring
   Colored sprinkles or toasted whole almonds (optional)

1. Sift the flour, cinnamon and salt onto wax paper. Reserve.

2. Crumble the almond paste into a medium-size bowl. Add the egg yolk, butter, sugar and vanilla. Beat until smooth.

3. Stir in the flour mixture and chopped almonds until well blended. Wrap the dough in aluminum foil or plastic wrap. Chill for 2 hours.

4. Preheat the oven to moderate (375°). Grease and flour a large cookie sheet.

5. Roll out half of the dough at a time on a lightly floured board to a ⅛-inch thickness. Cut out the dough with a floured 2¼-inch star-shaped cutter. Place on the prepared cookie sheet, ½ inch apart.

6. Bake in the preheated moderate oven (375°) for 10 minutes or until the edges are lightly browned. Transfer to a wire rack; cool. Store in a tightly covered container for up to 2 weeks.

7. Tint the Confectioners' Icing pale green with food coloring. Fit a pastry bag or cake decorator with a small round tip. Pipe frosting, outlining the star, ⅛-inch from the edge. Pipe a small amount of frosting in the center of the star; decorate with colored sprinkles or toasted almonds.

Confectioners' Icing: Stir 1½ tablepoons milk or water into 1 cup *sifted* 10X (confectioners') sugar. Add additional 10X sugar, if necessary, to make a fairly stiff but spreadable icing.

▨ ▣ ▢ *Double Mocha-Walnut Cookies*

Bake at 400° for 8 to 10 minutes.
Makes about 3 dozen double cookies.

Nutrient Value Per Cookie: 195 calories, 2 gm. protein, 11 gm. fat, 98 mg. sodium, 33 mg. cholesterol.

 2   **tablespoons instant coffee powder**
2½ **cups sifted all-purpose flour**
2½ **teaspoons baking powder**
 1 **cup very finely chopped or
       ground walnuts**
 1 **cup (2 sticks) butter, softened**
1½ **cups sugar**
 2 **eggs
       Creamy Chocolate Frosting
       (recipe follows)**

1. Mash the instant coffee to a fine powder. Reserve. Sift the flour and baking powder onto wax paper; add the walnuts.
2. Beat the butter, sugar, eggs and coffee in a medium-size bowl until smooth. Stir in the flour mixture until well blended.
3. Wrap the dough in foil. Chill for 1 hour or until firm enough to handle.
4. Preheat the oven to hot (400°). Grease 2 large cookie sheets.
5. Divide the dough in half. Roll out each half on a floured surface to a ⅛-inch thickness. Cut with a floured round 2¼-inch cookie cutter. Transfer to the prepared cookie sheets, ½ inch apart. Cut ½-inch rounds from the centers of half the cookies.
6. Bake in the preheated hot oven (400°) for 8 to 10 minutes or until lightly browned around edges. Transfer to wire racks; cool. The cookies then may be stored in a covered container for up to 2 weeks.
7. To serve: Sandwich two cookies together (1 solid cookie and 1 cut out cookie) with a thin layer of Creamy Chocolate Frosting. Pipe frosting on the cookie following the scalloped edge.

Creamy Chocolate Frosting: Heat ⅓ cup half and half and ¼ cup (½ stick) butter or margarine in a small saucepan just until boiling. Stir in 1 package (6 ounces) semisweet chocolate pieces and 1½ teaspoons vanilla until smooth. Beat in 2¼ cups *sifted* 10X (confectioners') sugar until smooth, thick and spreadable.

COOKIE STORAGE
● Store soft cookies in an airtight container, with a slice of apple on a piece of wax paper to keep the cookies soft and moist.
● Store crisp cookies in a container with a loose fitting lid. If the cookies soften, place them in a slow oven (300°) for a few minutes to make them crisp again.

▨ ▢ *Shamrock Sugar Cookies*

Bake at 375° for 7 minutes.
Makes 4 dozen cookies.

Nutrient Value Per Cookie: 79 calories, 1 gm. protein, 4 gm. fat, 21 mg. sodium, 6 mg. cholesterol.

 1 **cup butter-flavored vegetable shortening**
 1 **cup sugar**
 1 **egg**
½ **teaspoon vanilla**
2¼ **cups all-purpose flour**
 1 **teaspoon baking powder**
¼ **teaspoon ground ginger**
¼ **teaspoon salt
       Green decorating sugar**

1. Beat the butter-flavored vegetable shortening with the sugar, egg and vanilla in a bowl with an electric mixer at high speed until fluffy.

2. Combine the flour, baking powder, ginger and salt in a small bowl. Stir into the shortening mixture to make a stiff dough. Divide the dough in half; shape into two balls. Wrap in wax paper; chill for at least 2 hours.
3. Preheat the oven to moderate (375°).
4. Roll the dough out on a lightly floured board to a ¼-inch thickness. Cut cookies out with a 2½- or 3-inch shamrock-shaped cutter. Place 1 inch apart on ungreased cookie sheets. Sprinkle with decorating sugar.
5. Bake in the preheated moderate oven (375°) for 7 minutes or until light brown around the edges. Remove to wire racks to cool. Store in a tightly covered metal tin.

Cream Stars

Bake at 375° for 6 minutes.
Makes about 5 dozen sandwich cookies.

Nutrient Value Per Cookie: 59 calories, .51 gm. protein, 4.4 gm. fat, 39.28 mg. sodium, 16 mg. cholesterol.

1   *cup (2 sticks) butter, softened*
⅓   *cup heavy cream*
1   *teaspoon almond extract*
2   *cups sifted all-purpose flour*
    Granulated sugar
    Pastel Butter Filling (recipe follows)

1. Mix the butter, heavy cream, almond extract and flour in a large bowl until creamy. Shape into a ball; flatten slightly. Wrap in plastic; chill for 1 hour.
2. Preheat the oven to moderate (375°).
3. Roll dough on a well-floured pastry cloth with a floured stockinette-covered rolling pin to a ⅛-inch thickness. Cut into 2-inch stars with a cookie cutter. Transfer to wax paper heavily sprinkled with sugar; turn to coat both sides. Place on an ungreased cookie

sheet; prick cookies in 3 places with a fork.
4. Bake in the preheated moderate oven (375°) for 6 minutes or until slightly puffed. Cool on wire racks.
5. Sandwich the cookies together with Pastel Butter Filling.

Pastel Butter Filling: Combine ¼ cup (½ stick) softened butter, ¾ cup *sifted* 10X (confectioners') sugar, 1 egg yolk and ⅛ to ¼ teaspoon almond extract; mix until smooth. Divide into thirds; place in separate bowls. Tint yellow, green and pink with food coloring.

Log Jam Cookies

Bake at 350° for 17 minutes.
Makes about 4 dozen cookies.

Nutrient Value Per Cookie: 88 calories, 1 gm. protein, 3 gm. fat, 39 mg. sodium, 13 mg. cholesterol.

2⅓ *cups sifted all-purpose flour*
½   *teaspoon baking powder*
⅛   *teaspoon salt*
⅔   *cup butter or margarine, softened*
⅔   *cup sugar*
1   *egg*
2   *teaspoons vanilla*
1   *cup apricot preserves or seedless red raspberry jam*
    Confectioners' Icing (recipe follows)
⅓   *cup chopped pistachio nuts*

1. Sift the flour, baking powder and salt onto wax paper; reserve.
2. Beat the butter, sugar, egg and vanilla in a medium-size bowl until smooth; stir in the flour mixture until well blended.
3. Preheat the oven to moderate (350°).
4. Divide the dough into 4 equal parts. Shape each part into a roll 10 inches long and 1 inch in diameter. Transfer the rolls to a large ungreased cookie sheet, spacing about

1 inch apart. Flatten the rolls slightly.
5. Press a ¼-inch-deep trough down the center of each roll with the handle of a wooden spoon, leaving the ends solid to keep the filling in place.
6. Spoon the preserves into the trough, filling to the level of the dough.
7. Bake in the preheated moderate oven (350°) for 17 minutes or until light golden brown.
8. Remove from the oven. Cut the warm cookies into ¾-inch wide diagonal slices. Transfer the cookies to a wire rack; cool. Store in a tightly-covered container for up to 2 weeks.
9. Drizzle the Confectioners' Icing over the edges of the cookies; sprinkle the icing with chopped pistachio nuts.

Confectioners' Icing: Stir 1½ tablespoons milk or water into 1 cup *sifted* 10X (confectioners') sugar to make a smooth icing that flows easily from the tip of a spoon.

Stellas

Bake at 400° for 15 minutes.
Makes about 3½ dozen cookies.

Nutrient Value Per Cookie: 143 calories, 2 gm. protein, 10 gm. fat, 75 mg. sodium, 21 mg. cholesterol.

    1   cup very finely chopped pecans
    ½   cup granulated sugar
    ½   teaspoon ground cinnamon
    3   cups sifted all-purpose flour
    1½ cups (3 sticks) butter, softened
    1   cup dairy sour cream
    2   egg whites, slightly beaten
        Confectioners' Icing (recipe follows)
        OR: 10X (confectioners') sugar

1. Combine the pecans, sugar and cinnamon in a small bowl. Reserve.
2. Sift the flour into a medium-size bowl. Cut in butter until the mixture is crumbly. Stir

in sour cream. Work the dough with a spoon or your hands just until it holds together. Wrap in foil or plastic wrap; refrigerate for 6 hours.
3. Divide the dough into 4 equal parts. Work with one at a time, leaving the remainder refrigerated. The dough will be soft and sticky.
4. Sprinkle the work surface with flour, then heavily with sugar. Shape one fourth of the dough into a ball. Roll out to a round a little larger than 8 inches. Dough should be quite thin. Cut into an 8-inch circle. Refrigerate the scraps. Divide the circle into 8 equal wedges.
5. Brush the circle with beaten egg white. Sprinkle with the nut mixture. Roll up each wedge from the wide end, tucking the point underneath. Place 1 inch apart on ungreased cookie sheets. Repeat with the remaining dough. Brush the tops with egg white; sprinkle with the remaining nut mixture. Form the scraps of dough into a ball; roll out, cut into wedges and roll as above.
6. Bake in a preheated hot oven (400°) for 15 to 20 minutes or until light brown. Remove cookies to wire racks; cool. Store in a tightly covered container for up to 2 weeks.
7. To serve, drizzle with Confectioners' Icing; let stand to set. Or, sprinkle cookies with sieved 10X (confectioners') sugar.

Confectioners' Icing: Stir 1½ tablespoons milk or water into 1 cup *sifted* 10X (confectioners') sugar to make a smooth icing that will flow easily from the tip of a spoon.

Swiss Lemon Strips

Bake at 375° for 10 minutes.
Makes about 5 dozen cookies.

Nutrient Value Per Cookie: 110 calories, 1 gm. protein, 7 gm. fat, 64 mg. sodium, 28 mg. cholesterol.

1½ **cups (3 sticks) butter or margarine, softened**
1 **cup sugar**
¼ **teaspoon salt**
3 **egg yolks**
2 **teaspoons grated lemon rind**
3 **tablespoons lemon juice**
1 **tablespoon milk**
3½ **cups sifted all-purpose flour**
   Lemon Butter Cream (recipe follows)
⅔ **cup chopped pistachio nuts**

1. Beat the butter, sugar, salt and egg yolks in a large bowl until smooth. Beat in the lemon rind and juice and milk.
2. Stir in the flour until well blended.
3. Preheat the oven to moderate (375°).
4. Fit a large pastry bag with a ½-inch plain round tip. Fill with one quarter of the dough. Press out onto ungreased cookie sheets in finger lengths 3 inches long and ½ to ¾ inch wide, spacing about ½ inch apart. Dip your finger in flour; press down on each cookie where the pastry bag leaves a tail. Repeat with the remaining dough.
5. Bake in the preheated moderate oven (375°) for 10 minutes or just until the edges are a golden brown. Transfer to wire racks; cool completely. Store in a tightly covered container for up to 2 weeks.
6. Frost one end of the cooled cookies with Lemon Butter Cream; dip in or sprinkle with pistachio nuts.

Lemon Butter Cream: Combine ¼ cup (½ stick) softened butter or margarine, 1 teaspoon grated lemon rind, 1 tablespoon *each* lemon juice and milk, and 2 cups *sifted* 10X (confectioners') sugar. Beat until smooth.

◀◀◀ ⌛ *Merry Christmas Wreaths*

Bake at 350° for 12 minutes.
Makes about 3⅓ dozen cookies.

Nutrient Value Per Cookie: 52 calories, 0.9 gm. protein, 3 gm. fat, 29 mg. sodium, 20 mg. cholesterol.

1¾ **cups sifted all-purpose flour**
½ **teaspoon baking soda**
½ **cup (1 stick) butter or margarine, softened**
½ **cup sugar**
1 **egg**
1 **egg yolk**
1 **tablespoon grated orange rind**
1 **egg white, slightly beaten**
   Green sugar crystals
   Wedges of candied red and green cherries

1. Sift together the flour and baking soda onto wax paper. Reserve.
2. Beat the butter, sugar, egg, egg yolk and orange rind until smooth.
3. Stir in the flour mixture until well blended. Wrap in foil or plastic wrap. Chill for 1 hour or freeze for 15 minutes.
4. Preheat the oven to moderate (350°). Lightly grease 2 cookie sheets.
5. Divide the dough into four equal parts. Work with one fourth of dough at a time; keep the remaining dough refrigerated. Roll one fourth of the dough with hands on a lightly floured surface into a cylinder ¼ inch in diameter. Cut the cylinder into 10 equal pieces. Repeat with the remaining dough.
6. Roll each piece into a strip 6-inches long. Holding the strip close to the cookie sheet, quickly and gently form a small circle, overlapping the ends to form small tails. Place on the cookie sheets ½ inch apart. Brush with the egg white; sprinkle with the sugar crystals. Decorate the tails with wedges of candied cherries.
7. Bake in the preheated moderate oven (350°) for 12 minutes or until lightly browned. Transfer the cookies to wire racks; cool. Store in tightly covered containers for up to 2 weeks.

🍸 ▢ *Almond Macaroons*

Bake at 300° for 15 minutes.
Makes 2½ dozen cookies.

Nutrient Value Per Cookie: 81 calories, 2 gm.
protein, 3 gm. fat, 5 mg. sodium, 0 mg.
cholesterol.

1½ cups blanched almonds, toasted
1 cup sugar
2 large egg whites
½ teaspoon almond extract
Icing (recipe follows)
Red and green candied pineapple,
sliced unblanched almonds for garnish
(optional)

1. Grind the nuts to a fine powder in a food
   processor. Add the sugar; process just to
   combine.
2. Beat the whites until stiff, not dry. Fold in
   the almond mixture and extract until it
   becomes a smooth paste.
3. Preheat the oven to slow (300°). Cut 30
   rectangles, 3½ x 1½ inches, from brown
   paper. Divide the dough into 30 pieces.
   Shape each into a 2-inch-long roll. Flatten
   onto the paper to make a 2½ x 1-inch oval.
   Place the papers on a cookie sheet.
4. Bake in the preheated slow oven (300°) for
   15 minutes or until firm and dry on the
   surface. Cool completely on wire racks; turn
   off oven.
5. Frost the cookies with the Icing. Return to
   the cooling oven just until the surface of the
   frosting is firm. Decorate with optional
   garnishes.

Icing: Beat 1 egg white in a bowl until stiff. Add 1
cup 10X (confectioners') sugar, 1 teaspoon lemon
juice. Beat to a good spreading consistency.

🍸 *Pecan Cup Cookies*

Bake at 350° for 20 minutes.
Makes about 4½ dozen cookies.

Nutrient Value Per Cookie: 59 calories, 0.7 gm.
protein, 4 gm. fat, 20 mg. sodium, 15 mg.
cholesterol.

½ cup (1 stick) butter or margarine,
softened
¼ cup granulated sugar
2 eggs, separated
1¼ cups sifted all-purpose flour
1 cup ground or finely chopped pecans
¾ cup sifted 10X (confectioners') sugar
½ teaspoon vanilla
Confectioners' Icing (recipe follows)
Candied red and green cherries

1. Beat together the butter, granulated sugar
   and egg yolks until smooth.
2. Stir in the flour until well blended. Break
   off small pieces of dough. Press into 1-inch
   tart or hors d'oeuvre pans, forming a shell
   about ⅛ inch thick. If you have only a few
   tart pans, refrigerate the dough and filling;
   bake in small batches.
3. Preheat the oven to moderate (350°).
4. To make the filling, combine pecans, 10X
   sugar, vanilla and egg whites in a bowl. Beat
   until well blended.
5. Spoon a small amount of filling into each
   pastry-lined shell to come level with the
   edge. Place the tart pans on a cookie sheet.
6. Bake in the preheated moderate oven (350°)
   for 20 minutes or until filling is set and
   lightly browned. Transfer to wire racks; cool
   for 5 minutes. Carefully remove cups from
   the pans, gently easing out with the tip of a
   paring knife; cool completely.
7. Decorate the tops with Confectioners' Icing
   and candied red and green cherries.

Confectioners' Icing: Stir 1½ tablespoons milk or water
into 1 cup *sifted* 10X (confectioners') sugar to make
a smooth icing that will flow easily from tip of spoon.

▮ ◻ *Danish Spritz Cookies*

Bake at 350° for 8 to 10 minutes.
Makes 4 dozen cookies.

Nutrient Value Per Cookie: 70 calories, 1 gm. protein, 4 gm. fat, 39 mg. sodium, 27 mg. cholesterol.

1 cup (2 sticks) butter, softened
⅔ cup sugar
3 egg yolks
½ teaspoon almond extract
2½ cups sifted all-purpose flour
1 egg white, slightly beaten (optional)
   Chocolate shot and colored decorating
      sugar for garnish (optional)

1. Preheat the oven to moderate (350°).
2. Beat together the butter, sugar, egg yolks and almond extract in a large bowl with an electric mixer until fluffy. Stir in the flour, blending well.
3. Spoon the dough into a pastry bag fitted with a star tip or into a cookie press with a star plate. Press out the dough into 3-inch lengths, 1 inch apart, on ungreased cookie sheets. Gently push into wreaths, "S" shapes, candy canes or leave straight.
4. Bake in the preheated moderate oven (350°) for 8 to 10 minutes or until the edges are lightly browned.
5. If you wish, brush the warm cookies with egg white and sprinkle with chocolate shot or colored sugar. Cool on wire racks.

▮ ◻ *Almond Tartlets*

Bake at 325° for 20 to 25 minutes.
Makes 7 dozen cookies.

Nutrient Value Per Cookie: 57 calories, 1 gm. protein, 3 gm. fat, 23 mg. sodium, 12 mg. cholesterol.

1 cup blanched almonds
1 cup (2 sticks) butter, softened
½ teaspoon almond extract
½ teaspoon lemon extract
⅔ cup sugar
2 egg yolks
2 cups sifted all-purpose flour
1 jar (12 ounces) currant jelly or
   apricot preserves

1. Grind the almonds in a food processor or a blender to a fine powder.
2. Beat together the butter, almond extract, lemon extract, sugar and egg yolks in a large bowl with an electric mixer, until light and fluffy. Add the ground almonds and flour. Beat at low speed until a firm dough forms.
3. Preheat the oven to slow (325°).
4. Place small cupcake papers in 1-inch muffin pans (gem pans). Divide the dough into ¾-inch balls. Press one ball into each cupcake paper to cover the sides and bottom, hollowing out the center to form a tartlet.
5. Bake in the preheated slow oven (325°) for 20 to 25 minutes or until the edges are golden. Remove from the pans and cool completely on wire racks.
6. Spoon about ½ teaspoon jelly or preserves into each tart. If tartlets are to be stored for several days, do not fill them until you are ready to serve them.

MICROWAVE DIRECTIONS
650 Watt Variable Power Microwave Oven Directions: Prepare the tartlets as directed above, placing the papers in a 1-inch muffin pan to form the tartlets. Remove from the pan and arrange, just in the papers, 12 at a time, in a circle with 3 in the center, on a microwave-safe baking sheet. Microwave, uncovered, at full power for 1 minute and 40 seconds. Remove to a cooling rack. Cool and fill as directed above. If you wish, unbaked, formed tartlets may be frozen. Microwave, unthawed, as directed above when ready to use. Do not increase the time.

◄◄◄ 𝚼 *Neapolitan Cookies*

Bake at 350° for 10 minutes.
Makes about 6 dozen cookies.

Nutrient Value Per Cookie: 75 calories, 1 gm.
protein, 4 gm. fat, 49 mg. sodium, 16 mg.
cholesterol.

   4   cups sifted *all-purpose flour*
   1   teaspoon baking powder
  ¼   teaspoon baking soda
  ¼   teaspoon salt
 1¼   cups (2½ sticks) butter or margarine,
        softened
   1   cup firmly packed light brown sugar
  ½   cup granulated sugar
   2   eggs
  ½   teaspoon vanilla
  ½   teaspoon almond extract
 1½   squares (1 ounce each) unsweetened
        chocolate, melted and cooled
        Red and green food coloring
   2   tablespoons chopped pistachio nuts
   2   tablespoons chopped candied red cherries
        Milk

1. Sift the flour, baking powder, baking soda
   and salt onto wax paper. Reserve.
2. Beat together the butter, brown and
   granulated sugars, eggs, vanilla and almond
   extract in a large bowl until smooth.
3. Stir in the flour mixture until well blended.
   Divide dough into 5 equal parts. Combine 2
   parts to make 1 larger portion. Place each
   portion in 4 small bowls.
4. Stir the chocolate into the large portion.
   Tint one small portion pink with red food
   coloring; another with green food coloring.
   Leave the fourth part plain. Stir the pistachio
   nuts into the green, cherries into the pink.
   Cover; chill for 2 hours.
5. Shape the green dough into a long roll
   about 2 inches in diameter. Roll between 2
   sheets of wax paper to a rectangle about
   11 x 4 inches. Brush the top lightly with
   milk. Repeat with the plain dough; place on

top of the green dough. Repeat with pink
dough; place on top of the plain dough.
With a ruler and knife, cut the rectangle to
exact size. Wrap in aluminum foil or plastic
wrap. Chill 1 hour or freeze 30 minutes.

6. Divide the chocolate part in half. Roll each
   half between sheets of wax paper to an
   11 x 6-inch rectangle. Divide chilled layered
   dough in half, lengthwise. Place a layered
   half on one of the chocolate rectangles.
   Brush with milk; wrap chocolate around the
   layered dough, pressing gently to form a
   long block. Repeat with the remaining
   chocolate and layered dough. Rewrap in
   aluminum foil or plastic. Freeze for 1 hour.
   The dough may be stored in the refrigerator
   for up to 1 week, or frozen for up to 1 month.
7. Preheat oven to moderate (350°).
8. Cut the dough into ¼-inch slices. Place on
   ungreased cookie sheets ½ inch apart.
9. Bake in the preheated moderate oven (350°)
   for 10 minutes or just until set. Cookies
   should not brown, except on the bottom, to
   keep colors bright. Transfer to wire racks;
   cool completely. Store in tightly covered
   containers for up to 2 weeks.

𝚼 *Sandbakels (Swedish Almond Cookies)*

**A very tender cookie dusted with 10X
(confectioners') sugar.**

Bake at 350° for 8 minutes.
Makes 3 dozen cookies.

Nutrient Value Per Cookie: 80 calories, 1 gm.
protein, 5 gm. fat, 40 mg. sodium, 10 mg.
cholesterol.

  ⅓   cup blanched slivered almonds
   4   whole unblanched almonds
  ¾   cup (1½ sticks) butter, softened
  ¾   cup sugar
   1   egg white

1¾ **cups** sifted **all-purpose flour**
10X (confectioners') sugar

1. Combine the slivered and whole almonds in the container of an electric blender or food processor; cover. Whirl until finely ground.
2. Beat together the butter and sugar in a small bowl until light and fluffy; beat in the egg white. Stir in the flour until well blended.
3. Shape the dough into a ball; cover with plastic wrap. Chill for 2 hours.
4. Preheat the oven to moderate (350°).
5. Press the dough by rounded teaspoonfuls into 2½-inch shell-shaped tins.
6. Bake in the preheated moderate oven (350°) for 8 to 10 minutes or until golden brown. Remove the cookies to a wire rack. Sprinkle with 10X (confectioners') sugar. Cool.

▣ ▢ *Morning Kisses (Chocolate Nut Meringues)*

Bake at 350° for 15 minutes.
Makes about 6 dozen cookies.

Nutrient Value Per Cookie: 33 calories, less than 1 gm. protein, 2 gm. fat, 2 mg. sodium, less than 1 mg. cholesterol.

2 **egg whites, at room temperature**
¾ **cup superfine sugar**
1 **cup plus 3 tablespoons ground walnuts (about 1¼ cups walnut pieces)**
2 **ounces (½ package) sweet cooking chocolate, grated**
   Superfine sugar
   Candied red cherries, halved

1. Preheat the oven to moderate (350°). Grease cookie sheets; dust with flour, tapping off excess.
2. Beat the egg whites in a medium-size bowl until frothy. Gradually beat in the sugar until the meringue forms stiff peaks. Fold in

the walnuts and chocolate.

3. Shape the meringue into balls, using a level teaspoon for each cookie. Roll in additional sugar. Place 2 inches apart on the prepared cookie sheets. Press a cherry half into each.
4. Bake in the preheated moderate oven (350°) for 15 minutes or until firm on outside. Remove from cookie sheets; cool on racks.

Note: Make these on a cool dry day.

▣ ▢ *Pecan Wafers*

Bake at 350° for 12 to 15 minutes.
Makes 5 dozen cookies.

Nutrient Value Per Cookie: 38 calories, 0 gm. protein, 2 gm. fat, 14 mg. sodium, 2 mg. cholesterol.

3 **egg whites**
⅛ **teaspoon salt**
1¼ **cups firmly packed light brown sugar**
3 **tablespoons melted butter**
1 **teaspoon vanilla**
2 **tablespoons all-purpose flour**
1 **cup finely chopped pecans**
   Corn syrup, red and green sugar for garnish (optional)

1. Cover cookie sheets with aluminum foil; grease the foil with vegetable shortening. Preheat the oven to moderate (350°).
2. Beat the egg whites with the salt in a medium-size bowl with an electric mixer until stiff.
3. Combine the sugar, butter, vanilla and flour in a bowl. Fold the mixture into the egg whites just until uniformly combined. Fold in the nuts.
4. Drop by slightly rounded teaspoonfuls, 3 inches apart, on the prepared cookie sheets.
5. Bake in the preheated moderate oven (350°) for 12 to 15 minutes or until the centers and edges are evenly colored. Cool on foil.

If not crisp when cooled, return to oven for 2 to 3 minutes. Store in an airtight container.

6. If you wish, brush two parallel lines of syrup in each direction on the cookies while they are warm. Sprinkle red sugar over one line in each direction, and green over the others.

◻ Frozen Chocolate Cookie Cakes

Bake at 350° for 10 minutes.
Makes 2 dozen cookies.

Nutrient Value Per Cookie: 149 calories, 1 gm. protein, 10 gm. fat, 64 mg. sodium, 35 mg. cholesterol.

1   cup sifted all-purpose flour
½ teaspoon baking soda
⅛ teaspoon salt
½ cup (1 stick) butter
6   squares (1 ounce each) semisweet chocolate
¼ cup light corn syrup
⅓ cup granulated sugar
1   teaspoon vanilla
1   egg
1   cup heavy cream
2   tablespoons 10X (confectioners') sugar
2   teaspoons orange-flavored liqueur Candy decorations for garnish (optional)

1. Preheat the oven to moderate (350°). Cover the cookie sheets with aluminum foil; grease with vegetable shortening.
2. Sift together the flour, baking soda and salt.
3. Heat the butter, chocolate, corn syrup and sugar in a medium-size saucepan over low heat until the butter and chocolate are melted. Stir until smooth; cool for 5 minutes.
4. Stir the vanilla, egg and flour mixture into the chocolate mixture. Beat until smooth.
5. Drop the mixture by level teaspoonfuls, 2

inches apart, onto the prepared cookie sheets. Spread with a small spatula into an even circle, 1½ inches in diameter.
6. Bake in the preheated moderate oven (350°) for 10 minutes or until the cookies have flattened and become firm. Cool them completely on the foil on a wire rack.
7. Remove the cookies from the foil and match into stacks of three cookies each.
8. Beat the cream with 10X (confectioners') sugar and liqueur in a small bowl until stiff. Spoon into a pastry bag fitted with a large star tip. Pipe a star onto each cookie in each of the stacks. Reassemble the stacks, pushing the cookies together until they are about ¼ inch apart. Sprinkle the top star with candy decorations, if you wish.
9. Place the cookies in a deep dish or pan. Cover tightly; freeze until ready to serve.

◳ ⏦ ◻ Chocolate Pecan Refrigerator Cookies

A great make-ahead, nutty chocolate cookie. The dough can be kept frozen for up to 1 month.

Bake at 350° for 10 minutes.
Makes about 7½ dozen cookies.

Nutrient Value Per Cookie: 76 calories, 0.8 gm. protein, 5 gm. fat, 39 mg. sodium, 10 mg. cholesterol.

3   cups sifted all-purpose flour
½   cup unsweetened cocoa powder
1¼ cups (2½ sticks) butter or margarine, softened
1½ cups sifted 10X (confectioners') sugar
1   egg
1   teaspoon vanilla
1   cup finely chopped pecans
1   container (16.5 ounces) milk chocolate frosting Pecan halves

1. Sift together the flour and cocoa powder onto wax paper. Reserve.
2. Beat together the butter, 10X (confectioners') sugar, egg and vanilla in a large bowl until smooth.
3. Stir in the flour mixture until well blended. Divide the dough in half. Shape each half into a roll 1½ inches in diameter. Wrap in plastic wrap. Chill for 2 hours or freeze for 1 hour.
4. Roll each cylinder of chilled dough in chopped pecans, shaping as round as possible. Freeze briefly if too soft.
5. Preheat the oven to moderate (350°).
6. Cut the rolls into ¼-inch slices. Place on ungreased cookie sheets, ½ inch apart.
7. Bake in the preheated moderate oven (350°) for 10 minutes or until firm. Store in tightly covered containers for up to 2 weeks.
8. Decorate with frosting piped through a pastry bag or cake decorator. Garnish with pecan halves.

Chocolate-Bourbon-Currant Squares

Just a small piece of this very rich, chocolatey cake goes a long way.

Bake at 325° for 35 minutes.
Makes 40 squares.

Nutrient Value Per Square: 175 calories, 2 gm. protein, 12 gm. fat, 12 mg. sodium, 54 mg. cholesterol.

½ **cup bourbon**
½ **cup currants**
14 **squares (1 ounce each) semisweet chocolate**
1 **cup (2 sticks) sweet butter**
6 **eggs, separated**
1⅓ **cups granulated sugar**
¾ **cup sifted all-purpose flour**

1⅓ **cups ground toasted walnuts**
10X (confectioners') sugar
Walnut halves, if you wish

1. Preheat the oven to slow (325°). Grease and flour a 13 x 9 x 2-inch baking pan.
2. Pour the bourbon over the currants in a small bowl; set aside and let soak while preparing the cake batter.
3. Melt the chocolate and butter in the top of a double boiler over hot, not boiling, water; stir until blended. Cool slightly.
4. Beat together the egg yolks and sugar in a medium-size bowl until pale yellow and thickened. Beat in the cooled chocolate mixture. Combine the flour with the ground walnuts in a small bowl; stir into the batter. Stir in the soaked currants with liquid.
5. Beat the egg whites until soft peaks form; gently fold into the cake batter. Pour into the prepared pan.
6. Bake in the preheated slow oven (325°) for 35 minutes or until the top feels firm to the touch. Cool thoroughly on a wire rack. Chill in the refrigerator for at least 2 hours for ease in cutting.
7. Sprinkle the chilled cake with 10X (confectioners') sugar. Cut into squares; top each with a walnut half, if you wish. Store leftover cake in the refrigerator; serve at room temperature for better flavor.

TO TOAST WALNUTS
Place the shelled walnuts in a baking pan and bake in a preheated moderate oven (350°) for 10 minutes. Cool.

MAKE-AHEAD TIP
The baked squares may be wrapped in aluminum foil and frozen. Thaw at room temperature.

☐ *Coconut Flake Cookies*

Bake at 325° for 15 minutes.
Makes 5 dozen cookies.

Nutrient Value Per Cookie: 44 calories, 0 gm.
protein, 3 gm. fat, 23 mg. sodium, 9 mg.
cholesterol.

> 1   cup sifted **all-purpose flour**
> $\frac{1}{8}$ teaspoon salt
> $\frac{1}{8}$ teaspoon ground cinnamon
> $\frac{1}{8}$ teaspoon ground nutmeg
> $\frac{1}{2}$ cup (1 stick) butter, softened
> $\frac{1}{4}$ cup firmly packed dark brown sugar
> 1   egg yolk
> $\frac{1}{2}$ teaspoon vanilla
> $\frac{1}{4}$ teaspoon almond extract
> 2   teaspoons grated orange rind
> 2   teaspoons grated lemon rind
> 2   egg whites, slightly beaten
> 2   cans (3½ ounces each) flaked coconut
>   Red and green candied pineapple,
>   cut into ¼-inch cubes, for garnish

1. Preheat the oven to slow (325°). Grease cookie sheets with vegetable shortening.
2. Sift together the flour, salt, cinnamon and nutmeg onto wax paper.
3. Beat together the butter, brown sugar, egg yolk, vanilla, almond extract, orange and lemon rinds in a medium-size bowl with an electric mixer until fluffy. Add the flour mixture; beat at low speed until smooth.
4. Drop the dough by half-teaspoonfuls into the beaten whites; toss in the coconut to coat evenly. Place 1 inch apart on the prepared cookie sheets. Press 1 candied pineapple cube into the center of each cookie.
5. Bake in the preheated slow oven (325°) for 15 minutes or until the coconut is golden. Transfer to wire racks to cool.

☐ *Fruit and Nut Cookies*

Bake at 350° for 15 minutes.
Makes 4½ dozen cookies.

Nutrient Value Per Cookie: 95 calories, 1 gm.
protein, 4 gm. fat, 51 mg. sodium, 17 mg.
cholesterol.

> $\frac{1}{2}$ cup dried apricots, diced
> 1   cup boiling water
> 2   cups sifted **all-purpose flour**
> 1   teaspoon baking powder
> $\frac{1}{2}$ teaspoon baking soda
> $\frac{2}{3}$ cup butter, softened
> 1   cup sugar
> 1   teaspoon grated orange rind
> 1   teaspoon grated lemon rind
> 2   eggs
> 1   tablespoon lemon juice
> $\frac{1}{2}$ cup dairy sour cream
> $\frac{1}{4}$ cup diced candied orange peel
> $\frac{3}{4}$ cup diced candied pineapple
> $\frac{2}{3}$ cup chopped walnuts
>   Frosting (recipe follows)
>   Apricots, candied pineapple and
>   walnuts for garnish (optional)

1. Combine the apricots and 1 cup boiling water in a small bowl. Set aside for 10 minutes. Drain well. Reserve.
2. Preheat the oven to moderate (350°). Lightly grease cookie sheets with vegetable shortening.
3. Sift together the flour, baking powder and baking soda onto wax paper.
4. Beat together the butter, sugar, orange and lemon rinds, eggs and lemon juice in a large bowl with an electric mixer until fluffy.
5. Stir in the flour mixture and sour cream until blended. Fold in the apricots, candied orange and pineapple and walnuts. Drop by tablespoonfuls, 1½ inches apart, onto the prepared cookie sheets.
6. Bake in the preheated moderate oven (350°) for 15 minutes or until the edges are

golden and the centers feel firm to the touch. Remove to racks to cool completely.

7. Spread the cookies with Frosting and garnish with more apricots, pineapple and walnuts, if you wish.

Frosting: Blend in a small bowl 1¼ cups 10X (confectioners') sugar, 1 tablespoon light corn syrup, ¼ teaspoon vanilla and 1½ tablespoons hot water until blended and a good spreading consistency.

Lace Cookie Sundaes

Try the cookies by themselves, without ice cream and chocolate sauce. It may take a few tries to master the technique of making these delicate cookies.

Bake at 350° for 5 to 7 minutes.
Makes 12 servings.

Nutrient Value Per Serving: 486 calories, 7 gm. protein, 26 gm. fat, 178 mg. sodium, 55 mg. cholesterol.

¼   cup (½ stick) butter
6   tablespoons unblanched almonds,
*   finely ground*
¼   cup sugar
2   tablespoons all-purpose flour
1   tablespoon heavy cream
3   pints vanilla ice cream
*   Rich Chocolate Sauce (recipe follows)*

1. Preheat the oven to moderate (350°). Grease 2 baking sheets.
2. Melt the butter in a small heavy saucepan. Add the almonds, sugar, flour and cream. Cook, stirring, for 1 minute.
3. Place 8 rounded ½ to ¾ teaspoonfuls of batter, spacing far apart, on each sheet.
4. Bake in the preheated moderate oven (350°) until the cookies are lightly browned around the edges, but still slightly bubbly in

the center, 5 to 7 minutes. They should spread to be about 4 inches in diameter.

5. Cool the cookies on the sheets for about 1 minute, until the edges are firm enough to lift with long thin spatula. Working quickly, remove the cookies to wire racks. If the cookies become too difficult to remove, return the sheet to the oven for about 1 minute to soften. Repeat until all the batter is used.
6. Scoop out 12 medium-size balls of ice cream. Place on a wax paper-lined pan. Flatten slightly. Place in freezer.
7. To serve, sandwich 2 cookies together with 1 flattened scoop of ice cream. Serve with a tablespoon of Rich Chocolate Sauce.

Rich Chocolate Sauce: Combine 1 can (13 ounces) evaporated milk and 2 cups sugar in a small saucepan. Bring to boiling; boil for 1 minute. Add 4 squares (1 ounce each) unsweetened chocolate. When melted, beat with a hand mixer until smooth and creamy. Remove from the heat. Add ¼ cup (½ stick) butter and 1 teaspoon vanilla. Cool. Store leftover sauce in a jar in the refrigerator.

> **PLEASE NOTE:**
> **Do not attempt to make these cookies in hot, humid weather, as the cookies will absorb moisture from the air and become limp. To store the cookies, layer carefully between sheets of wax paper in a container with a tight-fitting lid.**

▲ **Crispy Bow Tie Cookies**

Crispy Bow Tie Cookies

Makes about 2 dozen cookies.

Nutrient Value Per Cookie: 61 calories, 1 gm. protein, 1 gm. fat, 6 mg. sodium, 23 mg. cholesterol.

2 eggs
2 tablespoons granulated sugar
2 cups sifted all-purpose flour
2 tablespoons vanilla
1 teaspoon grated lemon rind
Vegetable oil for frying
10X (confectioners') sugar

1. Beat together the eggs and sugar in a medium-size bowl until the mixture is light and fluffy. Stir in 1½ cups of the flour, the vanilla and lemon rind until blended. Shape into a ball.
2. Turn the dough out onto a lightly floured surface. Knead until the dough is smooth and elastic, about 8 minutes; add as much of the remaining flour as necessary to prevent sticking. Cover with plastic wrap. Let rest for 5 minutes.
3. Divide the dough into 4 equal portions. Roll one fourth of the dough to a ⅛-inch thickness. Keep the remaining dough covered with plastic wrap while working with the one-fourth. Cut into 5 x 1½-inch strips with a pastry wheel or pizza cutter. Make a lengthwise slit about 1-inch long in center of each strip. Pull one end through the slit to make a bow tie. As you work, keep the bow ties covered with plastic wrap. Repeat with the remaining dough.
4. Pour vegetable oil into a large saucepan or Dutch oven to a depth of 4 inches. Heat the oil until it registers 375° on a deep-fat frying thermometer or until a 1-inch cube of white bread turns golden brown in about 50 seconds. Transfer 3 or 4 cookies to the hot oil with a metal spatula. Fry the cookies for a total of 3 minutes or until golden, turning once. Drain on paper toweling; cool. Keep unfried bow ties covered with plastic wrap. Fry the remaining cookies.
5. Store in a tightly covered container. Sprinkle with 10X (confectioners') sugar just before serving.

Scottish Shortbread Cookies

Use this recipe to make small individual cookies or larger ones for the Strawberry Shortbread (recipe follows). Serve these cookies with ice cream, fresh fruit or just by themselves with a glass of milk.

Bake at 300° for 30 minutes.
Makes about 1½ dozen cookies.

Nutrient Value Per Cookie: 167 calories, 2 gm. protein, 10 gm. fat, 103 mg. sodium, 27 mg. cholesterol.

1 cup (2 sticks) butter or margarine, softened
½ cup sugar
2½ cups sifted all-purpose flour

1. Beat together butter and sugar in a large bowl until smooth. Gradually work in the flour with a wooden spoon to make a stiff dough. Shape into a ball; flatten. Wrap in wax paper. Refrigerate for 30 minutes.
2. Preheat the oven to slow (300°).
3. Roll the dough out on a lightly floured surface to a ¼-inch thickness. Cut into 3-inch rounds with a scalloped cookie cutter. Transfer the cookies with a wide spatula to a cookie sheet, spacing 1 inch apart.
4. Bake in the preheated slow oven (300°) for 30 minutes or just until pale golden. Remove to a wire rack; cool completely. Store in a tightly covered container.

▲Mocha Lace Roll-Ups

🍸 *Mocha Lace Roll-Ups*

Bake at 325° for 9 minutes.
Makes about 1¾ dozen.

Nutrient Value Per Serving: 125 calories, 2 gm. protein, 10 gm. fat, 29 mg. sodium, 22 mg. cholesterol.

- ½ **cup sifted *all-purpose flour***
- ½ **cup ground blanched almonds**
- ¼ **cup light corn syrup**
- ¼ **cup granulated sugar**
- ¼ **cup (½ stick) butter or margarine**
- 1 **square unsweetened chocolate**
- ½ **teaspoon vanilla**
- 1 **cup heavy cream**
- 2 **tablespoons 10X (confectioners') sugar**
  Chopped pistachio nuts

1. Preheat the oven to slow (325°).
2. Combine the flour and almonds. Combine the corn syrup, sugar, butter and chocolate in a small heavy saucepan. Cook, stirring constantly, until the mixture comes to a boil and the chocolate is melted. Remove from the heat; stir in the vanilla. Stir in the flour mixture gradually until well blended.
3. Drop the mixture by rounded teaspoonfuls about 3 inches apart onto ungreased cookie sheets; bake no more than 6 at a time.
4. Bake in the preheated slow oven (325°) for 9 minutes. Remove to a wire rack; cool for 1 to 1½ minutes. Scoop up the warm cookies with a large metal spatula; quickly roll around a wooden spoon handle (at least ½ inch in diameter). Hold a few seconds until the cookie stiffens. (If the cookies cool too quickly or are too brittle to work, return to a warm oven briefly to soften.) Slide the cookie off the handle onto a wire rack to cool completely.
5. Beat the heavy cream with 10X (confectioners') sugar until stiff. Pipe into the ends of cookies. Dip the ends into the chopped pistachios.

▼ ▢ *Strawberry Shortbread*

Two large Scottish shortbread cookies are the basis for this dessert.

Bake at 300° for 30 minutes.
Makes 8 servings.

Nutrient Value Per Serving: 493 calories, 5 gm. protein, 31 gm. fat, 241 mg. sodium, 62 mg. cholesterol.

1 recipe Scottish Shortbread Cookies, prepared through step 1 (page 000)
1 quart strawberries
1 tub (8 ounces) frozen whipped topping, thawed

1. Prepare the shortbread recipe through step 1.
2. Line a cookie sheet with aluminum foil.
3. Divide the dough in half. Roll out each half between 2 sheets of wax paper into a 9½-inch circle. Peel off the top sheets of paper. Invert the dough onto the lined cookie sheet. Remove the second sheets of paper. Outline an 8-inch circle on each round. Then with a teaspoon as a guide, cut a scalloped edge on each cookie. Remove the trimmings. Prick cookies with a fork. Score one circle with a knife into 8 equal triangles. Refrigerate for 30 minutes. Preheat the oven to slow (300°).
4. Bake in the preheated slow oven (300°) for 30 to 35 minutes or until pale golden. Cool on the cookie sheet on a wire rack for 5 minutes. Cut through the score lines on the one cookie; leave the second cookie whole. Transfer both to a wire rack to cool.
5. Reserve 7 or 8 whole strawberries for garnish. Halve or slice the remaining strawberries.
6. Place the whole shortbread cookie on a serving plate. Top with the cut strawberries and topping. Arrange the shortbread triangles on an angle on the topping with the points meeting in the center and the scalloped edges out. Garnish with the reserved whole berries. The shortbread may be refrigerated for up to 1 hour before serving.

8. The Best Course: Dessert Pies, Fruits, Ice Cream and Calorie-light Sweets

*W*hether a meal is for family or friends, it is always nice to plan a special ending. Serve an irresistible pie, a fabulous fruit dessert, or a meltingly delicious ice cream dessert for that special flourish! Dessert should complement the other courses yet not repeat the other foods. A heavy main course is best followed by a light dessert, like sherbet, while a heavier dessert, like pie, would be fine after a light meal. Family and guests should leave the table with a *satisfied* not a *stuffed* feeling.

Tempt young and old alike with the tantalizing aroma of a freshly baked pie cooling in the kitchen. Old favorite recipes, regional favorites and new discoveries are included here.

No matter what the season, there is always a variety of fresh and dried fruits in the market. Why not use them to create marvelous light desserts like Lime Soufflé, Ribbon Bavarian, Summer Fruit Compote or Bananas Flambé.

When summer rolls around, dessert seems to become synonymous with ice cream. Serve up variety with such cooling delights as Piña Colada Ice Cream Waffles, Pineapple Mint Sorbet and Fresh Strawberry Ice Soda.

In our think-thin society, dessert is frequently passed up by those who are watching their weight. But one can be weight-conscious and still enjoy a great dessert. Here we offer a selection of fabulous calorie-light desserts made with low-fat ingredients, hardly any sugar and lots of fresh fruit. These rich-tasting desserts are all under 160 calories per serving. So...dig in!

Pies

◀*Clockwise from Top:* **Strawberry-Almond Tart (page 252), Strawberry-Orange Shortcakes (page 263) and Port Wine Gelatin with Strawberries (page 262).**

▯ Green Apple Pie

The original English ancestor of this pie was the Marlborough Pie, traditionally made with applesauce, as apples were dried for long keeping over the winter. This version departs from the traditional by layering tender apple slices with creamy lemon custard.

Bake at 400° for 15 minutes; then at 350° for 30 minutes.
Makes 6 servings.

Nutrient Value Per Serving: 669 calories, 7 gm. protein, 37 gm. fat, 475 mg. sodium, 183 mg. cholesterol.

3 **medium-size Granny Smith or Greening apples**
¼ **cup apple juice or cider**
3 **tablespoons sugar**
1 **package (11 ounces) piecrust mix**
3 **eggs**
⅔ **cup sugar**
½ **teaspoon ground cinnamon**
1 **tablespoon lemon juice**
1 **cup light cream or half and half**
2 **tablespoons butter or margarine, melted**
1 **tablespoon milk**
2 **tablespoons sugar**
   Whipped cream and apple slices (optional)

1. Pare, quarter and core the apples; cut into very thin slices. Combine with the apple juice and the 3 tablepoons sugar in a large saucepan. Cook, gently stirring occasionally, until the apple slices are translucent and just tender, about 5 minutes.
2. Preheat the oven to hot (400°).
3. Prepare the piecrust mix following label directions for a 9-inch pastry shell with a high fluted edge. Roll out the remaining half of the pastry; cut out 6 large "leaves." Mark each "leaf" with the back of a knife to simulate veins; reserve.
4. Beat the eggs in a large bowl until foamy. Stir in the apple slices and any remaining syrup, the ⅔ cup sugar, the cinnamon, lemon juice, cream and butter. Pour the filling into the pastry shell. Brush the pastry leaves with milk; sprinkle with the 2 tablespoons sugar. Arrange on the filling, like spokes in a wheel. (Or you may roll out the pastry, cut vents, and cover the pie completely.)
5. Bake in the preheated hot oven (400°) for 15 minutes. Lower the oven temperature to moderate (350°) and continue baking 30 minutes longer. The filling may be a little

soft in the center, but will set as it cools. Cool on a wire rack. Garnish with whipped cream and apple slices, if you wish. Serve at room temperature. Keep any leftovers refrigerated.

PIE-MAKING TIPS
- To ensure a light, flaky pastry, handle the dough as little as possible. Dough that is overhandled will become tough.
- Always roll pastry dough from the center to the edge; never roll back over the dough toward the center. This will help to make your crust even in size and thickness.
- As you roll out the dough, turn it gently to prevent sticking.
- Be sure to fit the dough *loosely* in the pie plate. If the dough is stretched tight, it will shrink during baking.
- For lattice pies as well as pastry shells, turn the edges of the dough *under* and pinch to form a stand-up edge. There is no need to seal in juices as there is with most double-crust pies.
- To catch any run-overs during baking, slide a piece of aluminum foil on the oven rack below the pie.
- Trimmings from pastry can be re-rolled, cut, sprinkled with sugar and cinnamon and baked for extra treats.

Spiced Raisin Pie

Akin to the Pennsylvania Dutch "Rosina Boi," or, with the addition of chopped nuts, sometimes know as "Funeral Pie." The latter customarily brought as a gift of food to a bereaved family.

Bake at 425° for 40 minutes.
Makes 6 servings.

Nutrient Value Per Serving: 698 calories, 6 gm. protein, 27 gm. fat, 633 mg. sodium, 65 mg. cholesterol.

- **1 package (12 ounces) seedless raisins**
- **1 cup firmly packed light brown sugar**
- **½ teaspoon salt**
- **2 cups water**
- **2 tablespoons butter or margarine**
- **1 tablespoon grated lemon rind**
- **½ teaspoon ground cinnamon**
- **2 tablespoons cornstarch**
- **¼ cup lemon juice**
- **2 tablespoons water**
- **1 package (11 ounces) piecrust mix**
- **1 egg, beaten**
  Vanilla ice cream (optional)

1. Combine the raisins, sugar, salt, the 2 cups water and butter in a large saucepan. Bring to boiling; lower the heat slightly. Cook, stirring occasionally, for 5 minutes. Stir in the lemon rind and cinnamon. Remove from the heat.
2. Blend the cornstarch with the lemon juice and 2 tablespoons water in a small bowl until smooth; stir into the raisin mixture. Cook, stirring constantly, until the mixture thickens and bubbles, 1 minute.
3. Preheat the oven to hot (425°).
4. Prepare the piecrust mix, following label directions for a 9-inch double-crust pie. Line a 9-inch pie plate with the pastry; spoon in the raisin filling.
5. Cut top crust into ½-inch strips. Weave over filling in a lattice design. Trim overhang to 1 inch; fold under, flush with rim. Pinch to make a stand-up edge; flute.
6. Brush the beaten egg over the pastry for a shiny crust.
7. Bake in the preheated hot oven (425°) for 40 minutes or until the juices bubble up and the pastry is golden brown. Cool on a wire rack. Serve warm with scoops of vanilla ice cream, if you wish.

▲*Clockwise from left:* **Spiced Raisin Pie (page 244), Lemon Sponge Pie (page 246) and Green Apple Pie (page 243).**

PROTECT CRIMPED EDGE
If the pastry edge is browning too quickly, cover it with strips of aluminum foil.

▮▯ Sour Cream-Walnut Pie

Originally made with native black walnuts, this is a kissin' cousin of the famed pecan pie.

Bake at 350° for 40 minutes.
Makes 8 servings.

Nutrient Value Per Serving: 601 calories, 7 gm. protein, 37 gm. fat, 355 mg. sodium, 189 mg. cholesterol.

½ *of an 11-ounce package piecrust mix*
⅓ *cup butter or margarine*
½ *cup firmly packed light brown sugar*
4 *eggs*
¾ *cup granulated sugar*
¼ *teaspoon salt*
½ *cup light or dark corn syrup*
¾ *cup dairy sour cream*
1 *cup broken walnuts*
1 *teaspoon vanilla*
½ *cup heavy cream, whipped*
  Walnut halves (optional)

1. Prepare the piecrust mix, following label directions for a 9-inch pastry crust with a high fluted edge. Chill.
2. Preheat the oven to moderate (350°).
3. Combine the butter and brown sugar in the top of a double boiler over simmering water. Heat, just until the butter is melted.
4. Beat the eggs slightly in a medium-size bowl. Beat in the granulated sugar, salt, corn syrup and sour cream, just until smooth. Pour into the butter mixture, stirring until well blended. Cook over hot, not boiling, water, stirring constantly, for 5 minutes. Remove from the heat; stir in the walnuts and vanilla. Pour the mixture into the pastry shell.
5. Bake in the preheated moderate oven (350°) for 40 minutes. The filling will be a little soft in the center, but do not overbake. Cool on a wire rack. Garnish with whipped cream and walnut halves, if you wish. Serve at room temperature. Keep any leftovers refrigerated.

▯ Lemon Sponge Pie

This Amish specialty from Pennsylvania has a layer of lemon custard topped with lemon sponge cake.

Bake at 350° for 35 minutes.
Makes 6 servings.

Nutrient Value Per Serving: 367 calories, 7 gm. protein, 19 gm. fat, 293 mg. sodium, 201 mg. cholesterol.

½ *of an 11 ounce package piecrust mix*
4 *eggs, separated*
⅔ *cup sugar*
2 *tablespoons all-purpose flour*
1 *tablespoon grated lemon rind*
⅓ *cup lemon juice*
⅔ *cup milk*
2 *tablespoons butter or margarine, melted*
  Whipped cream and lemon slices
  (optional)

1. Prepare the piecrust mix, following label directions for a 9-inch pastry shell with a high fluted edge; chill.
2. Preheat the oven to moderate (350°).
3. Beat the egg whites in a large bowl until foamy. Add 2 tablespoons of the sugar slowly, beating until the meringue forms soft peaks.
4. Beat the egg yolks and the remaining sugar in a medium-size bowl until thick and light. Beat in the flour, lemon rind and juice, milk and butter until smooth. Fold into the meringue until no streaks of white remain. Pour into the pastry shell.
5. Bake in the preheated moderate oven (350°) for 35 minutes or until the top is golden brown. Do not overbake. Cool on a wire rack. Serve warm or chilled. Garnish with whipped cream and lemon slices, if you wish. Refrigerate leftovers.

FREEZING PIE SHELLS

Make 2 pie shells, use 1 and freeze the other for future use.

● **Wrap unbaked pie shells in aluminum foil and freeze. To use, thaw the unbaked shell at room temperature for about 30 minutes and use in the recipe as directed.**

● **Cool a baked pie shell before wrapping and freezing. Warm the frozen shell in a preheated moderate (375°) oven for 10 minutes, if you wish.**

Glazed Apple-Apricot Pie

Bake at 450° for 15 minutes; then at 350° for 40 minutes.
Makes 8 servings (one 9-inch pie).

Nutrient Value Per Serving: 317 calories, 2 gm. protein, 13 gm. fat, 147 mg. sodium, 15 mg. cholesterol.

  1 cup dried apricots, halved
  ⅔ cup hot water
  2 pounds apples (5 to 6), such as Cortland or Rome Beauty, pared, cored and thinly sliced (about 6 cups)
  ½ cup granulated sugar
  1 tablespoon cornstarch
  2 teaspoons lemon juice
  1 teaspoon ground cinnamon
  ¼ teaspoon ground nutmeg
  ½ of an 11-ounce package piecrust mix
  3 tablespoons unsalted butter or margarine, melted
  2 tablespoons apple jelly
     10X (confectioners') sugar

1. Combine the apricots and hot water in a bowl. Let stand for 5 minutes; drain.

2. Combine the apricots, apples, sugar, cornstarch, lemon juice, cinnamon and nutmeg in a large bowl; toss to mix thoroughly. Let stand for 10 minutes.

3. Preheat the oven to very hot (450°).

4. Prepare the piecrust mix, following label directions for a 9-inch pastry shell with high fluted edge.

5. Measure 2 cups of the apple-apricot mixture; set aside. Spoon the remaining fruit into the prepared pie shell. Remove the apple slices from the reserved apple-apricot mixture, and arrange in an overlapping pattern around the outside edge. Place the reserved apricot pieces in the center. Cover the apricots with a square of aluminum foil to prevent browning.

6. Bake in the preheated very hot oven (450°) for 15 minutes. Lower the oven temperature to moderate (350°). Continue to bake for 40 minutes or until the apples are tender, basting the apples with melted butter several times. Cool on the wire rack.

7. Melt the jelly in a small saucepan over low heat. Brush over the pie. Just before serving, dust the pie lightly with 10X (confectioners') sugar.

Three-Flavor Pie

Mince, apple and cranberry combine perfectly in this pie.

Bake at 425° for 40 minutes.
Makes 6 servings.

Nutrient Value Per Serving: 463 calories, 3 gm. protein, 15 gm. fat, 431 mg. sodium, 9 mg. cholesterol.

  ½ of an 11-ounce package piecrust mix
  ¼ cup unsifted all-purpose flour
  ⅓ cup sugar
  1 tablespoon butter
  3 medium-tart apples
     Mincemeat-Cranberry Filling (recipe follows)

1. Preheat the oven to hot (425°).
2. Prepare the piecrust mix, following label directions for a single-crust 9-inch pastry shell with a high fluted edge. Sprinkle 2 tablespoons of flour over the crust.
3. Combine the remaining flour and sugar in a small bowl. Cut in the 1 tablespoon butter with a pastry blender until the mixture has the texture of small peas. Reserve.
4. Prepare the Mincemeat-Cranberry Filling.
5. Spread the Mincemeat-Cranberry Filling in the bottom of the pastry shell.
6. Pare the apples; cut into quarters. Cut the quarters into wedges, ½-inch thick at the outer edge. Lay the wedges over the mince-meat in 2 concentric circles. Cover the center with 3 or 4 wedges. Sprinkle the reserved sugar mixture over the apples.
7. Cover the edge of the pastry with a 2- or 3-inch strip of aluminum foil to prevent excessive browning.
8. Bake in the preheated hot oven (425°) for 30 minutes. Remove the aluminum foil. Bake another 10 to 15 minutes or until the edge of the pastry is golden brown.

Mincemeat-Cranberry Filling: Crumble 1 box (9 ounces) mincemeat into a small saucepan. Add 1 cup water and 3 tablespoons sugar. Stir to combine. Bring to boiling; boil for 1 minute. Stir in 1 cup cranberries (fresh or thawed frozen berries). Remove from the heat.

▲*From the top:* **Ribbon Bavarian (page 261), Cream Stars (page 227) and Three-Flavor Pie (page 247).**

🍸 🏠 *Pear Crumb Pie*

A gem of a pie from the Northwest, where pear and apple orchards crisscross the land. Crunchy crumbs top the juicy pears.

Bake at 400° for 40 minutes.
Makes 6 servings.

Nutrient Value Per Serving: 564 calories, 4 gm. protein, 22 gm. fat, 298 mg. sodium, 31 mg. cholesterol.

½ *of an 11-ounce package piecrust mix*
1 *cup sifted all-purpose flour*
⅓ *cup firmly packed light brown sugar*
⅓ *cup butter or margarine*
2½ *pounds firm-ripe Anjou or Bosc pears*
1 *tablespoon lemon juice*
⅔ *cup granulated sugar*
1 *teaspoon ground cinnamon*
¼ *teaspoon ground mace*
1 *tablespoon all-purpose flour*
  10X (confectioners') sugar
  Ice cream (optional)

1. Prepare the piecrust mix, following label directions for a 9-inch pastry shell with a high-fluted edge; chill the crust while preparing the filling.
2. Combine the 1 cup flour and the ⅓ cup brown sugar in a small bowl. Cut in the butter with a pastry blender until coarse crumbs form; reserve the brown sugar topping.
3. Preheat the oven to hot (400°).
4. Pare, quarter and core the pears. Slice into a large bowl; sprinkle with the lemon juice.

5. Combine the granulated sugar, cinnamon, mace and flour in a small bowl; sprinkle over the pears. Toss gently to mix well; spoon into the prepared pastry shell. Sprinkle with the reserved brown sugar topping.

6. Bake in the preheated hot oven (400°) for 40 minutes or until the juices bubble up and the top browns. If the pie is browning too quickly after 20 minutes of baking, cover the top loosely with aluminum foil; remove the foil 5 minutes before the end of the baking time. Cool on a wire rack. Sprinkle the cooled pie with 10X (confectioners') sugar. Serve with ice cream, if you wish.

Chocolate Chiffon Pie

Makes 8 servings.

Nutrient Value Per Serving: 626 calories, 10 gm. protein, 38 gm. fat, 398 mg. sodium, 262 mg. cholesterol.

¼ cup (½ stick) butter or margarine
2 cans (3½ ounces each) flaked coconut, toasted
3 envelopes unflavored gelatin
2 cups sugar
1 teaspoon salt
2⅔ cups water
4 squares unsweetened chocolate
6 eggs, separated
2 teaspoons vanilla
½ teaspoon cream of tartar
1 cup heavy cream, whipped
Maraschino cherries and candles (optional)

1. Melt the butter in a medium-size saucepan. Stir in the coconut; remove from the heat. Press the mixture against the side and bottom of 9-inch pie plate. Refrigerate.

2. Combine the gelatin, 1 cup of the sugar, the salt, water and chocolate in a saucepan.

Place over low heat until the chocolate melts and the sugar dissolves. Remove from the heat.

3. Beat the yolks slightly in a medium-size bowl. Stir a little hot chocolate mixture into the yolks; return to the saucepan. Heat, stirring occasionally, just until boiling. Transfer to a bowl; cool over ice water, stirring occasionally, until the mixture mounds. Add the vanilla.

4. Beat the egg whites and cream of tartar in a large bowl until foamy. Gradually beat in the remaining 1 cup sugar until the meringue forms stiff glossy peaks; do not underbeat. Fold the meringue into the chocolate mixture; chill briefly. Mound into the coconut shell. Refrigerate until firm, about 4 hours.

5. Garnish with whipped cream and maraschino cherries and candles, if you wish.

▲**Chocolate Chiffon Pie**

▯ ▢ *Nectarine and Plum Custard Tart*

Bake crust at 450° for 13 minutes; bake tart at 350° for 35 minutes.
Makes 8 servings.

Nutrient Value Per Serving: 311 calories, 3 gm. protein, 19 gm. fat, 155 mg. sodium, 99 mg. cholesterol.

½ of an 11-ounce package piecrust mix
4 to 5 nectarines
3 red or purple plums
¼ cup firmly packed light brown sugar
⅔ cup heavy cream
2 tablespoons granulated sugar
2 egg yolks
⅛ teaspoon ground nutmeg
2 tablespoons coarsely chopped pecans

1. Prepare the piecrust mix following label directions. Roll out on a lightly floured surface to a 12-inch circle. Fit and press into a 9-inch tart pan with a removable bottom or a 9-inch pie plate. Prick the bottom with a fork. Chill for 30 minutes.
2. Preheat the oven to very hot (450°).
3. Place a square of aluminum foil in the crust; add dried beans or rice to weight crust.
4. Bake in the preheated very hot oven (450°) for 5 minutes. Carefully remove the aluminum foil and beans. Bake the shell 8 minutes longer or until lightly browned. Cool slightly on a wire rack. Leave the oven on at 450°.
5. Cut the nectarines into quarters or sixths. Cut the plums into quarters. Arrange the nectarines, skin-side down, spoke-like in bottom of crust around the outside edge. Arrange the plums, skin-side up, spoke-like in a circle next to the nectarines. Fill the center with the remaining fruit. Sprinkle with 2 tablespoons of the brown sugar.
6. Place the tart in the very hot oven (450°). Immediately lower the oven temperature to moderate (350°). Bake for 15 minutes.
7. Meanwhile, mix together the cream, granulated sugar, egg yolks and nutmeg in a small bowl until well combined.
8. Pour the cream mixture over the fruits in a tart. Continue to bake in the moderate oven (350°) for 15 minutes.
9. Sprinkle with the remaining 2 tablespoons brown sugar and the pecans.
10. Continue to bake for 5 minutes or until the custard is set in the center. Cool on a wire rack. Serve slightly warm.

▯ *Thin Apple Tart*

This dramatic apple tart is large enough to feed a crowd. The important piece of kitchen equipment for this recipe is a pizza pan.

Bake crust at 425° for 8 minutes; bake tart at 425° for 25 minutes.
Makes 16 servings.

Nutrient Value Per Serving: 276 calories, 2 gm. protein, 13 gm. fat, 218 mg. sodium, 5 gm. cholesterol.

1½ packages (11 ounces each) pie crust mix
1 jar (12 ounces) apricot preserves
6 large tart apples, pared, cored and thinly sliced
   10X (confectioners') sugar

1. Preheat the oven to hot (425°).
2. Prepare the piecrust following label directions. Roll out on a lightly floured surface to make a circle 17 inches in diameter. Gently fold dough over into quarters to form a triangle; transfer to a 14-inch pizza pan. Unfold and gently press the dough into pan so it fits evenly. Trim the edges, leaving a ½-inch overhang. Turn under to make a stand-up edge; flute.

3. Bake the tart crust in the preheated hot oven (425°) for 8 minutes or until lightly browned. Remove from the oven. Leave the oven temperature at hot (425°).
4. Heat the preserves in a small saucepan over low heat. Force through a sieve with the back of the spoon into a small bowl.
5. Brush the pastry with half of the strained preserves. Arrange the apple slices, over-lapping, in circles over the crust.
6. Bake in the preheated hot oven (425°) for about 25 minutes or until the apples are tender and lightly browned. Remove from the oven. Turn the oven to broil.
7. Brush the apples carefully with the remaining preserves. Sprinkle the top lightly and evenly with the 10X (confectioners') sugar. Place the tart very briefly under the broiler, just long enough to glaze the top; watch very carefully so the top does not become too dark. Serve warm or at room temperature. (A pizza cutting wheel makes slicing easier.)

▲Thin Apple Tart

🍸 🍽 *Pear Cream Tart*

Bake shell at 425° for 12 minutes.
Makes 8 servings.

Nutrient Value Per Serving: 287 calories, 4 gm. protein, 12 gm. fat, 316 mg. sodium, 114 mg. cholesterol.

½ **of an 11-ounce package piecrust mix**
⅓ **cup sugar**
3 **tablespoons cornstarch**
½ **teaspoon salt**
2 **cups milk**
3 **egg yolks, slightly beaten**
1 **teaspoon almond extract**
1 **can (16 ounces) pears**
¼ **cup currant jelly**

1. Preheat the oven to hot (425°). Prepare the piecrust mix following label directions. Fit into a 9-inch tart pan with a removable bottom. Prick surface with a fork.
2. Bake in the preheated hot oven (425°) for 12 minutes or until golden brown. Cool in the pan on a wire rack.
3. Combine the sugar, cornstarch and salt in a small saucepan. Gradually stir in the milk until the mixture is smooth; stir in egg yolks.
4. Bring to boiling over medium-low heat, stirring constantly; boil for 1 minute only. Remove from the heat; stir in the almond extract; pour into a medium-size bowl. Place a piece of plastic wrap directly on the surface of the hot mixture to prevent a skin from forming; refrigerate until cold.
5. Spoon the cold filling into the pastry shell. Drain the pears; slice; pat the slices on paper toweling. Arrange the slices on the filling. Heat the currant jelly in a small saucepan over very low heat until melted. Cook, stirring constantly, for 3 minutes. Brush over the pears to glaze them. Refrigerate the tart until ready to serve.

▼ Strawberry-Almond Tart

This tart has a very flavorful almond crust.

Bake crust at 375° for 15 minutes.
Makes 8 servings.

Nutrient Value Per Serving: 381 calories, 6 gm. protein, 19 gm. fat, 23 mg. sodium, 57 mg. cholesterol.

- ¾ **cup plus 2 tablespoons unsifted all-purpose flour**
- ⅓ **cup blanched whole almonds, ground or very finely chopped**
- 3 **tablespoons sugar**
  Pinch of salt
- 6 **tablespoons cold unsalted butter**
- 1 **egg yolk, slightly beaten**
- 2 **pints strawberries, hulled**
- ½ **cup red currant jelly**
- ¾ **cup sliced or slivered almonds, toasted**

1. Preheat the oven to moderate (375°).
2. Combine the flour, ground almonds, sugar and salt in a medium-size bowl. Cut in the butter with a pastry blender or two forks until the mixture resembles coarse crumbs. Add egg yolk; toss with a fork until well blended. Form a ball.
3. Press the dough over the bottom and sides of a 9 x 1-inch fluted tart pan with a removable bottom.
4. Bake in the preheated moderate oven (375°) for 15 minutes or until the crust is golden. Cool on a wire rack for 10 minutes. Remove the sides of the pan. Cool the crust completely on a wire rack.
5. Arrange the whole strawberries, stem-end down, over the crust.
6. Melt the jelly in a small saucepan over low heat. Brush carefully over the strawberries. Sprinkle the toasted almonds over the strawberries. Let stand at room temperature until ready to serve.

▲Chocolate-Pecan Chess Tart

▼ Chocolate-Pecan Chess Tart

Bake at 425° for 10 minutes; then 325° for 35 minutes.
Makes 8 servings.

Nutrient Value Per Serving: 584 calories, 6 gm. protein, 34 gm. fat, 265 mg. sodium, ·177 mg. cholesterol.

- 1⅓ **cups piecrust mix**
- 1 **egg yolk**
- 1 **tablespoon water**
- 3 **eggs**
- 1 **cup sugar**
- ½ **cup firmly packed light brown sugar**
- ½ **cup chocolate-flavored syrup**
- ¼ **cup milk**
- ¼ **cup (½ stick) butter or margarine, melted**
- 2 **tablespoons cornstarch**
- 1 **cup pecan halves**
- ½ **cup heavy cream**
  Chocolate cutouts (optional)
  Green grapes dipped in melted chocolate (optional)

1. Combine the piecrust mix, egg yolk and the 1 tablespoon water. Prepare the crust, following label directions. Pat into a 9-inch fluted tart pan with a removable bottom. Preheat the oven to hot (425°).
2. Beat the eggs slightly in a medium-size bowl. Stir in the sugars, chocolate syrup, milk, butter and cornstarch. Pour into the prepared tart shell. Arrange pecan halves on top.
3. Bake in the preheated hot oven (425°) for 10 minutes. Lower the oven temperature to slow (325°). Continue baking for 35 minutes or until the center is almost set but still soft; do not overbake. Cool on a wire rack.
4. Remove the tart from the pan. Decorate with whipped cream rosettes. Add the chocolate cutouts, and green grapes dipped in melted chocolate, if you wish.

Fruit Desserts

Bananas Flambé

A dramatic dessert for any time of the year.

Makes 4 servings.

Nutrient Value Per Serving: 332 calories, 2 gm. protein, 9 gm. fat, 90 mg. sodium, 23 mg. cholesterol.

1 package (10 ounces) frozen raspberries, partially thawed
2 tablespoons orange-flavored liqueur or orange juice
2 tablespoons granulated sugar
3 tablespoons butter
1 tablespoon light brown sugar
4 ripe bananas, peeled and halved lengthwise
Orange-flavored liqueur for flambéing

1. Place the raspberries, liqueur and granulated sugar in the container of an electric blender. Whirl until smooth. Strain through a fine sieve.
2. Melt the butter in a heavy skillet; add the brown sugar. When the sugar has dissolved, add the bananas. Sauté on each side for 3 minutes. Add the raspberry mixture; reheat.
3. Warm a little liqueur in a small saucepan. Carefully ignite it with a long kitchen match. Carefully pour the flaming liquid over the bananas in the skillet. Carefully spoon the bananas and the flaming sauce into 4 individual shallow dessert bowls.

▼ Stuffed Peaches

There is a tasty surprise inside these peaches.

Bake at 375° for 18 to 20 minutes.
Makes 6 servings.

Nutrient Value Per Peach: 305 calories, 3 gm.
protein, 8 gm. fat, 13 mg. sodium, 32 mg.
cholesterol.

> 6 **large ripe peaches**
> 1 **cup almond macaroon biscuit crumbs***
> ½ **teaspoon vanilla**
> 1 **tablespoon unsalted butter, melted**
> ⅔ **cup apricot preserves**
>   **Lemon leaves (optional)**

1. Preheat the oven to moderate (375°).
2. Drop the peaches, a few at a time, into boiling water. Let stand for 15 seconds. Lift out with a slotted spoon. Peel off the skins. Halve; remove the pits. Scrape out ½ tablespoon of pulp from the center of each peach half to enlarge the seed cavity. Reserve the pulp; you should have 6 tablespoons.
3. Set aside 2 tablespoons of the almond macaroon crumbs. Combine the remaining crumbs, vanilla and the reserved peach pulp in a small bowl. Place the mixture into the center of each peach half, dividing evenly. Fit the halves together to make 6 whole peaches. Trim a thin slice from each peach, if necessary, to allow the peach to sit evenly. Place in a baking dish. Brush the peaches with the melted butter.
4. Bake in the preheated moderate oven (375°) for 18 to 20 minutes or just until tender. Cool to room temperature.
5. Heat the apricot preserves in a small saucepan. Strain through a sieve into a bowl. Cool to room temperature.
6. Place the cooled peaches in serving dishes. Brush with the apricot glaze; sprinkle with reserved almond macaroon crumbs. Tuck lemon leaves in the top of each peach, if you wish.

*Note: If almond macaroon biscuits are not available, combine ½ cup vanilla wafer crumbs, ½ cup ground almonds and ½ teaspoon almond extract in a small bowl. Use as directed for the almond macaroon biscuit crumbs.

MICROWAVE DIRECTIONS
650 Watt Variable Power Microwave Oven
Ingredient Changes: Eliminate butter.
Directions: Prepare peaches and stuff as in above recipe. Place in a microwave-safe pie plate or baking dish. Cover tightly. Microwave at full power for 2 minutes. Place preserves in a small microwave-safe bowl. Microwave along with peaches for 3 minutes longer or until peaches are tender. Let both stand 5 minutes. Stir preserves. Strain, if you wish. Spoon preserves over peaches.
Nutrient Value Per Peach: 288 calories, 3 gm. protein, 6 gm ft, 13 mg. sodium, 27 mg. cholesterol.

▼ ▢ Peach (or Apple) Crisp

Bake at 375° for 20 minutes.
Makes 4 servings.

Nutrient Value Per Serving: 406 calories, 4 gm.
protein, 15 gm. fat, 173 mg. sodium, 23 mg.
cholesterol.

> 1 **can (1 pound, 5 ounces) peach or apple pie filling**
> 1 **cup all natural ready-to-eat cereal**
> ¼ **teaspoon ground cinnamon**
> 3 **tablespoons butter, melted**
>   **Ice cream (optional)**

1. Preheat the oven to moderate (375°).
2. Spread the pie filling in an 8-inch pie plate.
3. Toss together the cereal, cinnamon and melted butter in bowl. Spoon over the filling.
4. Bake in the preheated moderate oven (375°) for 20 minutes or until bubbly and the topping is lightly browned. Serve warm with ice cream, if you wish.

Summer Fruit Compote

Makes 10 servings.

Nutrient Value Per Serving: 249 calories, 2 gm. protein, 1 gm. fat, 13 mg. sodium, 0 mg. cholesterol.

> **Rind of 1 orange (no white pith), slivered**
> 4 **cups water**
> 1¼ **cups sugar**
> ½ **cup light corn syrup**
> 1 **slice (¼ inch thick) lemon**
> 6 **peaches, peeled, quartered and pitted**
> 6 **apricots, halved and pitted**
> 6 **plums, quartered and pitted**
> 2 **cups dark sweet cherries, stemmed and pitted**
> 1 **cup blueberries**
> ½ **pint strawberries**

1. Combine the orange rind and 1 cup of the water in a small saucepan. Bring to boiling; boil for 1 minute. Drain; reserve rind.
2. Combine the remaining 3 cups water, sugar, corn syrup and lemon slice in a large saucepan. Bring to boiling over medium heat, stirring until the sugar dissolves. Lower the heat; simmer, uncovered, for 5 minutes.
3. Add the peaches to the syrup. Simmer until the peaches are tender but firm, 5 to 10 minutes. Remove with a slotted spoon to a large heatproof bowl.
4. Add the apricots to the syrup. Simmer until tender but firm, 5 to 10 minutes. Remove with a slotted spoon to the bowl with the peaches.
5. Add the plums, cherries, blueberries and strawberries to the same bowl.
6. Stir the reserved orange rind into the syrup. Simmer for 5 minutes. Remove the saucepan from the heat. Let stand, covered, for 5 minutes. Pour over fruits in the bowl. Let cool completely. Cover; refrigerate overnight.
7. To serve, spoon the fruit and liquid into dessert bowls or glasses.

Spiced Rhubarb

Bake at 400° for 25 minutes.
Makes 6 servings.

Nutrient Value Per Serving: 145 calories, less than 1 gm. protein, less than 1 gm. fat, 2 mg. sodium, 0 mg. cholesterol.

> 1 **pound fresh rhubarb, trimmed and cut into ½-inch pieces OR: 1 package (1 pound) frozen cut rhubarb, thawed**
> 1 **cup sugar**
> 1 **2-inch piece stick cinnamon**
> 4 **whole cloves**
> 2 **whole allspice**
> 1 **4-inch strip orange rind (orange part only)**

1. Preheat the oven to hot (400°).
2. Toss the rhubarb with the sugar in a 2-quart shallow baking dish with a cover. Add the cinnamon, cloves, allspice and orange rind; cover.
3. Bake in the preheated hot oven (400°) for 10 minutes. Uncover; stir gently to dissolve the sugar; cover. Bake 15 minutes longer or until the rhubarb is tender, but not mushy. Remove the dish to a wire rack; leave covered; cool completely. Refrigerate several hours to mellow the flavors.
4. To serve, remove the spices and orange rind. Spoon the rhubarb into individual compote dishes or over vanilla ice cream.

◼ 🍸 ⬜ *Honeyed Fruit Compote*

The actual preparation time for this dessert is just minutes.

Makes 6 servings.

Nutrient Value Per Serving: 81 calories, 1 gm. protein, 0.4 gm. fat, 2 mg. sodium, 0 mg. cholesterol.

 2   **pints starwberries, hulled**
 ¼   **cup honey**
 1   **tablespoon grated orange rind**
 1   **tablespoon orange liqueur, or to taste (optional)**

1. Combine the strawberries, honey and orange rind in a bowl; mix well. Let stand for 30 minutes to 1 hour at room temperature.
2. Arrange the strawberries, stem-end down, in a shallow serving dish. Pour the honey mixture over. Refrigerate for up to 1 hour.
3. To serve, sprinkle with the orange liqueur and serve with whipped cream or sour cream on the side, if you wish. For a decorative touch, garnish with an orange peel rose.

⦀ 🍸 *Lime Soufflé*

This soufflé freezes beautifully. When it is firm, wrap in plastic wrap and freeze. Let stand at room temperature for 30 minutes to soften slightly before serving.

Makes 8 servings.

Nutrient Value Per Serving: 259 calories, 7 gm. protein, 12 gm. fat, 84 mg. sodium, 192 mg. cholesterol.

 1   **cup evaporated milk**
 1   **envelope unflavored gelatin**
 1   **cup fresh lime juice (about 8 limes)**
 5   **eggs, separated**
 1   **cup granulated sugar**
 ⅓   **cup grated lime rind (about 4 limes)**
 ¼   **teaspoon cream of tartar**
 ½   **cup heavy cream**
 ½   **teaspoon vanilla**
 1   **tablespoon 10X (confectioners') sugar**
     Lime slices (optional)

1. Prepare a collar for a 4-cup soufflé dish: Tear off a length of aluminum foil long enough to encircle the dish. Fold in half lengthwise. Fasten to the dish with tape or string so the collar is 2 inches higher than the rim.
2. Heat the evaporated milk in a heavy saucepan over low heat until heated through.
3. Sprinkle the gelatin over the lime juice in a measuring cup; let stand to soften.
4. Beat together the egg yolks and ½ cup of the granulated sugar in a small bowl at high speed until very thick and light, about 8 minutes.
5. Slowly pour the hot evaporated milk into the egg yolk mixture, beating until well

▲ *Clockwise from left:* **Chocolate Velvet Cake (page 200), Lime Soufflé (page 256), Raspberry Roll (page 210), Bread Pudding (page 271) and Stuffed Peaches (page 254).**

combined. Return the mixture to the saucepan. Cook over low heat, stirring constantly, until the custard is thick enough to coat a spoon; do not let it boil or the mixture will curdle.

6. Remove the saucepan from the heat. Stir in softened gelatin mixture. Reserve 1 tablespoon grated lime rind for garnish. Stir the remaining rind into the custard. Set aside, stirring occasionally until the gelatin is dissolved, 3 to 5 minutes. Pour the mixture into a medium-size bowl. Refrigerate or set in a larger bowl of ice and water to speed setting Chill, stirring frequently, until the mixture is thick enough to mound when spooned.

7. When the custard begins to feel cool to the touch, beat together the egg whites and cream of tartar in a medium-size bowl until foamy. Slowly beat in the remaining ½ cup of granulated sugar, a tablespoon at a time, until the whites form soft peaks.

8. As soon as the custard is thick enough to mound, fold in one third of the beaten whites until well combined. Gently fold in the remaining whites until no streaks of white remain. Pour into the soufflé dish. Refrigerate for at least 4 hours.

9. To serve: Beat together the heavy cream, vanilla and 10X (confectioners') sugar in a small bowl until stiff. Carefully remove collar from the soufflé dish, freeing soufflé from the foil, if necessary, with a small knife. Spoon or pipe the cream on top. Garnish with the reserved lime rind and lime slices, if you wish.

▥ ▼ *Glazed Orange Soufflé*

Chill 4 hours.
Makes 8 servings.

Nutrient Value Per Serving: 430 calories, 7 gm. protein, 26 gm. fat, 70 mg. sodium, 253 mg. cholesterol.

> **Glazed Orange Decoration**
>   **(recipe follows)**
> 2 **envelopes unflavored gelatin**
> ½ **cup water**
> 5 **eggs, at room temperature**
> 1 **cup sugar**
> 2 **cups heavy cream**
> 1 **tablespoon grated orange rind**
> ½ **cup orange juice**
>   **Light corn syrup**

1. Prepare the Glazed Orange Decoration.
2. Sprinkle the gelatin over water in a small saucepan. Let stand for 10 minutes to soften. Place the saucepan over very low heat; stir to dissolve the gelatin. Cool.
3. Meanwhile, prepare the collar for a 4-cup clear glass soufflé dish: Measure off a length of aluminum foil long enough to encircle the dish; fold in half lengthwise. Fasten around the dish with tape or string; the collar should be about 2 inches higher than the rim of the dish.
4. Combine the eggs and sugar in a large bowl; beat with an electric mixer at high speed until very thick and light, 7 to 8 minutes.
5. Beat 1½ cups of the cream in a small bowl until stiff peaks form; refrigerate.
6. Combine the grated orange rind and juice with the cooled gelatin; pour into the egg mixture. Beat until well blended. Chill briefly, about 5 minutes. Stir frequently, just until the mixture is thick enough to mound when spooned. Fold in the whipped cream.
7. Brush the cooled and glazed orange slices with light corn syrup around the rind edge.

Press the orange slices firmly up against the side of the soufflé dish, reserving one slice. Pour the soufflé mixture into the dish; refrigerate for 4 hours, or until set.
8. Remove the collar gently, freeing the soufflé from the aluminum foil, if necessary, with a small paring knife.
9. Beat the remaining ½ cup of cream in a small bowl until stiff. Garnish the soufflé with the cream and reserved orange slice.

Glazed Orange Decoration: Combine ½ cup water and ½ cup sugar in a large skillet; simmer until the sugar is dissolved. Slice 1 juice orange into ⅛-inch slices; remove the seeds. Add the slices to the skillet. Simmer on medium-high heat for 5 minutes, turning the slices half way through. Transfer to a wire rack; cool.

▥ ▼ *Summer Pudding*

This is a classic English dessert made with fruit. Make a day ahead, refrigerate overnight; then unmold and serve with whipped cream.

Makes 6 servings.

Nutrient Value Per Serving: 274 calories, 4 gm. protein, 9 gm. fat, 135 mg. sodium, 28 mg. cholesterol.

> 14 **very thin slices white bread,**
>   **crusts removed**
> 3 **cups fresh or dry-pack frozen**
>   **raspberries**
> 3 **cups fresh strawberries, sliced**
> ⅔ **cup sugar**
> ½ **cup heavy cream, whipped**
>   **Strawberries and raspberries for**
>   **garnish (optional)**

1. Place 1 slice of bread in the bottom of a 1½-quart bowl. Arrange 10 slices, overlapping, around the side of the bowl. Set aside.
2. Combine the raspberries, strawberries and sugar in a medium-size saucepan. Cook over

medium heat, stirring constantly, until the sugar dissolves. Cool to room temperature.

3. Pour off a little of the fruit syrup; reserve. Pour the remaining fruit mixture into the bread-lined bowl. Cover with the remaining bread slices, cutting them to fit. Cover with a plate that fits just inside the bowl. Weight with several cans. Refrigerate overnight.

4. To serve, unmold onto a serving plate with a rim. Serve with whipped cream, reserved fruit syrup, and additional strawberries and raspberries, if you wish.

◀◀◀ 🍸 *Plum Charlotte*

A cool summer dessert, perfect for a large crowd. Make a day ahead and just add the meringue topping as the final touch.

Bake meringue at 450° for 3 to 4 minutes. Makes 10 servings.

Nutrient Value Per Serving: 356 calories, 7 gm. protein, 13 gm. fat, 60 mg. sodium, 203 mg. cholesterol.

- 2 *pounds red or purple plums, halved, pitted and sliced*
- 1¼ *cups sugar*
- 2 *packages (3 ounces each) ladyfingers*
- 2 *envelopes unflavored gelatin*
- ½ *cup cold water*
- 4 *eggs*
- 1 *cup heavy cream*
- 2 *egg whites*
- ¼ *teaspoon cream of tartar*
- 6 *tablespoons sugar*

1. Combine the plums and ¾ cup of the sugar in a large saucepan. Place over low heat just until plums yield some juice. Raise the heat; bring to boiling. Lower the heat; simmer until the plums are tender, about 10 minutes.

2. Force the plum mixture through a sieve.

Return 1 cup of the purée to a saucepan. Cook until reduced by half. Cool; set aside. Cool the remaining purée in large bowl.

3. Stand the ladyfingers upright around the side of a 10-inch springform pan. Cover the bottom of the pan with the remaining ladyfingers, fitting them neatly together.

4. Sprinkle the gelatin over the water in a small bowl. Let stand to soften, 5 minutes. Place the bowl in simmering water, stirring to dissolve the gelatin.

5. Beat the eggs in a large bowl until foamy. Gradually beat in the remaining ½ cup of sugar until very thick and light colored, 8 to 10 minutes.

6. Stir the dissolved gelatin into the plum purée in a large bowl. Fold in the egg mixture until well blended. Place in a large bowl of ice and water to speed setting. Chill, stirring often, just until the mixture is thick enough to mound slightly when spooned, about 5 minutes.

7. Beat the heavy cream in a small bowl until stiff. Fold into the plum-egg mixture until no streaks of white remain. Pour into the prepared pan. Spoon the reserved reduced plum purée over the top. Fold in partially to create a marbled effect. Refrigerate at least 4 hours or until set.

8. About 1 hour before serving, preheat the oven to very hot (450°).

9. Beat the egg whites in a small bowl with the cream of tartar until foamy. Gradually beat in the 6 tablespoons of sugar until the meringue forms stiff peaks. Pipe the meringue around the outside edge of the charlotte and across the top in a lattice pattern. Do not remove the sides of the pan.

10. Place the charlotte, with side of the pan, in the preheated very hot oven (450°) for 3 to 4 minutes or just until the meringue turns golden. Return immediately to the refrigerator until serving time.

11. To serve, remove the sides of the pan and place the charlotte on a serving plate.

◀◀◀ 🍸 *Orange Cream*

Makes 8 servings.

Nutrient Value Per Serving: 218 calories, 5 gm. protein, 13 gm. fat, 39 mg. sodium, 144 mg. cholesterol.

4 to 5 large navel oranges
1 envelope unflavored gelatin
3 eggs, separated
⅓ cup sugar
1 cup heavy cream
   Mint sprigs (optional)

1. Grate enough rind from the oranges to measure 2 tablespoons. Squeeze and strain enough juice to make 1 cup. Pare and section the remaining oranges into a small bowl for garnish; cover; refrigerate.
2. Sprinkle the gelatin over ¼ cup of the orange juice in a small saucepan; let stand 10 minutes to soften. Place the saucepan over very low heat until the gelatin dissolves, 2 to 3 minutes. Remove; cool.
3. Beat the egg yolks in a large bowl until light and fluffy. Add the sugar, a little at a time; continue beating until the mixture becomes thick and light. Add the orange rind and the remaining ¾ cup orange juice. Reserve.
4. Beat the egg whites in a small bowl until soft peaks form; refrigerate. Beat the heavy cream in another bowl until soft peaks form. Refrigerate.
5. Combine the cooled gelatin mixture with the yolk mixture. Place bowl in a larger bowl partially filled with ice and water. Stir just until mixture is thick enough to mound.
6. Fold the egg whites and heavy cream into the gelatin mixture until no streaks of white remain. Pour into a 4-cup serving dish. Refrigerate until set, about 3 hours. Garnish with the reserved orange sections and mint sprigs, if you wish.

> **LEMONS, LIMES AND ORANGES**
> **Should be grated before squeezing when a recipe calls for both grated rind and juice.**

◀◀◀ 🍸 *Strawberry Bavarian Cream*

A Bavarian cream is everybody's favorite, and this is an especially light one.

Makes 8 servings.

Nutrient Value Per Serving: 200 calories, 3 gm. protein, 13 gm. fat, 30 mg. sodium, 110 mg. cholesterol.

1 pint strawberries, hulled
2 eggs, separated
1 envelope unflavored gelatin
½ cup plus 2 tablespoons sugar
1 tablespoon freshly squeezed lemon juice
½ teaspoon vanilla
1 cup heavy cream
   Strawberries and whipped cream for garnish (optional)

1. Place the strawberries in the container of an electric blender or food processor. Cover; whirl until puréed.
2. Combine ¾ cup of the purée with the egg yolks in a medium-size saucepan. Stir in the gelatin and ½ cup of the sugar. Place over very low heat; stir until gelatin and sugar are dissolved. Transfer to a medium-size bowl.
3. Stir in the remaining strawberry purée, lemon juice and vanilla.
4. Set the bowl in a large bowl of ice and water. Refrigerate, stirring occasionally, until the mixture mounds slightly when spooned, about 30 minutes.
5. Beat the egg whites in a small bowl until foamy. Beat in the remaining 2 tablespoons of sugar, 1 tablespoon at a time, until the meringue forms soft peaks. Fold into the strawberry mixture.

6. Without washing the bowl and the beaters, beat the cream in the bowl until soft peaks form. Fold into the strawberry mixture.
7. Rinse a 5-cup ring or other decorative mold with cold water; shake out excess. Pour the strawberry mixture into the mold. Gently tap the mold on the counter to settle the mixture. Smooth the top with a spatula.
8. Refrigerate until set, 4 to 6 hours.
9. To serve: Very briefly dip the mold into a bowl of warm water. Invert a serving dish over the mold; turn right side up. Gently shake the mold to loosen; carefully remove the mold. Garnish with whipped cream and strawberry slices, if you wish.

🎴 🍸 *Ribbon Bavarian*

Makes 10 servings.

Nutrient Value Per Serving: 252 calories, 4 gm. protein, 16 gm. fat, 40 mg. sodium, 158 mg. cholesterol.

1 envelope plus 1½ teaspoons unflavored gelatin
¾ cup sugar
¾ cup water
4 egg yolks, slightly beaten

◀ Strawberry Bavarian Cream

4 egg whites
1½ cups heavy cream
¾ cup raspberry purée (one 10-ounce package frozen raspberries, thawed and puréed)
1 can (8¾ ounces) unpeeled apricot halves, drained and puréed (about ½ cup purée)
2 tablespoons lime juice
   Green food coloring (optional)
   Whipped cream (optional)

1. Combine the gelatin and sugar in a heavy medium-size saucepan. Stir in the water, then egg yolks. Cook, stirring until the gelatin is dissolved and the mixture is thickened. Do not allow to boil. Transfer to a large bowl. Cool to room temperature.
2. Beat the egg whites in a small bowl until stiff peaks form. Fold the egg whites into the cooled gelatin mixture.
3. Beat the heavy cream just until soft peaks form; do not overbeat. Fold into gelatin mixture. Divide the mixture into 3 equal portions (about 2 cups each).
4. Gently fold the raspberry purée into one portion; fold the apricot purée into another portion; fold the lime juice and food coloring, if using, into third portion.
5. Pour the raspberry mixture into a 7-cup glass bowl. Carefully spoon the apricot mixture in a layer over the top. Carefully spoon the lime in a layer on top of that. Cover; chill for 4 to 5 hours or until firm.
6. Garnish with whipped cream.

AN ENVELOPE OF UNFLAVORED GELATIN
Will gel 2 cups of liquid.

Port Wine Gelatin with Strawberries

A refreshingly tart dessert.

Makes 6 servings.

Nutrient Value Per Serving: 112 calories, 1 gm. protein, 0.2 gm. fat, 2 mg. sodium, 0 mg. cholesterol.

½ cup sugar
1 envelope unflavored gelatin
1⅓ cups cold water
½ cup ruby port wine
3 tablespoons freshly squeezed lemon juice, strained
1 pint strawberries, hulled and sliced

1. Sprinkle the sugar and gelatin over ⅔ cup of the water in a small heavy saucepan. Let stand for 1 minute. Place over low heat, stirring constantly, until the sugar and gelatin are dissolved. Remove from the heat.
2. Transfer the gelatin mixture to a bowl. Stir in the remaining ⅔ cup water, wine and lemon juice. Set in a bowl of ice and water to speed setting. Refrigerate, stirring occasionally, until the mixture is the consistency of unbeaten egg whites, 30 to 45 minutes.
3. Gently fold the strawberries into the thickened gelatin mixture.
4. Divide among 6 wine glasses or clear glass punch cups. Chill until completely set, 2 to 3 hours.

Palmier Shortcakes

Makes 6 servings.

Nutrient Value Per Serving: 564 calories, 5 gm. protein, 44 gm. fat, 351 mg. sodium, 55 mg. cholesterol.

2 medium-size nectarines or peaches, pitted and diced (about 1½ cups)
½ cup blueberries
2 to 3 tablespoons 10X (confectioners') sugar
1 cup heavy cream
12 Palmier Cookies (recipe follows)

1. Place the nectarines or peaches, blueberries and 10X (confectioners') sugar in a small bowl; toss to mix. Let stand for 30 minutes or until the juices run freely.
2. Beat the cream in a small bowl until stiff.
3. Spoon a dollop of whipped cream, reserving some for the top, on each of 6 palmiers; top with fruit, then another palmier. Garnish with the remaining whipped cream and fruit.

Palmier Cookies: Thaw 1 package (17¼ ounces) frozen puff pastry (2 sheets) following label directions. Sprinkle the work surface with granulated sugar; place the unfolded pastry sheets, end to end and overlapping ½ inch, on a sugared surface; moisten the overlapping edges to make them stick. Roll the pastry to a 24 x 10-inch rectangle, using sugar to keep pastry from sticking. Fold both short ends to almost meet in the center. Roll gently with a rolling pin to flatten to a rectangle. Fold the short ends again to meet in the center; roll gently to make a rectangle. Fold both short sides to meet together like a book with 8 layers. Refrigerate, covered, for 1 hour to relax pastry.
   Preheat the oven to hot (425°). Slice the pastry ⅜ inch thick on a lightly sugared surface. Arrange slices 3 inches apart on large cookie sheets. Bake for 12 to 15 minutes. Turn the palmiers on the cookie sheet with a wide spatula. Bake for 10 minutes longer or until golden brown and evenly glazed. Remove to wire racks; cool completely.

Store in a tightly covered container in a cool, dry place or in the freezer. Makes about 2 dozen. *Nutrient Value Per Cookie:* 388 calories, 4 gm. protein, 29 gm. fat, 335 mg. sodium, 0 mg. cholesterol.

WHIPPED CREAM
Place the beaters and bowl in the refrigerator along with the heavy cream to chill for 1 hour. Beat the heavy cream in the chilled bowl until stiff. For sweetened whipped cream, fold 2 tablespoons 10X (confectioners') sugar for each cup of heavy cream used into the whipped cream.

Strawberry-Orange Shortcakes

Bake at 450° for 10 to 12 minutes.
Makes 8 servings.

Nutrient Value Per Serving: 428 calories, 5 gm. protein, 24 gm. fat, 445 mg. sodium, 74 mg. cholesterol.

- 3 **pints strawberries, hulled and thinly sliced**
- ½ **to ¾ cup sugar, depending on tartness of the berries**
- 5 **tablespoons freshly squeezed orange juice, strained**
- 2 **teaspoons grated orange rind**
- 1¾ **cups unsifted all-purpose flour**
- 2 **tablespoons sugar**
- 1 **tablespoon baking powder**
- 1 **teaspoon salt**
- ⅓ **cup unsalted butter**
  OR: vegetable shortening
- ½ **cup cold milk**
  Unsalted butter or margarine
- 1 **cup heavy cream, whipped**
  Mint leaves for garnish (optional)

1. Combine the strawberries, the ½ to ¾ cup sugar, 3 tablespoons of the orange juice and 1½ teaspoons of the orange rind in a large bowl; toss gently to mix. Let stand for 30 minutes at room temperature.
2. Preheat the oven to very hot (450°).
3. Combine the flour, the 2 tablespoons sugar, baking powder and salt in a large bowl; stir to mix well. Stir in the remaining orange rind. Cut in the ⅓ cup butter with a pastry blender until the mixture resembles coarse crumbs.
4. Make a well in the center of the flour mixture. Pour in the milk and the remaining 2 tablespoons orange juice. Stir quickly and lightly just until the dough cleans the side of the bowl and sticks together.
5. Turn out onto a lightly floured board. Lightly sprinkle the dough with flour. Knead lightly about 7 times or just until the dough holds together. Lightly flour the surface again. Roll or pat out the dough to a thickness just less than ½ inch. Cut the dough into 2½-inch rounds with a floured biscuit cutter. Gather up the scraps; roll out and cut as before. You should have about 8 biscuits. Place the biscuits on an ungreased baking sheet about 1½ inches apart.
6. Bake in the preheated very hot oven (450°) for 10 to 12 minutes or until golden brown.
7. Split the hot biscuits in half. Lightly butter the bottom halves. Place the bottoms on dessert plates. Spoon about ¼ cup of the strawberry mixture over each bottom half. Cover with the top half. Spoon another ¼ cup over each. Garnish with a dollop of whipped cream, and with mint leaves, if you wish.

Blueberry Cream in Meringue Nests

The meringue nests and the blueberry purée for the cream can be made a day ahead.

Bake the meringues at 250° for 1 hour; let stand in the turned-off oven for 1½ hours. Makes 6 servings.

Nutrient Value Per Serving: 280 calories, 3 gm. protein, 15 gm. fat, 44 mg. sodium, 55 mg. cholesterol.

MERINGUE NESTS
- *3 egg whites, at room temperature*
- *¼ teaspoon cream of tartar*
- *⅔ cup superfine sugar*

FILLING
- *2 cups fresh or frozen blueberries*
- *2 to 3 tablespoons sugar*
- *1 teaspoon grated lemon rind*
- *2 teaspoons lemon juice, or to taste*
- *1 cup heavy cream*
  Blueberries, thin lemon slices and fresh mint for garnish

1. Preheat the oven to very slow (250°).
2. Cover a large cookie sheet with heavy brown paper. Outline six 3-inch circles on the paper, using a bowl or plate as a guide.
3. Beat the egg whites with the cream of tartar in a medium-size bowl until foamy. Beat in the sugar, 1 tablespoon at a time, until the meringue forms stiff glossy peaks.
4. Spread or pipe the meringue through a pastry bag fitted with a large decorative tip, inside the circle outlines, building up a rim around the edges.
5. Bake the meringue nests in the preheated very slow oven (250°) for 1 hour. Turn the oven off. Let the meringues cool in the oven with the door closed for 1½ hours. Remove from the oven; cool completely on a wire rack.

▶*Clockwise from bottom:* **Blueberry Cream in Meringue Nests (page 264), Palmier Shortcakes (page 262), Summer Fruit Compote (page 255), Nectarine and Plum Custard Tart (page 250) and Plum Charlotte (page 259).**

6. Store the nests in a tightly covered container in a cool, dry place or in the freezer.
7. Prepare the Filling: Place the blueberries in the container of an electric blender or food processor. Cover; whirl until smooth. Combine with the sugar in a saucepan. Bring to boiling; lower the heat; simmer for 8 to 10 minutes or until slightly thickened. Remove from the heat. Stir in the lemon rind and juice. Cool completely, stirring often. Transfer to a bowl. Cover; refrigerate until chilled.
8. Beat the cream in a small bowl until stiff. Gently fold into the blueberry purée until no streaks remain.
9. Spoon the blueberry cream into meringue nests. Garnish with blueberries, lemon slices and mint. Refrigerate the nests until serving time, up to 2 hours.

WHEN BEATING EGG WHITES
For the best volume, egg whites should always be at room temperature when you beat them. Be sure not to let any yolk get into the whites; fat in the yolks will decrease the volume.

✦ *Vacherine Stars with Lemon Crème*

Bake at 225° for 1 hour.
Makes 6 servings.

Nutrient Value Per Star: 368 calories, 4 gm. protein, 16 gm. fat, 282 mg. sodium, 59 mg. cholesterol.

4   egg whites, at room temperature
¼   teaspoon cream of tartar
1   cup sugar, preferably superfine
1½ teaspoons almond extract
**   Lemon Crème (recipe follows)**
**   Lemon slices**
**   Kiwi slices**
**   Fresh mint leaves**
**   Currant Sauce, optional (recipe follows)**

1. Preheat the oven to very slow (225°). Grease and flour 2 cookie sheets.
2. Using a 3½-inch star cookie cutter, make 3 star outlines in the flour on each cookie sheet.
3. Beat together the egg whites and cream of tartar in a large bowl until frothy. Beat in the sugar very gradually, allowing it to fill slowly "like snow." Beat until the meringue forms stiff glossy peaks. (This whole process should take 10 to 15 minutes.)
4. Beat the almond extract into the meringue. Transfer the meringue to a 16-inch pastry bag fitted with a #6 open-star pastry tube. Pipe out the meringue following the star outlines on each baking sheet. Repeat to make a second layer on each star.
5. Bake in the preheated very slow oven (225°) for 1 hour. Turn off the oven. Leave the meringues in the oven with the door closed until cool.
6. Place the meringues on individual dessert plates. Fill with the Lemon Crème. Garnish each with ½ lemon slice, ½ kiwi slice and mint leaf, if you wish. Pass the Currant Sauce, if you wish.

Lemon Crème: Combine 1 package (3¾ ounces) instant lemon pudding mix, 1 cup heavy cream and ¾ cup milk in a small bowl. Mix slowly with an egg beater until smooth. Let stand to thicken, about 5 minutes.

Currant Sauce: Melt 1 jar (10 ounces) currant jelly in a small heavy saucepan over low heat. Stir in 2 tablespoons cherry brandy. Cool.

Ice Cream Desserts

▨ ▼ *Piña Colada Ice Cream Waffles*

Toast the coconut at 350° for 10 minutes.
Makes 5 servings.

Nutrient Value Per Serving: 1045 calories, 14
gm. protein, 42 gm. fat, 666 mg. sodium, 152
mg. cholesterol.

1 **pint vanilla ice cream**
1 **can (4 ounces) flaked coconut**
1 **cup firmly packed light brown sugar**
½ **cup light corn syrup**
1 **teaspoon cornstarch**
¼ **cup cold water**
½ **cup chopped macadamia nuts**
1 **tablespoon butter**
1 **can (20 ounces) pineapple rings in their own juice, drained**

WAFFLES
2 **cups sifted all-purpose flour**
3 **tablepoons sugar**
2 **teaspoons baking powder**
¾ **teaspoon salt**
2 **eggs, separated**
1½ **cups milk**
¼ **cup vegetable oil**
½ **cup well drained crushed pineapple**

1. Scoop the ice cream into 5 balls. Place on a tray in the freezer.
2. Toast the coconut on a baking sheet in a preheated moderate oven (350°) for 10 minutes. Cool. Roll the ice cream balls in the toasted coconut. Return to the freezer.
3. Combine the brown sugar and corn syrup in a medium-size skillet. Cook over medium heat until the sugar dissolves. Dissolve the cornstarch in the cold water; stir into the skillet. Cook, stirring, until the mixture thickens and clears. Add the nuts, butter and pineapple rings. Cook just until the pineapple is lightly glazed. Keep warm while preparing the waffles.
4. Prepare the Waffles: Sift together the flour, sugar, baking powder and salt onto a sheet of wax paper; set aside.
5. Beat together the egg yolks, milk and vegetable oil in a medium-size bowl until well blended. Beat the egg whites until stiff; gently fold into the batter, along with the drained crushed pineapple.
6. Heat a waffle maker until medium-hot. Pour the waffle batter, 1 cup for 2 waffles, onto the waffle maker. Cook until the waffle maker stops steaming; the waffles should be cooked through and light brown. If not, close the waffle maker and cook a little longer.
7. Top each waffle with the coconut ice cream balls and pineapple rings and syrup.

Note: This recipe uses a double-waffle maker.

▨ ▼ *Vanilla Ice Cream with Bourbon Peaches*

Try the peaches with pound cake.

Makes 10 servings.

Nutrient Value Per Serving: 421 calories, 5 gm.
protein, 27 gm. fat, 76 mg. sodium, 203 mg.
cholesterol.

4 **egg yolks**
⅔ **cup sugar**
⅛ **teaspoon salt**
1⅔ **cups milk**
2⅔ **cups heavy cream**
1 **tablespoon vanilla**
   Bourbon Peaches (recipe follows)

1. Combine the egg yolks, sugar and salt in a heavy medium-size saucepan. Beat until well mixed and creamy.

2. Heat the milk in a small saucepan over low heat until bubbles appear around the edges of the pan. Gradually pour the milk into the egg mixture, stirring constantly. Cook over low heat, stirring constantly, until the custard mixture thickens enough to lightly coat a spoon; do not let the mixture boil or it will curdle. Remove from the heat; cool.
3. Stir the cream and vanilla into the custard mixture. Cover; refrigerate until chilled.
4. Place the custard mixture in the container of an ice cream freezer. Freeze according to the manufacturer's directions.
5. Serve with Bourbon Peaches.

Bourbon Peaches: Peel, pit and slice 8 to 10 firm-ripe peaches. Place in a small bowl. Add ¼ cup bourbon and ¼ to ½ cup sugar. Stir gently to mix well. Cover; refrigerate until serving time.

◀◀◀ ▼ ☐ *Refrigerator Strawberry Ice Cream*

Makes 3 quarts.

Nutrient Value Per Serving: 371 calories, 5 gm. protein, 25 gm. fat, 106 mg. sodium, 156 mg. cholesterol.

1½ *cups sugar*
¼ *teaspoon salt*
3 *tablespoons all-purpose flour*
2 *cups milk*
3 *eggs, slightly beaten*
2 *pints (4 cups) strawberries, hulled, halved*
3 *cups heavy cream*

1. Combine 1 cup of the sugar, salt and flour in a saucepan; gradually stir in milk. Cook, stirring until the mixture thickens and bubbles. Remove from the heat.
2. Stir half the hot milk mixture into the eggs in a bowl; stir back into saucepan. Cook, stirring constantly, 1 minute; do not boil.

Pour into a large bowl; cool.
3. Toss the strawberries with the remaining ½ cup sugar in a bowl. Let stand for 10 minutes. Remove 1 cup of the strawberries; chop them coarsely. Purée the remainder in an electric blender. Whirl. Add the chopped and puréed berries and 1½ cups heavy cream to the egg mixture. Refrigerate for 2 hours, until chilled.
4. Pour into a 13 x 9 x 2-inch metal pan. Freeze until partially frozen, about 1 hour.
5. Beat the remaining heavy cream in a bowl until stiff. Beat the partially frozen mixture in a chilled bowl with chilled beaters until smooth. Fold in the whipped cream quickly. Return to the metal pan; cover. Freeze until firm, stirring once or twice, for 4 hours.

◀◀◀ ▼ ☐ *Refrigerator Chocolate Ice Cream*

Makes 3 quarts.

Nutrient Value Per Serving: 483 calories, 6 gm. protein, 38 gm. fat, 119 mg. sodium, 207 mg. cholesterol.

1½ *cups sugar*
¼ *teaspoon salt*
3 *tablespoons all-purpose flour*
2 *cups milk*
4 *squares (1 ounce each) unsweetened chocolate*
4 *eggs, slightly beaten*
2 *pints (4 cups) heavy cream*
1 *tablespoon vanilla*

1. Combine the sugar, salt and flour in a large saucepan; gradually stir in milk and chocolate. Cook over medium heat, stirring constantly, until the chocolate is melted and the mixture thickens. Remove from the heat.
2. Stir half the chocolate mixture slowly into the eggs in a medium-size bowl; stir back

into the chocolate mixture in the saucepan. Cook over low heat, stirring constantly, for 1 minute; do not boil. Pour into a large bowl; cool. Stir in 2 cups of the heavy cream and vanilla. Refrigerate for about 2 hours or until chilled.

3. Pour into a 13 x 9 x 2-inch metal pan. Freeze until partially frozen, about 1 hour.
4. Beat the remaining cream in a bowl until stiff. Beat the partially frozen chocolate mixture in a chilled bowl with chilled beaters until smooth. Fold in the whipped cream quickly. Return to the metal pan; cover. Freeze until firm, stirring once or twice, for about 4 hours.

FOR ICE CRYSTALS
If your homemade ice cream develops ice crystals, whirl it in a food processor at 5-second pulses until smooth.

▦ ▼ *Pineapple-Mint Sorbet*

Makes 1 quart.

Nutrient Value Per ¼ Cup: 41 calories, 1 gm. protein, 0.3 gm. fat, 4 mg. sodium, 1 mg. cholesterol.

 2 cans (20 ounces each) crushed
 *   pineapple in syrup*
 ½ cup plain yogurt
 ¼ cup chopped fresh mint leaves

1. Combine the crushed pineapple with its syrup, yogurt and mint in a medium-size bowl. Working in batches, place in the container of an electric blender or food processor. Cover; whirl until puréed.
2. Pour the purée into the container of an ice cream freezer. Freeze according to the manufacturer's directions.

▦ ▼ ▢ *Citrus Ice*

Makes 6 servings (1½ cups).

Nutrient Value Per Serving: 84 calories, 0.3 gm. protein, 0 gm. fat, 1 mg. sodium, 0 mg. cholesterol.

 2 lemons
 2 limes
 1 navel orange
 ¾ cup water
 ½ cup sugar

1. Remove the outermost colored rind from the lemons, limes and orange, without the white part, with a swivel-bladed vegetable peeler. Place the rind in a medium-size bowl.
2. Cut the fruit in half. Squeeze the juice into a 2-cup glass measure; reserve 1 cup to use in this recipe.
3. Combine the water and sugar in a saucepan. Bring to boiling, stirring just until the sugar is dissolved. Remove from the heat. Pour in the reserved 1 cup citrus juice. Pour over the rind. Let stand for 15 minutes.
4. Strain; cool. Pour into a serving bowl. Freeze until solid.

▼ ▢ *Fresh Strawberry Ice*

This coarsely textured ice should not be frozen too hard. Serve by itself or scoop into an equally refreshing Fresh Strawberry Ice Soda.

Makes 6 servings.

Nutrient Value Per Serving: 159 calories, 1 gm. protein, 0.4 gm. fat, 1 mg. sodium, 0 mg. cholesterol.

 1 cup sugar
 1 cup water
 2 pints strawberries, hulled
 1 tablespoon freshly squeezed lemon juice

1. Combine the sugar and water in a small heavy saucepan. Bring to boiling over medium heat, stirring until the the sugar is dissolved. Lower the heat to very low; simmer for 4 minutes. Refrigerate the syrup until completely cooled.
2. Place the strawberries in the container of an electric blender or food processor. Cover; whirl until puréed. Combine the cooled syrup and strawberry purée in a medium-size bowl. Stir in the lemon juice.
3. Spoon into a 9-inch-square metal baking pan or other shallow pan. Place in the freezer for about 2 hours or until the mixture becomes slushy; stir every 30 minutes to break up any large ice crystals. Do not freeze too hard.

■ ♈ ☐ Fresh Strawberry Ice Soda

Makes 1 serving.

Nutrient Value Per Serving: 78 calories, 1 gm. protein, 1 gm. fat, 2 mg. sodium, 0 mg. cholesterol.

⅓ to ½ cup crushed strawberries
1 scoop Fresh Strawberry Ice (see recipe above) Club soda or seltzer water

Place the strawberries in a tall glass. Add Fresh Strawberry Ice. Fill the glass with soda. Serve immediately.

▨ ♈ "Roman Punch" Cups

Makes 8 servings.

Nutrient Value Per Serving: 205 calories, 1 gm. protein, 2 gm. fat, 44 mg. sodium, 7 mg. cholesterol.

▲*Left:* Fresh Strawberry Ice. *Right:* Strawberry Ice Soda.

This is not a punch at all, but nevertheless a favorite "cup" served at formal banquets in the White House during the nineteenth century. Make small scoops of lemon and orange sherbet, using about 1 pint each. Mix the sherbet in chilled sherbet glasses or scooped out oranges. Freeze. To serve, drizzle 2 tablespoons amber rum over each serving. Serve at once.

TO MAKE AN ICE CREAM MOLD
Chill a well-oiled mold in the freezer. (Shallow, plain designs are the best to work with.) Spoon the ice cream into the prepared mold. Cover with plastic wrap, pressing the wrap directly onto the ice cream. Freeze until firm, for 8 hours or overnight. To serve, place a towel wrung out in hot water over the bottom of the mold and turn out onto a chilled serving platter.

Other Desserts

◖◖◖ ❚ *Frozen Grand Marnier Mousse*

A spectacular centerpiece for the buffet desserts. Prepare the frozen mousse up to a week ahead, and decorate just before serving.

Makes 12 servings.

Nutrient Value Per Serving: 261 calories, 5 gm. protein, 18 gm. fat, 247 mg. sodium, 194 mg. cholesterol. (With orange juice—247 calories.)

- ⅓ **cup sugar**
- 1 **envelope unflavored gelatin**
- 2 **teaspoons cornstarch**
- 6 **egg yolks**
- 1 **cup milk**
- ⅓ **cup Grand Marnier or orange juice**
- 4 **egg whites**
- ¼ **cup sugar**
- 2 **cups heavy cream**
- 1 **pint strawberries, washed, hulled and halved**
- 2 **kiwis, pared and sliced**

1. Combine the ⅓ cup sugar, gelatin and cornstarch in a medium-size saucepan; add the egg yolk; beat until well blended. Gradually stir in the milk. Cook, stirring constantly, over medium heat, just until the mixture is slightly thickened. Remove from the heat; stir in the liqueur or orange juice.
2. Set the pan in a larger pan filled with ice and water. Chill, stirring often, until the mixture mounds when spooned.
3. While the mixture is chilling, beat the egg whites in a medium-size bowl with an electric mixer until foamy and double in volume. Beat in the ¼ cup sugar gradually until the meringue forms soft peaks.
4. Beat 1½ cups of the heavy cream in a small bowl until stiff. Fold the whipped cream, then the meringue into the gelatin mixture until no streaks of white remain. Turn into an 8-cup decorative mold; smooth the top. Wrap the mold with aluminum foil or plastic wrap. Freeze overnight or until firm. (The mousse can be frozen for up to 1 week.)
5. To serve, remove the mousse from the freezer. Loosen around the edges with a small spatula. Unmold onto a serving platter. Beat the remaining ½ cup cream in a small bowl until stiff. Pipe the whipped cream around the base and top of mousse. Garnish with the strawberries and kiwis.

◣ ◖◖◖ ❚ ◻ *Chocolate Mousse*

Makes 6 servings.

Nutrient Value Per Serving: 238 calories, 5 gm. protein, 14 gm. fat, 47 mg. sodium, 183 mg. cholesterol.

- 6 **squares (1 ounce each) semisweet chocolate**
- 4 **eggs, separated**
- 2 **to 3 tablespoons amaretto-flavored OR: Irish cream liqueur**
- 3 **tablespoons sugar**

1. Melt the chocolate in the top of a double boiler over barely simmering water. Remove from the heat. Cool the chocolate to lukewarm. Beat in the egg yolks, one at a time, beating well after each addition. Beat in the liqueur.
2. Beat the egg whites in a bowl until foamy. Gradually beat in the sugar until the meringue forms stiff peaks. Stir one third of the meringue into the chocolate. Gently fold the chocolate mixture into the remaining meringue until no white streaks remain. Spoon into 6 dessert goblets. Chill for at least 1 hour.

▨ ▥ ▼ *Espresso Tortoni*

Toast the almonds at 350° for 5 minutes.
Makes 6 servings.

Nutrient Value Per Serving: 225 calories, 2 gm.
protein, 16 gm. fat, 24 mg. sodium, 5 mg.
cholesterol.

- *2   tablespoons chopped almonds*
- *1   egg white*
- *1   to 1½ tablespoons instant espresso*
  powder
- *½   cup sugar*
- *1   cup heavy cream*
- *1   teaspoon vanilla*
- *¼   teaspoon almond extract*

1. Toast the chopped almonds on a baking sheet in a preheated moderate oven (350°) for 5 to 7 minutes. Cool. (The darker the toasted almonds, the more flavorful they will be. Be careful not to let them burn.)
2. Whip the egg white with the instant espresso powder in small bowl; gradually add 1 tablespoon of the sugar.
3. Beat the cream until stiff. Add the remaining sugar, vanilla and almond extract. Fold the cream into the egg white mixture; fold in the toasted almonds.
4. Transfer the mixture to a pastry bag fitted with a large open star pastry tip. Pipe into fluted-foil baking cups. Sprinkle with additional toasted almonds, if you wish. Freeze 2 hours or more.

YOU DON'T HAVE A PASTRY BAG?
Don't worry, you can spoon the mixture into the fluted-foil baking cups, swirling the tops decoratively.

◳ *Bread Pudding*

Bake at 325° for 1 hour.
Makes 10 servings.

Nutrient Value Per Serving: 285 calories, 7 gm.
protein, 9 gm. fat, 250 mg. sodium, 106 mg.
cholesterol.

- *¾   cup sugar*
- *3   eggs*
- *⅛   teaspoon salt*
- *1   tablespoon vanilla*
- *3   cups milk*
- *¼   cup (½ stick) butter, melted*
- *½   cup seedless raisins*
- *10   slices firm white bread, crusts removed*
- *⅓   cup strawberry or red raspberry*
  preserves
  Fresh strawberries, sliced

1. Reserve 1 teaspoon of the sugar. Combine the remaining sugar with the eggs, salt and vanilla in a large bowl. Gradually beat in the milk until well combined. Preheat the oven to slow (325°).
2. Brush the bottom and sides of an 11¾ x 7½ x 1¾-inch baking dish with some of the melted butter. Reserve 1 tablespoon of the raisins. Sprinkle the remaining raisins over the bottom of the baking dish. Pour the milk mixture over the raisins.
3. Cut the bread slices in half diagonally. Brush both sides of the bread triangles with butter.
4. Arrange the bread, slightly overlapping, on top of the milk mixture. Sprinkle with the reserved raisins and reserved sugar. Set the baking dish in a larger pan; place on oven shelf. Pour boiling water into the larger pan to come halfway up side of baking dish.
5. Bake in the preheated slow oven (325°) for 1 hour or until a knife blade inserted 1 inch from the edge comes out clean. Let stand for 15 minutes before serving.
6. Force the preserves through a sieve with the back of a spoon. Drizzle over the pudding. Serve with strawberries.

MICROWAVE DIRECTIONS
650 Watt Variable Power Microwave Oven
Ingredient Changes: Reduce butter from ¼ cup to
½ teaspoon.
Directions: Place ½ teaspoon butter in an 11¾ x
7½ x 1-inch microwave-safe baking dish. Microwave
at full power for 30 seconds or until butter is
melted. Brush over bottom of the dish. Place milk in
a microwave-safe bowl. Microwave at full power for
3 minutes, stirring once. Assemble bread pudding
according to the recipe above, without brushing
bread with butter. Microwave, uncovered, at full
power for 12 minutes, turning twice, or until the
center feels set. Let stand for 10 minutes.
Nutrient Value Per Serving: 246 calories, 7 gm. protein, 5 gm. fat, 206 mg. sodium, 94 mg. cholesterol.

▨ ▼ ▢ *Flan*

A smooth version of everyone's favorite.

Bake at 325° for 35 minutes.
Makes 8 servings.

Nutrient Value Per Serving: 338 calories, 8 gm.
protein, 18 gm. fat, 174 mg. sodium, 254 mg.
cholesterol.

1¼ cups sugar
2 cups milk
2 cups light cream
6 eggs
¼ teaspoon salt
2 teaspoons almond extract
Whipped cream (optional)

1. Heat ¾ cup of the sugar in a heavy skillet
   over low to medium heat until the sugar
   melts and forms a light brown syrup; stir to
   blend. Immediately pour the syrup into a
   heated 1½-quart round baking dish. Quickly
   rotate the dish to cover the bottom and side
   with syrup. Preheat the oven to slow (325°).
2. Heat the milk and light cream in a medium-
   size saucepan just until bubbles form
   around the edge of the pan.
3. Beat the eggs slightly in a large bowl. Beat

in the remaining ½ cup sugar, salt and
almond extract. Gradually stir in the hot
milk mixture. Pour into the prepared dish.
4. Set the dish in a shallow pan; pour boiling
   water into the pan to a depth of ½ inch.
5. Bake in the preheated slow oven (325°) for
   35 minutes or until a knife blade inserted 1
   inch from the edge comes out clean. Cool
   on wire rack; refrigerate for 4 hours or
   overnight.
6. To serve, run a metal spatula around the
   edge of the dish to loosen the custard.
   Invert onto a serving dish. Serve with
   whipped cream, if you wish.

Delicious Calorie-light Desserts

▼ ▢ *Peach Melba Crêpes*

The crêpes can be prepared ahead.

Makes 12 crêpes.

Nutrient Value Per Crêpe: 60 calories, 4 gm.
protein, 1 gm. fat, 49 mg. sodium, 46 mg.
cholesterol.

4 ounces (half of an 8-ounce package)
imitation low-calorie cream cheese
OR: Neufchatel cheese
1 fresh peach, peeled, pitted and sliced OR:
2 peach halves packed in juice, drained
1 tablespoon sugar OR: sugar substitute
equal to 4 teaspoons sugar (optional)
2 eggs
6 tablespoons skim milk
¼ cup sifted all-purpose flour
Dash of salt
Fruit Topping (recipe follows)

1. Prepare the crêpe filling: Combine the cream cheese, peach slices and sugar (or sugar substitute, if using), in the container of an electric blender or food processor. Cover; whirl until smooth. Chill.
2. Prepare the crêpes: Beat the eggs, milk, flour and salt in bowl until the batter is smooth.
3. Spray a 5- or 6-inch non-stick omelet or crêpe pan with non-stick vegetable cooking spray. Pour in about 1 tablespoon of the batter at a time, quickly rotating the pan to evenly spread the batter over the bottom. Cook over low heat until lightly browned, about 30 seconds. Flip, and cook the other side for 30 seconds. Slide the crêpe onto a plate. Continue until all the batter is used. Stack the cooled crêpes between wax paper.
4. Spoon a heaping tablespoon of crêpe filling across the center of each crêpe. Roll up. Arrange the crêpes, seam-side down, on a serving platter. Serve with Fruit Topping.

Fruit Topping: Brush 2 cups of thinly sliced fresh peaches with 2 tablespoons lemon juice. Surround the crêpes with the peach slices. Combine 1 cup fresh or frozen unsweetened, thawed raspberries and sugar substitute equal to 14 teaspoons sugar, if you wish, in the container of an electric blender or food processor. Cover; whirl until smooth. Drizzle the sauce over the crêpes.

⁅⁅⁅ 🍸 ⬚ *Fruited Rice Mold*

Makes 6 servings.

Nutrient Value Per Serving: 99 calories, 5 gm. protein, 0 gm. fat, 67 mg. sodium, 2 mg. cholesterol.

- **2   cups skim milk**
- **3   tablespoons uncooked white rice**
- **3   tablespoons orange liqueur**
    Pinch of salt
- **1   envelope unflavored gelatin**
- **¼   cup cold water**
    Sugar substitute equal to 10 teaspoons

sugar (optional)
- **1   teaspoon grated orange or lemon rind**
- **⅛   teaspoon ground nutmeg**
- **½   cup diced seeded orange slices**
- **½   cup blueberries**
- **½   cup seedless green grapes**
    Mint, orange slices and green grapes (optional)

1. Combine the milk, rice, orange liqueur and salt in the top of a double boiler. Place over simmering water. Cook, uncovered, stirring occasionally, for 25 minutes.
2. Sprinkle the gelatin over cold water to soften, about 1 minute. Add to the rice mixture; stir to dissolve. Add the sugar substitute, if you wish, orange rind and nutmeg.
3. Set the saucepan over a bowl of ice and water to speed setting. Stir until the mixture just begins to set. Fold in the diced orange, blueberries and grapes.
4. Generously spray a 3- or 4-cup mold with non-stick vegetable cooking spray. Spoon in the rice-fruit mixture. Cover; refrigerate overnight.
5. To unmold: Loosen the edges with the tip of a knife. Invert a serving plate over the mold. Turn the mold and plate right side up; shake gently to loosen. Carefully remove the mold. Garnish with mint and orange slices and green grapes, if you wish.

🍸 *Eclair Ring*

Picture one big eclair, shaped into a ring, spiked with chocolate filling and crowned with fruit. A dramatic lo-cal dessert that could easily be the star of a buffet table.

Bake at 400° for 10 minutes; then at 375° for 40 to 45 minutes.
Makes 12 servings.

Nutrient Value Per Serving: 151 calories, 7 gm. protein, 7 gm. fat, 161 mg. sodium, 98 mg. cholesterol.

⅔ *cup water*
½ *cup (1 stick) diet margarine*
   Pinch of salt
1 *cup* sifted *all-purpose flour*
4 *eggs*

COCO-CREAM FILLING
1 *cup part-skim ricotta cheese*
2 *tablespoons creme de cacao liqueur*
4 *teaspoons unsweetened cocoa powder*
1 *envelope unflavored gelatin*
¼ *cup cold water*
2 *egg whites*
¼ *cup sugar*
   Fresh raspberries (optional)

1. Preheat the oven to hot (400°). Spray a cookie sheet with non-stick vegetable cooking spray.
2. Combine the water, margarine and salt in a medium-size saucepan. Bring to boiling. Add the flour all at once. Stir vigorously with a wooden spoon until the mixture forms a thick smooth ball that leaves the side of the pan clean. Remove from the heat.
3. Beat in the eggs, one at a time, beating well after each addition, with a wooden spoon or electric mixer until the paste is shiny and smooth. Spoon the paste into a pastry bag without a tip. Pipe the paste into an 8-inch ring on the prepared cookie sheet. Or, if you do not have a pastry bag, shape the paste into an 8-inch ring with a large spoon and rubber spatula.
4. Bake in the preheated hot oven (400°) for 10 minutes. Lower the heat to moderate (375°). Bake for 40 to 45 minutes or until puffed and golden. Remove the ring to a wire rack. Make several slits in the side of the ring to let steam escape. While still warm, slice the ring in half horizontally with a serrated knife. Pull out and discard any moist pastry. Cool the halves on a wire rack.
5. Meanwhile, prepare the Coco-Cream Filling: Combine the ricotta, creme de cacao and cocoa powder in the container of an electric blender or food processor. Cover; whirl

until smooth. Transfer to a large bowl.
6. Sprinkle the gelatin over the cold water in a small cup; let stand to soften, 1 minute. Set the cup in a pan of simmering water; stir to dissolve the gelatin. Remove from the water. Cool to lukewarm.
7. Beat the egg whites in a small bowl until foamy. Beat in the sugar, 1 tablespoon at a time, until the meringue forms soft peaks.
8. Stir the dissolved gelatin into the chocolate mixture. Gently fold in the meringue until no streaks of white remain. Spoon the filling into the bottom of the eclair ring. Arrange the top of the ring over filling. Garnish the center with a mound of fresh raspberries, if you wish.

▨ ▾ *Velvety Crème Chocolate*

Bake cake layers at 350° for 20 minutes.
Makes 10 servings.

Nutrient Value Per Serving: 104 calories, 6 gm. protein, 2 gm. fat, 76 mg. sodium, 44 mg. cholesterol.

CAKE LAYERS
½ *cup* sifted *all-purpose flour*
¼ *cup unsweetened cocoa powder*
¼ *teaspoon ground cinnamon*
¼ *teaspoon salt*
3 *eggs*
⅔ *cup sugar*

CHOCOLATE CRÈME
1 *envelope unflavored gelatin*
3 *tablespoons unsweetened cocoa powder*
1 *tablespoon instant coffee*
   Pinch of ground cinnamon
¼ *cup water*
1 *cup cold skim milk*
2 *egg whites*
3 *tablespoons sugar*

YOGURT TOPPING
1 *envelope unflavored gelatin*
¼ *cup water*
1 *egg white*

1   **tablespoon sugar**
½   **teaspoon vanilla**
¾   **cup plain yogurt**
4   **to 6 large strawberries, quartered**
    Fresh mint leaves for garnish (optional)

1. Prepare the Cake Layer: Grease two 8-inch round cake pans; line the bottoms with wax paper, grease the paper. Preheat the oven to moderate (350°).

2. Sift together the flour, cocoa, cinnamon and salt onto a piece of wax paper.

3. Beat the eggs in a small bowl until foamy. Gradually beat in the sugar until thick and fluffy. Fold in the flour mixture. Spoon into the prepared pans, dividing evenly.

4. Bake in the preheated moderate oven (350°) for 20 minutes or until the tops spring back when lightly pressed with a fingertip. Cool in the pans on wire racks for 10 minutes. Loosen the edges; invert the cakes on the racks; cool completely. Place one layer on a serving platter. Cover; set aside. Wrap and freeze the second layer for another use.

5. Prepare the Chocolate Crème: Combine the gelatin, cocoa powder, instant coffee, cinnamon and water in a cup. Stir until the gelatin is softened. Place the cup in hot water; stir to dissolve gelatin.

6. Combine the cold milk and gelatin-cocoa mixture in a small bowl. Chill until the consistency of unbeaten egg whites.

7. Beat the 2 egg whites in a bowl until foamy. Gradually beat in the sugar until soft peaks form. Fold the chilled cocoa mixture into the beaten whites until no white streaks remain. Pour into a 1-quart metal mold or bowl, 6 to 7½ inches in diameter. Shake gently to remove any large bubbles. Refrigerate for several hours or overnight until firm.

8. To *un*mold, loosen the edges of the gelatin; quickly dip in warm water. Invert over cake layer, shake to loosen and carefully remove mold. Refrigerate until

surface of the mold has set again.

9. To prepare the Yogurt Topping: Sprinkle the gelatin over the water in small cup; let stand 5 minutes to soften. Set cup in hot water, stir to dissolve gelatin. Cool slightly.

10. Beat the egg white in a small bowl until foamy. Gradually beat in the sugar until the meringue forms soft peaks. Fold the gelatin mixture and vanilla into the yogurt in a medium-size bowl. Fold in the beaten white. Spoon the Yogurt Topping into the pastry bag fitted with large star tip. Pipe up and down over the side of the mold, but leaving top sides of mold uncovered. Pipe the topping on top of the mold in a small swirl. Garnish side and top with strawberries. Garnish each strawberry with fresh mint leaves, if you wish.

⋘ 𝚈 *Romanoff Roll*

Bake at 400° for 5 minutes.
Makes 10 servings.

Nutrient Value Per Serving: 128 calories, 6 gm. protein, 6 gm. fat, 146 mg. sodium, 147 mg. cholesterol.

¾   **cup sifted all-purpose flour**
1   **teaspoon baking powder**
5   **eggs, separated**
⅛   **teaspoon salt**
¼   **cup orange juice**
⅛   **teaspoon grated orange rind**
    Sugar substitute equal to 14 teaspoons sugar (optional)

CREAMY ROMANOFF FILLING
4   **ounces (half of an 8-ounce package) imitation low-calorie cream cheese**
2   **tablespoons orange-flavored liqueur**
⅛   **teaspoon ground cinnamon**
⅛   **teaspoon ground allspice**
2   **cups pressurized light whipped cream topping**
1   **cup coarsely chopped strawberries Strawberries for garnish (optional)**

1. Preheat the oven to hot (400°). Spray a 15 x 10 x 1-inch jelly-roll pan with non-stick vegetable cooking spray. Line only the bottom with wax paper; do not let the paper come up the sides of the pan. Generously spray the paper with non-stick vegetable spray.
2. Sift together the flour and baking powder onto a clean piece of wax paper. Reserve.
3. Beat together the egg whites and salt in a large bowl until soft peaks form.
4. Beat the egg yolks with the orange juice and orange rind in a large bowl until light and fluffy. Beat in the reserved flour mixture. Gently fold in the beaten egg whites until no streaks of white remain. Turn the batter into the prepared jelly-roll pan, spreading evenly.
5. Bake in the preheated hot oven (400°) for 5 to 7 minutes or until the top springs back when lightly pressed with a fingertip and a wooden pick inserted in center comes out clean. The cake should not be brown.
6. Loosen the cake around the edges with the tip of a knife. Invert onto a clean towel. Very carefully peel off the paper. (Use a knife to help peel off wax paper, if necessary.) Sprinkle the cake with the sugar substitute, if using. Starting at the short end, roll up the cake and towel together. Place the roll, seam-side down, on a wire rack. Cool completely.
7. Meanwhile, prepare the Creamy Romanoff Filling: Combine the cream cheese, liqueur, cinnamon and allspice in the container of an electric blender or food processor. Cover; whirl until smooth. Transfer to a medium-size bowl. Gently fold in the cream topping. If the filling is not firm enough to spread, refrigerate.
8. When the jelly roll is cool, unroll carefully. Spread the roll evenly with the filling; sprinkle with the strawberries. Reroll, without the towel. Place the roll, seam-side down, on a serving plate. Refrigerate, covered, until ready to serve. Garnish with additional strawberries, if you wish.

◀◀◀ 🍷 ☐ *No-Bake Black Forest Refrigerator Cake*

Prepare this easy-to-put-together cake, with store-bought ladyfingers and a no-bake chocolate filling, a day ahead. Unmold just before serving.

Makes 10 servings.

Nutrient Value Per Serving: 100 calories, 5 gm. protein, 2 gm. fat, 56 mg. sodium, 39 mg. cholesterol.

- **10 ladyfingers, split in half**
- **⅓ cup evaporated milk**
- **½ teaspoon lemon juice**
- **2 egg whites**
- **⅛ teaspoon salt**
- **2 tablespoons cold water**
- **2 tablespoons cherry-flavored liqueur OR: water**
- **1 envelope unflavored gelatin**
- **⅔ cup strong coffee**
- **4 ice cubes**
- **3 packages (.75 ounces each) chocolate reduced-calorie dairy drink mix**
- **2 teaspoons vanilla**
- **1 cup fresh or frozen cherries, thawed**

1. Line the bottom and long sides of an 8½ x 4½ x 2-inch glass loaf pan with one long sheet of wax paper, extending the ends of the paper several inches beyond the rims. Arrange 6 ladyfinger halves, flat side up, across the bottom, parallel to the short ends of the dish. Line each long side of the pan with 7 ladyfinger halves, standing up with the flat sides facing in. Set aside.

2. Place a medium-size bowl in the freezer along with the mixer beaters. Pour the evaporated milk into an ice cube tray. Place in the freezer until ice crystals form around the edge, about 25 minutes.

3. Scoop out the evaporated milk into the chilled bowl. Add the lemon juice. Beat with the chilled beaters until stiff. Reserve.

4. Beat the egg whites and salt in second bowl until stiff peaks form. Reserve.

5. Combine the cold water and cherry-flavored liqueur in the container of an electric blender. Sprinkle the gelatin over the liquid; allow to soften about 1 minute.

6. Meanwhile, heat the coffee to boiling in a small saucepan. Pour over the softened gelatin. Cover the container; whirl until the gelatin is dissolved. Add the ice cubes, chocolate dairy drink mix and vanilla. Cover; whirl until well mixed. Transfer to a large bowl. If the mixture has not begun to set, chill just until it does.

7. Fold the whipped evaporated milk and beaten egg whites into the chocolate mixture. Spoon the chocolate filling into the ladyfinger-lined baking dish.

8. With a serrated knife, carefully trim the ends of the ladyfingers even with the top of the filling. Sprinkle the trimmed pieces evenly over the top of the filling. Bring the

ends of the wax paper over the top; cover the entire top lightly with plastic wrap. Refrigerate overnight.

9. To unmold, carefully invert the dish onto a serving plate. Remove the dish and wax paper. Garnish the top of the cake with whole cherries. Serve immediately.

◀◀◀ ▼ *Peach-Filled Cheese Tart*

Love cheesecake? Try our low-calorie version.

Bake at 350° for 45 minutes.
Makes 10 servings.

Nutrient Value Per Serving: 103 calories, 8 gm. protein, 3 gm. fat, 205 mg. sodium, 112 mg. cholesterol.

> *4 eggs, separated*
> *1 egg white*
> *⅛ teaspoon salt*
> *1½ cups lowfat cottage cheese*
> *½ cup lowfat vanilla yogurt*
> *4 ripe peaches*
> *2 teaspoons lemon juice*
> *⅓ cup low-sugar strawberry spread*
> *Mint leaves (optional)*

1. Preheat the oven to moderate (350°). Generously spray bottom and sides of a 9-inch springform pan, 2½- to 3-inches deep, with non-stick cooking spray.

2. Beat together the 5 egg whites and salt in a large bowl until soft peaks form.

3. Combine the 4 egg yolks, cottage cheese and yogurt in the container of an electric blender or food processor. Cover; whirl until smooth. Transfer to a large bowl.

4. Gently fold the beaten egg whites into the cottage cheese mixture until no streaks of white remain. Spoon the batter into the prepared pan.

5. Bake in the preheated moderate oven (350°) for 45 minutes or until puffed and golden. Remove to a wire rack. Cool completely,

◀*Clockwise from center:* **Peach-filled Cheese Tart (page 277), No-Bake Black Forest Cake (page 276) and Romanoff Roll (page 275).**

away from drafts. (Cake will considerably as it cools.) Run a sharp knife around the edge. Loosen and remove the side of the pan. Cover and refrigerate.

6. Just before serving, peel, pit and thinly slice the peaches. Toss slices gently with lemon juice in a large bowl. Arrange the slices, overlapping, in circles on top of the cake.

7. Heat the strawberry spread in a small saucepan just until it becomes liquid. Strain; discard the fruit bits. Brush the liquid over the peach slices. Garnish the center of the tart with mint leaves, if you wish.

Marbled Jamaica Chomocha Pie

This spectacular pie looks and tastes like a lot of effort and calories, but it has neither!

Bake crust at 350° for 8 minutes.
Makes 10 servings.

Nutrient Value Per Serving: 155 calories, 7 gm. protein, 6 gm. fat, 187 mg. sodium, 6 mg. cholesterol.

1½ cups graham cracker crumbs
¼   cup (½ stick) diet margarine
4   tablespoons unsweetened cocoa powder
¼   teaspoon ground cinnamon
1   tablespoon unflavored gelatin
2   tablespoons cold water
¾   cup boiling water
4   ice cubes
½   cup skim milk
2   teaspoons rum flavoring
¾   cup part-skim ricotta cheese
5   envelopes (.75 ounces each) vanilla
*   reduced-calorie dairy drink mix*
½   teaspoon instant coffee
1   tablespoon hot water

1. Preheat the oven to moderate (350°).
2. Mix together the cracker crumbs, margarine, 2 tablespoons of the cocoa powder and cinnamon in a medium-size bowl with fingers until the margarine is blended throughout. Press firmly over the bottom and side of the 9-inch pie plate.

3. Bake in the preheated moderate oven (350°) for 8 minutes. Cool completely on a wire rack before filling.

4. Sprinkle the gelatin over the cold water in the container of an electric blender; let stand to soften, about 1 minute. Pour the boiling water over the gelatin. Add the ice cubes, milk and rum flavoring. Cover; whirl until the ice melts. Add the ricotta and dairy drink mix. Whirl until smooth. Transfer to a large bowl. Place the bowl in a pan of ice and water to speed setting. Chill, stirring often, until the mixture just begins to thicken.

5. Reserve ½ cup of the vanilla filling. Spoon the remaining filling into the pie shell. (Try to work quickly at this point as the filling will set very quickly.)

6. Dissolve the coffee in 1 tablespoon hot water in small bowl. Stir in the remaining 2 tablespoons cocoa and reserved ½ cup vanilla filling. Beat until smooth. Using a spoonful at a time, draw the coffee-cocoa mixture through the vanilla filling to create a marbling effect. Refrigerate, loosely covered, until the filling is completely set, several hours.

Piña Colada Crustless Pie

No baking, no crust (and no pastry calories) in this light and easy 2-layered pie—coconut and rum-pineapple.

Makes 10 servings.

Nutrient Value Per Serving: 96 calories, 4 gm. protein, 1 gm. fat, 54 mg. sodium, 1 mg. cholesterol.

3   cups skim milk
1   tablespoon cornstarch
*   Pinch of salt*
2   envelopes unflavored gelatin

3 tablespoons light rum
½ cup flaked coconut
1 can (20 ounces) crushed pineapple
  packed in juice, chilled
  Sugar substitute equal to 8 teaspoons
  sugar (optional)
  Fresh fruit and mint leaves (optional)

1. Combine 1½ cups of the skim milk, the cornstarch; and salt in a large saucepan. Cook, stirring constantly, over medium heat until the mixture is thick and bubbly, about 5 minutes.
2. Meanwhile, sprinkle 1 envelope of the gelatin over 2 tablespoons of the rum; let stand to soften, 1 minute.
3. Add the gelatin mixture to the skim milk mixture; stir to dissolve gelatin. Remove from the heat. Stir in the remaining 1½ cups of skim milk and coconut. Spoon into a 9-inch non-stick pie plate, or spray a regular pie plate with non-stick vegetable spray. Chill for several hours or until set.
4. Drain ¼ cup juice from the crushed pineapple into a small cup. Pour the remaining juice and pineapple into medium-size bowl. Sprinkle the remaining envelope of gelatin over ¼ cup of juice; let stand to soften, 1 minute. Set the cup in a pan of simmering water; stir to dissolve the gelatin. Remove from the heat.
5. Stir the dissolved gelatin into the crushed pineapple in the bowl, along with the remaining 1 tablespoon rum and sugar substitute, if you wish. Spoon the pineapple mixture over the coconut layer. Chill until almost set. Garnish with fresh fruit and mint leaves, if you wish.

◀◀◀ ▢ *Yogurt Fresh Fruit Pie*

A layer of yogurt cream topped with jewel-glazed fresh fruit.

Bake crust at 450° for 7 minutes.

Makes 10 servings.

Nutrient Value Per Serving: 142 calories, 3 gm. protein, 7 gm. fat, 128 mg. sodium, 4 mg. cholesterol.

½ of an 11-ounce package pie crust mix
1 can (8 ounces) pineapple chunks packed
  in pineapple juice
1 envelope unflavored gelatin
¼ cup cold water
  Sugar substitute equal to 16 teaspoons
  sugar (optional)
¾ cup low-fat plain yogurt
1 teaspoon vanilla
½ teaspoon ground cinnamon
¾ cup thinly sliced fresh peaches
¾ cup sliced strawberries
¾ cup blueberries

1. Preheat the oven to very hot (450°).
2. Prepare the piecrust mix, following label directions for 9-inch pastry shell with high fluted edge. Prick all over with a fork.
3. Bake in the preheated very hot oven (450°) for 7 minutes or until the pastry is golden brown. Cool on the wire rack.
4. Drain the juice from the pineapple chunks into a 2-cup glass measure. Reserve the chunks. Add enough water to juice to make 1 cup.
5. Sprinkle the gelatin over the ¼ cup cold water in a small cup; let stand to soften, 1 minute. Set the cup in a pan of simmering water; stir to dissolve gelatin. Pour the gelatin into the pineapple juice mixture. Add the sugar substitute, if using. Refrigerate until syrupy.
6. Reserve ¼ cup of the pineapple juice-gelatin mixture for glaze. Mix the remainder with the yogurt and vanilla. Spread the yogurt mixture over the bottom of the prebaked pie shell. Sprinkle with the cinnamon.
7. Arrange the drained pineapple chunks, peaches, strawberries and blueberries over yogurt mixture. Gently brush the fruit with the reserved ¼ cup pineapple juice-gelatin mixture. Refrigerate, covered, overnight.

9. Elegant Meals and Festive Parties for Holidays and Entertaining

$\int$deas for entertaining, from a rousing St. Patrick's Day Feast to a Lavish Wine and Cheese Spread, are outlined here, complete with menus, recipes and tips. (Recipes for the starred dishes can be found either following the menus or listed in the index.) Entertain in a way that lets *you* feel completely comfortable about all your arrangements. Your parties should work well for the space you have and the way you live.

Careful planning will help you run your parties smoothly. After deciding on the type of entertaining, be it formal dinner, patio barbecue or Sunday brunch, decide on the number of people to be invited. Inventory the number of people you can comfortably seat, whether at the table, in the living room or in the yard. Check that you have enough tableware for the number of guests you are serving. Choose a menu featuring dishes that may be prepared ahead and be sure your bar is well stocked if you are serving drinks. Make a kitchen schedule listing everything to be done before serving and when to do it. Check off items as you complete them.

The most important thing to remember is to keep things simple and be yourself. The purpose of your party is to give pleasure to yourself as well as your guests. Good company and good food make good times better!

ST. PATRICK'S DAY FEAST
(for 12)

Kilkenny Corned Beef*   Killybegs Horseradish Sauce*

Shannon Vegetable Platter*

Bantry Brown Bread*

Blarney Castle Parfaits*   Shamrock Sugar Cookies*

Dublin Irish Coffee*

You don't have to be Irish to enjoy a hearty corned beef dinner! Almost everything can be prepared ahead, so why not invite some friends to celebrate with you?

◄*Clockwise from left:* **Kilkenny Corned Beef with Killybegs Horseradish Sauce (page 282), Bantry Brown Bread (page 42) and traditional Irish Soda Bread and Shannon Vegetable Platter (page 282).**

▥ ♉ *Kilkenny Corned Beef*

Bake at 325° for 2 hours; then at 325° for 1 hour.
Makes 12 servings.

Nutrient Value Per Serving: 314 calories, 35 gm. protein, 15 gm. fat, 139 mg. sodium, 103 mg. cholesterol.

> 1 **piece corned beef brisket (about 5 pounds)**
>   **Boiling water**
> 1 **tablespoon mixed pickling spices**
> ½ **cup firmly packed light brown sugar**
> ⅓ **cup prepared mustard**
>   **Orange wedges**
>   **Watercress**
>   **Killybegs Horseradish Sauce (recipe follows)**
>   **Orange wedges and watercress (optional)**

1. Preheat the oven to slow (325F°).
2. Wash the corned beef brisket. Place in a large roasting pan on the oven rack. Cover the meat with boiling water; add the pickling spices; cover the pan with aluminum foil.
3. Bake in the preheated slow oven (325°) for 2 hours or until tender when pierced with a two-tined fork. Allow to cool in the cooking liquid. (This can be done the day before; refrigerate.)
4. Prepare the Killybegs Horseradish Sauce.
5. About 1 hour before serving, drain the cooked corned beef and place it in the roasting pan.
6. Bake in a preheated slow oven (325°) for 30 minutes.
7. Combine the brown sugar and mustard in a small bowl and spread the mixture over the corned beef. Bake for 30 minutes longer or until well glazed. Place on a platter. Garnish with wedges of orange and sprigs of watercress. Cut into thin slices and serve with Killybegs Horseradish Sauce.

Killybegs Horseradish Sauce: Combine 1 container (8 ounces) dairy sour cream with 2 tablespoons prepared mustard and 2 tablespoons prepared horseradish in a glass or ceramic bowl. Cover with plastic wrap and refrigerate for at least 2 hours to blend the flavors.

MAKE-AHEAD TIP
Cook the corned beef the day before; then return to the oven 1 hour before serving for the final glazing.

▥ ♉ *Shannon Vegetable Platter*

Makes 12 servings.

Nutrient Value Per Serving: 232 calories, 5 gm. protein, 8 gm. fat, 133 mg. sodium, 20 mg. cholesterol.

> 12 **medium-size boiling potatoes (about 4 pounds)**
> 2 **packages (1 pound each) baby carrots**
> 1 **large head green cabbage**
>   **Boiling water**
> ½ **cup (1 stick) butter or margarine**
> ¼ **cup chopped parsley**

1. Pare the potatoes and carrots. (This can be done the day before. Cover the vegetables with cold water in a bowl; refrigerate.)
2. Cook the potatoes and carrots, separately, in 2 saucepans of boiling salted water, for 15 minutes or until fork-tender. Drain. Return the saucepans to low heat; toss the vegetables over the heat to dry. Place on a heated serving platter and keep warm.
3. Cut the cabbage into 12 wedges. Soak in warm salted water in a large bowl for 1 minute. Drain. Arrange, overlapping, in a large skillet. Pour boiling water over to cover; cover the skillet; bring to boiling. Lower the heat; simmer for 3 minutes.

Remove the cabbage and drain on paper toweling. Arrange on the platter with the potatoes and carrots.

4. Heat the butter and chopped parsley in a small saucepan until bubbly. Pour over the vegetables to coat well.

🍸 *Blarney Castle Parfaits*

Makes 12 servings.

Nutrient Value Per Serving: 275 calories, 3 gm. protein, 10 gm. fat, 84 mg. sodium, 43 mg. cholesterol.

½ *gallon vanilla ice cream*
1 *bottle (12 ounces) green crème de menthe OR: 1½ cups light corn syrup combined with a few drops green food coloring and 2 teaspoons peppermint extract*

Scoop the ice cream into 12 parfait or sherbet glasses. Top with crème de menthe or the corn syrup mixture.

▲ **Blarney Castle Parfait (page 283) and Shamrock Sugar Cookies (page 226).**

🍸 *Dublin Irish Coffee*

Makes 1 serving.

Nutrient Value Per Serving: 192 calories, 1 gm. protein, 11 gm. fat, 13 mg. sodium, 41 mg. cholesterol.

Boiling water
1 *teaspoon sugar*
1 *ounce (2 tablespoons) Irish whiskey*
Hot coffee
Softly whipped heavy cream

Heat a heavy stemmed glass with boiling water; pour out the water. Combine the sugar and whiskey in a glass; stir in coffee to within 1 inch of the top. Pour whipped cream over the back of a spoon onto the coffee. Serve without stirring.

PREPARE IN ADVANCE
When you entertain, have the food prepared ahead whenever possible.
●**Appetizers should be made and refrigerated, if necessary.**
●**Most soups can be made and refrigerated, then reheated just before serving.**
●**Breads may be wrapped in aluminum foil, ready for warming.**
●**Make green salads (without the dressing) 1 or 2 hours ahead and refrigerate in a plastic bag or a glass bowl, covered with plastic wrap. Add the dressing just before serving.**
●**Prepare as much of the entrée ahead as possible. Have the ingredients and implements ready to use for any last-minute sauces or other cooking.**
●**The dessert should be made ahead ready to be served.**

MARVELOUS SPRING DINNER BUFFET
(for 8)

Assorted Cheeses   French Bread in Thin Slices

Asparagus Cream Soup*

Glorious Ham*

Spring Vegetable Salad*   Sautéed Cherry Tomatoes*

Fresh Strawberry and Rhubarb Pie*

Coffee with Amaretto and Whipped Cream

Celebrate the arrival of spring with a fabulous feast of the season! Tender young vegetables accompany a baked ham, topped with fresh mushrooms and shallots and wrapped in flaky phyllo pastry. It's an elegant make-ahead buffet—and it's *not* hard to do. We give you step-by-step directions on how to wrap phyllo around the ham. The soup and salad feature vegetables simply prepared; dessert is a no-bake garden-fresh fruit pie.

Glorious Ham

Perfect for a spring buffet, this boneless ham is easily sliced with an electric knife.

Bake at 350° for 1¾ hours.
Makes 24 servings.

    1 *pound mushrooms*
    ¼ *cup finely chopped shallots*
       OR: white part of green onions
    ¼ *cup (½ stick) unsalted butter or*
       margarine
    ½ *teaspoon salt*
       Pinch of white pepper
    1 *tablespoon lemon juice*
    1 *tablespoon all-purpose flour*
    ⅓ *cup milk*
    1 *egg, separated*
    1 *package (1 pound) phyllo or strudel*
       pastry leaves, thawed if frozen*
    1 *cup (2 sticks) unsalted butter, melted*
    1 *fully-cooked smoked boneless ham*
       (about 8 pounds)
       Sugar-frosted green seedless grapes and
       lemon leaves for garnish (optional)

1. Finely chop the mushrooms, half at a time, in a food processor, or by hand; set aside. Sauté the shallots in the ¼ cup butter in a large skillet for 1 minute. Stir in the chopped mushrooms, salt, pepper and lem-

◄*Clockwise from bottom:* **Asparagus Cream Soup (page 70), Spring Vegetable Salad (page 286), Glorious Ham (page 285) and Fresh Strawberry and Rhubarb Pie (page 287).**

on juice. Cook over medium-high heat until tender and most of the liquid has evaporated, about 7 minutes. Stir in the flour, then the milk, until smooth. Cook until bubbly and thickened. Remove from the heat; cool slightly. Refrigerate until cold. (Mushroom mixture can be cooked a day ahead.)

2. Stir egg yolk into the mushroom mixture.

3. Tear off four 18-inch lengths of wax paper. Overlap the long edge of two pieces of wax paper on a counter or table top. Unwrap the phyllo and place it on the wax paper. Cover the top with slightly dampened paper toweling to keep the phyllo from drying out. Overlap the other two pieces of wax paper on the counter. Lift 1 sheet of phyllo from the stack and place it on the wax paper. Brush the phyllo with the melted butter. Place another sheet of phyllo on top; repeat buttering and stacking the phyllo. When all the sheets are buttered, cut off the corners of the phyllo stack to form 4- to 5-inch triangles, thus removing excess pastry when you wrap the ham.

4. Preheat the oven to moderate (350°).

5. Place the ham on a rack in a large open shallow roasting pan. Brush with slightly beaten egg white. Cover the top of the ham with the mushroom mixture. Place the stack of phyllo over ham so that the length of the ham is covered by the length of the phyllo. Tuck the phyllo along the two long sides under the ham. Tuck the short ends of the phyllo under the ham. Brush the entire surface of the phyllo with egg white.

6. With the 4 phyllo triangles, cut out decorative pieces using fluted cookie cutters

or scissors. Arrange on top of the ham. Brush the pieces with egg white.

7. Bake the ham in the preheated moderate oven (350°) for 1¾ hours, turning the pan around midway through the baking time for even browning. If the phyllo browns too quickly on top, cover with a tent of aluminum foil. Transfer the ham to a platter using 2 wide pancake turners. Garnish the platter with frosted grapes and lemon leaves, if you wish.

*Note: Phyllo or strudel leaves can be found in the refrigerated or frozen foods sections of your supermarket.

LEFTOVER HAM
This ham will yield enough for several meals when you use it to serve 8. Wrap in aluminum foil and freeze in meal-size portions if you do not intend to use it right away. Remember to slice some ham for lunch-box sandwiches.

A BUFFET FOR 16
To serve up to 16 people, make the soup, salad, cherry tomato and pie recipes twice. There will be ample ham to serve 16 people with leftovers for seconds.

2,3   *Spring Vegetable Salad*

This salad may be made with any fresh vegetables available in your market. Blanch and chill the vegetables a day ahead.

Makes 8 servings.

Nutrient Value Per Serving: 279 calories, 3 gm. protein, 27 gm. fat, 265 mg. sodium, 0 mg. cholesterol.

½ *pound small zucchini, trimmed*
½ *pound small yellow squash, trimmed*
½ *pound green beans, trimmed and halved*
1 *small bunch broccoli, flowerets only*
1 *cup olive or vegetable oil*
⅓ *cup tarragon-flavored or white wine vinegar*
2 *teaspoons Dijon-style mustard*
¾ *teaspoon salt*
¼ *teaspoon pepper*
1 *can (13¾ ounces) artichoke hearts, chilled, drained and halved*
    Radish roses for garnish (optional)

1. Cook the zucchini and yellow squash in a large saucepan of boiling water for 5 minutes or just until slightly softened. Remove with a slotted spoon; run under cold water; drain; chill.
2. Add the green beans to the same boiling water; cook a few minutes just until crisp-tender. Remove with a slotted spoon to a bowl of cold water to stop further cooking. Drain; chill.
3. Drop the broccoli flowerets into the same boiling water; cook a few minutes just until crisp-tender. Drain; rinse with cold water; chill.
4. Combine the oil, vinegar, mustard, salt and pepper in a jar with a tight-fitting lid. Cover and refrigerate.
5. To serve, cut the zucchini and yellow squash into 3 x ½-inch strips. Arrange all the blanched vegetables and artichoke hearts on a platter. Shake the salad dressing and drizzle some over the vegetables. Garnish the platter with radish roses, if you wish. Pass the remaining dressing.

TO MAKE A RADISH ROSE
Wash and trim the radish, leaving some of the green leaves on if they are attractive. With a sharp knife, make 5 deep cuts (petals) all around the side of the radish. Place in a bowl of ice water for 15 minutes to make the petals open up.

Fresh Strawberry and Rhubarb Pie

Makes 8 servings.

Nutrient Value Per Serving: 346 calories, 4 gm. protein, 13 gm. fat, 180 mg. sodium, 21 mg. cholesterol.

1 **cup granulated sugar**
2 **tablespoons cornstarch**
1 **cup water**
1 **pound fresh rhubarb, washed and cut into 1-inch pieces OR: 1 package (1 pound) frozen unsweetened cut rhubarb**
1 **package (3 ounces) strawberry flavored gelatin**
2 **pints fresh strawberries, washed, dried and hulled**
   9-inch baked pie shell
½ **cup heavy cream**
1 **tablespoon 10X (confectioners') sugar**

1. Mix together the granulated sugar and cornstarch in a large saucepan. Stir in the water and rhubarb. Cook the mixture, gently stirring occasionally, just until the rhubarb is tender and the mixture is thickened and bubbly. Boil for 1 minute. Remove from the heat. Stir in the strawberry gelatin until it dissolves.
2. Refrigerate, stirring often, until the mixture mounds when dropped from a spoon. Stir the strawberries into the rhubarb mixture. Pour into the pie shell; spread evenly. Refrigerate while whipping the cream.
3. Beat the cream with the 10X (confectioners') sugar in a small bowl until soft peaks form. Spoon into a pastry bag fitted with a small rosette tip. Pipe the cream in a lattice pattern on top of the pie. Chill the pie for 4 hours or until set.

ELEGANT SUMMER DINNER ALFRESCO
(for 6)

Salmon Spread*   Party Rye Bread   Toast Points

Cold Cucumber and Yogurt Soup*

Grilled Cornish Game Hens*

Tomatoes Stuffed with Gruyère and Mozzarella*   Creamy Coleslaw*

Soufflé Bread*   Butter

Summer Pudding*

Red Bordeaux   Coffee

Entertaining needn't be confined to the dining room. A table on the patio, covered with a pastel or white tablecloth and set with your best linen napkins, flatware, china and glassware provides an elegant setting for your Summer Dinner Alfresco. An added bonus—the Grilled Cornish Game Hens and Tomatoes Stuffed with Gruyère and Mozzarella are cooked outside on the grill, so the chef can chat with the guests while cooking!

▐▌ ▢ *Grilled Cornish Game Hens*

Makes 6 servings.

Nutrient Value Per Serving: 547 calories, 47 gm. protein, 39 gm. fat, 655 mg. sodium, 192 mg. cholesterol.

 6   Cornish game hens (¾ to 1 pound each)
 1   teaspoon salt
 ½   teaspoon pepper
 ½   cup (1 stick) butter, melted
 3   tablespoons lemon juice
 1   teaspoon leaf rosemary, crumbled OR:
 **   1 tablespoon fresh rosemary, chopped**
 **   Fresh rosemary (optional)**

1. Truss the birds. Rub the skin with salt and pepper. Arrange on a barbecue spit, head to tail.
2. Combine the melted butter, lemon juice and rosemary in a bowl.
3. Attach the spit to an electric rotisserie. Grill the hens over hot coals, basting with the seasoned butter, 1 to 1¼ hours or until the meat is no longer pink near the bone. Garnish with fresh rosemary, if you wish.

▐▌ ▐▌ ▢ *Tomatoes Stuffed with Gruyère and Mozzarella*

Makes 6 servings.

Nutrient Value Per Tomato: 157 calories, 11 gm. protein, 10 gm. fat, 138 mg. sodium, 36 mg. cholesterol.

 6   medium-size ripe tomatoes
 **   Pepper**
 4   ounces Gruyère cheese, shredded
 4   ounces mozzarella cheese, shredded
 2   tablespoons finely chopped fresh basil

1. Cut a slice from the top of each tomato. Scoop out the pulp and seeds with a spoon. Turn the tomatoes upside down on a plate;

let drain for 30 minutes.
2. Season the insides of the tomatoes with pepper. Combine the Gruyère cheese, mozzarella cheese and basil in a small bowl; mix well. Fill the tomatoes. Wrap each in a 9 x 9-inch square of heavy-duty aluminum foil; seal tightly.
3. Place on a grill over moderately hot coals. Grill 20 to 25 minutes or until heated through.

> **MAKE-AHEAD TIP**
> **Make the stuffed tomatoes and wrap them as directed; then place in the refrigerator. Remove from the refrigerator 30 minutes before grilling to allow them to return to room temperature.**

▐▌ ▐▌ *Creamy Coleslaw*

Makes 8 servings.

Nutrient Value Per Serving: 317 calories, 3 gm. protein, 31 gm. fat, 381 mg. sodium, 27 mg. cholesterol.

 1   medium-size green cabbage (2 pounds)
 ½   cup chopped green onion
 1⅓ cups plain yogurt
 1⅓ cups mayonnaise
 2   teaspoons whole mustard seeds
 ½   teaspoon salt
 ¼   teaspoon pepper
 **   Radish and watercress (optional)**

1. Trim the outer leaves from the cabbage; quarter and core. Shred; you should have about 10 cups. Combine the cabbage and green onion in a large bowl.
2. Combine the yogurt, mayonnaise, mustard seeds, salt and pepper in a bowl. Pour over the cabbage; toss. Cover; refrigerate for several hours before serving.
3. Garnish with a whole radish and watercress, if you wish.

▲ *Clockwise from bottom left:* **Tomato Aspic Rectangles (page 290), basket of breads, Marinated Tomato-Rice Salad (page 84), Three Vegetable Relishes (page 291), Tuna-White Bean Salad (page 82), Chicken-Macaroni Salad (page 80), Green Potato Salad (page 81) and platter of cold cuts and vegetables.**

Help yourself to an entertaining idea! A salad bar is fun for guests and easy on the hostess. What could be simpler? You prepare these delectable salads and fixings ahead of time, chill, then set out just before the party starts. Everyone will love being able to pick and choose their favorites or create salads of their own. Your party will be the summer's most popular bash!

SUMMER SALAD BAR PARTY
(for 12 to 18)
Tomato Aspic Rectangles*   Three Vegetable Relishes*
Pickled Beet Salad*
Platter of Meats with Accompanying Breads*
Tossed Salad*   Assorted Dressings*
Fresh Fruit Salad with Tangerine Dressing*
Condiments*
Assorted Beverages

HOW TO SET UP YOUR SALAD BAR
- Make food *look* inviting with tempting textures and colors. Use interesting garnishes, such as the sunny Lemon Basket on our Tuna-White Bean Salad page 82.
- Offer lots of variety. Salads can be made with anything from fruit to pasta. Include tasty toppings for greens, like corn chips (for a Mexican-style salad) and croutons, plus a choice of dressings. Set out a large tray of assorted cold cuts and cheeses so guests can fix a chef's salad or small sandwiches.
- Stock up on beverages. Beer, wine and fruity sangria are ever-popular thirst-quenchers. For nondrinkers, have soft drinks and pitchers of juice on hand.
- Set up your salad bar in a logical order—starting with the plates and ending with an assortment of breads and butter. (Slice the bread ahead of time so it's easy to pick up as guests pass by.)
- Serve the salads in chilled bowls and platters—they'll keep longer.
- For an outdoor party, arrange platters on ice. Salads will stay cold and fresh.
- Refill the platters as needed or transfer salad that's running out to a smaller plate.

Tomato Aspic Rectangles

Make this cool refreshing aspic in a large pan; then just cut into individual servings.

Makes 18 servings.

Nutrient Value Per Serving: 36 calories, 3 gm. protein, 0.3 gm. fat, 311 mg. sodium, 0 mg. cholesterol.

- 3   *envelopes unflavored gelatin*
- 1   *can (18 ounces) tomato juice*
- 1   *can (35 ounces) whole tomatoes, undrained*
- 1   *cup chicken broth OR: water*
- 1   *cup diced celery*
- 1   *large onion, chopped (1 cup)*
- 1/4 *cup chopped fresh dill*
       OR: 1 tablespoon dried dillweed
- 3   *cloves garlic, sliced*
- 1   *tablespoon sugar*
- 1   *teaspoon salt*
- 1   *tablespoon lemon juice*
- 1/2 *teaspoon Worcestershire sauce*
       Leafy green lettuce
       Lemon slices and sprigs of dill
       for garnish

1. Sprinkle the gelatin over 1 cup of the tomato juice in a small bowl; let stand to soften.
2. Combine the remaining tomato juice, whole

tomatoes, chicken broth, celery, onion, dill, garlic, sugar and salt in a large saucepan. Bring to boiling. Lower the heat; simmer, uncovered, stirring occasionally, for 30 minutes. Remove from the heat. Stir in the softened gelatin mixture until dissolved. Cool slightly.

3. Work the tomato mixture through a food mill or sieve with a rubber spatula, into a large bowl. Discard the solid pulp. Measure the liquid and add enough water to make 6 cups. Stir in the lemon juice and Worcestershire.

4. Pour into a 13 x 9 x 2-inch baking pan. Cover; refrigerate overnight.

5. Cut the aspic into 18 rectangles, 3 x 2 inches. Transfer each with a small spatula onto a bed of lettuce on a platter or salad plate. Garnish with lemon slices and dill sprigs.

 *Three Vegetable Relishes*

These three colorful grated raw vegetables— radish, carrot and beet—are marinated in vinegar, and then individually flavored. Serve in small quantities as a relish or condiment.

Makes 6 servings of each relish.

Nutrient Value Per Serving Beet Relish: 80 calories, 1 gm. protein, 5 gm. fat, 133 mg. sodium, 0 mg. cholesterol.

Nutrient Value Per Serving Carrot Relish: 74 calories, 1 gm. protein, 5 gm. fat, 116 mg. sodium, 0 mg. cholesterol.

Nutrient Value Per Serving Radish Relish: 54 calories, 1 gm. protein, 5 gm. fat, 100 mg. sodium, 0 mg. cholesterol.

> *3 cups shredded pared carrots (about 6 medium-size carrots)*
> *3 cups shredded pared raw beets (about 3 medium-size beets)*
> *3 cups shredded radishes (about 24 medium-size radishes)*
> *1 cup white vinegar*
> *3 teaspoons salt*
> *4½ cups water*
> *½ cup orange juice*
> *6 tablespoons olive oil*
> *3 teaspoons sugar*
> *3 teaspoons grated orange rind*
> *¾ teaspoon ground nutmeg*
> *¾ teaspoon dried mint, crumbled*
> *¾ teaspoon ground cumin*
> *¾ teaspoon pepper*

1. Place the carrots, beets, and radishes in 3 separate bowls. Add ⅓ cup vinegar, 1 teaspoon salt and 1½ cups water to each bowl. Stir to mix. Cover; refrigerate for at least 1 hour. Drain each bowl separately; rinse under cold water. Return each vegetable to a separate bowl.

2. Pour ¼ cup of the orange juice into the carrots, and the remaining ¼ cup of orange juice into the beets. Stir 2 tablespoons of olive oil and 1 teaspoon of sugar into each bowl; toss well to mix.

3. Add 1½ teaspoons of the orange rind to the carrots and the remaining 1½ teaspoon of orange rind to the beets. Add the nutmeg to the carrots, the mint to the beets, and the cumin to the radishes. Add ¼ teaspoon pepper to each bowl. Toss each vegetable to mix well. Cover; refrigerate.

4. Just before serving, toss each vegetable and drain any excess dressing. Mound the vegetables into 3 separate serving bowls.

Pickled Beet Salad

Prepare this salad a day ahead so the eggs have a chance to lightly pickle and turn an attractive shade of pink. This salad goes very well with herring.

Makes 12 servings.

Nutrient Value Per Serving: 82 calories, 4 gm. protein, 3 gm. fat, 260 mg. sodium, 114 mg. cholesterol.

8	*medium-size beets*
10	*medium-size carrots, pared*
5	*hard-cooked eggs, shelled*
1	*medium-size onion, grated*
6	*tablespoons cider vinegar*
2	*teaspoons sugar*
1	*teaspoon salt*
1/4	*teaspoon pepper*

1. Cook the beets in enough boiling salted water to cover in a medium-size saucepan until fork-tender, about 25 minutes. Drain. When cool enough to handle, slide off the skins with your fingers. Cut the beets into 1-inch cubes; you should have about 3 cups.
2. Cook the carrots in enough boiling salted water to cover in a large saucepan until tender, about 10 minutes. Drain. When cool enough to handle, cut into 1/2-inch cubes.
3. Coarsely chop 3 of the hard-cooked eggs. Combine the beets, carrots, chopped eggs, grated onion, vinegar, sugar, salt and pepper in a medium-size bowl. Toss to blend well.
4. Make a well in the center of the beet salad. Place the remaining 2 whole hard-cooked eggs in the well. Cover with the salad. Refrigerate, covered, overnight.
5. To serve, remove the whole pickled eggs. Toss the salad again. Arrange the salad on a serving platter. Cut the whole eggs into thin slices; overlap the slices down the center of the salad. Serve well chilled.

Platter of Meats with Accompanying Breads

Include a platter of cold cuts so your guests can create their own Chef's Salad. Be sure to garnish the platter with colorful vegetables, such as radish roses, celery brushes, broccoli flowerets and endive. Include any or all of the following.

> *Sliced roast beef*
> *Sliced roast chicken*
> *Sliced turkey*
> *Sliced smoked ham*
> *Thinly sliced salami or pepperoni*
> *Shredded Cheddar cheese*
> *Basketful of breadsticks, small dinner*
>   *rolls and assorted breads*

CELERY BRUSHES
Wash and trim celery, cut into 3-inch pieces. With a sharp knife, on one end, make many 1-inch deep cuts at right angles. Place in a bowl of ice water for 15 minutes to spread the celery "bristles."

Tossed Salad Ingredients

Prepare any or all of the following ingredients ahead of time and keep them well wrapped in the refrigerator until ready to arrange the salad bar. Greens should be washed and dried; endive separated into leaves. Vegetables should be washed and peeled, when appropriate, and cut into serving pieces. Each can be arranged in individual serving dishes or crocks, or you can group them on platters. Serve assorted dressings (recipes follow) and Basic Vinaigrette and variations, page 75 alongside.

Romaine lettuce
Iceberg lettuce
Boston lettuce
Bibb lettuce
Spinach leaves
Belgian endive
Shredded cabbage
Watercress
Chopped parsley
Blanched broccoli flowerets
Peeled blanched finger carrots
Sliced green onions
Alfalfa sprouts
Sliced radishes
Sliced mushrooms
Little carrot sticks
Sliced summer squash
Cherry tomatoes
Tomato wedges
Diced sweet red pepper
Diced avocado
Blanched asparagus spears
Celery sticks
Artichoke hearts
Finely chopped red onion
Diced cucumber
Croutons
Cheese cubes

◀◀◀ ▼ ⬜ Blue Cheese Dressing

This dressing will be more pungent if made a day or two ahead.

Makes about 3 cups.

Nutrient Value Per ¼ Cup: 112 calories, 5 gm. protein, 9 gm. fat, 281 mg. sodium, 24 mg. cholesterol.

8 ounces blue cheese
1 cup dairy sour cream
1 cup plain yogurt
½ teaspoon lemon juice

Crumble the blue cheese in a medium-size

bowl. Add the sour cream; blend together with a fork. Stir in the yogurt and lemon juice. Refrigerate, covered, for several hours or up to 2 days.

◀◀◀ ▼ Fresh Fruit Salad with Tangerine Dressing

Makes 12 servings.

Nutrient Value Per Serving: 191 calories, 2 gm. protein, 1 gm. fat, 12 mg. sodium, 0 mg. cholesterol.

1 medium-size ripe pineapple, peeled, cored and cut into 1-inch cubes
1 small ripe honeydew or crenshaw melon, halved, seeded and scooped into melon balls
1 small ripe canteloupe, halved, seeded and scooped into melon balls
5 medium-size bananas, cut diagonally into ½-inch-thick slices
3 large oranges, peeled, sectioned and seeded
3 cups seedless green grapes (about 1 pound)
1 pint strawberries, hulled
2 red Delicious apples, cored and cut into thin wedges
1 can (6 ounces) frozen tangerine juice concentrate, partially thawed
2 tablespoons fresh lime or lemon juice
¼ cup sugar (optional)

1. Combine the pineapple, melon balls, banana, orange, grapes, strawberries and apple in a large bowl.
2. Combine the tangerine juice, lime juice and sugar, if you wish, in a small screw-top jar. Cover; shake well to blend. Pour over the fruit salad. Toss to coat. Cover; refrigerate for several hours.
3. Just before serving, toss again.

◀◀◀ 🍴 ▢ *Thousand Island Dressing*

This homemade salad dressing has great fresh flavor. Prepare it a day or two ahead.

Makes about 3¾ cups.

Nutrient Value Per ¼ Cup: 183 calories, 1 gm. protein, 18 gm. fat, 394 mg. sodium, 13 mg. cholesterol.

1½ *cups mayonnaise*
½ *cup finely chopped sweet pickle*
½ *cup finely chopped dill pickle*
½ *cup thinly sliced green onion*
⅓ *cup tomato paste*
⅓ *cup lemon juice*
¼ *cup dry white wine (optional)*
2 *tablespoons Dijon-style mustard*
1 *tablespoon anchovy paste (optional)*

Combine all the ingredients in a medium-size; bowl. Stir to mix well. Cover; refrigerate. Stir well before serving.

BUFFET TIPS
● The buffet table should have plenty of space for the guests to flow around it freely.
● Arrange the table in a sequence for easy serving and carrying; plates first, entrée and accompaniments next, tableware and napkins last.
● Wrap each set of tableware in a napkin for easy carrying.
● Bread should be buttered in advance.
● Place the proper serving utensils next to each dish.
● Be sure each guest has seating and table space. Card tables and individual fold-up tables work well.
● You may choose to seat guests at the dining table. Set the table with napkins and tableware so the guests won't have to pick them up at the buffet table.

▶ *Clockwise from bottom:* **Roast Chickens with Herbs (page 296), Salmon-Cucumber Pâté (page 62), Creamy Herb Dip (page 59), Sour Cream-Walnut Cake (page 202), Cream of Pumpkin Soup with Cinnamon Croutons (page 72), Crisp Cranberry Relish (page 297), Chicken Pan Gravy (page 296) and buttered cubed sweet potatoes with brussels sprouts.**

Condiments

To complete your salad bar, include an attractive selection of any or all of the following condiments. Arrange some in individual serving dishes and crocks and others on a platter.

Mustard
Mayonnaise
Sour cream
Horseradish
Taco sauce
Black olives
Green olives
Dill pickle slices
Sweet gherkins
Raisins
Pickled pearl onions
Pickled herring
Bacon bits
Chopped hard-cooked eggs
Chopped nuts
Capers
Mango chutney
Spiced peaches
Dates

AUTUMN HOLIDAY BUFFET

Bountiful Enough for Thanksgiving

(for 10 to 12)

Salmon-Cucumber Pâté*

Creamy Herb Dip*   Assorted Raw Vegetables

Cream of Pumpkin Soup with Cinnamon Croutons*

Roast Chickens with Herbs*   Chicken Pan Gravy*

Mushroom-Herb Stuffing* or Fruited Brown Rice Stuffing*

Buttered Cubed Sweet Potatoes and Brussels Sprouts

Crisp Cranberry Relish*   Hot Buttered Rolls

Sour Cream-Walnut Cake*

Coffee   Tea

A Thanksgiving feast with a difference! Instead of the usual turkey, try two magnificent Roast Chickens with Herbs. This buffet might start a whole new tradition in your house!

⊻ Roast Chickens with Herbs

Try chicken instead of turkey for Thanksgiving; it's quicker.

Roast at 375° for 2½ hours.
Makes 12 servings.

Nutrient Value Per Serving: 497 calories, 49 gm. protein, 32 gm. fat, 599 mg. sodium, 178 mg. cholesterol.

> 2 **roasting chickens (5 to 6 pounds each)**
> 2 **teaspoons salt**
> ½ **teaspoon pepper**
>   **Mushrooms Herb Stuffing (recipe follows)**
>   **OR: Fruited Brown Rice Stuffing (recipe follows)**
> ½ **cup (1 stick) butter or margarine**
> 1 **tablespoon Dijon-style mustard**
> 2 **cloves garlic, finely chopped**
> 1 **tablespoon chopped parsley**
> 1 **teaspoon leaf rosemary, crumbled**
> 1 **teaspoon paprika**
> ½ **teaspoon leaf thyme, crumbled**
>   **Chicken Pan Gravy (recipe follows)**
>   **Grapes and watercress (optional)**

1. Preheat the oven to moderate (375°).
2. Sprinkle the chicken cavities with salt and pepper. Reserve the livers for the Mushroom Herb Stuffing, if you wish.
3. Stuff the neck and body cavities lightly with either Mushroom Herb Stuffing or Fruited Brown Rice Stuffing. Skewer the neck skin to the back; close the body cavity and tie the legs to the tail. Place the chickens breast-side up on the rack in a large roasting pan.
4. Blend the butter, mustard, garlic, parsley, rosemary, paprika and thyme in a small bowl. Rub part of the butter over the birds.
5. Roast in the preheated moderate oven (375°) for 2½ to 3 hours or until tender, basting and brushing with the remaining herb butter every 30 minutes. Remove the strings and skewers. Transfer the chickens to a heated serving platter; keep warm. Let stand for 15 to 20 minutes before carving. Reserve the roasting pan with drippings.
6. Meanwhile make the Chicken Pan Gravy.
7. Garnish the platter with grapes and watercress, if you wish. Serve with gravy, buttered cubed sweet potatoes and Brussels sprouts.

Chicken Pan Gravy: Measure 4 tablespoons drippings from the roasting pan into a large saucepan. Pour off the remaining excess drippings from the roasting pan. Add 1 cup boiling water to the pan; stir to loosen the brown bits. Pour into a 4-cup measure. Add chicken broth or water to measure 2½ cups. Set aside. Stir ⅓ cup all-purpose flour into the drippings in the saucepan to make a smooth paste. Cook, stirring constantly, for 1 minute. Gradually stir in the reserved broth and ½ cup white wine or dry vermouth. Cook, stirring constantly until the sauce thickens and bubbles, 3 minutes. Taste for seasonings; add more, if you wish. Makes 12 servings.
Nutrient Value Per Serving: 22 calories, 1 gm. protein, 0.4 gm. fat, 85 mg. sodium, 0.2 mg. cholesterol.

◥ ⊻ ◻ Mushroom-Herb Stuffing

Double this recipe to stuff 2 chickens.

Makes 6 servings (enough to stuff one 5- to 6-pound roasting chicken).

Nutrient Value Per Serving: 238 calories, 6 gm.

protein, 11 gm. fat, 606 mg. sodium, 27 mg. cholesterol.

2 chicken livers (optional)
5 tablespoons butter or margarine
1 medium-size onion, chopped, (½ cup)
2 cups coarsely chopped mushrooms
¼ cup chopped parsley
1 package (8 ounces) herb-stuffing mix
½ teaspoon leaf marjoram, crumbled
¾ cup boiling water

1. Sauté the livers, if you wish, in butter in a skillet for 5 minutes or until they lose their pink color. Remove to a board and chop.
2. Sauté the onions and mushrooms in the butter in the same skillet until the onions start to brown very slightly. Remove the skillet from the heat; stir in the parsley, stuffing mix, marjoram and chicken livers, if using. Add the water; toss lightly to moisten evenly.

▮▮ *Fruited Brown Rice Stuffing*

Be sure to double this recipe for 2 chickens.

Makes 6 servings (enough to stuff one 5- to 6-pound roasting chicken).

Nutrient Value Per Serving: 423 calories, 7 gm. protein, 23 gm. fat, 651 mg. sodium, 21 mg. cholesterol.

1 small onion, chopped (¼ cup)
4 tablespoons butter or margarine
1 cup brown rice
2 cups chicken broth or water
¼ cup chopped parsley
½ to 1 teaspoon salt
½ teaspoon leaf sage, crumbled
1 cup sliced celery
1 cup diced dried apricots

1 cup pecan halves, coarsely chopped, (optional)
½ cup raisins

1. Sauté the onion in butter in a large saucepan until soft, about 5 minutes. Stir in the rice. Add the broth; bring to boiling. Lower the heat; cover. Simmer, covered, until the rice has absorbed all the liquid, about 40 minutes. Remove from the heat.
2. Stir in the parsley, salt, sage, celery, apricots, pecans and raisins.

▮▮▮▮ *Crisp Cranberry Relish*

Be sure to add the apple and celery no more than an hour or two before serving to ensure the relish is crispy.

Makes 12 servings (3 cups).

Nutrient Value Per Serving: 86 calories, 0.2 gm. protein, 0.1 gm. fat, 13 mg. sodium, 0.0 mg. cholesterol.

1 package (12 ounces) fresh or frozen cranberries
1 cup sugar
2 teaspoons grated lemon rind
1 tablespoon lemon juice
1 cup diced green eating apple
1 cup sliced celery

1. Place half the cranberries in the container of a blender or food processor. Turn on and off until the cranberries are evenly chopped. Transfer to a bowl. Repeat with the remaining berries.
2. Stir in the sugar, lemon rind and juice. Refrigerate, covered, overnight or for up to 1 week.
3. Add the apple and celery 1 to 2 hours before serving.

▲*From top:* **Tomato Eye-Opener (page 299), Golden Coffee Bread (page 52) and Cheese and Blueberry Crêpe Triangles (page 299).**

NEW YEAR'S DAY BRUNCH
(for 6 to 8)
Tomato Eye Opener with Celery and Lime Garnish*
Frozen Spirits*
American Caviar Sampler*
Cheese and Blueberry Crêpe Triangles*
Cinnamon Sugar
Sour Cream   Preserves   Golden Coffee Bread*
Fruit Arrangement
Coffee or Tea

For a different New Year's celebration or whenever you feel like "putting on the Ritz," set out this elegant brunch, complete with American caviar and a bottle of spirits encased in ice. Best of all, preparation couldn't be simpler—even the crêpes can be made ahead!

⚊ ⚌ ⍦ *Tomato Eye-Opener*

Makes about 8 servings.

Nutrient Value Per Serving: 38 calories, 2 gm. protein, 0.2 gm. fat, 640 mg. sodium, 0 mg. cholesterol.

> **6 cups tomato juice**
> **⅓ cup lime juice**
> **4 to 5 teaspoons prepared horseradish**
> **1 teaspoon Worcestershire sauce**
> **6 to 8 drops liquid red pepper seasoning**
> **1 teaspoon salt, or to taste**
> **Frozen Spirits (optional; recipe follows)**
> **Celery sticks**
> **Lime wedges**

1. Combine the tomato juice, lime juice, horseradish, Worcestershire sauce, red pepper seasoning and salt in a large pitcher. Chill.
2. To serve, let each guest who wishes add their own Frozen Spirits to taste (provide a shot glass for measuring). Stir with a celery stick; garnish with a lime wedge. Add ice cubes, if you wish.

Frozen Spirits: Place a bottle, fifth or quart of American vodka or Aquavit in an empty ½-gallon milk carton or plastic container or large juice can, allowing about 1-inch space all around the bottle; add cold water to fill the container. Place upright in the freezer overnight or until the water is frozen solid (alcohol will not freeze). Remove to room temperature for 20 to 30 minutes to loosen the container. Remove the container and return the block of ice with the bottle to the freezer until ready to serve. Place on a folded napkin or towel on a deep plate or in a shallow bowl to catch the melting ice.

⚊ ⍦ *American Caviar Sampler*

Makes 8 servings.

Nutrient Value Per Serving: 67 calories, 7 gm. protein, 4 gm. fat, 468 mg. sodium, 82 mg. cholesterol.

Arrange about 2 ounces each of black lumpfish caviar, salmon caviar and golden whitefish caviar (or caviar of your choice) on a serving plate. Garnish with chopped hard-cooked egg white and yolk, chopped green onion and lemon wedges. Chill. Accompany with toast points.

⚌ ⍦ *Cheese and Blueberry Crêpe Triangles*

Make the crêpes ahead and freeze for up to 2 weeks. Make the filling the day before.

Makes 8 servings.

Nutrient Value Per Serving: 298 calories, 16 gm. protein, 16 gm. fat, 521 mg. sodium, 179 mg. cholesterol.

BATTER
1½ cups milk
3 eggs
1 cup sifted all-purpose flour
½ teaspoon salt
3 tablespoons butter, melted

FILLING
1 pound cream-style cottage cheese
7½ ounce package farmers cheese,
**   at room temperature**

1   **egg yolk**
2   **tablespoons sugar**
¼   **teaspoon ground cinnamon**
    Butter or margarine
1   **cup fresh or frozen blueberries**
2   **tablespoons melted butter or margarine**
    Cinnamon sugar
    Sour cream
    Strawberry or cherry preserves

1. Prepare the Batter: Place the milk, eggs, flour and salt in the container of an electric blender; whirl for 1 minute or until smooth. Whirl in the butter. Cover. Refrigerate for 30 minutes or until ready to use.

2. Prepare the Filling: Beat the cottage cheese and farmers cheese in a small bowl until smooth. Beat in the egg yolk, sugar and cinnamon. Refrigerate.

3. Heat a 7- or 8-inch skillet over medium-high heat. Grease lightly. Pour 3 tablespoons of the batter into the pan, rotating quickly to spread the batter evenly. Cook over medium heat until lightly browned, for about 1 minute. Flip over; cook for 30 seconds. Remove to a plate. Repeat with the remaining batter to make about sixteen 6-inch crêpes; stack with wax paper between them.

4. Spread about 3 tablespoons of the filling on 8 crêpes; sprinkle 1 tablespoon blueberries over each. Fold in quarters. Arrange on an ovenproof platter. Fill the remaining crêpes with plain filling; arrange on a platter. Brush lightly with melted butter.

5. To serve, heat the crêpes in a preheated moderate oven (350°) for 10 to 15 minutes. Serve with cinnamon sugar, sour cream and preserves.

A VERY SPECIAL DINNER PARTY
(for 6 to 8)
Appetizer Cheesecake Fingers*
Gazpacho*   Garlic Croutons
Boneless Roast Pork with Basil and Mushroom Stuffing*
Mashed Potato Casserole Parmesan*
Hot Buttered Broccoli with Toasted Almond Slices
Glazed Orange Soufflé*
Sparkling Rosé Wine   Coffee   Tea

This is a gourmet dinner to serve to the boss or to serve friends or family on a very special occasion. Best of all, most of the preparation for this dinner is completed ahead of time. You can enjoy your dinner party with a minimum of last-minute fuss.

AT A SIT-DOWN DINNER
- It's nice to serve the appetizer in the living room with cocktails.
- If you don't have someone to help you serve the meal, put the soup on the table just before the guests are seated, to make serving less complicated.
- Have a rolling cart or a tray nearby to make the removal of dishes easier.

⚑ Roast Pork with Basil and Mushroom Stuffing

Bake at 325° for about 2½ hours.
Makes 10 servings.

Nutrient Value Per Serving: 389 calories, 26 gm. protein, 30 gm. fat, 299 mg. sodium, 90 mg. cholesterol.

½ **pound medium-size mushrooms**
½ **cup finely chopped fresh basil leaves**
1 **small onion, finely chopped (¼ cup)**
½ **teaspoon salt**
¼ **teaspoon pepper**
1 **rolled boneless pork loin (about 3¼ pounds)**
1 **can (13¾ ounces) chicken broth**
1 **teaspoon butter**
2 **tablespoons all-purpose flour**
Fresh basil leaves for garnish

1. Select a few nice mushrooms for garnish. Trim the stems. Wash and flute the tops, if you wish, reserving the scraps. Set aside.
2. Wash, trim and chop the remaining mushrooms. Add the scraps if you fluted the mushrooms for garnish.
3. Reserve 2 tablespoons of the chopped basil. Combine the remaining chopped basil, chopped mushrooms, onion, ¼

teaspoon of the salt and pepper in a bowl.
4. Preheat the oven to slow (325°).
5. Unroll the pork roast; lay flat on a counter. Starting in the center of the meat and holding a knife parallel to the counter, cut the thick part of the loin through the center and almost in half. Fold the piece back like a book to increase the size of the loin by one third.
6. Spread the basil-mushroom mixture over the meat. Reroll. Tie at 3-inch intervals with string. Place in a shallow roasting pan. Sprinkle the remaining salt over the top. Pour ¼ cup of the chicken broth around the roast. Refrigerate the remaining broth.
7. Roast the pork in the preheated slow oven (325°) for 2½ hours or until a meat thermometer registers 170°.
8. Just before the roast is done, sauté reserved mushrooms for garnish in the butter in a heavy saucepan until golden. Remove the mushrooms; set aside.
9. Reserve ½ cup of the refrigerated chicken broth. Pour the remaining broth into the saucepan in which the mushrooms were sautéed. Bring to boiling.
10. Remove the roast to a warmed serving platter; keep warm. Pour off fat from the roasting pan. Add the hot chicken broth to the pan. Stir, scraping up the browned bits from the roasting pan. Bring to boiling on top of the stove.
11. Meanwhile, stir the flour into the remaining ½ cup chilled chicken broth until smooth. Gradually add to the boiling broth in the roasting pan, stirring rapidly with a wire whisk. Cook until smooth and thickened. Fold in the reserved 2 tablespoons chopped basil. Spoon some gravy over the roast. Pour the remainder into a sauce-boat. Garnish the roast with the reserved mushrooms and fresh basil leaves.

◀ Roast Pork with Basil and Mushroom Stuffing

MICROWAVE DIRECTIONS
650 Watt Variable Power Microwave Oven
Ingredient Changes: Omit 1 teaspoon butter. Increase flour from 2 to 3 tablespoons. Brush pork with browning liquid, if you wish.
Directions: Prepare and roll roast as directed, using all the mushrooms in the filling. Place roast, fat-side down, in a 11½ x 7 x 2-inch microwave-safe baking dish. Do not sprinkle with salt or add chicken broth. Microwave, uncovered, at full power for 15 minutes. Turn roast over; brush with browning liquid, if you wish. Sprinkle with the ½ teaspoon salt. Microwave at full power for 20 minutes or until meat thermometer inserted in center of roast registers 165°. Remove roast to serving platter; cover loosely with foil and set aside until it reaches an internal temperature of 170°, about 5 minutes. Drain fat. Add all but ½ cup broth to the baking dish. Microwave at full power for 3 minutes. Stir 3 tablespoons flour into the reserved ½ cup broth. Whisk into the broth in the baking dish. Microwave at full power for 3 to 4 minutes, stirring once, until the mixture comes to boiling. Fold in the reserved basil. Serve as above.

FOR A MASHED POTATO CASSEROLE Early in the day, make your favorite mashed potatoes to serve 8. Spoon three quarters of the mixture into an ovenproof casserole or soufflé dish. Using a pastry bag with a large star tip, pipe the remaining quarter decoratively over the top. Sprinkle grated Parmesan cheese over the top, cover and refrigerate. Remove from the refrigerator 1 hour before baking to bring to room temperature. Bake, covered, in a slow oven (325°) for 45 minutes or until warmed through. Remove the cover and run under the broiler to brown the top.

LAVISH WINE AND CHEESE SPREAD
(for 12)
Cheese (8 ounces per person)
2 pounds Brie or Camembert   1 pound Gorgonzola or Bleu
1 pound Goat Cheese or Emmenthaler
2 pounds Fontina or Port Salut
Crusty French Bread   Plain Unsalted Crackers
Unsalted Almonds
Strawberries and Grapes
Wine (3½ glasses per person)
California Zinfandel (4-liter bottle)   Dry White Wine (1-liter bottle)

Guide to Popular Cheeses

For buying information and description of two dozen popular cheeses, including the ones used in our spreads, see the chart at right. You can serve any combination of cheeses, so why not try some new ones along with your old favorites? Experiment and enjoy!

Pop the cork, put out the food and join the fun! It's that easy, whether you throw a Lavish Wine and Cheese Spread party or a Budget Wine and Cheese Bash. Be sure to check the Start-to-Finish Party Tips and, if you are feeling adventuresome, select several cheeses you've never tasted before from the cheese chart.

BUDGET WINE AND CHEESE BASH
(for 12)
Cheese (6 ounces per person)

2 pounds Cheddar or Swiss   1 pound Colby or Brick Cheese

1½ pounds Muenster or Monterey Jack

Sesame Seed Wafers

Pear and Apple Wedges   Carrot and Celery Sticks

Wine (2½ glasses per person)

Spritzer Punch:

1.5 liters Chablis and 2 bottles Club Soda

CHEESE	ORIGIN	AVE. PRE-PACKAGED WEIGHT	TASTE	TEXTURE
Bel Paese	Italy	8 oz.	milk, sweet	creamy, soft
Brick	U.S.	8 oz.	salty, somewhat nutty flavor	semi-soft; irregular holes
Brie	France	8 to 16 oz.	wild honey-like flavor; herbed, peppered also	creamy smooth
Camembert	France U.S.	8 to 16 oz.	mild to strong	creamy smooth
Cheddar (Red)	U.S.	6 to 16 oz.	rich, nutty flavor; mild to sharp	firm to hard
Cheddar (White)	U.S.	6 to 16 oz.	mild to pungent; garlic, pepper, wine, etc.	firm to hard
Colby	U.S.	1 lb., 2 lb wheels, 8 to 16 oz.	sweetish, similar to Cheddar	soft, but firm
Edam	Holland U.S.	8 or 16 oz. rounds	buttery, clean tasting	firm, supple
Emmenthal	Switzerland	8 oz.	nutty	firm, supple with moist holes
Fontina	Italy Denmark	8 oz.	sweetish, nutty	firm, supple; dotted with small holes
Goat Cheese (Chèvre)	France U.S.	8 oz. cylinder	mild to pungent	soft, crumbly
Gorgonzola	Italy	4 or 6 oz.	savory; verging on sharp	veined cheese; softer and creamier than most bleus
Gouda	Holland U.S.	7 oz. wedge 8 oz. round	mild, creamy and buttery	firm, but smooth
Gourman-dise	France	5¾ oz. round	processed Gruyère types: cherry, garlic, walnut	smooth, spreadable
Havarti	Denmark	10 oz.	clean, piquant flavor	supple, half-firm
Jarlesburg	Norway	6 to 8 oz.	nutty and sweet	firm, supple
Monterey Jack (variations)	U.S.	7 to 16 oz.	light, mild Cheddar flavor; caraway, jalapeño pepper, etc.	supple, resilient
Muenster	Denmark U.S.	6 oz.	robust	semi-soft, supple
Port Salut	France	7½ oz. round	buttery, piquant	semi-soft, resilient
Rondelle	France	3.52 oz. round	double cream cheese; pepper, garlic or herbs	rich and creamy
Swiss and Swiss type	Switzerland U.S.	7 oz.	sweet and nutty	slightly supple

START-TO-FINISH WINE PARTY TIPS
● Plan ¼ to ½ pound cheese per person.
● Serve the cheese at room temperature. Take soft cheese out of the refrigerator half an hour ahead; hard cheese two to three hours ahead. To prevent the cheese from drying out, leave it in its wrapper.
● Do not put strong cheeses next to mild ones.
● Chill the white and rosé wines. Serve the red at room temperature.
● Sprinkle pear and apple wedges with lemon juice to keep the fruit white.
● Store leftover cheeses individually wrapped in airtight plastic in the coldest part of the refrigerator. Recork and refrigerate the wine on its side.

WINE BUYING
● Buy inexpensive wines in a store with a large turnover to avoid getting old wines. Be sure the corked bottles are stored on their sides to keep the cork moist.
● When trying a new wine, buy only one bottle, try it and then buy more if you like it.
● Choose wine from a producer whose wines you have tried and liked before if you are undecided.

WINE SERVING
● Less expensive wines should be consumed shortly after you purchase them.
● White and rosé wines should be refrigerated just until chilled, for 1 to 2 hours.
● Light red wines may be chilled only slightly.
● Full-bodied red wines are always served at room temperature.

Festive Drinks

 Make-Ahead Punch

Make this delicious citrusy punch for either the kids or the adults, depending on whether you use the ginger ale.

Makes 20 servings.

Nutrient Value Per Serving (4 ounces): 141 calories, 0 gm. protein, 0 gm. fat, 3 mg. sodium, 0 mg. cholesterol.

1½ cups sugar
1   cup lemon juice
4   cups orange juice
2   cups brandy OR: 2 cups rum
*   OR: 1 bottle (28-ounces) ginger ale*

1. Combine the sugar and lemon juice in a medium-size saucepan. Cook over medium heat until the sugar dissolves. Cool to room temperature. Store in a covered container in the refrigerator.
2. To serve, combine the chilled sugar syrup, orange juice and either brandy, rum or ginger ale in a large punch bowl. Serve over ice.

 Sangria

A fruity wine punch, made with either red or white wine.

Makes about 2 quarts.

Nutrient Value Per Cup: 214 calories, 1 gm. protein, 0 gm. fat, 10 mg. sodium, 0 mg. cholesterol.

⅓ **cup sugar**
⅓ **cup water**
½ **cup orange juice**
¼ **to ⅓ cup brandy**
½ **lemon, sliced and seeded**
1 **small orange, sliced and seeded**
1½ **quarts red or white wine, chilled**
1 **bottle (12 ounces) club soda, chilled**
    (optional)
    Ice cubes

1. Combine the sugar and water in a large clear glass pitcher; stir to dissolve the sugar. Add the orange juice, brandy, lemon and orange slices and wine. Refrigerate for 1 hour.
2. Just before serving, add the club soda, if using, and ice cubes.

◣ ◖◖◖ 🍸 *Winter Fruit Cider*

Makes about 2 quarts.

Nutrient Value Per Serving: 246 calorie, 1 gm. protein, less than 1 gm. fat, 16 mg. sodium, 0 mg. cholesterol.

Water
1 **package (8 ounces) dried mixed fruit**
2 **cans (6 ounces each) frozen apple juice**
    concentrate, thawed
1 **cup brandy**
1 **bottle (28 ounces) ginger ale**
    Ice cubes

1. Add water to just cover the dried fruit in a small saucepan. Bring to boiling; cover and simmer for 10 minutes; remove the fruit to a small bowl; refrigerate the fruit and liquid separately.
2. Combine the chilled liquid, apple juice and brandy in a punch bowl. Spoon in the fruit; add the ginger ale and ice cubes.

◣ ◖◖◖ 🍸 *Mocha Eggnog*

Makes 1½ quarts.

Nutrient Value Per Serving: 514 calories, 7 mg. protein, 35 gm. fat, 97 mg. sodium, 338 mg. cholesterol.

2 **cups heavy cream**
2 **tablespoons instant granulated coffee**
5 **tablespoons chocolate-flavored syrup**
5 **eggs, separated**
⅓ **cup sugar**
¾ **cup bourbon whiskey**
¼ **cup brandy**

1. Stir together the cream, coffee and chocolate syrup in a 4-cup measure.
2. Beat together the egg yolks and sugar in a large bowl until the mixture is thick and lemon-colored. Stir in the whiskey, brandy and the cream mixture. Chill.
3. Just before serving, beat the egg whites in a large bowl with an electric mixer on high speed until soft peaks form. Fold the egg whites into the cream mixture.

Index